AmongUS

AmongUS

Essays on Identity, Belonging, and Intercultural Competence

Edited by

Myron W. Lustig
San Diego State University

Jolene Koester
California State University, Sacramento

 LONGMAN

An imprint of Addison Wesley Longman, Inc.

New York • Reading, Massachusetts • Menlo Park, California • Harlow, England
Don Mills, Ontario • Sydney • Mexico City • Madrid • Amsterdam

Editor-in-Chief: Priscilla McGeehan
Acquisitions Editor: Michael Greer
Marketing Manager: Megan Galvin-Fak
Full Service Production Manager: Mark Naccarelli
Project Coordination and Text Design: Nesbitt Graphics, Inc.
Electronic Page Makeup: Nesbitt Graphics, Inc.
Cover Designer/Manager: Nancy Danahy
Senior Print Buyer: Hugh Crawford
Printer and Binder: Maple-Vail Book Manufacturing Group
Cover Printer: The Lehigh Press

Library of Congress Cataloging-in-Publication Data

AmongUS: essays on identity, belonging, and intercultural competence
/ edited by Myron W. Lustig and Jolene Koester.
        p. cm.
    ISBN 0-321-04920-9
    1. Pluralism (Social sciences)—United States. 2. Group identity—
United States. 3. Intercultural communication—United States.
4. United States—Ethnic relations. 5. United States—Race
relations.   I. Lustig, Myron W.   II. Koester, Jolene.   III. Title:
AmongUS.
E184. A1A65 2000
306'.0973—dc21   99-31067
                                                        CIP

Please visit our website at http://www.awlonline.com

ISBN 0-321-04920-9

12345678910—MA—02010099

Contents

Preface   *ix*
Prologue   *xiii*

PART ONE

Cultural Identity: Who Are We?

1   Myron W. Lustig and Jolene Koester, *The Nature of Cultural Identity*   3

2   Patricia Covarrubias, *Of Endearment and Other Terms of Address: A Mexican Perspective*   9

3   Mei Lin Swanson Kroll, *My Name Is. . .*   18

4   Michael John Lewis, *Something to Tell You*   24

5   Samuel M. Edelman, *To Pass or Not to Pass, That Is the Question: Jewish Cultural Identity in the United States*   33

6   Alfred J. Guillaume, Jr. *To Be American, Black, Catholic, and Creole*   41

7   Wen Shu Lee, *In Search of My Mother's Tongue: From Proverbs to Contextualized Sensibility*   48

PART TWO

Inside/Outside: Belonging to Multiple Cultures

8   Young Yun Kim, *On Becoming Intercultural*   59

9   Tadasu Todd Imahori, *On Becoming "American"*   68

10   Keturah A. Dunne, *La Güera*   78

11   Peter O. Nwosu, *Cultural Problems and Intercultural Growth: My American Journey*   84

12   Chevelle Newsome, *Finding One's Self in the Margins*   93

13   Ringo Ma, *"Both-And" and "Neither-Nor": My Intercultural Experiences*   100

14   William J. Starosta, *dual_consciousness @USAmerican.white.male*   107

PART THREE

Othering: Racism and Prejudice AmongUS

15   Myron W. Lustig and Jolene Koester, *Cultural Biases and Intercultural Communication*   119

16   Richard Morris, John Sanchez, and Mary E. Stuckey, *Why Can't They Just Get Over It?*   134

17   Mark Lawrence McPhail and Karen Lynette Dace, *Black as We Wanna Be: From Identity Politics to Intercultural Competence*   148

18   Gale Young, *Leonard's Yard: Pulling at the Roots and Responsibilities of My Whiteness*   161

19   Veronica J. Duncan, *A Whole Lot of Milk with a Drop of Chocolate: An African American Woman's Story*   172

20   Elane Norych Geller, *The Holocaust and Its Lessons: A Survivor's Story*   179

21   Ann M. Bohara and Patrick McLaurin, *Friends and Partners*   186

PART FOUR

Crossing Cultures: Negotiating Intercultural Competence

22   Myron W. Lustig and Jolene Koester, *Negotiating Intercultural Competence*   197

23   Donal Carbaugh and Saila Poutiainen, *By Way of Introduction: An American and Finnish Dialogue*   203

24   Zhong Wang and Rui Shen, *Acculturation in a Foreign Land*   213

25   Thomas J. Knutson, *Tales from Thailand: Lessons from the Land of Smile*   221

26   Charles A. Braithwaite, *Roast Mutton, Fry Bread, and Tilt-a-Whirls: Cultural and Intercultural Contact at the Navajo Nation Fair*   232

27   Vicki Marie, *Living in Paradise: An Inside Look at the Micronesian Culture*   239

28   Thomas M. Steinfatt, *The Shower*   254

About the Authors   *263*

Preface

This book of essays is a tool that, our students tell us, helps people learn about living and communicating in an intercultural world. It was created with the assistance and collaboration of colleagues and friends from many disciplines.

Approach

What makes this book different from other collections of readings about intercultural communication is the centrality of lived experiences by individuals engaged in communication with culturally different others. Common to all the writers is a personal and active engagement in working through the issues of cultural identity and intercultural communication in the United States. Although many of the authors are scholars in their own right, their ideas on these pages are anchored primarily in personal experience. Thus, although the authors are informed by a deep knowledge and understanding of intercultural communication, their own voices are the bases for the claims they make about intercultural relationships. The essays allow readers to feel, experience, and understand what the authors have experienced.

The impetus for creating this book came from our students, who said that they find traditional textbooks useful but incomplete. Missing is the opportunity to understand what happens in the minds, hearts, and behaviors of individuals who come from culturally disparate backgrounds yet are attempting to communicate with one another. Our students challenged us to provide extended examples—not just myriad short vignettes—that illustrate the substantive concepts and ideas. They recognized, as we do, that those involved in intercultural communication don't always react to cultural differences with a purely detached and intellectualized response. They wanted a richer sense of the stress and distress, the passion and compassion that inevitably accompany many real-world intercultural interactions. We believe strongly that theory and research provide essential anchors for a substantive understanding of intercultural phenomena, but we also agree with our students that the emotional links to these ideas come from a deep understanding of their own and others' lived experiences. The essays in this book are intended to provide that emotional link.

Using the Book

AmongUS is intended for the general student reader. Although grounded in a scholarly understanding of intercultural communication, each essay is written in an easy-to-read narrative style and with a minimum of footnotes and references.

This book can be used as an independent text for courses about human interactions in the multicultural United States of the twenty-first century. Because we are communication scholars, the focus of our own teaching is the creation and interpretation of symbols, messages, and meanings. However, the essays provide a rich source of materials to teach a broad array of sociological, psychological, and interpersonal concepts that apply to educational, business, and cultural settings.

AmongUS can also be used to complement texts that are grounded in a more scholarly treatment of theories and constructs. Combining this anthology of essays with a more traditional textbook provides an intellectual framework through which students can understand both the experiences of those living among us and the concepts that undergird them. In our own teaching of intercultural communication we have used the essays in *AmongUS* to complement the ideas in another book we authored and Longman published, *Intercultural Competence: Interpersonal Communication Across Cultures.*

Organization of the Book

AmongUS begins with a prologue that affirms our central goal: to provide, for the twenty-first century inhabitants of the United States, examples from individuals whose intercultural experiences give insights into how to achieve an effective and fair multicultural society. In such a society unique cultural identities are celebrated and maintained within a common national boundary.

Each of the four major sections of the book contains seven essays. Each section begins with an overview essay, which provides a substantive exposition of a major theme: identity, belonging to multiple cultures, racism and prejudice, and negotiating intercultural competence. Each essay includes a brief introductory paragraph to focus the reader's attention and put the writer's ideas in context.

The placement of each essay within the book is, to some extent, arbitrary. As with all human encounters, the experiences of the essays' authors do not fall neatly into discrete categories without any overlap. Thus we encourage you to read and impose your own mental frameworks on the issues exemplified by the lived experiences portrayed on these pages.

The first section of the book is entitled "Cultural Identity: Who Are We?" Its overview essay discusses how an individual develops a cultural identity and her or his relationship to social and personal aspects of the individual. This essay provides a framework for understanding the remaining six essays, in which the authors describe experiences that affirm or deny essential elements of their cultural identities.

"Inside/Outside: Belonging to Multiple Cultures" is the theme of Part Two. One of our respected colleagues in communication, Young Yun Kim, prepared the overview essay for this section, in which she presents a theoretical perspective on understanding the transformations individuals experience when they interact and live within multiple cultures. The essays that follow then present stories about grappling with cultural identities that are anchored in multiple cultural frameworks.

Part Three, "Othering: Racism and Prejudice AmongUS," explores the pernicious and invidious consequences of discrimination. The section begins with an essay that addresses the important background understandings about human cognitive processes that are the basis for racism, prejudice, ethnocentrism, and discrimination. The authors of the remaining essays in Part Three speak directly to their personal experiences in reacting to and resolving the "othering" that has been directed toward them.

Part Four, the final section of the anthology, is entitled "Crossing Cultures: Negotiating Intercultural Competence." The opening essay provides a scholarly approach to intercultural competence and offers useful tools to achieve competent communication with culturally diverse people. The remaining essays are case studies of individuals attempting to make sense of and function appropriately and effectively within different cultural environments.

Appreciation and Assistance

Our deep appreciation goes to those who contributed the essays that form the messages of this book. The authors have been willing to present personal insights into their lives that help to achieve the goal of providing models for effective and appropriate intercultural interactions with others. Their deep commitment to the celebration of cultural differences as a means of forging a fully functioning multicultural society is evident in their work. We thank and acknowledge the work of Ann Bohara, Charles Braithwaite, Donal Carbaugh, Patricia Covarrubias, Karen Dace, Veronica Duncan, Keturah Dunne, Samuel Edelman, Elane Geller, Alfred Guillaume, Tadasu Todd Imahori, Young Yun Kim, Thomas Knutson, Mei Lin Kroll, Wen Shu Lee, Michael Lewis, Ringo Ma, Vicki Marie, Patrick McLaurin, Mark McPhail, Richard Morris, Chevelle Newsome, Peter Nwosu, Saila Poutiainen, John Sanchez, Rui Shen, Thomas Steinfatt, Mary Stuckey, William Starosta, Zhong Wang, and Gale Young.

In addition, we thank the individuals who reviewed the essays at various stages of their inception and preparation. Specifically, we would like to acknowledge the contributions of Fred Casmir, Pepperdine University (retired); Patricia Covarrubias, University of Washington; Keturah Dunne, San Diego, California; Samuel Edelman, California State University, Chico; Michael R. Elkins, Texas A&M University, Kingsville; Reeze L. Hanson, Haskell Indian Nations University; Robert Hertzog, Indiana University East; Beatriz McWilliams, Miracosta College; Candice Thomas-Maddox, Ohio University; and Gale Young, California State University, Hayward.

We acknowledge, as well, the important contributions made by our students. They have inspired and encouraged us to find additional ways to translate theory and research into powerful examples.

We hope that you appreciate and learn from these essays. Enjoy!

Myron W. Lustig
Jolene Koester

Prologue

We are here, now, on the cusp of the twenty-first century. We have crossed a great divide, are standing with our backs to a gaping chasm, the bridges from there to here destroyed. We can't go back—don't want to go back—but we appreciate the memories.

We are optimistic, but also very concerned, about the future before us. We have made a fantastic leap from there to here. We have progressed from sea ships to spaceships, from motorcars to microchips. We have survived a century that has been both mundane and mad; life in the twentieth century was good for more people than it was in any previous century, yet more people were murdered in wars and organized mayhem during the twentieth century than ever before.

We in the United States are in the midst of a great social experiment, and few examples show us how to proceed, much less how to succeed. The goal of this social experiment is easily articulated but difficult to achieve: to become an effective and functional multicultural society. How do we create a single nation with many cultures? How can U.S. Americans live, thrive, and interact peacefully? How do we maintain our unique cultural identities and still maintain a common national identity?

It is easy to find negative examples: people who are intolerant of those from other groups, people who equate "different" with "inferior" and perhaps "threatening," people who measure others only and always by standards that put themselves at the top of the hierarchy.

Much harder to find are positive examples, useful clues, and helpful suggestions about what it means and what is required to build something that heretofore has not existed: a multicultural United States of America, with the many cultures living together in harmony, living as equals, living among other U.S. Americans, living AmongUS.

The essays in this book are designed to help develop a road map toward that goal. They are written by people who have struggled with the inherent tensions of living AmongUS, who have faced enormous and sometimes overwhelming challenges to their cultural identities, who have given voice to their longing for belonging, who have confronted prejudices and discrimination and learned to survive and thrive, and who have been at the forefront of the negotiations that must be resolved peacefully if we are to live AmongUS as interculturally competent communicators.

AmongUS

PART ONE

Cultural Identity

Who Are We?

The Nature of Cultural Identity[1]

Myron W. Lustig and Jolene Koester

How do people come to identify themselves as belonging to a particular culture? How and when does a child begin to think of herself as a Latina, a Jewish American, or a Korean American? How are some people defined as "not members" of a culture?

One's cultural identity—the self-concept of a person who belongs to a particular cultural group—has a powerful effect on one's intercultural communication. As part of the socialization process, children learn to view themselves as members of particular groups. Children in all cultures, for example, are taught to identify with their families. As a child becomes a teenager and then an adult, the development of vocational and avocational interests creates new groups with which he or she can identify. "Baseball player," "ballet dancer," or "scientist" may become important labels to describe the self.

Another feature of socialization is that people are taught about groups to which they do not belong, and they often learn that certain groups should be avoided. This tendency to identify as a member of some groups, called *ingroups,* and to distinguish these ingroups from *outgroups,* is so prevalent in human thinking that it has been described as a universal human tendency.[2]

The Nature of Identity

Related to the distinction between ingroup and outgroup membership is the concept of one's *identity,* or self-concept. An individual's self-concept is built on cultural, social, and personal identities.[3]

Cultural identity refers to one's sense of belonging to a particular culture or ethnic group. It is formed through a process that results from membership in a particular culture, and it involves learning about and accepting the traditions, heritage, language, religion, ancestry, aesthetics, thinking patterns, and social structures of a culture. That is, people internalize the beliefs, values, and norms of their culture and identify with that culture as part of their self-concept.

Social identity develops as a consequence of memberships in particular groups within one's culture. The characteristics and concerns common to most members of such social groups shape the way individuals view their characteristics. The types of groups with which people identify can vary widely and might include perceived similarities such as age, gender, work, religion, ideology, social class, place (neighborhood, region, and nation), and common interests. For instance, those baseball players, ballet dancers, and scientists who

3

strongly identify with their particular professions likely view themselves as "belonging" to "their" group of professionals, with whom they share similar traits and concerns.

Finally, *personal identity* is based on individuals' unique characteristics, which frequently differ from those of others in their cultural and social groups. You may like cooking or chemistry, singing or sewing; you may play tennis or trombones, soccer or stereos; you may view yourself as studious or sociable, goofy or gracious; and most assuredly you have abilities, talents, quirks, and preferences that differ from those of others.

For ease and clarity we have chosen to present aspects of a person's identity as separate categories. There is a great deal of interdependence, however, among these three aspects of identity. Characteristics of people's social identities inevitably are linked to preferences shaped by their cultural identities. Similarly, how people enact their unique interests is heavily influenced by their cultural identities. Thus, for example, a teenage girl's identity will likely be strongly linked to her culture's preferences for gendered role behaviors, as well as to her social class and her personal characteristics and traits.

The Formation of Cultural Identity

Cultural identities often develop through a process involving three stages: unexamined cultural identity, cultural identity search, and cultural identity achievement.[4] During the *unexamined cultural identity* stage one's cultural characteristics are taken for granted, and consequently there is little interest in exploring cultural issues. Young children, for instance, typically lack an awareness of cultural differences and the characteristics that differentiate one culture from another. Teenagers and adults may not want to categorize themselves as belonging to any particular culture.[5] Some people may not have explored the meanings and consequences of their cultural membership but may simply have accepted preconceived ideas about it that were obtained from parents, their community, the mass media, and others. Consequently, some individuals may unquestioningly accept the prevailing stereotypes held by others and may internalize common stereotypes of their own culture and themselves. Scholars have suggested that the cultural identities of many European Americans, in particular, have remained largely unexamined, a consequence of the power, centrality, and privilege the European American cultural group has had in the United States.[6] As Judith Martin, Robert Krizek, Thomas Nakayama, and Lisa Bradford suggest,

> This lack of attention to white identity and self-labeling reflects the historical power held by Whites in the United States. That is, Whites as the privileged group take their identity as the norm or standard by which other groups are measured, and this identity is therefore invisible, even to the extent that many Whites do not consciously think about the profound effect being White has on their everyday lives.[7]

Cultural identity search is a process of exploration and questioning about one's culture to learn more about it and to understand the implications of membership in that culture. By exploring the culture individuals can learn about its strengths and may come to a point of acceptance of both their culture and themselves. For some individuals a turning point or crucial event precipitates this stage, whereas for others it begins with a simple growing awareness and reinterpretation of everyday experiences. Common to this stage is an increased social and political awareness, along with an increased desire to learn more about one's culture. Such learning may be characterized by an increase in discussions with family and friends about cultural issues, independent reading of relevant sources, enrollment in appropriate courses, or attendance at cultural events such as festivals and museums. There may also be an emotional component of varying intensity to this stage involving tension, anger, and perhaps even outrage directed toward other groups. These emotions may intensify as people become aware of and wrestle with the effects of discrimination on their present and future lives and the potential difficulties in attaining educational, career, and personal objectives.

Cultural identity achievement is characterized by a clear, confident acceptance of oneself and an internalization of one's cultural identity. Such acceptance can be calmly and securely used to guide one's future actions. People in this stage have developed ways of dealing with stereotypes and discrimination so they don't internalize others' negative perceptions and are clear about the personal meanings of their culture. This outcome contributes to increased self-confidence and positive psychological adjustment. Table 1 on page 6 provides sample comments from individuals in each of the three stages of cultural identity development.

Characteristics of Cultural Identities

Once formed, cultural identities provide an essential framework for organizing and interpreting our experiences of others. This is so because cultural identities are central, dynamic, multifaceted components of one's self-concept.

Cultural identities are central to a person's sense of self. Like gender and race, your culture is "basic" because it is broadly influential and is linked to a great number of other aspects of your self-concept. These core aspects of your identity are likely to be important in the bulk of your interactions with others. Most components of your identity, however, become important only when they are activated by specific circumstances. For many people the experience of living in another culture or interacting with a person from a different culture triggers a new awareness of their own cultural identities. When a component of your identity becomes important, your experiences are filtered through that portion of your identity. Because cultural identities are central, most experiences are interpreted or "framed" by cultural membership.

Because cultural identities are dynamic, your cultural identity—your sense of the culture to which you belong and who you are in light of it—exists

Table 1 STAGES IN THE DEVELOPMENT OF CULTURAL IDENTITY

Stage	Sample Comments	Source of Comments
Unexamined Cultural Identity	"My parents tell me about where they lived, but what do I care? I've never lived there."	Mexican American Male
	"Why do I have to learn who was the first black woman to do this or that? I'm just not too interested."	African American Female
	"I don't have a culture. I'm just an American."	European American Male
Cultural Identity Search	"I think people should know what black people had to go through to get to where we are now."	African American Female
	"There are a lot of non-Japanese people around me and it gets pretty confusing to try and decide who I am."	Japanese American Male
	"I want to know what we do and how our culture is different from others."	Mexican American Female
Cultural Identity Achievement	"My culture is important and I am proud of what I am. Japanese people have so much to offer."	Japanese American Male
	"It used to be confusing to me, but it's clear now. I'm happy being black."	African American Female

Source: Adapted from Jean S. Phinney, "A Three-Stage Model of Ethnic Identity Development in Adolescence," *Ethnic Identity: Formation and Transmission among Hispanics and Other Minorities,* ed. Martha E. Bernal and George P. Knight (Albany: State University of New York Press, 1993) 61-79.

within a changing social context. Consequently, your identity is not static, fixed, and enduring; rather, it is dynamic and changes with your ongoing life experiences. In even the briefest encounter with people whose cultural backgrounds differ from your own, your sense of who you are *at that instant* may well be altered, at least in some small ways. Over time, as you adapt to various intercultural challenges, your cultural identity may be transformed into one that is substantially different from what it used to be. The inaccurate belief that cultural identities are permanent, that "once a Chinese American, always a Chinese American," ignores the possibility of profound changes that people may experience as a result of their intercultural contacts.

Cultural identities are also multifaceted. At any given moment you have many "components" that make up your identity. For instance, a specific person may simultaneously view herself as a student, an employee, a friend, a woman, a southerner, a daughter, a Methodist, a baby boomer, and more. Similarly, there are typically many facets or components to your cultural identity.

Many people incorrectly assume that an individual could—or perhaps should—identify with only one cultural group. However, as Young Yun Kim suggests:

> If someone sees himself or herself, or is seen by others, as a Mexican American, then this person's identity is [commonly] viewed to exclude all other identities. This tendency to see cultural identity in an "all-or-none" and "either-or" manner glosses over the fact that many people's identities are not locked into a single, uncompromising category, but incorporate other identities as well.[8]

Given our increasingly multicultural world, in which people from many cultures coexist and in which the United States has become a country where individuals from many cultures live and interact, the multifaceted characteristic of cultural identity is even more important.

The cultures with which you identify affect your views about where you belong and who you consider to be "us" and "them." A good place to begin talking about your own cultural identity is to describe yourself in terms of the culture (or cultures) to which you belong. Is this relatively easy for you to do? Have you always been aware of your cultural background, or have you experienced events that lead you to search for an understanding of your cultural identity? Do you find your cultural identity primarily in one cultural group or in several cultural groups? How does your cultural identity shape your social and personal identity? Does your cultural identity result in a strong sense of others as either in or out of your cultural group? If so, were you taught to evaluate negatively those who are not part of your cultural group? Conversely, do you sometimes feel excluded from and evaluated negatively by people from cultures that differ from your own? The answers to these questions will help you understand the possible consequences, both positive and negative, of your cultural identity as you communicate interculturally.

NOTES

1. Excerpted and adapted from Myron W. Lustig and Jolene Koester, *Intercultural Competence: Interpersonal Communication Across Cultures,* 3rd ed. (New York: Longman, 1999).

2. Marilyn Brewer and Donald T. Campbell, *Ethnocentrism and Intergroup Attitudes* (New York: Wiley, 1976).

3. Our labels are analogous to Triandis's tripartite distinction among one's collective self, public self, and private self. See Harry C. Triandis, "The Self and Social Behavior in Differing Cultural Contexts," *Psychological Review* 96 (1989): 506–520. See also Henri Tajfel, *Differentiation Between Social Groups* (London: Academic Press, 1978); Henri Tajfel, *Human Groups and Social Categories: Studies in Social Psychology* (Cambridge: Cambridge University Press, 1981).

4. Our discussion of the stages of cultural identity draws heavily on the works of Jean S. Phinney, particularly Jean S. Phinney, "A Three-Stage Model of Ethnic Identity Development in Adolescence," in *Ethnic Identity: Formation and Transmission Among Hispanics and Other Minorities*, ed. Martha E. Bernal and George P. Knight (Albany: State University of New York Press, 1993), 61–79. See also Jean S. Phinney, "Ethnic Identity in Adolescents and Adults: Review of Research," *Psychological Bulletin* 108 (1990): 499–514; Jean S. Phinney, "Ethnic Iden-

tity and Self-Esteem: A Review and Integration," *Hispanic Journal of Behavioral Sciences* 13 (1991): 193–208.

5. Frances E. Aboud, "Interest in Ethnic Information: A Cross-Cultural Developmental Study," *Journal of Cross-Cultural Psychology* 7 (1977): 289–300; Frances E. Aboud, "The Development of Ethnic Self-Identification and Attitudes," in *Children's Ethnic Socialization*, ed. Jean S. Phinney and Mary Jane Rotheram (Newbury Park, CA: Sage, 1987), 32–55; Frances E. Aboud, *Children and Prejudice* (New York: Basil Blackwell, 1988).

6. See, for example, Richard D. Alba, *Ethnic Identity: The Transformation of White America* (New Haven, CT: Yale University Press, 1990); Theodore W. Allen, *The Invention of the White Race: Racial Oppression and Social Control* (New York: Verso, 1994); Russell Ferguson, "Introduction: Invisible Center," in *Out There: Marginalization and Contemporary Cultures*, ed. Russell Ferguson, Martha Gever, T. M. Trinh, and C. West (Cambridge: MIT Press, 1992), 9–14; Ruth Frankenburg, *White Women, Race Matters: The Social Construction of Whiteness* (Minneapolis: University of Minnesota Press, 1993); Judith N. Martin, Robert L. Krizek, Thomas K. Nakayama, and Lisa Bradford, "Exploring Whiteness: A Study of Self Labels for White Americans," *Communication Quarterly* 44 (1996): 125–144; Thomas K. Nakayama and Robert L. Krizek, "Whiteness: A Strategic Rhetoric," *Quarterly Journal of Speech* 81 (1995): 291–309.

7. Judith N. Martin, Robert L. Krizek, Thomas K. Nakayama, and Lisa Bradford, "Exploring Whiteness: A Study of Self Labels for White Americans," *Communication Quarterly* 44 (1996): 125.

8. Young Yun Kim, "Identity Development: From Cultural to Intercultural," in *Interaction & Identity*, ed. Hartmut B. Mokros (New Brunswick, NJ: Transaction, 1996), 350.

Patricia Covarrubias speaks of a sorrow arising from a sudden rupture from the only language she knew. She was just eight years old when her parents moved the family from Mexico to California. This essay describes the language of her culture and the special use of many terms of endearment (nicknames, pet names) that are so central to her identity and feelings of belonging. Patricia eloquently describes how the loss of her Spanish nicknames and the Americanization of her name to "Pat" denied her a sense of self, which she later found after a journey to reclaim "Patricia" and her return sojourn to Mexico.

2 | Of Endearment and Other Terms of Address: A Mexican Perspective

Patricia Covarrubias

"This old man, he played two, he play knick-knack on my—" The singing jerked to a halt. It was my first day of school in my new country. As the school principal and I entered the third-grade classroom, Mrs. Williams ceased her piano playing and came toward me. With a hand on my shoulder, she steered me to face the children who were sitting in a large circle on small wooden chairs in a large circle. "Class, this is *Pat*." With that introduction I had been rechristened. In one unexpected and infinitesimal moment, all that I was and had been was abridged into three-letter, bottom-line efficiency: *Pat*. Mrs. Williams could not have imagined that her choice of address, imposed on me in 1960, just two weeks after my mother, my brother, and I immigrated to the United States to join my father, would be a name I would revile for the rest of my life.

Yet I am not ungrateful to Mrs. Williams. She facilitated, inadvertently, an important pivotal point in my life. In calling me *Pat,* in that hair-splitting instant, she prompted what became one of my primary life themes: understanding the profound and enduring personal and social consequences of the terms people use to address one another. As a recent doctoral student in communication, I join those who suggest that address forms are unique vocabularies in and through which people strategically align themselves in reference to other people. But in that fractional childhood moment, all I could understand was that with a simple *Pat* Mrs. Williams had crammed me into a space I did not fit. I was suddenly at the mercy of a word that did not describe me. With a single syllable she invaded a private way of being and made it accessible publicly, on her terms. I knew I was not *Pat*, but I did not know enough English to defend myself.

From the moment I stepped into my new American world, the alien *Pat* separated me not only from myself but also from the classmates who would make up so much of my social life through elementary, junior high, and high school. For weeks, months, years I struggled to convey who I "really" was, using the most direct channel available to humans: speech. But I continually failed. I lacked the lexicon. I lacked the syntax. I lacked the defiance. Like a mute patient who holds the solution to a crime and wants to speak but is unable to do so, I gagged on my urge to argue for my real name, for the real me. By the time I acquired enough English and enough courage to assert my personhood, I was off by too much to catch up. Over time, the people who composed so much of my social world had formed impressions of the person they thought I was. *Pat* became a composite of my awkward utterances, their imaginations, and some destructive stereotypes.

During those early years I was in some in-between space, some hollow whose depth I did not comprehend for decades. Yet I realized from the beginning that I could not surrender to the gap that alienated me from myself and from everyone else. I sensed early on that integration and reintegration would come at a cost, but that they would come. I did not lose hope. I did not stop striving. Nor did I stop hearing my parents' admonitions for grit. Instinctively and by design, I set out to recover that which had been overtaken, without losing entirely the moment at hand.

Curiously, it was in the public sphere that the reintegration of my intimate, real self began to occur. Reintegration crystallized recently when I returned to Mexico for seven months to conduct ethnographic fieldwork for my doctoral dissertation. Since we left in December 1959 I had returned to Mexico only four or five times and only for brief visits. One absence lasted 16 years. Moreover, I had never returned alone. It was only against the backdrop of my recent stay that I have finally been able to answer my own questions: "What specifically did *Pat* take away from me?" and "Can I finally make peace with her?" For me to understand what I had lost, I first had to find out what I had possessed prior to our immigration.

My given name is Patricia Olivia Covarrubias Baillet, and I was born to a world shaped, in great measure, by what people call themselves and each other. Titles, first names, surnames, nicknames, terms of endearment, terms of estrangement—they all reflect and constitute a particular Mexican way of being. In my childhood world, people used terms of address not only to point to particular people but also to form particular relationships and to evoke complementary emotions.

As a child I was seldom called *Patricia*. To address someone by his or her first name *a secas* (literally "dryly" but connoting "alone") is perceived by most Mexicans as cold and distant. First names alone are generally reserved for reprimand or censure or to underscore formality. Therefore, in most conversations a variety of pointing terms are used to personalize one's communication with another and to affirm intimacy, friendship, esteem, and *confianza,* which is a blend of trust, respect, confidentiality, and unity.

In keeping with the Mexican penchant for avoiding formal names in favor of more personalized address when *confianza* is desired, at school and elsewhere in my world I was *Pati, Paty,* or *Patty* (the Spanish diminutives for *Patricia*). Only on formal occasions, such as at the presentation of school diplomas, are students addressed by their full names. All Mexicans have at least two last names, the first for their father's family name and the second for their mother's. As the Mexican expression goes, people have **two** parents. In the Maddox Academy annuals for 1958 and 1959, I am listed as *Covarrubias Baillet, Patricia Olivia*.

My grandmothers and great-grandmother were generous deployers of nicknames and other terms of endearment. They cajoled, hugged, bathed, dressed, played with me, took me to school, sang and read to me. They lathered me also with an abundant array of forms of address. To my paternal grandmother and great-grandmother, with whom I lived for a time, I was *Patricita, Pato* (duck), *Patita* (little duck or little foot), *la Patricita, la niña* (the girl), *la chiquita* (the little one). My mother's mother had her own selection. In addition to *Paty* and *Patricita,* she called me *mi rosita de Castilla* (my rose of Castille), *mi rosita de Jericó* (my rose of Jericho), *mi orquídea* (my orchid). I, in turn, had a term for these women who were additional mothers to me: *mamá*. My maternal grandmother was *Mamá Mary* or *Mamita Mary* (*mamita* is the diminutive for *mamá* and *Mary* is the diminutive for *María*). My paternal grandmother was *Mamá Lupe* (*Lupe* is the diminutive for *Guadalupe*).

Utterances were never spoken without the inclusion of some endearing term of address or reference, and it is those terms that anchor my memory to particular events. For instance, before leaving for work as a government secretary, Mamá Lupe, with whom I had lived for a year, always had some admonition on my behalf. "*Hay que pelarle las uvas a la Patricita,*" she'd tell her mother. My great-grandmother *Abuelita Sarita* (*abuelita* is the diminutive for *abuela,* meaning grandmother; *Sarita* is the diminutive for *Sara*) in turn responded, "*Sí Lupe.*" Once my grandmother had left, my great-grandmother was true to her word. She would sit at the wooden kitchen table and, with the sharpest corner of her longest fingernail, peel one grape at a time so the skins would not aggravate my lifelong colitis. At other times she painstakingly peeled the cooked black beans one by one so that I could eat something I especially enjoyed because of their color. Many evenings when my grandmother had returned from work she loved to tease me about getting married, or more specifically about not getting married. Sara, who was widowed before age 30 and raised three children by herself, would sweep her arm up in the air saying, "*No niña ¿para qué te casas? ¡No te cases!*" [No child, why get married? Don't get married!] Then she would laugh and gather me into her arms.

My maternal grandmother also feasted me with a glossary of nicknames. For Mamá Mary, inspiration came from the world of fragrances. Beautiful scents were her arsenal against the odors of a city that was well on its way to becoming the most populated in the world. Before donning her military nurse's uniform, her daily ritual involved anointing herself with the essence of lavender, jasmine, gardenia, or rose. *"Toma mi Rosita de Castilla, Toma mi Rosita de Jericó,"* [Here, my little rose of Castille, my little rose of Jericho] she would say, handing me a clean, folded handkerchief infused with perfume. The handkerchief was meant for me to bury my nose in as we passed sewers, exhaust fumes, or unbathed people. On lonely Saturday evenings she would blast music from the radio and invite me to dance around her tiny apartment. *"¡Ven mi orquídea, vamos a bailar!"* [Come my orchid, let's dance!] she'd exclaim, grabbing me with one hand. With the other hand she clutched a large uncapped bottle of cologne, with whose liquid orange flowers she splashed the walls as we danced to *"Las Bicicletas"* (a particularly animated Mexican song).

At home, to my mother, I was *hija* (daughter) or *mija* (contraction of *mi hija,* meaning my daughter). To my brother I was *manita* (diminutive of the term *mana,* which itself is a diminutive for *hermana,* meaning sister). My brother and I shared a bedroom; our nightly ritual involved kissing each other good night. *"Buenas noches manita"* my brother would say, pecking my cheek before climbing into his bed. Then, as we both lay in the dark, I would often say, *"Güero* (a common nickname for fair-complected people), *cuéntame un cuento"* [Güero, tell me a story]. When the tales were exhausted or when sleep weighted his eyes, *Güero* would speak into the shadowy space connecting our beds. *"Buenas noches manita, ya tengo mucho sueño"* [Good night little sister, I'm very sleepy].

In the Mexico of my early childhood, terms of address and of reference were an integral part of my history. Whether I was at school or at home, my name assured me a place in the universal continuum. I was *Patricia* because *Mamá Lupe* wanted it so; the *Mamá Lupe* who more than 20 years before my birth had left the town of Cárdenas to participate in the presidential campaign of Lázaro Cárdenas. I was *Olivia* because that was *Mamá Mary's* choice; the *Mamá Mary* whose family ranch had been confiscated by the government during the Revolution of 1910 and whose family was disbanded forever in the ensuing chaos. I had a father, *Covarrubias,* whose ancestors had come from northern Spain and settled in Mexico City. I had a mother, *Baillet,* whose father's family emigrated from France and settled in Puebla and who had served in the Mexican military until his death.

Having a name does not grant me claims to idealism. My Mexican childhood was not perfect, but I had a secure cultural footing. In the network of rituals, myths, and traditions that has characterized many Mexicans from ancient to modern times, I held appointed office. I was daughter, granddaughter, great-granddaughter, sister, niece, cousin, pupil, Catholic, playmate. I lived in a world where public and private domains routinely exchanged places. Thus, while I had a generalized public function as defined by my status and role, I also had a differentiated intimate space. It was in this intimate space that my uniqueness was largely shaped and sustained by the banquet of terms of address that were meant exclusively for me. So it was for the first eight years of my life.

A few days before Christmas 1959 I experienced a concentrated outpouring of address forms unlike any other I had yet known. In a nervous stream, the sounds from my grandmothers' lips overflowed: *"Patricita," "Patty," "Paty," "Patita," "mi rosita," "mi orquídea," "mi niña," "mi niñita."* We had gathered at the train station for a final good-bye and it would be my last feast of spoken endearments for a long time.

I didn't know it at the time, but I was just a few days away from a pivotal moment. Two weeks after our final parting from Mexico City, I was introduced to Mrs. Williams and her third-grade class in California. "Class, this is *Pat*." I still cannot hear that phrase without my stomach cramping. With a single turn of the tongue, my mother's and my father's surnames vanished, my first name and its variations were razed, and the affect and history associated with them were dimmed. For the next eight years—in elementary, junior high, and high school—I was *Pat*. When last names were required I was *Pat C.* because others could not or would not try to pronounce *Covarrubias*.

I do not recall ever having been asked during my years in primary education how I wanted to be addressed. I did not resist. There were fiercer battles to win. There was the language barrier and the loneliness that provoked. There was the sorrow resulting from the school principal's decision to place me in classes targeted for students with learning disabilities, including mental retardation. (Thanks to my parents' intervention the placement did not last long). And there was the frustration of the school's decision to send me to remedial speech classes, where I spent tedious hours in a closet-sized room practicing the pronunciation of words ending in *ch*: *"Catch, which, such, finch, march, fetch, cinch, conch, sandwich, catch, which, such, finch, march. . . ."* It seems some Hispanics tend to say *sh* instead of *ch*, but it took the therapist months to figure out I was not one of them. Yet there were other obstacles.

In a decision made strategically for my brother's and my benefit, only a few months after my arrival in Mrs. Williams's third-grade classroom my parents decided to move to another small California town. The new town had schools known for exceptionally high academic standards. It also had virtually no Hispanic residents. It was my parents' design for us to grow up where we would be obliged to learn English as quickly as possible and, thus, to learn to defend ourselves. But, as with Mrs. Williams, I did not know *what*—or more specifically *who*—awaited me in the new town. On a prematurely hot spring morning, Barry Hanna confronted me.

Barry remained a classmate for the next three years. His eyes were sky blue, resolute, and mean. From the moment of my arrival he made it his self-appointed duty to expose me to a prolific set of new terms of address that humiliated, confused, and hurt me. To Barry I was "spic," "beaner," "taco," "taco eater," "mex," "wetback," "green card," "stupid Mexican," and "lazy Mexican." For a long time I didn't understand what some of those expressions meant. They were in neither the textbooks nor the dictionary.

Barry was a relentless terrorist. With calculated slyness and regularity he would turn around from his school desk so only I could see him, lift the middle finger of his right hand, and point it straight at me. In predictably random attacks he approached me in the playground scowling, "Beaner, go home!" One day at recess, with his lips in a snarl exposing large yellow teeth, he reached toward my ear and tried to yank my pierced earring off my left ear. "Indian!" he scowled. (Pierced earrings were not yet fashionable in the United States but an accessory most Mexican women wear and are seldom seen without.) For weeks I wept, pleading with my mother to let me remove the earrings. Eventually she relented. I still did not know enough English to defend myself.

At the time I knew nothing about the controversial *bracero* program, rat-infested underground border tunnels, or immigration reform efforts. I knew something about injury, confusion, and disconnection. I knew that I was terrified to go to school and face the tyranny of Barry's epithets. When I finally figured out their meanings, I asked my father *"¿Por qué?"* [Why?] *"Porque son ignorantes y mediocres. Porque son ignorantes y mediocres,"* ["Because they are ignorant and mediocre,"] he repeated with infuriating calm. I would have felt consoled if he had said, "Because they're racist, prejudiced, bad." But those terms were never uttered in my parents' home.

For my father, a human being's maximum sin was to be ignorant and mediocre. Ignorance and mediocrity, he claimed, prevent people from behaving according to the highest order of integrity, honor, knowledge, and wisdom. In fact, until I reached adulthood, on more occasions than I want to remember he sanctioned me, saying, *"No seas mediocre"* [Don't be mediocre] and *"No seas ignorante"* [Don't be ignorant]. So my father's quiet response did not soothe my childhood hurt and frustration, but it did prepare me for other, larger battles.

From my father's words and examples, I learned to view ignorance and mediocrity—whether mine or someone else's—as something I could do something about. My father's approach also helped me to realize that others' failings need not become my own. As a little girl I craved for my parents to smother me with pity; as an adult, I am strengthened by their injunction: *"No te hagas la víctima. No te dejes."* [Don't play the victim. Don't yield to them/it]. In my parents' eyes one was a social casualty only by choice. Whether right or wrong, that is what they said and that is how they lived. In spite of Mrs. Williams and Barry Hanna, I learned to eliminate victimization as an option for confronting life's battles. And there has never been a shortage of battlegrounds.

One such battleground came as a surprise. When I was an undergraduate major in French language and literature my struggles involved the school's Hispanic community. On multiple occasions members of various Hispanic organizations challenged my choice of academic discipline. "Why do you study French?!" one demanded to know. "You're Chicana! We're never going to win the war this way!" This second-generation compatriot did not realize I **was** trying to win a war and that **he** was adding to my challenges. Once again, my intimate "I" was appropriated publicly, this time by one from whom I least expected it. I was saddened that he, whose cultural history included the oppressive reduction of individuals to easy stereotypes, should have thought I ought to abide in **his** preferred terms and conceptualizations of personhood. For him, I seemed to be but a category of person. I was still someone who was fighting for terms that fit. Yet things were changing. Some victories lay ahead. I was about to take a crucial step in the recovery of the intimate "I," of *Patricia*. Curiously, this change occurred in the most public of contexts, the mass media.

Immediately after finishing a master's degree in French language and literature I began an internship in the newsroom of the number-one-rated television station in northern California. With less than a year of unpaid training I was hired and given the opportunity to present news stories on air. I remained there as news reporter for the next several years. But the fight for my name followed me like a crawling plague. I was tired of it, but practice and fatigue had made me bold. Besides, by now I had mastered English.

In my private life I was married to an Anglo-Saxon man who supported my use of the name *Covarrubias*. But professionally there was dissent. The senior anchor, who was especially sensitive to being embarrassed on the air, frequently tripped and stuttered in pronouncing my name when introducing my early news stories. "Patricia Co—Corr—Corva . . . ias has more on that." After a particularly problematic show, he stormed into the newsroom and decreed, "Patricia, that name has got to go! I suggest something more pronounceable." I felt hot coals in my stomach as I grabbed onto my father's words, *"Porque son ignorantes."* "Yes, ignorance is something I can do something about," I repeated mentally in an attempt to douse my own flames. So I engaged every news anchor in pronunciation drills. "Co-va-rru-bi-as, Covarrubias. See, it's very phonetic."

My battle also pertained to my first name. I was willing to accept *Patricia, Trish, Trisha, Patrish,* even *Patrisher* (someone's sense of humor). But *Pat* was no longer an option. And so, for my name to fit on the screen, it had to be typed on fonts slightly smaller than those used on other reporters' names. On every aired report *Patricia Covarrubias* stretched from one end of the television set to the other. My family and I took great pleasure in that.

After nearly 20 years, at last I had rid myself of the imposed persona. I was no longer crammed into a name that was not mine. But after so much time living in a fiction, I could no longer identify clearly the parts that would enable complete self-reintegration. The missing dimensions were indeed obvious, but I didn't see them. The search took much longer than it should have. However, self-discovery and synthesis were the unexpected dividends of my recent doctoral fieldwork in Mexico.

In the port of Veracruz, I called the construction company where I recently spent seven months collecting ethnographic data. *Chabela* (diminutive of *Isabel*), the 33-year-old secretary of the CEO, answered the phone. *"¿Hola manita? ¿Cómo estás Paty?"* she exclaimed on hearing my voice, adding, *"¡Que gusto de oir tu voz mana!"* [Hello *manita* how are you Paty? What a pleasure to hear your voice *mana*!]. *Manita, Mana, Patty,* there they are again each time I call Mexico, the sounds from my early childhood. The subjective, perhaps inefficient, soft vocabularies of María, Guadalupe, and Sara.

It is not out of ghostly nostalgia that I call as often as I can. It is more to satisfy a physical need to feel close to a world bent on recreating the structures and emotions of family at every turn. I am fulfilled hearing and speaking the language that requires people to pay more than passing glances at each other. I am filled as I yield and am yielded to by terms with particular intimates in mind.

During my stay in Mexico, I observed and experienced hundreds of such interactions with intimates. *"¿Linda niña, que haces por aquí?"* [Pretty girl, what are you doing around here?] the company owner greeted me with a hug when we ran into each other at work one morning. *"Muñeca te sirvo un café"* [Doll, I'll serve you some coffee] offered Nieves, the dean of architecture at a local university, at our initial interaction. Subsequent interactions included the terms *mi reina* my queen, *mi amor* my love, and *corazón* [heart or dear heart].

At a reunion with a male friend I had not seen since our teenage years, he rushed to embrace me, remarking, *"¡Patita, Patita, no lo puedo creer!"* [Patita, Patita (diminutive of *Patricia*), I can't believe it!"]. A female relative christened me *Pata* (a name she made up for me). The wife of the couple with whom I lived drew me into her family by calling me *Patricha* (a name she created for me) and *hija* (daughter) or *mija* (contraction for my daughter). In the public market I was frequently called *"güera"* and *"güerita."* On a particular occasion in a public office when I was asked my name, out of habit I responded, *"Patricia Covarrubias."* Somewhat perturbed, the receptionist asked, *"¿Covarrubias qué?"* Not so indirectly I was being reminded that I have a mother as well. *"Baillet,"* I sputtered quickly.

Moreover, my age and social status had earned me some culturally traditional forms of address for which I was not prepared. For the first time in my life I was addressed as *señora,* in recognition of my marital status and perhaps my age. Although I resisted it as politely as possible, I was sometimes called *Licenciada,* in recognition of the fact that I have a college education, and *Maestra (teacher)* because of the workshops I presented. In formal situations I was systematically addressed as *Doctora* despite my efforts to explain I was not yet a "doctor." In seven months I was called *Patricia* on only a handful of occasions and almost always at initial introductions. Routinely I was *Paty or Patty.*

My fieldwork in Mexico was intended to focus on others' ways of speaking. Naively, I never imagined it would result in the rediscovery and recovery of my own speaking style. As others were generous and inventive in their use of forms of address with me, I reciprocated. Expressions came easily and naturally. We drew on a common pool of linguistic possibilities and added our own variations. We were mutually intelligible. I felt socially integrated—or rather, reintegrated. This was a new feeling for me. It was this feeling that *Pat* had displaced so many years before.

"Thanks, Pat," smiled the ticket agent in Los Angeles as I received my boarding pass. I had just cleared U.S. customs and was on my final flight home. Home? I had left "home" when the Veracruzanos and I embraced for the last time. Yes, they are my *home,* they are my history. But in a matter of hours I would rejoin another part of my history, the non-Mexican husband who understands my need for a name of my own. In a matter of days, I would again conjoin with the fellowship of intimates in whose joyous transitions and silent collapses we often partake. Soon I would reconnect with the community of mentors whose guidance and support are not contingent on my ability to fit within their slotted social restraints. They are my history as well.

"Have a good flight, Pat," said the ticket agent. I started laughing. He never knew why.

Chang Hee Yoon was adopted from a Korean orphanage as an infant. Her name was changed to Mei Lin Swanson Kroll, and she was raised in Minnesota. This essay describes the evolution of her identity as a Korean and her reactions to the ignorance and stereotyping she still encounters. Her story provides a meaningful touchstone for individuals born into one culture and socialized in another.

3   My Name Is. . .

Mei Lin Swanson Kroll

My name is Yoon, Chang Hee—and my name is Mei Lin Swanson Kroll. There's obviously a story here, and also a metaphor for my life. I was born in Seoul, South Korea, and was named Yoon, Chang Hee in an orphanage. I was then transracially adopted at the age of five months, and my parents changed my name to Mei Lin Swanson Kroll.

Mei Lin is actually a Chinese name, but my parents thought it sounded Asian and would be easy for non-Asians to say; they didn't realize that Koreans wouldn't name their children with Chinese names. Swanson was my mother's name; she's Swedish and Norwegian. Kroll is my father's name; we're not sure what he is, but he's Slovenian, English, and maybe German or Polish. I know my parents were trying to be culturally sensitive when they named me Mei Lin, but they didn't realize how difficult it in fact would be for people to say my name properly. I still don't see why some people have such a hard time trying to pronounce it. You say it just like it looks. Mei Lin. It's two words: the first like the month of May, and the second like the American name, Lynn. But people have a tendency to add a "g" at the end of my name, because they think all Asian names have *g*s. They also call me My Lin, Mee Lynn, My Ling, Mia Lim, Mee Ling, Marylyn, Elle, and my own favorite, Melon. So I've found the name to be a bit of trouble.

When I was experiencing an identity crisis in my first year of college, I came across my naturalization papers while I was getting ready to apply for a passport. I saw my orphanage-given name and suddenly had a very strong emotional reaction. That was really all I had when I came to this country: that name. And my parents overlooked it and chose another one. So I began to use Yoon, Chang Hee in writing and in speaking. I've thought about changing my name legally and I still may do it. I want to tell you more about myself, about how I've arrived at these names, and about my sense of identity in a transracial family and in a racist society. It's been quite a journey.

When I was young, I knew that I was adopted and was Korean. I also knew other adopted Koreans and other families with adopted kids, so I thought I was pretty normal. In fact, when I was about three or four I came home one day to tell my mother a big secret—something I'd just figured out. I asked her, very confidentially, "Did you know there are some families who don't have any adopted kids?" She said she did know that. I said, "You know, they're just plain white."

In fact, in grade school, my two best friends were adopted Koreans. We thought we were pretty special, like we had a secret language. We often teased other kids and made up things about our relationships. One day we told them we were really sisters. Another day we were cousins. Another day we were friends, just all from different families. It made a difference, obviously, for there to be several of us. I later met Korean adoptees who didn't live near others. They grew up in suburbs with few kids of color, and they always felt alone and outside. I also had the good fortune to have a Korean woman as my day-care provider. I consider her now my godmother. She took care of me during the day and taught me to eat Korean food, sing Korean nursery rhymes, and count in Korean. I loved her and came to love Korean food. I consider her a very important part of the development of my positive cultural identity.

When I was in junior high my parents sent me to a preteen Korean group. I went for several years, enjoying the food and joining in discussions about Korean culture, activities, groups, and (especially) Korean food. But as I got older, I got tired of it. I told my parents I was tired of the same old questions over and over: "How does it feel to be Korean?" "How does it feel to be adopted?" My parents reluctantly let me quit. Looking back, I think that was the beginning of my turning my back on my Korean identity and culture.

Ever since I was little there was always some kind of teasing going on because I was Korean and didn't look like everyone else. My mother tells me that on the first day of public school I came home indignant because some kid had called me Chinese and said I peed in my Coke. My parents were very concerned and asked me how I felt and what I did. I said, "Well, I hit him." They thought that ended that; I'd learned to stand up for myself. They didn't know that the teasing went on all the time and that I was storing up some negative reactions about being different. Once some friends and I were talking about stupid things we had done. I was telling a story about jumping and flipping on my parents' bed. While I was jumping up and down and having the time of my life, I decided to flip over forward. I accidentally overrotated, fell off the bed, hit my mouth on the wall, and started to bleed. My friend then said, "Oh, is that why your face is so flat?" She and another girl just laughed. I just sat there embarrassed and acted as if I didn't hear a thing. I've been told that I look like a Chinese porcelain doll. Some have even asked if I could see out of my eyes. The list goes on and on, but I began in junior high and throughout high school to let people make those comments and pretend I didn't hear or they didn't really say what they said. I think that subconsciously I decided to drop the Korean side of myself and try to fix the other side—the reasons I was teased. I decided to "fix" it by wanting to be white, to be "just like everyone else."

I also felt like an outsider at times within my own family, especially my extended family. It wasn't as direct or as deliberate as the incidents in school, but it happened nevertheless. Once one of my cousins was diddling with her fingers and discovered that when she put her two index fingers together, they parted from each other at the tips. Everyone else decided to put their fingers together to see what it looked like. I knew exactly where this was going. I put my fingers together under the table, where no one could see. When I put my two fingers together, it looked like someone put crazy glue on them—straight together to the end. There was no separation, not even slightly. I pretended something was in my eye and got up and left—and went to the bathroom where no one could see my tears. I often still feel like an outsider when my extended family gets together, such as when the out-of-town cousins come to visit. Someone always mentions that "the Krolls have a distinct look." Last I checked I was a Kroll too. But they start to point out similarities: who has what eyes, lips, smile, hair thickness, and so on. If someone doesn't fit that mold, it is for some peculiar reason. I never fit. But we don't talk about it—like I'm not there or I don't count. But I feel it—I don't fit, the oddball even in my own family.

When kids get to high school they become concerned with fitting in. I went to a high school that was pretty racially diverse, but I spent my time with a kind of "in" athletic crowd, mostly from my neighborhood, and mostly white. I didn't want to spend time with people who looked like me. I didn't want to spend time with other Asians—I acted like they were foreigners—even other adopted Koreans. An adopted Korean boy asked me to a dance; I said no and avoided him like the plague. I even tried to avoid talking to other Asians. I was so self-conscious and thought that everyone else was looking at us, lumping us together, when I was determined to be like everyone else—not Asian.

In the summer after high school and before college this assimilation plan of mine started to come apart. First it changed because of something positive; then my first year of college demolished it completely. When I finished high school, I was introduced to a group of Koreans by a former high school friend who was Korean. I wouldn't have given him the time of day in high school, but he came often into the Chinese restaurant where I worked so I agreed one night to go with him to somebody's house after work. What I found was so intriguing and amazing—I didn't have to explain or adjust myself to fit in. We all shared this invisible bond. We all had gone through similar experiences in school—and I had thought I was the only one feeling this way because I was adopted. I realized this was a race issue, not just an adoption issue. People pick out differences in how we look. But now I felt like I belonged. I opened up to Koreans, and to Korean culture and to other Asians. I had a whole new appreciation for being Korean and for Korean culture. I had a new set of friends and they were like me!

In the fall I went away to a college about 70 miles from my home. I went with a group of kids from my high school, but I looked forward to meeting other people. I didn't expect what I found: a new level of stereotyping and racism, beyond teasing. One of my classes was taught by a professor who talked about cultural sensitivity in her classes. On the very first day of class, she asked a Japanese man in the front row if he had a camera. She then looked around the room and at the four Asians in the room—including me—and asked, "I mean, come on, all you Japanese people have nice cameras, right?" All of a sudden she began to laugh, a signal for the rest of the class to laugh too. I just kept looking down at my notebook, while everyone else waited for more jokes. I realized this was just the beginning.

Winter break was coming up and everyone was getting restless. This professor handed out something to several of us; at first I thought it was our grades. Then I saw it was a map. It was an invitation to come to her house for Thanksgiving. I was going up to thank her but decline after class, when I realized only Asian students had received these invitations. She commented to another (white) student who looked curious that she was inviting the Japanese students because they couldn't afford to fly all the way home for Thanksgiving. The ironic thing was that on the first day of class she had us fill out cards telling her where we came from, our name, address, and why we wanted to take the class. My name is Kroll—my address was 70 miles away, I don't have a Korean or a Japanese accent. But she couldn't see me as a person—just a stereotype—and what she automatically assumed about all Asians was applied to us, though only one of the four Asians in that class was Japanese.

It was even harder on a social level. One night my friends from high school talked me into going to a party. I tried to mingle, but people spoke to me v . . . e . . . r . . . ry slo-o-o-w-ly, e-nun-ci-a-ting every word. No one asked me to dance. There wasn't another person of color in the entire room. I had enough; I wanted to go back to the dorm and told my friends so. They asked why I wanted to leave. I told them I didn't feel comfortable and had heard someone whispering to another "and they can't even speak English." One of my friends said to me, "Well, Mei, at least you're not black." I couldn't believe it. I just stood there in total shock while the rest of them kept bouncing to the music and sipping Old Milwaukee beer.

I began to go home every weekend and to spend my free time with my Korean friends. They could understand, so I didn't have to explain. It began to hit me that all the effort I had put into being white wasn't worth it, and of course it didn't really work. Wow! Like a ton of bricks! I had other choices. I knew I had to get off that campus and go to the people who could help me be myself. That would be a better way to get through college. As the year was coming to a close I began hauling my stuff back home, nearly three to four weeks before school actually ended. I just couldn't wait to get off that campus and I looked forward to not ever seeing those people again.

The following year I transferred to a college nearer my home. I got to know more Koreans and spent more of my time, in fact almost all my free time, with other Koreans. I took Korean language classes, as well as classes in Asian history, race and gender relations, and intercultural communication. Things were much better—not because the transfer meant that I would avoid all prejudice, racism, and discrimination. But I was better able to face it because I had the family and friends who are my support network.

I do still encounter incidents and people who don't understand Koreans or Korean culture. At work I was hanging out in the kitchen tossing French fries back and forth with a cook who is African American. He said, "Hey, don't be doing any of that Kung-fu stuff on me! I know you Chinese people!" I said, "Um, I'm not Chinese. I'm Korean." He said, "What's the difference?" like it was unimportant. I said, "It's a big difference. What's the difference between a Jamaican and a Nigerian?" He said, "I don't know." "The difference is culture! Different languages, food, values, beliefs, traditions, music, ways of life!" I've found ways to respond and not just be silent and keep my feelings bottled up inside.

I'm also reminded that people know so little when they expect me to know everything Asian and every aspect of Asian cultures. I was talking to another student who was telling me how amazed he was by the dinner an Asian woman had made for him recently. I asked him what she made. He started to describe it, because he didn't know the name. He was describing it as chicken with red, sweet sauce all over it. I immediately said, "Oh, that's got to be sweet and sour chicken." He said, "Wow! How did you know? Do your parents own a Chinese restaurant?" I said, "Uh, not quite, but I did work in a Chinese restaurant." Then he moved on to the next dish. He described this soup with all kinds of greens and said it was Japanese soup. I said, "Well, you got me there. I don't know what kind of soup that is." He had an unsettled look on his face and insisted that I must know. He said, "This soup is Japanese, though. What do you mean, you don't know?" And I said back, loudly, "I don't know means I don't know. I'm Korean and I worked in a Chinese restaurant. How does that make me a Japanese authority?"

My Korean friends understand and have similar experiences all the time. We recall similar experiences from high school, where practically all our friends were white or of another color. We were all pretty "Americanized." There were times when we hated to be Korean, because we looked so different from our friends. In college most of us changed and began to identify with and spend our time with other Koreans. We can relate to each other better, because we don't have to explain ourselves. I identify more strongly with my Korean heritage and culture, which makes me actually feel in place, comfortable with who I am. All of these experiences that I've written about have made me a stronger person and determined to succeed—to prove wrong the people who underestimated me.

My mother and I were talking once and she told me that when she went to Norway to visit her relatives she could feel that bond, not so much because her relatives were Scandinavian, but because this was who she was. She felt at home and understood herself better by seeing them and learning which parts of Scandinavian culture had become part of her. I could relate because that's how I feel about being with Koreans. I think everyone should visit where they originally came from. I don't mean it has to be a physical visit to another land—but merely soul searching—meet people of a similar background and ethnicity, read books about your ethnicity, the country you originate from, whatever it takes to get a better understanding of who you are. If you go, if you find a place, a book, or a person that awakens your inner self or an unrecognized part, you will discover something deep inside that is inexplicable, something priceless. I know my identity and who I am because I know who I am not. I wish others the same.

In this essay Michael Lewis offers insights into the experiences of many gays and lesbians as they seek to establish cultural, social, and personal identities within a larger society that does not accept or affirm their sexual preferences. His stories provide insights into the denial that many people are forced to experience to "get along." Michael also provides an understanding of the significance that "otherness" plays in shaping one's identity.

Something to Tell You

Michael John Lewis

She had come to her brother's house to heal. Her oldest son had died in a car accident on his way back to college after a family celebration of his twentieth birthday. The center had fallen out of her life. All her assumptions and beliefs about the way her life would be had been transformed into myth. She was floating in a universe without rules. Anything could happen. She was on the edge. Of all her family she was closest to her brother. They always had been close. They looked alike and thought alike. They had even been born on the same day, exactly four years apart. For a short time during childhood their height evened out and everyone thought they were twins. She came to her brother's house to grieve and to breathe air not filled with visions of her son. She knew that her brother would support her, hold her, listen to her, and help her move on. Her friends back home found the subject of such loss uncomfortable and avoided her and, if not her, the subject of her son's death. Her husband was inconsolable, locked in his own grief. She loved him and she believed in his love for her; but in this she felt alone.

The two weeks with her brother were nearly over. They had shared tears and long evenings of walks through the neighborhood. She had been very moved by a book that her brother's friend had shared with her when she first arrived. Her brother and his friend had helped her begin to see the faint outlines of purpose once again. She could talk of her son and her own future with feelings other than pain alone. It was her last night. Tomorrow she would fly home to resume her life. After dinner, she and her brother decided to take one last walk while Donald cleaned up the kitchen. It was a beautiful evening, cool and breezy, with the electric indigo sky of dusk in the far west. The conversation centered on her husband and how she might best help him when she returned home. As they rounded the corner of the far point of their walk, her brother broke the train of their conversation.

"I have something I have been wanting to tell you, Sis. I'm gay. Donald's not my friend or roommate; he's my partner. I hope you realize how hard it is for me to talk about this. I've been trying to get up the nerve for years. I wanted to tell someone in the family and I chose you."

She smiled at her brother and grabbed and squeezed his arm with her long nails the way she did when she was in high school and he was her nerdy little brother. "I'm so happy that you finally said something to me. To tell you the truth I've been a little hurt that you didn't say something a long time ago." She wasn't sure where to go next. She had waited so long for her brother to say something, she didn't know what to say. "I love you," she finally said.

"I love you, too, Sis. I'm so relieved. I was so afraid what you might say. You know what a lot of people say about gay and lesbian people. I was prepared for the worst and you gave me the best. Thank you."

"What are you saying? No one has ever been mean to you, have they?" Suddenly she was the older sister. No one was going to pick on her little brother.

"Big time," he responded matter-of-factly, his mind fixed on the concerns he would have to address as he continued the process of coming out. "But right now I would like to talk about Mom and Dad. I have thought and thought for years and years about this. I don't know if I should tell them or not. I really would like to tell them. But, I am so afraid that they would never talk to me again. Do you know if they have any idea about this? I keep thinking that they must have figured this out by now. I'm pushing forty and I've been living with Donald for almost fifteen years. They know we own our house together. I never talk about getting married. I keep thinking that they would have put two and two together by now. What do you think I should do?"

"Well, I don't think they have figured it out. Dad keeps asking me why I think you haven't gotten married and wishing you would settle down and have children. Mom never says anything. We have never spoken about it. But somehow I think deep down she knows, but she doesn't want to, if you know what I mean. A mother knows. But I wouldn't tell them; I really wouldn't. They're getting older and I just don't think they could handle it. They come from a different generation and I just don't think they would understand. Especially Dad. Maybe after he is gone you could try to tell Mom. But she probably would just blame herself and think that you're the way you are because she did something wrong. But, you know how much they both love you and how proud they are of you."

Her brother felt silenced. He understood his sister's words exactly. He couldn't disagree with them. He couldn't agree with them. "I know how much they love me. But they don't know me."

Different

I always knew
Sitting there in the kitchen
Around the big yellow table
   Mother
     Father

Football Hero Brother
Beauty Queen Sister
and Me
I always knew I was different
Smart
Left-handed
and Different
Still
Not like the rest of you
The perfect family
Happy then around our yellow table
Not like you
Different

Symbol

They rose early in the morning to get ready. Graduation day. It had taken four years for the two of them to earn their degrees. Teachers by day; graduate students by night. Through it all they had supported each other—through the tuition bills, late dinners, no dinners; through the months when the money ran out long before payday; through the pressure of papers and presentations and studying while still being prepared for their own classrooms of third and fourth graders at 8:00 A.M. each morning. Credit cards charged to the max, they had made it to this day, ready to face the future together. Kathy turned on the iron while Jan put on the coffee. They had to be out of the house in two hours to be on time at the stadium. Kathy began pressing their graduation robes, sipping her coffee between passes over the blue rayon. Jan brought the dog out for his morning run and returned just in time to shower and dress. They were ready. Their fresh robes hung on hangers. The dog was in the yard. As they were about to walk out the door each pulled a corsage from behind her back. This would be their last private time together before the ceremony, their only chance to express how they felt about each other and their achievement. "I love you," Kathy whispered as she pinned the corsage on the lapel of Jan's navy jacket. "I love you, too," Jan whispered back. "Thanks for everything— the big things and the little ones, too."

Kathy and Jan managed to position themselves so they could walk together into the stadium and be seated together. It was hard not to hold hands. The friends and family members of their classmates, cheering, clapping, and stomping their approval of their graduates' accomplishments, surrounded them. No one was there to cheer for Kathy and Jan. Kathy had a strained relationship with her family and Jan's mother was too ill to make the trip. Their friends couldn't take time off from work to be there. For the moment, they had each other. They sat in silence.

The graduation program began, a series of speakers and music all leading to the awarding of diplomas. Kathy and Jan recognized some of the speakers from their years at the university. Both tried hard to listen patiently to each presentation, but it was difficult not to think about all that had brought them to this place and where they might go from here. Suddenly a new presenter was before them at the podium, a graying woman looking out at the crowd over half glasses. Her academic robes were jet black with beautiful royal blue velvet chevrons on each sleeve. Around her neck and flowing down the front of her robes was a silk scapular brightly decorated with the colors of the rainbow: red, orange, yellow, green, blue, indigo, and violet bands running the length of the scapular, the lines of the colors shifting and blending as she talked. On the breast of her robes were two pins, the glittering red ribbon of AIDS awareness and a large, pink, inverse triangle, the Nazi symbol of hatred and death transformed into the defiant symbol of liberation for gay and lesbian people. Kathy and Jan had never seen her before. Her presence before the crowd electrified them. They listened to each word she said, hoping she would never leave the podium. They felt suddenly that they really belonged to the university and to the ceremony. Jan began waving at the speaker, smiling and crying softly while pointing to the place on her own breast where the same pins were fixed. Kathy turned to Jan and hugged her, holding her until they were called to rise for their diplomas.

A Eulogy: About Bob

My friend Bob died suddenly last winter of a heart attack at age 71. He had a wonderful service at a local cathedral. His two sisters came from out of town to attend his funeral. Bob's colleagues from work attended in force. And Bob's friends from the gay and lesbian community attended. There were three eulogies for this magnificent man, all from people who had worked with Bob over the years. The words from his eulogists focused on Bob's considerable professional accomplishments, sly humor, and many good deeds. No one mentioned that Bob was gay, that a gay man had died—a gay man who had lived his life as honestly as he could through a time when there was no safe place for homosexuals in America.

Bob was born in San Jose in 1925, the only son, between two sisters. His father, a piano mover, died while Bob was a young man, and the family moved frequently around California, Oregon, and Washington. Bob had an early interest in the arts, singing and dancing in school and amateur productions and becoming a viola virtuoso, eventually playing part-time with a philharmonic orchestra in the 1950s. Bob was drafted in World War II, serving in combat zones in the Pacific theater. He served honorably and, in subsequent years, made much high humor of the military's "don't ask; don't tell" policy. Following his military discharge, Bob attended San Francisco State University on the G.I. bill. He earned his degree and his credentials as a teacher of the blind. Bob taught in special education classrooms in California's Central Valley through the 1950s, when he moved to New York City to earn his doctorate in education, specializing in programs for the blind. Along the way Bob dated a number of men, eventually meeting the love of his life and enjoying a long-term relationship that resolved into a long-distance friendship when his lover became an Episcopal priest.

Upon earning his doctorate Bob began a long and distinguished career in university teaching. He was the recipient of numerous federal research and training grants and was richly honored in his field. He retired from two universities and still was teaching part-time at a local university at the time of his death. He remained connected with his professional discipline and with the community around him. No one mistook him for "old." He loved opera and show tunes—he would walk out of any store or restaurant that was playing rock music. He was a terrible housekeeper. He loved a good meal, good Scotch, and a good joke. He drove 200 miles a week to visit two frail and elderly colleagues who were without family and lived in nursing homes. He served as legal guardian for one, agonizing over the decision to allow the medical amputation of her foot necessitated by advanced diabetes.

In his later years his personal life centered on the Episcopal Church. He seemed to volunteer as many hours a week there as I work for pay. One of his volunteer efforts through his church was with the AIDS Interfaith Network. Through the Network, Bob began assisting a gay man who was very ill with AIDS. Art had been a bartender at a local gay bar. He was in his late 50's, too ill to work, and living in a rooming house for people with AIDS. What Art needed, Bob was there to supply: rides to his many medical appointments and to the drug and grocery stores; reminders to take medication; getaway vacations; restaurant meals; holiday plans. They were an unlikely pair, so different and so in tune with each other. The moment Bob became his Network volunteer, Art began to improve—slowly at first, and then dramatically. I would kid the two of them that they really were an "item" and, in a way, they were. However, friendship, compassion, and service defined their relationship, rather than passion—the same friendship, compassion, and service that Bob brought to all he did.

Art was with Bob the day he died. Bob had undergone bypass surgery and had returned home to recuperate. It was Art's turn to take care of Bob. Art had taken Bob's car to the drugstore to pick up Bob's medication: he was gone 45 minutes. a church deacon had dropped by to look after Bob while Art was out. When Art returned, Bob had died in his sleep, while taking a nap.

I miss Bob terribly. I grieve, too, for Art, who has lost his mainstay. And I grieve for gay and lesbian people who even in death are denied the truth about their lives.

Love you, Bob.

Ten True Stories from Work and School

A guy I worked with for years walked with me to the parking garage. On the way he talked about how cool he was and that he had no problem with gay people and that he had all these gay friends. He made sure I knew he was straight. I listened politely. As we got to the garage he said he had heard rumors about my being gay and turned to ask me, "Are you gay?" I looked him straight in the eye and said, "Yes, I'm gay. I'm not going to deny who I am." With this, Mr. Cool slipped on the curb and fell on his butt.

When I was new on a job and new to the city I attended an informal welcoming party for new employees. A senior employee struck up a conversation with me, eventually asking me where I was living. When I told him, he replied, "Why are you living there? That's where all the blacks, Asians, and gays live." What a set-up! I was afraid to blast him away with a "Duh!" Instead, I said sweetly, "I know. I hope to save enough money to buy a house there." Till the day he retired I don't think he said another five words to me.

When I was a sophomore in high school, our class took a bus trip to a religious house for a spiritual retreat of several days. On the way home, my classmates decided to have some sport with me. Led by a particularly vicious boy, my classmates composed and sang a little song that made fun of me and my gayness. I really felt I would die, trapped on that bus with all those boys laughing at me. Even some of the teachers were laughing. Not one adult tried to help or to stop the abuse. The event was so traumatic that, as I look back on it, I realize that it affected my behavior and emotional life for a number of years thereafter. Ironically, my high school—actually a prep school—has been very successful in tracking me down over the years to solicit donations but I never give a cent. When the thirtieth anniversary of my graduation approached, I received an invitation to an event that asked us to bring our spouses or domestic partners. How times have changed. I didn't know whether to laugh or cry.

After I'd been at a job for a few years, a manager called me into his office and shut the door. "People say you're gay," he said flat out, without any preliminary niceties. "I can't help what people say," I shot back. Then he said, "So and so said he saw you last weekend on Polk Street." "Really?" I replied. "What was so-and-so doing on Polk Street?" The manager roared with laughter and subsequently always treated me with great respect, even affection.

I have a professional relationship with a talented and honored woman. We work together often and have a slight friendship going, although we live in different cities. When we are in each other's city, we sometimes dine out and go to the theater, symphony, or opera. Recently an issue began developing in our relationship that I don't know how to handle. I am very open with her about being gay. She knows my partner well and we have introduced her to gay culture. At first she appeared to adore everything about the gay community. Lately, though, she has made it very clear that she adores gay men, but that lesbians are a different matter. She also has begun to compliment my partner and me on how masculine we are and commented that we don't "appear" to be "gay." The subtext here is that appearing to be "gay" is a bad thing, a putdown of my more colorful and fabulous comrades. I have tried to model for her that the gay community is diverse and that its diversity is its strength. She hasn't picked up on it so I'm beginning to avoid her when I can.

One of our graduate students was completing a series of observations in preschool settings. She was doing research on the topic of sex-role stereotyping in young children. During one of her observations the preschool teacher asked the children to name and discuss their favorite colors. One little girl picked pink and then told her classmates that she loved pink and that pink was for girls. She elaborated that boys could not select pink unless they were faggots. When her teacher delicately tried to move her away from her premise, the girl insisted that faggots were bad and that she knew this to be true because her daddy had told her so.

I had interviewed for a top position with a company noted for its emphasis on traditional family values, meaning gays need not apply. I was surprised when I made it to the final cut. I was called back for a second interview and invited to a dinner party to which I could bring a guest. I knew that the company management valued entertaining as part of the corporate image and that the dinner was all about checking out my wife. I wasn't brave enough to come out and I was too proud to pretend to be a bachelor. So I went to the second interview and declined the dinner, making some excuse. Of course I didn't get the job. I've always wished since that I had been a little braver.

My lover of seventeen years had been laid off during the real estate slump. His medical benefits were about to be terminated. I knew my employer did not offer domestic partner benefits, but I decided to make a statement. My union rep had told me that management had been claiming during negotiations that domestic partner benefits really were not an issue, because no one had ever asked for them. So I went over to the benefits office and calmly explained to the clerk that I was there to register my gay domestic partner for benefits as my spouse. I was speaking to the manager of benefits in about 20 seconds. He was oh so nice to me and explained why my request was just not possible and how he would do it in an instant if he could. "Nice" just doesn't cut it for me any more.

Going to college saved my life. I grew up in a small farm town. You've heard of the "small-town girl"? Well, I was the small-town lesbian. Like most gay people, I thought I was the only one on earth, kind of like a space alien dropped from the sky into this farm family. In college I learned that I was not alone and that I had a community from which I could draw strength and pride. I am deeply grateful to my alma mater for supporting gay and lesbian studies and a gay and lesbian student organization.

Over the years I became very aware of the office gossip about my lesbianism and the jokes about my appearance: short, combed hair; no makeup; pleated trousers with plaid man-tailored shirts. State workers in downtown

Sacramento have a long tradition of coming to work in costume when Halloween falls on a workday. One Halloween I showed up at work with my short hair "styled" and decked out in a silk dress, nylons, and heels. My coworkers were so amused that the event now has become legend. But that's not all: The following year my coworkers surprised me on Halloween by all showing up at work dressed as ME!

Let's Dance

I'm a middle-aged gay man at the end of the century. I have lived with and loved the same man for 22 years. I have survived the epidemic. It is a privilege to be able to look back—and to look ahead. I come from the generation of gay and lesbian people who escaped persecution through building our lives in the large cities of our nation. We created gay communities, our own families, and our own culture. We pursued our own music, visual arts, dance, humor, design, literature, theater, politics, newspapers, magazines, charities, clubs, and places of worship. When AIDS attacked, it was a galvanized, united gay community that fought back. We refused to be silent about our lives and to be ashamed of who we are. We built a life apart because no one else would have us, outsiders to all but our own community.

Over the years we turned much of the pain of oppression, rejection, and loss into gay pride. Scratch gay pride in someone my age and you'll usually find some measure of anger, hurt, and pain. It takes a lifetime for gay and lesbian people to overcome the negative stereotyping of their families, communities, religious leaders, and the media to live a life in the sun. I recently told my much older brother that I considered being gay the most important and transforming part of my identity, that I love being gay, and that I am grateful that I have had the opportunity to live a gay life. He absolutely could not believe what I was saying. He really thought that I should *want* to be like him, even though he understood that I could not. This, perhaps, is heterosexism at its most basic—that gay and lesbian people should feel sorry for who they are and try as best they can to be like straight people.

One price I pay for my own experiences is that I don't trust straight people, a kind of "heterophobia." I'm not proud of this, but it's true for me. I have close straight friends, but as a whole I don't trust straight people to represent my interests, my point of view, or me. At worst I really believe that they want to kill me or put me into a camp somewhere; at best, I think they have their own interests in mind and use gay and lesbian people to further their own agenda. I have been waiting nearly 50 years for my most basic civil rights. In many of the 50 states it is still perfectly legal to refuse me a lease on an apartment or to fire me because I am gay.

While I have been waiting, a new generation of gay and lesbian people has grown into the community—our own Gen Xers. And they couldn't be more different from their elders. In *The Rise and Fall of Gay Culture* (New York: Hyperion, 1997), Daniel Harris writes about members of this generation, who appear to have a stronger affiliation with people their own age than with people who share their sexual identity. This is a generation whose members are much more comfortable with who they are and much less likely to feel "different" or "apart" because of their sexual identity. While Harris's characterization of these gay youth and young adults certainly does not hold for every Xer, I have observed the phenomenon he reports in the urban dance clubs of the gay community. These clubs historically have been exclusively gay, often exclusively male or female on certain nights of the week. If straight clientele appeared at the door they would be denied admission outright or made to feel uncomfortable enough to leave. Xers now attend these clubs in mixed groups: men, women, straight, gay, and bisexual. They look alike, dress alike; some are tattooed and pierced alike. They hang as a group, dance as a group, and socialize across gender, race, and sexual orientation without awkwardness or apology. They are apparently comfortable with themselves and with each other. They are special and beautiful. It is pleasant to guess that this phenomenon is a result of the success of the civil rights and gay movements of the last 25 years. Perhaps we did some good.

It is both gratifying and a little weird to have lived long enough to see "gay" characterized as "cool" and "lesbian" as "chic." Corporations are stumbling over themselves to advertise in what is perceived as a lucrative gay and lesbian niche market. Gay and lesbian themes have jumped from art films to big box office productions. Gay and lesbian characters populate television comedies, and a gay sensibility can be perceived in much of popular culture. We seem poised for a new age of acceptance and inclusion of gay and lesbian people within the mainstream culture. Perhaps the enemies of equal rights for gay and lesbian people have been so virulent in their attacks over the past few years because we are, in fact, winning. But when we do win, what of the community and culture built on the premise of otherness? What will come of that when freedom finally arrives?

Samuel Edelman describes his personal choices in nurturing and sustaining his Jewish cultural and religious identity in the face of the many pressures to assimilate and thereby blur the lines separating Jews from their non-Jewish neighbors and friends. Through descriptions of his journeys to Central Europe and to his hometown in Pennsylvania, Sam explains the alternative possibilities facing Jews in the United States. This essay also provides a larger framework for understanding the experiences of people who must live among and interact with those from more dominant cultural groups.

5

To Pass or Not to Pass, That Is the Question: Jewish Cultural Identity in the United States

Samuel M. Edelman

Not long ago, with only a few weeks between them, I took two voyages into my past. On the first I toured Poland, the Czech Republic, and Germany with 27 professors of the Holocaust. On the second I returned to my hometown in central Pennsylvania to see my parents and to show my children where their father grew up. I returned from these trips a changed man.

In Poland I discovered memorials to millions of dead Jews. Before World War II Poland had a Jewish population of 3.8 million people; today it is 2,500. Yet with almost no Jews remaining, I also found a schizophrenic Poland—anti-Semitic to the core, yet curious about and searching for a culture that is as Polish as Poland but was eradicated. Poland seems to have a split personality. Much of the wall graffiti is violently anti-Jewish, blaming communism and all of Poland's ills on phantom Jews, on the ghosts of the murdered. Newspapers, politicians' speeches, and Polish parish priests' sermons rail against hidden Jews; during the last presidential election, one of the candidates was "accused" of being Jewish. At the Auschwitz-Birkenau death camp several Polish skinheads even confronted us as we toured. I was stunned by the anger in their words and actions. Yet other Poles forcefully confronted the skinheads, who were ultimately carted off by the police.

The most disturbing image burned into my mind was a sight in the beautiful city of Krakow. Before the war Krakow had one of the oldest and most distinguished Jewish communities in Europe. Now only a hundred or so elderly

Jews remain. Krakow boasts of its Jewish section, its fine shops, its restaurants, a cemetery, and an ancient synagogue that is now a museum. It was there that I heard a *klezmer* band playing hauntingly beautiful Jewish melodies. Yet the *klezmer* band had no Jewish members. Jewish culture, burned alive in Auschwitz and Treblinka, was now on display in Krakow at a living museum without Jews.

In Poland I also witnessed a Jewish renaissance without Jews. In Warsaw, Krakow, Lublin, and other places there were Jewish film festivals, Jewish cultural festivals, and Yiddish readings. There were searches for Jewish roots by thousands of young Poles who had discovered that they had Jewish grandparents or that one of their parents was Jewish.

One warm evening we were relaxing at an outdoor café in Warsaw after visiting Jewish cemeteries, monuments, and synagogues. A young man overheard our discussion and asked if any of us were Jewish. Two of us were, and we said so. He asked if he could join us, and we welcomed him. It turned out that he was 36 years old and his father had died a few weeks earlier. Going through his father's papers he had discovered a packet of letters and other family materials; one of the letters was addressed to him. In the letter his father confessed that he was a survivor of one of the worst killing sites in Europe. After his escape, his father was protected and hidden by a young Polish woman, with whom he eventually fell in love and then married after the war. Because of the rampant anti-Semitism in Poland, his father hid his Jewish heritage from his children. Now, as he came closer to death, his father wanted to reveal his roots to his son, hoping that he would search out other Jews, find out more about being Jewish, and decide for himself what to be.

The man's father's death and his discovery of his own Jewish roots were emotionally overwhelming. He asked us if we knew where he could go to learn more about Jews and his heritage. It so happened that we had just returned from the Warsaw Jewish Documentation Center, and we suggested that he go there to discover more. I heard later that he did, indeed, go and began to discover his long-lost Jewish connections.

The man was not alone in his yearning to discover his identity. While anti-Semitism in Poland was growing without Jews, so, too, was interest in all things Jewish. A Jewish journalist told us that to have Jewish roots was "in" among Polish liberals. We learned that the phenomenon of this man's discovery was happening all over the country. The Jewish renewal without Jews was both puzzling and exciting, just as anti-Semitism without Jews was puzzling and disturbing.

My second journey was to my hometown, Altoona, Pennsylvania. When I lived there 40 years ago it was a small community of about 49,000 people in the middle of coal and railroad country. There were roughly five hundred Jewish families, two synagogues, two kosher butchers, and a few kosher bakers. *Yiddishkeit,* or Jewishness, thrived. There was also the standard anti-Semitism of small towns, such as the yearly swastika that was chalked on the sidewalk, soaped on the window, or painted on the front door. And there was the name calling—"Jew-boy," "Kike," "Christ killer"—coupled with periodic cross burnings by would-be Kluxers.

Today the Jewish population of Altoona is substantially reduced. Though there are still two rabbis and two buildings, the synagogues have had to put aside their religious differences to combine into one religious school. There is a struggle to keep going. The Reform and Conservative Jewish cemeteries sit side by side, never to meet formally.[1] There are no butcher shops for kosher meat, and no kosher bakeries. There seems to be a tiredness about the place. What is most frightening is the significant part of the Jewish population that is no longer Jewish. Friends and acquaintances with whom I grew up have married non-Jews and have given up their culture and religion—their children are being raised as Christians. Most of my school friends have either converted to Christianity, have become gastronomic Jews who eat ethnic foods on Saturday night or Sunday morning, or—worse yet—are nothing. They are Jews without Judaism; Jews without culture; Jews without history; Jews at best vaguely aware of their heritage. Only a handful remain practicing Jews. Most are lost forever. A few have spouses who converted to Judaism, and fewer still have spouses who helped their children grow up as Jews even though they did not convert.

These two voyages both point to a common image of Judaism and Jewish culture in the United States at the beginning of the twenty first century. Jewish culture, religion, and life are at a crossroads in the United States. One path leads to Altoona and Poland, to anti-Semitism without Jews. The other path leads to Jewish renewal and renaissance. One path leads to Jews passing as non-Jews and disappearing; the other leads to community and continuity.

In my parents' time, those who gave up their heritage were in the minority. For my generation, the size of that group grew significantly. Among today's college students, the number of Jews who are lost to Judaism is more than double that of my generation. Many demographers believe that if the trend continues, the Jewish population in the United States will decline until the middle of the twenty first century, when it will be negligible. Thirty years ago the Jewish population in the United States was 5.8 million people; today, after the arrival of Jewish immigrants from many parts of the world and a sizable increase in the total number of U.S. residents, the Jewish population is essentially unchanged. Where there should have been a substantial net increase, there is none. Zero population growth, coupled with a massive rate of assimilation, is the basis for the fear that within the next 25 years Jewish culture will disappear from America. Ironically, anti-Semitism is probably at its lowest point ever in the annals of the United States. Jewish intellectual, political, and economic power in the United States is strong. Yet the very existence of Jewish culture is facing its greatest threat.

Assimilation has always been a significant part of Jewish life in America, from the first recorded Jewish settlement in 1654 until today. Each wave of immigrants, and the successive generations of their children, has had to choose between passing as non-Jews or publicly embracing and maintaining their Jewish roots as Jewish Americans.[2]

For the Jewish community in the United States, there are four competing choices in dealing with assimilation and its benefits and threats. One choice, of course, is anchored in the vision of the Protestant majority: the United States ought to be a "melting pot," and any hint of foreignness is a threat to American culture and should be eliminated. Like the view often expressed in Europe following the French revolution and the Napoleonic period, the goal of this choice is the disappearance of Jews—both as a culture and as a religion—into the larger society. The force at play is the attractiveness of Americanization, which is sufficiently seductive that Jews will turn their backs on their "other" culture and eventually disappear. The disappearance of Jewish culture, or ethnocide, is happening all over America. Many American Jews have intermarried and, for a variety of reasons—laziness, a desire to pass, ignorance—watch passively as their children grow up with no Jewish education, intermarry again, and finally lose all touch with their heritage.

The second competing choice about how to deal with assimilation is one emphasized by such Jewish leaders as Rabbi Mordechai Kaplan, the founder of the Reconstructionist Jewish Movement. This choice involves an equilibrium between mainstream America and traditional Jewish values. These two sets of values are not antithetical but flow, one into the other, like a balancing act between particularist and universalist perspectives. Kaplan's view is that Jewish culture, history, and religion—important ingredients in the maintenance of Judaism—can easily live side-by-side with American values and culture. This choice verges on what one might call intercultural communication. Some communication scholars might term this approach "biculturalism."

As an example of this second choice to being Jewish in the United States, consider the experiences of one of my very close Jewish friends. More than 15 years ago he met a Catholic woman. They started to date, fell in love, and eventually were married by a Reform rabbi who wanted to keep intermarried families in the orbit of Judaism. After a few years, they had two girls in quick succession. He was ambivalent about his roots, but she was not about hers and felt a tension between them and her obligations to her children. They struggled with such issues as whether to have a Christmas tree in their house and whether to celebrate Christmas and Easter with her parents. They argued over what messages of ambivalence and inclusiveness would be sent to their children if they permitted both religions in the household. Their decision was to give up all Christian practices, even though she had not converted. This was a wrenching decision for her, which she did for the sake of her children. She also knew that because she had not converted to Judaism, the children would not be considered Jewish under Jewish law unless they chose to convert themselves. She therefore opted to have the girls educated in the synagogue, and when they were older she encouraged them to go through the ceremony of conversion. Recently they completed the conversion ceremony, and both had their Bat Mitzvot in the synagogue. Now she, too, is beginning to study to convert.

The third and fourth choices for dealing with assimilation both involve a separation from American culture, but in very different ways. The third choice involves living in the United States while rejecting secular American values. This alternative is adopted by ultra-Orthodox Jews such as the Hasidism. The Hasidic approach places physical and psychological barriers around the Jewish community to separate it from what its members view as the profane. Television is restricted, pop culture is avoided, and anything not Jewish—according to *halacha,* or strict Jewish law—is not permitted. This ideology, which is similar to that of the Amish and other separationist communities, is at the center of the Hasidic way of dealing with secular American values.

The fourth choice, while not rejecting American culture, involves leaving the United States for a political, cultural, linguistic, and religious existence as a Jewish majority in Israel. This Zionist approach encourages as many Jews as possible to make *aliyah* and emigrate to Israel. The horrors of the *Shoah* (the Holocaust) the unwillingness of the allies and others to save European Jewry, the antagonisms among Jewish political groups that left them splintered and ineffective, and the creation of the State of Israel by the United Nations in 1948 all acted as catalysts for many American Jews to propose Zionism to combat assimilation and extermination. It is mind-numbing to realize that, had a Jewish nation existed, millions of Jews could have survived the *Shoah*. The success of the State of Israel is an important and critical counterbalance to assimilation, conversion, intermarriage, indifference, and anti-Semitism in America and throughout the world. An economically developed, intellectually advanced, and politically stable Israel suggests that Zionism has been successful in achieving its broad goals. The core belief of Zionism is that what happened to Europe's Jews should never happen again. Connection to this idea and to Israel has become a secular religion for many American Jews. While Zionism initially held that one should make *aliyah* to Israel, it now supports the idea that one also serves who stays in America and fights in support of Jewish communities under threat throughout the world.

Another useful typology for understanding the American Jewish community is provided by Daniel J. Elazar.[3] Elazar describes American Jewry as seven concentric circles that radiate outward from a core of committed Jews toward a vague sense of Jewishness on the fringes. At the core are the "integral" Jews, for whom Jewishness is a central factor in their lives and a full-time concern. Elazar estimates that they represent 5 percent of the Jewish population in the United States. Surrounding the core is a second group of U.S. Jews, the "participants," who regularly engage in Jewish life and who view expressions of their Jewishness as important but not full-time activities. They may be officers in Jewish organizations, participants in pro-Israel activities, contributors to Jewish educational experiences, or professionals employed by Jewish agencies. Elazar estimates that they represent from 10 to 20 percent of U.S. Jews.

The third circle is made up of "associated" Jews, who are affiliated with Jewish institutions or organizations in some concrete way but are not very active in them. This group is made up of synagogue members whose activities are limited to High Holy Day services, participation in Jewish rites of passage, and memberships in Jewish social and political organizations such as Hadassah and B'nai B'rith. Elazar suggests that this group is fairly large, making up about 30 to 35 percent of the Jewish population.

The fourth circle, "contributors and consumers," consists of Jews who make periodic donations to Jewish causes and occasionally use the services of Jewish institutions, but who are at best minimally associated with the Jewish community. He estimates that 25 to 30 percent of Jews are in this circle.

The fifth circle includes what Elazar calls the "peripherals," who are recognizably Jewish in some way but are completely uninvolved in Jewish life. They have no interest in participating in Jewish experiences and rarely make donations to Jewish causes. About 15 percent are in this circle.

The sixth circle, the "repudiators," are Jews who actively deny their Jewishness. Some are extremely hostile to all things Jewish, while others simply react with hostility to their Jewish origins. This group, which once was very large but has experienced an extensive decline, now makes up less than 5 percent of U.S. Jews.

Finally, there is a group Elazar labels "quasi-Jews." They are neither fully inside nor entirely outside the Jewish community. They may have intermarried but have some connection to a personal Jewish label. They make up about 5 to 10 percent of the population.

Growth at both the core and on the periphery of Judaism is increasing. The core grows as young Jews return to Jewish religious life and become *Baal Teshuva,* conforming to Jewish laws and rituals. The proselytizing activities of some of the more aggressive fundamentalist groups, such as the Lebavitcher Hasidim, have been very successful with disaffected Jewish youth. There is also substantial population growth among Orthodox Jews, especially among the ultra-Orthodox. The movement toward religious return and revival, coupled with a phenomenal birth rate, contributes to growth in the core. Simultaneously, however, the intermarriage rate among those in the third and fourth circles of Jewish involvement, who comprise the majority of the U.S. Jewish population, is also on the rise. The intermarriage rate among these Jews— who often label themselves Conservative, Reform, or Reconstructionist Jews— now approaches 57 percent.

Intermarriage has both positive and negative consequences. Although increasing numbers of young Jews are intermarrying, there is also a growing number of their non-Jewish spouses who are converting to Judaism. The rate of conversion has been increasing in the last decade, but the relative numbers are still small. Of greater interest is the number of non-Jewish spouses in intermarried couples who join a Jewish communal group as quasi-Jewish participants. This phenomenon is most evident in rural or small Jewish congregations that exist where the Jewish population is relatively isolated from mainstream Jewish communities. For example, my own community of Chico, California, has one small synagogue and a congregation that dates back to the early days of the gold rush. Over the last 20 years the membership has tripled to about 90 families. Until recently we had an active religious school but only a part-time rabbi, who did not live in the community, to provide our religious services. Now we have a rabbi who lives here. A significant proportion of those who affiliate with the synagogue come from intermarried families in which the non-Jewish spouse is the catalyst for involvement of both the children and the Jewish spouse. Many of these men and women support Jewish communal and religious involvement despite resistance from their Jewish spouses. These Jewish affiliate members, as I call them, are integral to the development and maintenance of Jewish life in our community. This is the reality of what some of us call frontier Judaism.

Colleagues from other small and rural communities report observations similar to mine in Chico. This suggests to me that the most peripheral areas of Jewish involvement may provide the greatest potential for the future of Jewish America. It is because of these non-Jewish yet affiliated members of intermarried couples that Jewish life is transmitted to a new generation of Jews hitherto thought lost to Jewish life. If the Chico phenomenon is typical, then it is clear that a rethinking of the age-old negative vision of intermarriage must be undertaken.

I view myself as among the ranks of what Elazar calls the "integral Jew." I have taken a roundabout path to this place I am now in. Growing up in my hometown, I defined myself in terms of my Jewishness. I never denied it, and sometimes flaunted it. There was even a time when I thought seriously about becoming a rabbi; I still have dreams of doing that. I became, instead, a communication professor. I have experienced various incidents of anti-Semitism. One such incident occurred when I ran for township supervisor in Pennsylvania. Though it was a close race, it was only as election day approached that I discovered a secret my campaign staff and friends had been keeping from me: flyers accusing me of being part of a Zionist conspiracy and a "Christ-killer" had been distributed throughout the district. I doubt that I lost many votes because of these smears, but I did feel pain. I truly felt like an outsider.

I explored the option of making *aliyah* to Israel. I did not move there because, at the time, I couldn't find work and my wife didn't want to go. Nevertheless, I regret that I didn't immigrate, for when I am in Israel I feel truly at ease and not "the other." Instead, I choose to identify as a Jew in the United States, not only in my home but also in my work. Over the last 20 years I have gradually spent more and more time researching and studying Jewish subjects related to communication studies. I now identify more with my Jewish work than with my disciplinary involvement in communication. As I became successful in teaching and researching such subjects as the Holocaust and Israeli public address, I experienced a greater sense of ease. I also feel lucky to have supportive colleagues and friends who have encouraged me to do my own thing. My mentor at Penn State, Gerald Phillips, felt bitter that his peers in the communication discipline never provided him with similar latitude to work on Jewish topics.

Today I coordinate a Jewish studies program and am working toward developing a field of study called Jewish rhetoric. My wife is Jewish and my children are being educated and brought up in the Jewish faith. Even though I live in a small California town, I bring my Jewishness with me. I define myself through it and see the world through Jewish eyes. I am what I am. *Hineni,* here I am. I am content.

Being Jewish to me requires participation in a community, involving oneself in the rituals, ceremonies, and frames of reference that are typically Jewish. There are many types of Jews in the United States, but at the heart of all is the concept of the community—*klal yisrael,* the community of Israel, and *am yisrael,* people of Israel.[4] For many Jews in the United States passing has become a way of life. It is not hard to do. One simply has to choose not to be observant and not be a part of the Jewish community. To be Jewish is to be active, at least to some extent, in the community. Even though the religious law defines Jewishness based on the mother's religion, it is clear that actual affiliation goes far beyond that definition.

The second most defining event for Jews in the twentieth century, that of the *Shoah* or the Holocaust, eliminated the choice of passing. To pass or not to pass was no longer the choice of the Jew; rather, the Nazis said that you were Jewish no matter what. The first most defining event for Jews in the twentieth century was the creation of a Jewish homeland in the State of Israel, which also rejected the idea of passing. Only those who take the action of declaring themselves to be a part of *klal yisrael* can be a citizen of Israel.

As I consider friends and relatives in my old hometown, many of whom have intermarried and have found it easier to reject their connections to their Jewish communal heritage, I see Jews who are as lost to me as my relatives who perished in the *Shoah.* The legacy for their children will be empty synagogues, museums to a culture that disappeared, cemeteries covered with weeds, and *klezmer* music without Jews to play it. Their legacy will be to succeed in doing what the Nazis failed to complete in Europe. Judaism will continue in the United States, but the declining number of those willing to make the choice for communal involvement and against disappearance concerns me.

To be accepted fully by mainstream America has been a benefit that many generations of Jewish immigrants have sought and are finally achieving. Time will tell if Jewish Americans thrive or die because of such kindness.

NOTES

1. Reform and Conservative Judaism are separate movements. In the United States they comprise the two largest denominations.

2. There have been four waves of Jewish immigrants to the United States: the initial Sephardi Jews (Spanish origin), who immigrated prior to the birth of the United States; the immigration of German and central European Jews in the first third of the nineteenth century; the largest wave, of almost 3 million immigrants from Eastern Europe, between 1882 and 1914; and the most recent wave, after World War II, that has included survivors of the Holocaust and, more recently, Jews from the Soviet occupied lands, Jews from Arab lands, Iranian Jews, and Israelis.

3. Daniel J. Elazar, *Community and Polity: The Organizational Dynamics of American Jewry* (Philadelphia: Jewish Publication Society, 1976).

4. These terms refer not to the State of Israel but to the Biblical children of Israel, or all who call themselves Jewish.

Our cultural identities come from multiple sources. That is the theme of Alfred Guillaume's story about who he is, what he believes, and what values he tries to instill in his sons. The title of this essay describes the major cultural influences that shaped his identity. In the essay Alfred describes how race, nationality, culture, and religion interact in unique ways to produce beliefs and values that guide his personal and professional choices.

6   To Be American, Black, Catholic, and Creole

Alfred J. Guillaume, Jr.

I am a 50-year-old American. I am black, Roman Catholic, and Creole. This is how I describe myself 50 years in the making. As a young boy growing up in the South I was made to believe that I was different. Images of America did not mirror me. The segregated South wanted me to believe that I was inferior. The Catholic Church taught me that all of God's people were equal. My French Creole heritage gave me a special bond to Native Americans, to Europeans, and to Africans. This is the composite portrait of who I am. I like who I am and can imagine being no other.

What I've accomplished professionally I owe to discipline, a good education, and opportunity. I thank my parents, whose values concerning education shaped my life; they instilled in me the notion that hard work breeds success and opens doors to opportunity. Today I am a senior administrator at Indiana University. I am fortunate that my life has been a wonderful adventure.

I'm an American. I was born in New Orleans, Louisiana, whose sophisticated elegance and alluring exoticism make it America's most European city and also its most Caribbean. Natives call it the Big Easy. From its founding, New Orleans has been a land of dichotomies, of piety and hedonism, a Catholic city that revels in music, food, and good times.

I'm an African American. Just within my lifetime people of African ancestry have been called colored, Negro, black, and sundry derogatory terms that I categorically reject. I am proud to have been born black. My people paid a heavy price through toil and suffering to make America. Their unparalleled creative contributions shaped American culture.

I am Catholic. I thought everyone was Catholic until I went to school and learned that there were Protestants. The nuns taught my schoolmates and me to pray for them and for all other non-Catholics. My values were formed in large part by my religious faith. As a child I dreamed of becoming a priest. I left my parents at age 12 to study for the priesthood with the Josephite Fathers in New York. I made my first long journey on a train with five other seminarians from my parish. I will never forget the memorable sights along the way and my arrival at Grand Central Station and the Port Authority. The bustle of people made it feel like a carnival.

I am Creole. I trace my ancestry to Africa, to Europe, and to Native America. I am proud of my multiethnic ancestry. America is a nation of immigrants. Some came willingly; others came in shackles. The native peoples also call this land home. Race dominates American thought. In an era of increased intolerance; of rapid retreats from affirmative action, civil rights, and human rights; of tightened immigration laws; of fast-paced retrenchment from obligations to the poor and the homeless, America is becoming a society of "us" and "them." But America is not and has never been a land of clearly defined racial groups. Racial groups are not monolithic.

The word *Creole* is used to define Europeans who came to the Americas. But *Creole* also refers to blacks in the Americas, mixed-blood people whose ancestry can be traced to Africa as well as to Europe. Such is my family: gumbo people, a blend of Africa, Europe, and Native America. The first languages of my maternal grandparents were French and Creole, a kind of pidgin French. I regret that my siblings and I never learned to speak the language. We lived in the city and the language was spoken primarily in the rural areas. My mother understood the language but never spoke it to us. Speaking English correctly was important, particularly without the melodic Creole accent so characteristic of natives of southern Louisiana. Yet even without the language, I speak with a regional accent. On my paternal side were the Houma Indians. Pictures of my great-great-grandmother in Indian dress are prized family possessions.

I grew up in the segregated South. My parents shielded us from racism. Our upbringing, our religion, and our schooling protected us. We lived in a middle-class neighborhood, attended a Catholic elementary school run by a black order of nuns called the Holy Family Sisters, and went to Mass at a black Catholic church. We lived in a cocoon in our black, Catholic, Creole world. Because of all the support Creole society provided, it seemed that segregation did not affect us. It was not until the sixties, during my teenage years, that I became fully aware of the dehumanizing effects of segregation.

Creole society could not totally isolate us from racial prejudice. I remember sitting with my maternal grandmother in the colored section of the bus, behind the "Colored Only" sign, when a white patron removed the sign and put it behind us, forcing us to stand and relinquish our seat to him. I remember the separate water fountains, the separate entrances to restaurants, the separate playgrounds, the separate schools and churches. In department stores and other businesses, blacks did menial work; the salespeople and bosses were white. I remember the day my dad took me with him to the post office, where he worked. At the desks and the service counters were only whites; I asked my dad to show me his office. I had no notion then that only whites had offices.

My first recollection that black meant being inferior occurred one morning as I walked to school. In the segregated South, only white children were bused to school. A young white boy, about my own age—eight or so—yelled out the window of the yellow school bus, "Hey, chocolate boy!" When I related this story to my maternal great aunt her response to me was, "Cher (My dear), you a pretty chocolate boy." Since then I have always taken a particular delight in being "chocolate."

It was not until the sixties, during the civil rights movement, that I began to call myself black. I had always thought of myself as Negro or Creole. As Creoles we grew up believing that we were "different." I remember my maternal grandmother's shock when she saw me sporting an Afro. She wondered why I wanted to make my hair nappy. She firmly believed that we were descendants of France, not Africa—to her I was not black but brown. I didn't understand then, though I understand now, why she could not call herself black. After all, her parents spoke French; she grew up speaking French and Creole; she was Catholic; most of the people in her family were medium brown to fair-skinned. She herself was considered "high yellow" and gave birth to two fair skinned blonde girls.

In the sixties, of course, black was "beautiful," as young blacks shouted it with Stokely Carmichael. James Brown urged us to "Say it loud, 'I'm black and I'm proud.'" We marched with Martin Luther King, Jr., and felt a renewed pride in being black. Throughout the South, in sit-ins and on freedom rides, we sang exuberantly, "We Shall Overcome." In New Orleans I worked tirelessly in voter registration drives to teach blacks the preamble to the Constitution so they would be eligible to vote, only to have them denied that right repeatedly. We marched on city hall and were arrested when we refused to disband. I remember one sweltering day, passing my paternal grandmother's home on my way to jail, waving to her from a police car, singing freedom songs. Right up until her death years later, she recalled that day with horror.

Though the message of segregation was hatred and subjugation, my parents taught my four siblings and me never to feel inferior to whites. We never heard a disparaging word in our home about white people. Rather than thinking that whites were superior, we grew up believing that we were special. We were Americans. And not only were we colored, we were Creole and Catholic. My father took particular delight in repeatedly saying that each of us was a jewel; we were five dazzling jewels, and each was different. My parents taught us to believe in ourselves above all else, and that we were never to forget where we came from. We were never to forget those who helped us along the way. "Never burn bridges once you cross them," my dad would say. "You never know when you might have to cross them again." My parents taught us to have pride always but never to hate or deride another human being. We were taught to respect elders and treat all individuals with dignity. We were never to make fun of those less fortunate and were to be thankful for the graces we did have.

Neighborhoods in New Orleans today are more segregated than I remember as a child. Typical of housing patterns that date back to the eighteenth and nineteenth centuries, and because of the common practices of miscegenation during those historical times, whites and blacks lived in close proximity to each other when I was growing up. Our neighborhood was mixed. In a string of modest shotgun houses, white and black families lived adjacent to each other. Our next door neighbor, Miss Gladys, was white. Babette, an old white lady who walked with a limp that scared the children in the neighborhood, lived around the corner. She was always admonishing us to be good and chastised us if she caught us playing in the streets.

Most neighborhoods had two Catholic churches, and ours was no exception. There was St. Francis Cabrini for whites and St. Raymond for blacks. If blacks attended a white church, they sat in special seating in the back and sometimes would be denied communion. It was particularly hard for me, as a little boy, to understand why black and white Catholics should be separated. I believed that God did not segregate the races in Heaven. I prayed for forgiveness for those white Catholics who stood on the church steps citing biblical chapter and verse to prove that God meant the races to be separate. In our own black Catholic church the white priest spoke of God's love for all of humanity during his Sunday homily. As he glanced toward the congregation he said, "Negroes are beautiful in God's eyes. What I see in the church this morning are many hues and colors, as beautiful as the most magnificent flower garden." I was an altar boy at that Mass and those words made a deep impression on me. To this day they remain a source of comfort to me whenever I face the harshness of racism.

My brothers and sisters and I received our religious values from our parents, particularly our mother, who is religious and devoted to the Church. My dad, no matter how exhausted from the day's work—he sometimes worked two jobs—would, without fail, kneel at his bedside, saying his nightly prayers. Often we would find him asleep on his knees. Priests and nuns were frequent visitors to our home. My mom took the nuns for Sunday afternoon rides (at that time nuns did not drive). My brother and I were altar boys; we hated funerals, but we loved weddings because of the tips we received from the grooms. I remember the Monday night parish rosary, which rotated from home to home, and the Tuesday night novenas to Our Lady of Perpetual Help. I would also occasionally accompany my mother to the seasonal novenas to St. Jude, the patron saint of hopeless cases, and to the Shrine of St. Ann, where the devoted climbed stone steps to make the Stations of the Cross on their knees. When the neighborhood where St. Ann's shrine was located grew increasingly black, the Church tried to close the shrine and rebuild it in the white suburbs. Today there are two shrines to St. Ann, one in black New Orleans and the other in white Metairie.

Education was stressed in my family. My siblings and I knew from an early age that we would go to college. My dad would tell us that we could be anything we wanted in life, even bums, but he insisted that we be educated bums. We used to laugh at this idea, but now we understand his wisdom. He finished only high school, but he was an avid reader. He subscribed to the *Readers' Digest of Condensed Books,* and the *Encyclopedia Britannica* was prominently displayed in the living room. He earned a living as a postal clerk. One of eight children, my father shined shoes on Canal Street at age nine when his father died. My mom was a school teacher who taught piano and the sixth grade. My parents taught us that everything was within our reach, because success depended on our hard work and persistence. My dad taught us never to give up, that the word "can't" is not in the dictionary. We were Guillaumes, he would say, and a Guillaume never gives up. He exhorted us never to accept mediocrity. He encouraged us in our schoolwork always to aim for an *A.* "It is far better to aim high and miss the mark," he would say, "than aim low and make it." We understood that to mean that if we studied for an *A* and failed, then our reward would be a *B* or no less than a *C.* But if we studied for a *D* and succeeded, the results would be disastrous. He also taught us never to complain about what we didn't have. When we did complain he would say endlessly, "I complained because I had no shoes, until I saw the man who had no feet." I consider myself blessed to have had parents who valued education and who understood the limitless potential education affords.

Most of my formative education was in black schools, from kindergarten through college, and by all measures of assessment I received an excellent education. I spent my first three years of high school studying for the priesthood in Newburgh, New York, with the Josephite Fathers, whose apostolic mission is among African Americans. I finished my senior year in New Orleans with the Josephites at a black Catholic high school for boys. To many, Saint Augustine High was the best high school in the city. The school prided itself on its academics as well as its athletics. It produced many sports championships in the black leagues and graduated the first black presidential scholar. Perennially, it had the highest number of National Achievement Scholars for Negro students among the city's high schools. Its students earned scholarships to prestigious eastern colleges and universities.

Like our mother, all five of us graduated from Xavier University of Louisiana, which is a small, predominantly black Catholic university that was founded in 1913 by the Sisters of the Blessed Sacrament, an order of religious nuns established by Katherine Drexel of Philadelphia. Xavier has a history of excellence in training black teachers and pharmacists, and it is widely recognized for its strong music curriculum. Many of its graduates sang on the opera stages of Europe when discrimination did not permit them to perform in the United States. Xavier is now nationally recognized for its science programs; it consistently sends more blacks to medical and dental schools than does any other institution of higher learning in the United States, and it continues to train a large number of this nation's black pharmacists. Katherine Drexel has been beatified by the Catholic Church, the first step toward sainthood.

Growing up in New Orleans was fascinating. It is affectionately called the Crescent City because of the bend in the Mississippi River that shapes it; jazz and blues singers mournfully lament "Do you know what it means to miss New Orleans?" It has a unique flavor among American cities. It has been memorialized in literature dating from the earliest journeys of travelers to the New World who spoke of its pesky insects, its insufferable heat, and its beautiful women: black, white, and all the muted shades in between. A city nestled in the swamps and bayous of southern Louisiana, it is as enchanting as it is mysterious, blending Native American, African, European, and Caribbean cultures. Music, food, and good times are synonymous with New Orleans.

New Orleanians love to eat. Recipes that blend Native American, African, and European culinary tastes and spices treat the palate to a symphony of pleasure. Gumbo, crawfish etouffee, shrimp creole, jambalaya, stuffed crabs, soft-shell crabs, seafood boil, raw oysters, coushaw (an indigenous squash), mirliton, catfish, stuffed bell peppers, andouille, grits, pain perdu (homemade French bread or French toast), corn soup, red beans, and rice are the foods with which I grew up. You can't leave the home of a New Orleanian without first having something to eat.

Festivals and parties are also very much a part of New Orleans life. The carnival season of debutante balls, masked parties, and parades begins with the feast of the Magi on January 6. The biggest party of the year is Mardi Gras, the hedonistic carnival before Lent, in which New Orleanians feast and dance one last time before the 40 days of fasting and abstinence that precede Easter. My family, like many others, would wear colorful costumes sewn by my mother and watch the parades, yelling, "Hey, mister, throw me something." As young adults we also attended the debutante balls. Other popular festivals included the French Quarter Festival and the Jazz and Heritage Festival, perennial favorites that rival Mardi Gras.

I consider myself a citizen of the world. I have traveled to many countries in Europe, Africa, Asia, and the Americas, and I feel at ease wherever I am. My comfort with other cultures stems, in part, from my ability to speak French and to communicate passably in Spanish. After spending almost my entire high school years studying for the priesthood in the seminary, I had no idea what I wanted to study as a college student. My mother advised me to study what I enjoyed most. Because I liked French in high school, she suggested that I study languages in college. That was perhaps the best advice I've ever been given. Thanks to my parents' sacrifice and support, I was able to study French and Spanish through immersion. As an undergraduate I spent summers in Mexico and in French-speaking Canada. Later, as a graduate student, I studied and traveled in France and French-speaking Africa. In many ways my pursuit of French as an educational goal was, perhaps unconsciously, a way for me to recapture my lost Creole French heritage.

In the United States I am black. In Europe and abroad I am also black, but not in the same way. Race dominates American culture. In my own country I am black and American; abroad I am American and black. There is a distinction. In many places I have traveled, I am not a minority. Skin color is not a major distinctive attribute. In Brazil, where there is a panorama of skin tones and hues, race is not determined by skin color. Some Brazilians consider me white. Cultural identity is more aptly defined by racial groups, such as the blacks in Bahia and the Indians in the Amazon.

As an administrator and a professor at three different universities, I have confronted prejudice. Most of it was subtle. There are some who feel discomfort in accepting a black authority figure. I sometimes wonder whether individuals would respond to me differently as an administrator if I were white. I have noticed that some first-time visitors to my office are surprised to see a black vice chancellor. Our images of power in America show a white male in positions of authority.

Curiously, in northern California, where there is little ethnic and racial diversity, less attention was paid to my racial background. When I was appointed vice president of a midwestern Catholic university, the public and the university press highlighted the fact that I was the university's first black academic vice president. The alumni and the black community took special pride in my appointment. In admissions literature that reached out to African Americans and other minorities, I was prominently featured. When I was appointed provost and vice president at Humboldt, no mention of my race was made in the university's press releases.

Living in Humboldt County was less of a cultural adjustment than I had at first imagined. I suspect that my southern accent, coupled with my expressive and chatty manner, quickly marked me as a nonlocal. I was often asked how I liked it here, since there were so few blacks living in this part of California. When I first arrived, a kind, elderly couple was concerned that I might feel awkward at Mass because there were no black Catholics in the parish. They mentioned their own uneasiness when, during a visit to New Orleans, they were the only whites at Mass in a black Catholic church. I imagine they wanted to let me know that they understood what it is like to be a minority. The couple did not understand that my biggest transition to living in northern California was living in a rural community; it had nothing to do with race. Until then I had always lived in big cities.

I am divorced with two sons, ages 19 and 11. I know that each is trying to find his place in a society that is increasingly multicultural but whose power base remains white. As young black men they struggle with the stereotypical images of what being black connotes in America. This is particularly true for my older son, who learned bitterly what it meant to be black when, as a young boy of 11, he was stopped by campus police at a midwest university and escorted off campus because he did not belong there. He was afraid to tell them that his father was the vice president. My younger son, to my knowledge, has not yet experienced racism at its ugliest. He remains open and accepting of others. He hates talk of black people and white people and proudly boasts that all people are the same. For him the important quality in a person is whether he or she is nice.

I am raising my sons as my parents raised me. I teach them that it is less important that the world sees you as black, and it is more important that the world recognizes you as a person of strength and integrity. As my father taught me, I teach them to be strong and independent, to be individuals. I tell them that they are jewels, that there are no others like them, that they have unique gifts of self, and that they should be willing to share their gifts of self with others. Color is not important; character is. They are special and they honor their father and their heritage.

Wen Shu Lee's quest to understand herself and her relationship with her mother takes her to a rich source of cultural beliefs and values: the proverbs with which she was raised. The proverbs illustrate how Wen Shu's mother taught her daughter important values to guide her life. This essay exemplifies the importance of using proverbs to understand the deeply seated beliefs, values, and norms of a culture.

7 In Search of My Mother's Tongue: From Proverbs to Contextualized Sensibility

Wen Shu Lee

My mother was born in Taiwan, into the Chen family, in 1935. Her birth name is Shu Jen. Unlike English names, Chinese names have specific meanings. *Shu* means feminine virtue, and *Jen* means truth. Her parents expected her to abide by virtues appropriate for women and to honor truth in her conduct.

My grandfather was a redwood carpenter/artisan of the Han ethnicity. A housewife, my grandmother was half Han and half aborigine. Together with her eight sisters and brothers, my mother went through three major changes in Taiwanese history: the colonization of Taiwan by Japan from 1895 to 1945, the domination of Taiwan by Chiang Kai-Shek's nationalist party from 1945 to 1988; and democratic movements and multiparty politics from 1988 to the present. These political shifts have had a profound impact on my mother's speech. Let me elaborate.

During the Japanese colonization period, the Taiwanese language was the tongue of the colonized and Japanese was the official language. Taiwanese children spoke Taiwanese (or Fujianese[1]) at home, but they were expected to learn Japanese at school. My mother was the seventh child in her family to go to Japanese school, but only during the first grade, so her Japanese remained elementary. Her older siblings, however, could speak and read Japanese fluently. With the end of the Japanese control in 1945, Chiang Kai-Shek sent nationalist troops from mainland China to take over Taiwan. Mandarin became the official language, and Taiwanese remained a "substandard" language. This time, my mother had to learn Mandarin. My father was a "mainlander" and spoke Mandarin with a slight Shengdong accent, so my mother eventually became fluent in Mandarin.

Growing up in Taiwan in the 1960s, I was proud of my Mandarin. Even though my mother spoke Taiwanese with her siblings, I didn't take advantage of the bilingual environment. I could understand Taiwanese, but I couldn't speak it well. It was not until after 1983, when I came to the United States and learned about the relationship between power and language, and 1988, when the Taiwanese power movement became public, that I realized that I had learned to speak the tongue of the ruling elite. For 20 years I was unaware of my scorn for Taiwanese and, hence, my mother and her family.

This awareness also came when I began reading womanist literature, especially Alice Walker's (1983) *In Search of Our Mothers' Gardens*.[2] Like many black women, Chinese/Taiwanese women have remained oppressed for generations. They had to suffer through footbinding.[3] They could neither inherit property nor initiate a divorce. They had to obey codes of conduct that kept them silent and uneducated. While some progress has been made in Chinese women's rights, many inequalities remain.[4] Centuries of suffering have made Chinese women strong and persistent.[5] As one of them, I have yet to unlearn the internalized linguistic and gendered oppression. My unlearning begins with a search of my mother's tongue. Treating it seriously and reflecting on its implications, I write this essay to honor my mother and women like her.

Taiwanese/Chinese Proverbs and Their Meanings

My mother is an expert in proverbs, in both Taiwanese and Mandarin. Compared to ordinary speech, the proverb in Taiwanese and Mandarin, like the proverb in English (e.g., He who pays the piper calls the tune), is economical and precise. It contrasts in style and form with the daily colloquial. Like food, proverbs are full of colors, spices, and flavors. They take us right into the heart of a culture. The following are a few proverbs used by my mother. Because literal translation does not do justice to their richness, I will try to situate them relationally and socially in the world where my mother and many women of her generation live.

Gua Naa Ge Sho Gin

This is a Taiwanese proverb. Translated literally it means "bringing a basket to fake burning deity money." So you can grasp its meaning in a deeper sense, I will share with you some aspects of Taiwanese women's lives.

On the first and fifteenth day of each lunar calendar month, many Taiwanese women of my mother's and grandmother's generations, married or unmarried, would go to a Buddhist or Taoist temple to pay tribute to Heaven. They usually would bring a basket containing items necessary for the worship ceremony, including incense, deity money, food, and fresh fruit and flowers. Young unmarried women would go to the temple accompanied by matronly figures—mothers, aunts, sisters-in-law. The ceremony followed a routine: set up food and flowers on a worship desk; light the incense and hold it in one's hands; kneel in front of the deities and pray to them; ask the deities for some assistance in aspects of daily life; *kao tao* (bow) to the deities; stand up and stick incense in a sand-filled urn; and go to a tower, which is like a huge fireplace, to burn deity money. Deity money is made of paper with gilded patterns on it. Therefore, it is called *gin* [gold]. Women burn *gin* to send money to the deities and spirits so they will have money to get things they like. This is a way to show gratitude and respect.

In the old days young women were not allowed to go to public places. The only place where lovers could see each other (in a literal sense) was at the temple. Therefore, the proverb *gua naa ge sho gin* describes a situation in which a woman would go to the temple for the covert purpose of seeing her lover, all in the name of burning *gin*/deity money to pay tribute to heaven.

My mother often used this proverb during my college days. Young men who were interested in me would come to our house to visit my parents. They would bring presents. After these eager visitors left my mother would usually say, in a teasing way, *gua naa ge sho gin*! When my mother got to know some of them well, she would say this proverb when they were present. A few of them were rendered speechless with red, awkward faces. Others were able to appreciate the humor and laugh out loud. It was funny because my parents' house was like the temple and my young friends were the pious believers coming to pay tribute. Their gifts were the basket. But as a matronly figure, my mother teasingly communicated to them, "You bring me presents, but I know you are not here to pay tribute to me. You are faking burning deity money. You are here to see my daughter!"

We may use this proverb analogously in a U.S. context. Let us look at a hypothetical case. Julie and Sandra first became friends a few years ago, when they were volunteering for an AIDS health campaign for local schools. After the campaign was over they spoke on the phone occasionally and went to the movies together a few times. Though their relationship had begun to wane and they had not seen each other for more than four months, Julie suddenly called and invited herself to Sandra's house for a visit. Sandra was not sure what Julie wanted but agreed that Julie could come to the house on a Saturday afternoon. Julie showed up with a bouquet and a beautiful work of art from New Mexico. Sandra was touched by Julie's gifts, and she introduced Julie to her husband, Jeff. While they were sipping tea in the family room, Sandra noticed that Julie did not really talk to her at all. Instead, she was asking Jeff about his work and his company. Julie wanted to know if Jeff's company was hiring, and she let it be known that her boyfriend, Kevin, was a very competent engineer who happened to be in the job market. At this moment, Sandra could say that Julie was "bringing a basket to fake burning deity money."

Mon Laa Gien Se Ko
The literal translation of this Taiwanese proverb is "groping for little clams [in the river] and washing one's [under]pants at the same time." It is similar to an

English proverb, "To kill two birds with one stone." Its folksy aura has to be explained further.

Before Taipei was urbanized its largest river, Dan Shui He, had a lot of little clams. My mother has told me that until the 1950s people could still go to the river and dig up little clams, called *laa* in Taiwanese, for dinner. This proverb describes the fact that people were so eager to grope for *laa* that they forgot to pull the bottoms of their pants up. Because they went deeper and deeper into the water, they ended up washing their underpants too. Comically, these people accomplished two things at the same time.

My mother uses this proverb often. The market where my mother goes daily to pick up fresh produce is a place for women to chat with friends in the neighborhood. "Market talk," however, only lasts a few minutes, because shopping for the day's meals is more important. Mrs. Wang, one of the neighborhood women, is famous for being the "broadcast station"—she tells everyone about everyone else's business. Standing in a corner of the market with her little shopping cart full of such items as eggs, vegetables, tofu, and fish, Mrs. Wang often "kidnaps" one or two women and just chatters away for at least half an hour. So my mother would later tell me that "The broadcast station today *mon laa gien se ko* (groped for little clams [in the river] and washed her [under]pants at the same time) again in the market!"

Di Sai Na Ge Tsai

This proverb is in Taiwanese. "Di sai na" refers to a pig sty; "ge tsai" means to tie a silk ball on the door. Together they describe a situation in which people make a big production out of something undesirable. There are two things in the Chinese culture that may help explain this proverb. First, a pig sty was a place rural people considered unsightly and stinky. Second, on important occasions (e.g., Chinese New Year, weddings, grandparents' birthdays, one-month celebration of a newborn baby), people would put red silk balls and ribbons on the main entrance of a household to enhance the aura of celebration. Nobody in his or her right mind would put red silk balls and ribbons in a pig sty. To celebrate something so stinky is utter stupidity and lacking in taste! This is a very funny proverb. My mother often uses it when she observes some unwise act in her relatives. For example, after his wife passed away her oldest brother just let his house go. It was so messy that my mother and her sisters could not even walk into the house to visit. One day my mother got word from her sisterly gossip network that their oldest brother had purchased a new sofa for his messy house. She just said that her oldest brother was "*di sai na ge tsai* (tying up red silk balls and ribbons in a pigsty)!"

Jia Lan Ji Gin, Hing Lan Shi Nu

This Taiwanese proverb means "eating one Chinese pound of things from others, giving four Chinese ounces of things in return." Let me explain its meaning by sharing with you an aspect of my mother's world.

Taking after her grandmother of aborigine blood, my mother is good at mathematics. She worked as a bookkeeper for her sister for a few years. When my older brother and I were born she had to resign to take care of us at home. In the 1960s banks in Taiwan did not give loans to middle- and lower-class people. To help raise money, people living in the same neighborhood would start a collective, which is called *huei ya* in Taiwanese.

A person with a good reputation who needed money could start a collective. She or he was called "the head of the collective," or *huei tao*. A *huei tao* would ask 24 (or any number divisible by 12) people to join the collective. Those who joined were often friends and relatives. A stranger could join only if a friend or relative in the neighborhood vouched for him or her.

The *huei tao* would collect a fixed sum of money from each member—for example 1,000.00 new Taiwan dollars (N.T.). A month after the money was collected members would go to the *huei tao*'s house for a meeting. Those who needed money could place a bid. The expectation was that the more people needed money, the higher the bids went. The person giving the highest bid—for example, 100 N.T.—would gather 1,000 N.T. from the huei tao and 1,000 N.T. minus 100 N.T.—that is, 900 N.T.—from each of the 23 other members. The person who got his or her bid was called "dead," and those who had not were called "alive." A month later another meeting would be held again at the *huei tao*'s house, and those who were "alive" could place a bid. The person with the highest bid—for example, 150 N.T. this time—would collect that month's money from everybody. That is, he or she would get 1,000 N.T. from the *huei tao* and the "dead" person, and 850 N.T. from each of the remaining 22 members. The upshot is that the later you placed a bid, the more money you would get from the collective.

Many people became confused by how the collective operated. Given her reputation as a smart and reliable person, my mother became many of our family friends' "financial consultant." She would tell them when to place their bids and roughly how much to bid. A lot of them were able to get married, buy houses, or retire early because of my mother's assistance. On important occasions—for example, the Mid-Autumn festival (or the moon festival) and Chinese Lunar New Year—those who were assisted by my mother would come by the house bringing gifts for my family. After they left, my mother would assert in Taiwanese, "jia lan ji gin, hing lan shi nu (eating one Chinese pound of things from others, giving four Chinese ounces in return)."

This proverb means that a gift from another person is so generous that one cannot possibly match its value. However, one should do one's best to return some to honor the principle of reciprocity. Recall that the financial assistance rendered by my mother over the years far exceeded the value of the gifts she received. This proverb marked my mother's humility because she asserted that it was those who brought gifts who were generous. It also marked her belief in reciprocity. A few days after a person's visit, my mother would bring something to his or her house to reciprocate the goodwill. I am very proud of my mother in this regard. She taught us that it is important to help others without taking credit, and we learned to uphold the principle of reciprocity with our friends and relatives.

Proverbs About Women and Men

My mother is a strong woman, as are all of her sisters. They may be critical of men, but they often endorse values engineered by a patriarchal system. This reveals itself when they use gender-oppressive proverbs uncritically.

Zhu Bu Fei Fei Dao Gou

Translated literally, this Mandarin proverb means "A pig is not fat, but a dog is." For Chinese farmers in the old days, pigs were valuable because they brought cash to the family and were also an important source of food. Dogs, in comparison, were useless. One could neither sell nor eat dogs.[6] To many Chinese, sons are like pigs and daughters are like dogs. So it is very important to have sons who are smart and successful. If sons are not as smart as daughters, instead of praising their daughters' accomplishments, Chinese people often lament the fact that sons do not do as well. This proverb embodies a centuries-old patriarchal Chinese sentiment.

My grades were always far better than those of my brothers. When it was announced in the newspaper that I had passed the national high school entrance examination and was admitted to the best girls' high school in Taiwan, I remember my mother saying "Zhu bu fei fei dao gou (Pigs are not fat, but dogs are)!" to a relative. I was fifteen years old. It was the first time I sensed that my mother valued boys and girls differently. She loved me and wanted the best for me, but she also wished that it was her sons, rather than her daughter, who excelled at school. It hurt my feelings, but I did not bring this up.

Years later, I finally understood what this proverb meant to my mother when she told me about her own schooling. My grandfather was quite wealthy when I was born. But during the Japanese occupation, when my mother was a little girl, he had been forced to close down his business. Throughout my mother's childhood, she and her family had to endure poverty. My mother had to beg my grandmother for the money to pay for her elementary school tuition. Often before giving my mother the money my grandmother would say that girls should not go to school, that it was a waste of money. To make matters worse, my mother's teacher would remind her in front of the other children that she had not paid her fees. It was humiliating. In comparison, my mother not only let me go to school, she also tried to give my two brothers and me free time to study. For this I am grateful. But the proverb always brings a little sadness to me.

Jia Ji Sui Ji, Jia Gou Sui Gou

This proverb in Mandarin appears in an essay by Hsieh Ping-ying (1940/1992) in which she described her parents' reaction when she refused an arranged marriage. Its literal translation is "follow a cock [rooster][7] if you are married to the cock [rooster], and follow a dog if you are married to the dog" (p. 161). A woman, once married, is to obey her husband regardless of what he does to her. When a Chinese woman complains about her husband's drinking or womanizing, others would use this proverb to remind her that she must to be patient and tolerant. There is nothing she can do about it. It is her fate!

My mother and my sister-in-law have a stormy relationship. Caught in between, my older brother would either avoid the issues by coming home late or take my mother's side by listening to her complaints and scolding his wife. If he ever took his wife's side, my mother would accuse him of lacking filial piety. In the past few years, many conflicts have occurred and my sister-in-law became "solely responsible" for our family discord. If I sensed injustice, I would take my sister-in-law's side to argue with my mother. I would remind her that my sister-in-law had to endure so much to be with my brother. My mother would then automatically take my sister-in-law's credit away by using this proverb: she *has* to follow the rooster because she's married to the rooster. She has to endure. Her endurance is her *fate* rather than her *merit*!

The relationship between mother-in-law and daughter-in-law has traditionally been a sore point in Chinese families. This is certainly true in my family. Matronly figures often have oppressive attitudes toward younger women, and women of different generations are pitted against each other. Because matronly figures themselves have to suffer many years as daughters-in-law, it is only right that they be compensated for their suffering. But instead of resisting and changing a patriarchal system, they often form coalitions with men in the family (e.g., their sons) to denigrate younger women. I have often argued with my mother on this point. Perhaps I managed to persuade her to reconsider a little bit. At least she no longer demeans my sister-in-law in our conversations. But I know there's still a long way to go.

Nan Ren Si Le Yan Jing Xian Lan, Nu Ren Si Le Zui Ba Xian Lan

This Mandarin proverb criticizes both men and women. Literally, it says that "after men die, their eyes get rotten first; after women die, their tongues get rotten first." It carries a centuries-old wisdom about the tensions between women and men. Men often treat women as visual objects. They have mastered the art of voyeurism.[8] They can look at women in whatever way they want, as long as they do not get caught.[9] But Chinese women have also mastered the art of surveillance. That is, they do not make overt eye contact with men. Instead they look out of the corners of their eyes to check the corners of men's eyes. Over the centuries, such a tension between women and men has resulted in a proverb that warns men that their eyes, no matter what, get rotten first when they die.

Conversely, women love to gossip about men (and other women). Often family discord is blamed on "women's tongues." It is better for women to be quiet. When they have a lot to say they are called either "long-tongue" women or women with sharp teeth. Don't they have anything profound to say? Why are they always portrayed as "trivial and divisive"? Can't they be articulate and eloquent? Never in the proverbial sense!

My mother has used the first part of the proverb often, especially when my two brothers were adolescent. She cautioned them not to commit "visual offenses," and urged them to grow up to be honest and good men. My mother, on the other hand, never disciplined me by invoking the second half of the proverb. I guess she supported a strong tradition in her family—women can rightfully talk about their men, children, and family affairs. When my mother and her sisters get together to chat about life, one of my aunts often holds down my mother's hands (so that my mother can't gesture) and says to her, "You shut up. You get quiet. You listen to me!" They talk, interrupt each other, and laugh at their men, feeling that if their tongues get rotten after they die, it will be a small price to pay!

From Proverbs to Contextualized Sensibility

Dressed in her traditional, tight-fitting *qi pao,*[10] attending public functions, my mother has always been polite and proper. When my father was alive she never contradicted him in front of others. When others asked for her opinions, she would often defer to my father. In this regard, my mother performs as a traditional and docile Chinese woman. But through the colorful, humorous, and sometimes painful aspects of her communication with me, I am finally able to see her merits as well as her limits. Her proverbs defy the stereotype of Chinese women commonly held in the Western societies.

I encourage you, my reader, to learn deep codes (e.g., proverbs) used by people from different cultures. It will enable you to move beyond oversimplified knowledge—ignorance, prejudice, stereotype—and begin to cultivate a more *contextualized sensibility,* which for me means the ability to sense another individual's being in multiple contexts. By knowing about the contexts in which my mother uses colorful and saucy words, for example, you learn to see through my eyes that she is smart, strong, funny, folksy, humble, and honorable, although she cannot quite understand the impact of centuries-old patrilineal ideology on her views of women. My mother has done her best. I have come to understand that we cannot change things overnight.

Intercultural issues are complex. They demand an equally complex mind that can move beyond oversimplified views of "other" people. Contextualized sensibility, from my perspective, is one of the best and most enjoyable ways to get to know people from different cultures—especially those who tend to remain in a culture's background. They have a lot to say; we just need to find ways to hear them. Now that I have shared with you my mother's proverbs, what about yours? I look forward to learning about them.

NOTES

1. Taiwanese is a dialect from the Fu Jian province in China. The majority of Taiwanese people are descendants of Fujianese settlers who immigrated from China to Taiwan in the seventeenth and the eighteenth centuries.

2. "Womanist" is a term that was first advanced by Alice Walker (1983). It differs from feminist: "Womanist is to feminist as purple to lavender" (p. xii). It denotes "black feminist or feminist of color" (p. xi). A womanist is not only mature and capable but also loves other women and sometimes men. A womanist is not a separatist. She loves music, art, life and especially herself. I argued elsewhere (in press) for extending the meaning of "womanist" to include women and men of all colors (including white women, because whiteness is not a noncolor) who work together to end multiple forms of oppression. That is, a womanist is not just concerned about gender issues but also works to end oppression created by race, class, sexuality, and nationality.

3. I have discussed elsewhere (Lee, 1997) a brief history of footbinding in China and the rhetoric of the antifootbinding movement.

4. For example, in Taiwan, unless mothers can prove that their husbands are unfit for parenting (e.g., have committed adultery), fathers are given custody of their children in divorce proceedings.

5. For stories and scholarship about Chinese women, see Li (1992), Teng (1996), Waltner (1996), the fall 1996 issue of *Feminist Studies,* and the winter 1997 issue of *Journal of Women's History.*

6. It has been a custom among Cantonese people that eating puppies in the winter can boost men's potency. However, this custom is not widely endorsed by Taiwanese people.

7. In English one of the meanings denoted by "cock" is penis. In Chinese, however, it does not carry this meaning at all. I keep "cock" in Hsieh Ping-ying's essay, but I add "rooster" to remind the audience of its true meaning in this proverb.

8. Voyeurism is defined as "the practice of obtaining sexual gratification by looking at sexual objects or acts, esp. secretively" (*The Random House Dictionary of the English Language,* p. 1602).

9. I am aware that this interpretation is heterosexual in nature. However, men can also treat men as visual objects. Heterosexism has been a norm in Chinese culture, but since the 1990s it has been challenged in both Hong Kong and Taiwan. An existing Mandarin term, *tong zhi* (literally translated as comrade), has been appropriated to denote homosexuals. *Nu tong zhi* (or female comrade) means lesbian, and *nan tong zhi* (or male comrade) refers to gays.

10. Qi means Manchurian and *pao* means gown. *Qi pao* is a traditional tight-fitting dress for Chinese females. Its style comes from the Manchus, who ruled China from 1644 to 1911. *Qi pao* is worn by Susie Wang in the famous movie *Susie Wang's World.*

REFERENCES

Hsieh, P. (1940/1992). The family prison. In Li Yu-Ning (Ed.), *Chinese women through Chinese eyes* (pp. 156–166). New York: M. E. Sharpe.

Lee, W. S. (1997). Patriotic breeders or colonized converts? A postcolonial feminist approach to antifootbinding discourse in China. In D. Tanno & A. Gonzalez (Eds.), *Communication and identity across cultures* (pp. 11–33). Los Angeles: Sage.

Li, Y. (Ed.). (1992). *Chinese women through Chinese eyes.* New York: M. E. Sharpe.

Teng, J. E. (1996). The construction of the "traditional Chinese woman" in the Western academy: A critical review. *Signs, 22,* 115–151.

Walker, A. (1983). *In search of our mother's gardens: Womanist prose.* San Diego: Harcourt.

Waltner, A. (1996). Recent scholarship on Chinese women. *Signs, 21,* 410–428.

PART TWO

Inside/Outside

Belonging to Multiple Cultures

8 On Becoming Intercultural

Young Yun Kim

Issues of "cultural identity" produce some of the most volatile responses in many societies.[1] Hardly a day passes without reports of some new incidents of identity conflict. The politics of cultural identity have been played out throughout the world, from Northern Ireland to Bosnia, from the Middle East to Russia, from Africa to North, Central, and South America. Questions are still being raised concerning the autonomy of French-speaking Quebec in Canada, while issues involving aborigines and new immigrants persist in Australia. In the United States, wide-ranging views are voiced on the historically embedded intergroup relations—from the pronouncement of Louis Farrakhan during his visit to Iran: "You can quote me: God will destroy America at the hands of the Muslims" (*Time,* February 26, 1996, p. 12), to President Clinton's call for reconciliation and unity: "Long before we were so diverse, our nation's motto was *E Pluribus Unum*—out of many, we are one. We must be one—as neighbors; as fellow citizens; not separate camps, but family" (*Weekly,* 1995, p. 1851).

Against this contemporary milieu of identity politics, some basic questions need to be posed concerning the meanings that each of us holds about cultural identity. Is rigid adherence to the culture of our youth feasible or desirable? Is cultural identity in its pure form more a nostalgic notion than a reality? Can the desire for some form of collective uniqueness be satisfied without resulting in divisions and conflicts among groups? At what point do we cross the line from rightful and constructive claims for group identity to disastrous collisions and undue prejudice directed against one another? How can a society of multiple cultural identities such as that of the United States support and give confidence to all groups while upholding the communal values and responsibilities that transcend allegiance to each group? Can a society achieve this goal despite the increasing trend of disunity and "unbounded and unwholesome pluralism" (Etzioni, 1993, p. 217)?

Sam Rayburn, former speaker of the United States House of Representatives, used to say that "any jackass can kick a barn door down, but it takes a carpenter to build one." Today more than ever we need carpenters among us who can help bridge the chasms created by contentious identity politics. Ultimately our answers to the above questions have to be found, not in public policies but in the willingness and ability of each of us to get out of the conventional habit of solely defining ourselves in terms of a single cultural identity. In so doing, we may strive for a mental outlook that integrates, rather than separates, humanity. We need an outlook on self and others that is not locked in the provincial interests of our own group membership, where we can see ourselves as part of a larger whole that includes other groups.

Identity as an Evolving Entity

Let me call this integrative self-other orientation an "intercultural identity"—identity that conjoins rather than divides. As Adler (1982) described it, the identity of an intercultural person is based "not on belongingness, which implies either owning or being owned by culture, but on a style of self consciousness that is capable of negotiating ever new formations of reality. He [She] is neither totally *a part of* nor totally *apart from* his [her] culture; he [she] lives, instead, on the boundary" (p. 391). The idea of intercultural identity is grounded in the premise that an individual's identity can be *achieved* as much as it is *ascribed* by birth or by society. This emphasis on what we can achieve with respect to our identity counters, as well as complements, the conventional ascription-based view of cultural identity. The conventional view tends to treat cultural identity as an immutable, *a priori* human condition that profoundly affects the experience of an individual. Erikson's (1950, 1969) early framework placed group identity at the "core" of the individual and yet also in the core of his or her "common culture." Erikson further viewed the process of identity development as one in which the two identities—of the individual and of the group—are merged and integrated into one. Many other investigators have echoed Erikson's conception of cultural identity as integral to an individual's identity, because it offers a sense of historical continuity and embeds one in a "larger" collectivity composed of one's group. As such, cultural identity is seen as a "genuine culture" (Yinger, 1986) and thus an inherent moral force that, when denied or compromised, results in a debasement of the individual or the group. An array of studies have, in fact, linked negative cultural identity to a variety of undesirable psychological and social consequences, including poor self-image (e.g., Tajfel, 1978) and alienation (e.g., Blackwell & Hart, 1982). Individuals who fail to develop a healthy cultural identity have been reported to be more prone to think of themselves as misperceived by others, more likely to view chance as a major determinant of events, more influenced by peer conformity pressure, and more likely to fall into substance abuse and other self-destructive behaviors.

Even though theoretical and research insights have served us well in promoting a social-political consciousness that calls for a greater equity and respect among cultural groups, they have also contributed to a general downplaying of the rich variation in the way individuals experience their identity at any given time. The notion that cultural identity is unchangeable has led to the unfortunate consequence of exaggerating its uniformity, permanence, and deterministic influence on individuals who happen to be affiliated with a particular ethnic group by ascription. Too often, a person is viewed as "belonging to" one and only one cultural identity, glossing over the multifaceted and varied nature of identity experienced by those whose lives crisscross multiple sets of boundaries. It is not surprising, then, that the viability of the ascription-based conception of cultural identity is increasingly challenged in recent years by scholars who argue for the need to understand the complexity of the way cultural identity is enacted across psychological, relational, and situational contexts (e.g., Brewer & Gardner, 1996; Hecht, Collier, and Ribeau, 1993; Thornton, 1996).

To this growing voice I add my own emphasis on the dynamic and evolving nature of cultural identity. I argue that cultural identity is not only an ascriptive entity; it is also subject to change through life experiences. In a series of works that examine the process of cross-cultural adaptation of immigrants and sojourners I have theorized that prolonged and cumulative experiences of communication between individuals of differing cultural backgrounds bring about systemic, adaptive changes in the individual's psyche. One such change is the gradual transformation of identity, from the original ascribed cultural identity to one that is increasingly intercultural in nature (Kim, 1988, 1995a, 1995b, in press).[2] I explain this phenomenon of identity transformation in terms of a "stress-adaptation-growth dynamic," a psychological movement that is rooted in conflict between the natural inertia of old mental habits and the inherent drive to maximize life chances by adapting to new ways of dealing with unfamiliar challenges. The stress-adaptation-growth dynamic plays out not in a smooth, arrow-like linear progression, but in a cyclic "draw-back-to-leap" pattern, similar to the movement of a wheel. Each stressful event is responded to with a "draw back," which, in turn, activates adaptive energy to help reorganize one's psyche and "leap forward." Because growth of some parts always occurs at the expense of others, the movement follows a pattern that juxtaposes novelty and confirmation, attachment and detachment, progression and regression, integration and disintegration, construction and destruction. The state of misfit, stress, and heightened awareness serves as the very force that propels us to strive to overcome the predicament and partake in active learning of the new cultural elements. This is possible as we engage in forward-looking moves, striving to meet the challenge by making adjustments in our existing internal structure. In this adaptive struggle, some aspects of the new life conditions are incorporated into our psyches, thereby increasing psychic growth—our overall fitness to adapt to external realities. As the creative forces of "self-reflexivity" lead us to develop new ways of handling problems, the periods of stress subside (Jantsch, 1980).

Note that the stress, adaptation, and growth experiences are not unique to immigrants or sojourners who relocate to a different society. The same experience is broadly shared by anyone living in a multicultural society who is willing to confront and manage the challenges of intercultural encounters across ethnic, racial, and cultural lines. Whether we are at home or abroad, the same three-pronged dynamic of stress-adaptation-growth helps us move in the direction of increased chances of success in meeting the demands of intercultural contacts.

Correlates of Identity Development

One of the long-term consequences of undergoing the intercultural transformation process is an *individualization* of identity, which is a self-conception and a conception of others that transcends conventional social categories such as race, ethnicity, and culture. Individualization allows a life that is lived without rigid constraint due to the grip of conventional social categories. Such an orientation generates a heightened self-awareness, a sense of authenticity, a feeling of certainty about one's place in the world, and a sense of personal power to fix one's sights and chart a course. An individualized identity further allows the enactment and pursuit of socially constructive ends, such as the attitudes of tolerance, mutuality, and cooperation in search of meaningful relationships across group boundaries (Waterman, 1992). Capturing some of these elements of individualized identity are the words of Muruddin Farah, a Somali novelist who traveled widely in Africa, Europe, and North America: "One of the pleasures of living away from home is that you become the master of your destiny, you avoid the constraints and limitations of your past and, if need be, create an alternative life for yourself. That way everybody else becomes *the other,* and you the center of the universe" (in Glad, 1990, p. 65).

Accompanying the individualization of identity is a parallel psychological development, *universalization,* which is "a new consciousness, born out of an awareness of the relative nature of values and of the universal aspect of human nature" (Yoshikawa, 1978, p. 220). As we reach an advanced level of identity development, we become better able to see, with clarity, the oneness and unity of humanity. We are better able to feel compassion and sensitivity for people who are different. It becomes easier for us to locate the points of difference and contention as well as the points of commonality, complementarity, and consent. In so doing, cultural parochialism can be overcome and a wider circle of inclusion can be reached. Like hikers climbing a mountain who finally see that all paths below present unique scenery but ultimately lead to the same summit, we are able to attain a perspective of a larger whole. With such an outlook we can experience the humanity in all people beyond apparent polarities and opposites. We can rise above the hidden grips of the culture of our childhood and discover that there are many ways to be "good," "true," and "beautiful" without being blinded by what is called the "paradigmatic barrier" (Bennett, 1986).

In a subtle manner, the individualization and universalization of identity present us with a special kind of *freedom*—freedom to make deliberate choices for actions, to exercise spontaneous empathy, to "imaginatively participate in the other's world view" (J. Bennett, 1977, p. 49) and to appreciate "outsidedness" through the ability to view the other from the perspective of a disinterested outsider (Harris, 1993, p. 93). Even though such a sense of personhood must be hard won through many moments of inner crisis, it represents an uncommon achievement of personal and social integration through the successful resolution of a process in which we struggle and triumph over the constraints of rigid social categorization. In this self-liberating process, our identity is transformed into something that will always contain the old and the new, side by side, forming "a third kind." In a sense, the development of an intercultural personhood is a continuous struggle of searching for the authenticity in self and others across group boundaries. Consistent with Erikson's (1969) notion of "transcendence" in describing "self-actualizing" people and with Ricoeur's (1992) idea of a "transcendental ego," intercultural personhood is a way of life that embraces and incorporates seemingly divergent cultural elements into one's own unique worldview. This conception of identity development is very much in agreement with what has been described as the development of "double perspective" and "stereoscopic vision" (Rushdie, 1992), "cultural reflexibility" or "cultural relativistic insight" (Roosens, 1989), and "moral inclusiveness" (Opotow, 1990). All of these concepts characteristically show an increased self-knowledge that is less encumbered by the hidden grips of culture and allows broader and less categorical perceptions.

Intercultural Persons

The contemporary world of a tightly knit intercultural communication web offers ample cases of individuals who have attained a significant level of intercultural personhood. Numerous firsthand accounts witnessing the reality of intercultural identity transformation can be found in the form of case histories, memoirs, biographical stories, and essays of self-reflection and self-analysis available in popular books and newspaper and magazine articles and on radio and television programs. Among the more widely known are such prominent figures as Seiji Ozawa (the director-conductor of the Boston Symphony Orchestra and a Japanese American), Colin Powell (the former chairman of the Joint Chiefs of the United States and the son of immigrants from the Dominican Republic), and Kofi Annan (the United Nations secretary-general and a native of Ghana). There are many more lesser known individuals whose life experiences span multitudes of cultural domains—Peace Corps volunteers, missionaries, exchange students, and immigrants and refugees, as well as those ordinary citizens of multicultural societies such as the United States who have embraced a truly inclusive and integrated life that crosses various ethnic boundaries.

The stories of "intercultural persons" bear witness to our theoretical understanding of intercultural identity development and offer a special insight into the ebb and flow of psychic transformation and the eventual emergence of a personhood beyond the confines of a particular cultural identity. Even though no two individuals travel an identical path in becoming intercultural, the intensity of experiences in crossing cultures offers everyone opportunities for full blossoming of the uniquely human capacity to face challenges, to learn from them, and thereby to grow into a greater self-integration. We learn that experiences requiring adaptive challenges bring about a special privilege to think, feel, and act beyond the boundaries of a single culture and beyond "either-or" categorization. Russian exile Edward (in Glad, 1990) noted, "having lived now in three countries—USSR, the USA, and France—I really am able to answer the question: 'Which is best?' All of them have become part and parcel of my own personal history" (p. 50). Equally instructive is the final story in Salman Rushdie's book of short stories, *East, West* (1996). The story ends with the narrator's declaration: "I . . . have ropes around my neck, I have them to this day, pulling me this way and that, East and West, the nooses tightening, commanding, *choose, choose.* I buck, I snort, I whinny, I rear, I kick. Ropes, I do not choose between you. . . . I choose neither of you, and both. Do you hear? I refuse to choose" (p. 211).

Stories such as these remind us that becoming an intercultural person does not necessarily entail a "surrendering" of our personal and cultural integrity. Muneo Yoshikawa (1978) offered a particularly pointed and thoughtful testimonial to this point. Born in Japan, Yoshikawa taught at a university in the United States for many years and examined his own intercultural evolution as follows:

> I am now able to look at both cultures with objectivity as well as subjectivity; I am able to move in both cultures, back and forth without any apparent conflict. . . . I think that something beyond the sum of each [cultural] identification took place, and that it became something akin to the concept of "synergy"—when one adds 1 and 1, one gets three, or a little more. This something extra is not culture-specific but something unique of its own, probably the emergence of a new attribute or a new self-awareness, born out of an awareness of the relative nature of values and of the universal aspect of human nature. . . . I really am not concerned whether others take me as a Japanese or an American; I can accept myself as I am. I feel I am much freer than ever before, not only in the cognitive domain (perception, thoughts, etc.), but also in the affective (feeling, attitudes, etc.) and behavioral domains. (p. 220)

Yoshikawa's thoughts are echoed in an essay by Glenn Loury (1993), whose reflection on his own life experiences as a black American eloquently depicts the true meaning of a universalized and individualized identity orientation:

> I have had to confront the problem of balancing my desire not to disappoint the expectations of others . . . with my conviction that one should strive to live life with integrity. . . . I no longer believe that the camaraderie engendered among blacks by our collective experience of racism constitutes an adequate basis for any person's self-definition. . . . The most important challenges and opportunities that confront me derive not from my racial condition, but rather from my human condition. I am a husband, a father, a son, a teacher, an intellectual, a Christian, a citizen. In none of these roles is my race irrelevant, but neither can racial identity alone provide much guidance for my quest to adequately discharge these responsibilities. The particular features of my social condition, the external givens, merely set the stage of my life, they do not provide a script. That script must be internally generated, it must be a product of a reflective deliberation about the meaning of this existence for which no political or ethnic program could ever substitute. . . . In my view, a personal iden-

tity wholly dependent on racial contingency falls tragically short of its potential because it embraces too parochial a conception of what is possible, and of what is desirable. . . . Of course there is the constraint of racism also holding us back. But the trick . . . is to turn such "nets" into wings, and thus to fly by them. One cannot do that if one refuses to see that ultimately, it is neither external constraints nor expanded opportunity but rather an indwelling spirit that makes this flight possible. (pp. 7–10)

Forging an Intercultural Path

To the extent that intercultural identity is of value both to us individually and to the integration of a multicultural society such as the United States, we may accept and appreciate the real possibility that a part of who we are and what we are may be changed as we engage ourselves with those who are different from us. To be willing to undergo personal transformation, in turn, means that we recognize the necessity to be open to new experiences that may transform us. It further means that we accept that we cannot realistically choose between keeping the original identity intact and adapting to the increasingly intercultural milieu in which we live. We need to be mindful that embracing new cultural elements means not "throwing away" or "being disloyal to" our original cultural heritage but subjecting it to numerous intercultural tests and ultimately enriching it. We need to be guided by a foresight that there is a larger, reconstituted self at the end of our struggle to cross cultural boundaries. This foresight helps us to replace some of our short-term anxieties and reservations with optimism and resolve—a realization that most of us in most circumstances are capable of finding ways to face and overcome the challenges of intercultural interactions, including the most contentious of identity politics.

As members of an intercultural society, our true strength no longer lies in insisting on who we were in the past and who we are at the moment. Instead, our true strength resides in affirming and challenging our "uncommitted potentiality for change" (Bateson, 1951/1972, p. 49). In moments of inner calm, we must let our victorious personality spring forward with flashes of creative insights beyond exclusive cultural loyalty. This very idea was pointed out by Vaclav Havel, former president of the Czech Republic, in his remarks on the occasion of his receiving the Philadelphia Liberty Medal.

> It logically follows that, in today's multicultural world, the truly reliable path to coexistence, to peaceful coexistence and creative cooperation, must start from what is at the root of all cultures and what lies infinitely deeper in human hearts and minds than political opinion. It must be rooted in self-transcendence. Transcendence as a hand reached out to those close to us, to foreigners, to the human community, to all living creatures, to nature, to the universe, transcendence as a deeply and joyously experienced need to be in harmony even with what we ourselves are not, what we do not understand,

what seems distant from us in time and space, but with which we are nevertheless mysteriously linked because, together with us, all this constitutes a single world. Transcendence is the only real alternative to extinction. (Havel, 1995, p. 113)

The process of becoming intercultural, of course, is never easy or complete. Yet each step taken on this path is a new formation of life—a true reward for having withstood the test of continual tides of self-doubt and cynicism that are rooted in the habitual mental posturing of "us and them." This personal accomplishment is not an extraordinary phenomenon that only exceptional individuals achieve. It is simply an incident of the normal human mutability that all of us possess, manifesting itself as we stretch ourselves out of the old and familiar. The experiences of those who have already achieved a great deal of intercultural identity transformation bear witness to the human capacity for self-renewal. Even under extreme conditions of cultural estrangement, they have been able to revise their original cultural constitution and construct a life of their own that embraces a broad spectrum of human conditions. My own intercultural journey in the United States, which began in 1970 when I was a graduate student from Korea, gives me a sense of assurance and gratitude in joining them in the often arduous but ultimately rewarding path of becoming intercultural.

NOTES

1. The term "cultural identity" is employed broadly as a generic term that is interchangeable with other commonly used terms including "national," "ethnic," "ethnolinguistic," and "racial" identity, and more generic concepts such as "social" and "group" identity. In this sense, the present use of the term "culture" includes common ethnic, linguistic, racial, and historical backgrounds. Correspondingly, the term "intercultural identity" is employed throughout this essay interchangeably with "interethnic," "interracial," and "intergroup" identity, as well as with other terms such as "meta-identity," "multicultural identity," or "transcultural identity"—all of which indicate a nondualistic, metacontextual definition of self/others rather than rigid boundedness within any particular group category.

2. The theoretical ideas and case illustrations presented in this essay are based on the author's previous writings, including *Communication and Cross-Cultural Adaptation: An Integrative Theory* (1988) and *Becoming Intercultural: An Integrative Theory of Communication and Cross-Cultural Adaptation* (in press). For a more condensed presentation of her theory see Kim (1995a, 1995b).

REFERENCES

Adler, P. (1982). Beyond cultural identity: Reflections on cultural and multicultural men. In L. A. Samovar & R. A. Porter (Eds.), *Intercultural communication: A reader* (3rd ed.) (pp. 389–408). Belmont, CA: Wadsworth.

Bateson, G. (1951/1972). *Steps to an ecology of mind: Collected essays in anthropology, psychiatry, evolution, and epistemology.* New York: Ballantine.

Bennett, J. (1977, December). Transition shock: Putting culture shock in perspective. In N. C. Jain (Ed.), *International and intercultural communication annual* (Vol. 4, pp. 45–52). Falls Church, VA: Speech Communication Association.

Bennett, M. (1986). A developmental approach to training for intercultural sensitivity. *International Journal of Intercultural Relations, 10,* 179–196.

Blackwell, J. E., & Hart, P. S. (1982). *Cities, suburbs, and blacks: A study of concerns, distrust, and alienation.* Bayside, NY: General Hall.

Brewer, M., & Gardner, W. (1996). Who is this "we"? Levels of collective identity and self-representations. *Journal of Personality and Social Psychology, 71,* 83–93.

Erikson, E. H. (1950). *Childhood and society.* New York: W. W. Norton.

Erikson, E. H. (1969). Growth and crises of the healthy personality: Readings. In H. Chiang & A. H. Maslow (Eds.), *The healthy personality* (pp. 30–34). New York: Van Nostrand Reinhold.

Etzioni, A. (1993). *The spirit of community: Rights, responsibilities, and the communitarian agenda.* New York: Crown.

Glad, J. (Ed.). (1990). *Literature in exile.* Durham, NC: Duke University Press.

Harris, M. (1993, April). Performing the other's text: Bakhtin and the art of cross-cultural understanding. *Mind & Human Interaction, 4,* 92–97.

Havel, V. (1995, January/February). A time for transcendence. *Utne Reader, 53,* pp. 112–113.

Hecht, M. L., Collier, M. J., & Ribeau, S. L. (1993). *African American communication: Ethnic identity and cultural interpretation.* Newbury Park, CA: Sage.

Jantsch, E. (1980). *The self-organizing universe: Scientific and human implications of the emerging paradigm of evolution.* New York: Pergamon.

Kim, Y. Y. (1988). *Communication and cross-cultural adaptation: An integrative theory.* Clevedon, England: Multilingual Matters.

Kim, Y. Y. (1995a). Cross-cultural adaptation: An integrative theory. In R. L. Wiseman (Ed.), *Intercultural communication theory* (pp. 170–193). Newbury Park, CA: Sage.

Kim, Y. Y. (1995b). Identity development: From cultural to intercultural. In H. Mokros (Ed.), *Interaction & identity* (pp. 347–369). New Brunswick, NJ: Transaction.

Kim, Y. Y. (in press). *Becoming intercultural: An integrative theory of communication and cross-cultural adaptation.* Thousand Oaks, CA: Sage.

Loury, G. C. (1993). Free at last? A personal perspective on race and identity in America. In G. Early (Ed.), *Lure and loathing: Essays on race, identity, and the ambivalence of assimilation* (pp. 1–12). New York: Allen Lane/Penguin.

Opotow, S. (1990). Moral exclusion and inclusion. *Journal of Social Issues, 46,* 1–20.

Ricoeur, P. (1992). *Oneself as another* (K. Blamey, Trans.). Chicago: University of Chicago Press.

Roosens, E. E. (1989). *Creating ethnicity: The process of ethnogenesis.* Newbury Park, CA: Sage.

Rushdie, S. (1992). *Imaginary homelands: Essays and criticism 1981–1991.* New York: Penguin Books.

Rushdie, S. (1996). *East, West: Stories.* New York: Vintage Books.

Tajfel, H. (Ed.). (1978). *Differentiation between social groups: Studies in the social psychology of intergroup relations.* London: Academic Press.

Thornton, M. (1996). Hidden agendas, identity theories, and multiracial people. In Maria P. P. Root (Ed.), *The multiracial experience: Racial borders as the new frontiers* (pp. 101–120). Thousand Oaks, CA: Sage.

Waterman, A. S. (1992). Identity as an aspect of optimal psychological functioning. In G. R. Adams, T. P. Gullotta, & R. Montemayor (Eds.), *Adolescent identity formation* (pp. 50–72). Newbury Park, CA: Sage.

Yinger, J. (1986). Intersecting strands in the theorisation of race and ethnic relations. In J. Rex & D. Mason (Eds.), *Theories of race and ethnic relations* (pp. 20–41). New York: Cambridge University Press.

Yoshikawa, M. (1978). Some Japanese and American cultural characteristics. In M. H. Prosser, *The cultural dialogue: An introduction to intercultural communication* (pp. 220–239). Boston: Houghton Mifflin.

Tadasu Todd Imahori's essay illustrates, in very concrete terms, Young Yun Kim's argument that extensive intercultural communication experiences can be the catalyst for an individual's adaptive changes. Todd's journey from Japan to the Midwestern United States to San Francisco and back to Japan is a case study in cultural adaptation and change. Through all the stages of change and constancy, Todd shows how individuals seek to "fit in," as well as to maintain core elements of their identities.

9

On Becoming "American"

Tadasu Todd Imahori

I was born in Japan as Tadasu Imahori. In the fall of 1978, at a college campus in the U.S. Midwest, I was ordering pizza on the phone. Though I attempted to say "Tad," a shortened version of my first name, the person taking my order heard "Todd." That's when I decided that I would become "Todd Imahori." In that instant, as I readily accepted a familiar "American" name as my own, my cultural adaptation process started. I was content if people remembered my "American" nickname, even if they mispronounced my last name, made fun of it, or didn't even try to remember it. Such an attitude toward my own name truly reflected my earnest desire to "fit in," to become "American."

In those early days of my cultural adaptation to the United States, I wanted to *adapt myself* to the "American" culture. Twenty years later, I see my adaptation process as much more complex. A few years ago I had the following phone conversation with a hotel reservation clerk:

"May I please have your name sir?"
"Yes. It's Todd Imahori, and the last name is spelled I-M-A-H-O-R-I."
"Oh, come on, is this a crank call?"
"What?"
"I'm saying, are you pulling my leg?"
"Why do you think I am joking?"
"Well, a name spelled like that . . ."

At that moment, I surmised that the reservationist thought my last name was spelled "I-M-A-H-O-R-E," which could be read "I'm a whore." I had previously encountered others who had made fun of my last name in this way.

"Oh, so you wouldn't think this is a crank call if I had a name like Johnson, or Smith?"

"No, not that, but we get a lot of crank calls, and your name just . . ."

"My name is just what, not white? Not American? You've offended me, and I would like to speak to your supervisor right now."

After many years of trying to become "American" I had acquired a very different attitude toward my own name. I had developed a keen awareness of what *my* being "American" was supposed to look and sound like: I was forever to be an "other American," no matter how much I adapted. Madrid (1988) best described that awareness of and frustration with being an "other" in the United States:

> There was a myth, a pervasive myth, that said if we only learned to speak English well—and particularly without an accent—we would be welcomed into the American fellowship.
>
> Senator Sam Hayakawa notwithstanding, the true text was not our speech, but rather our names and our appearance, for we would always have an accent, however perfect our pronunciation, however excellent our enunciation, however divine our diction. That accent would be heard in our pigmentation, our physiognomy, our names. We were, in short, *the other*. (p. 56)

Today, as my cultural adaptation continues, I am simultaneously torn and excited by my multiple cultural identities. I am also frustrated with my never-ending status as the "other." Let me, then, present the tale of my journey through four stages of the cultural adaptation experience: (a) trying to become "American" and dealing with the "Japanese" or "American" choice; (b) becoming an "other American" and acquiring a "minority" identity; (c) becoming an "other Japanese" and being aware of a "majority" perspective; and (d) becoming "intercultural" and moving among the multiple identities of "other Japanese," "other American," "majority," and "minority."

Throughout this essay I will use quotation marks around terms that categorize people to indicate that such categories are overgeneralizations and need to be considered cautiously. I will use the term "American" to designate the culture and the people of the United States of America because that is the term "mainstream America" uses to refer to itself, and that was what I and others expected me to acquire and become in my adaptation process. Although the term should include other cultures and people located in all American (North, Central, and South) regions, I elect to use it because it best represents my own consciousness about "who and what" I tried to be in my adaptation processes. I will also use the terms "majority" and "minority" to refer to the two cultures defined by the relative differences in membership size, economic wealth, access to resources, and overall social power as defined by the larger culture.

Becoming "American"

To describe my adaptation to "American" culture, it would be helpful to describe myself before my journey to the United States. I grew up as the first son of a middle-class family. I am a "third-generation" sojourner in the United States. Both my grandfather and my father lived in the United States for a few years. I accompanied my father as a newborn baby and lived for one year in the United States. My grandfather didn't talk much about his life in New York, where he lived in 1930s, but he once told me how hard it was for him to find a place to live because of racism. This was the only "negative" thing about the United States that I heard growing up in Japan. My father, mother, and older sister spoke mostly positively about the United States. In school I was taught that the United States was a country to be followed and modeled after, and my generation was supposed to learn from it. I grew up thinking of the United States as a kind of utopia and I yearned to go there.

One direct effect this desire had on me was that I focused more on English than on other academic subjects and sought "American" cultural icons. During the 1970s I listened to "American" rock music, grew my hair long, and wore bell-bottom blue jeans. I intently watched "American" TV shows that were available in Japan. I felt very ready to come to the United States when I first arrived in 1978.

In my early stages of cultural adaptation I was mostly concerned with my English proficiency. Speaking English like an "American" was my criterion for successful cultural adaptation (or "assimilation"). I didn't know about the myth Madrid (1988) pointed out, but I knew my ability to speak English would facilitate my adaptation. I surrounded myself with "Americans" and for at least a year tried not to use the Japanese language or interact with other "Japanese." Within a year I mastered conversational English pretty well. Along with language skills, I also acquired the "American" lifestyle. I now had a mustache and a fashionable hair style. I had become almost "American." My "American" friends had accepted me as one of them; at least that's what I thought. One friend said, "Todd, you're more American than most Americans"—whatever that meant. I was happy, for a while, with my accomplishment: my amazing transformation from a "Japanese" to an "American."

My cultural adaptation, however, was subconsciously targeted to a specific sector of the United States. I was culturally immersed in the "white" youth culture of the late 1970s. I studied at a university in the Midwest, where nearly all of the students were "white." My "American" friends were mostly "whites." The English I acquired had a standard Midwestern "white" accent. The college lifestyle I maintained was that of "white men." In my consciousness at that time, that was "America." The subconscious belief that "white America" was "America" started early. I can't recall learning English in Japan from "nonwhite" native speakers. "Americans" I knew in Japan—in person, on TV, or in the movies—were almost exclusively whites.

Looking back, with the academic and personal sense-making frameworks I have since developed, I believe that my status in Japan before coming to the United States contributed to my subconscious adaptation to "mainstream America." I was a "mainstream Japanese": "male," "young," "middle-class," and "well-educated." Those who are in the "dominant" group, as I was, tend to have less awareness of their power and group identity. Thus, as a person who stood at the top of the "Japanese" social hierarchy without much awareness of doing so, it was easy for me to adapt to those who shared the same lack of awareness about their "mainstream" status in the United States. I took for granted that what I represented was "Japanese." My "mainstream American" counterparts also assumed that they represented the "American" culture and readily taught me what they regarded as "American." In the beginning phase, my cultural adaptation was thus focused on assimilating to a new national culture.

Although I was subconsciously adapting only to "white America" and thinking it was "America," it didn't take long for me to realize that most of my associations were with "white America." I had lost touch with others, particularly "people of color" and "women." Consequently, I denied a part of myself as a "person of color" as I developed into "almost white," or more specifically, an "almost white male." I remember a conversation with one of my "white" college classmates:

"Todd, you're okay, you are like honored white."
"What does that mean, 'honored 'white'?"
"Well, it means that you are like 'white,' you are like many of your people who have become doctors, teachers, and earned your status."

These types of statements, made by those who supposedly had accepted me, created dissonance in my sense of identity. I began to feel a need to be even more "American" to be accepted fully. However, the more "American" I tried to be, the greater the hindrance in my background. I was not even sure whether my background was a barrier because I was a "foreigner" (i.e., "non-U.S. born") or because I was a "Japanese" (i.e., someone who was "nonwhite").

The following incident illustrates my uncertainty. I was once traveling on a motorcycle with a "Japanese" friend. As we rode through the Appalachian Mountains, it started snowing. We found a strip mall to shelter ourselves from the snow and were drinking hot coffee on a bench inside the mall when a sheriff's deputy approached us. The following conversation ensued.

Deputy: Where are you from, boy?
Todd: We're traveling from Ohio, sir.
Deputy: No, I mean, where are you really from?
Todd: Well, I guess, then, we are originally from Japan, and now we are both studying at XXX university.
Deputy: I thought so. It's dangerous for your kind to be here.

He then ordered us to follow his squad car as he "escorted" us to a rundown motel outside of town. In his mind he was probably doing us a "favor" by protecting the "outsiders." That made me angry. But I wasn't sure whether I was being treated as an "outsider" because I was "Japanese" or because I was a "foreigner" (that is, I didn't speak English well enough).

Even though these kinds of incidents gave me the sense that I might never be accepted as an "American," I spent nearly 14 years struggling to become one. During the period from 1978 to 1991, I was often confronted with the question of "American or Japanese." My "American" students enjoyed asking me, "Do you now consider yourself an American or a Japanese?" I was bewildered by their question almost every time. I usually answered "I'm both: I'm still Japanese, but not quite fully Japanese, and at the same time I'm almost American. I'm culturally schizophrenic, like Jekyll and Hyde." I often asked myself a similar question: "How much do I want to be an American? How Japanese do I want to remain?"

In answering these questions I constantly experienced a paradox: The more I tried to become "American," the more different I felt because of my "Japanese" background; the more I tried to stay "Japanese," the more I realized how much I had changed since coming to the United States. I was torn between "American" and "Japanese." The torment was hard on me. In retrospect, it was a relatively simple set of choices, because I was dealing with only two possibilities.

Becoming an "Other American"

Carrying the dissonance with my identities as "American" and "Japanese," I moved from the Midwest to California in 1992. There I met many others who shared a similar sense of identity dissonance. They were also "Asian Americans," mostly second generation or later. Although they were born in the United States and grew up in a way that I thought of as "American," they expressed frequently the sense that they were never quite "at home."

Ronald Takaki (1993), a sansei (third-generation) "Japanese American" professor, relates the following story:

> I had flown from San Francisco to Norfolk and was riding in a taxi to my hotel. . . . My driver and I chatted about the weather and the tourists. . . . The rearview mirror reflected a white man in his forties. "How long have you been in this country?" he asked. "All my life," I replied, wincing. . . . With a strong southern drawl, he remarked: "I was wondering because your English is excellent!". . . Somehow I did not look "American" to him; my eyes and complexion looked foreign. (p. 1)

Thomas Nakayama (1997), a yonsei (fourth-generation) "Japanese American" scholar, writes:

> "Do you speak English?" This question always dis/orients me; I am lost when asked this question. Why wouldn't I speak the language of my parents, the language of my country? The simple response "Of course I do" does not usually dis/orient the questioner's assumption that one needs European ancestors to be "American." (p. 17)

I, too, am used to strangers complimenting my English or questioning me about whether I speak English. At times compliments or questions come after they learn that I grew up speaking Japanese, not English. At other times, they *assume*—as they did with Takaki and Nakayama—that I am a "foreigner." When I found this daunting similarity between my experiences and those of Takaki and Nakayama, I was no longer uncertain about the reason why I wasn't fully accepted as "American." I knew that my culture and my "foreign" status are the same to the "racist American" society.

As a result of this realization, I have come to appreciate my "Japanese American" experiences. What I share with the "Japanese American" experience is the assumption on the part of strangers that I am a "Japanese born Japanese." What I also share with them is the alienated feeling I experience when I encounter people who assume that I am not an "American." However, my experience is different from theirs because the strangers' assumption about me *happens* to be correct; for most "Japanese Americans" (and many other "nonwhite Americans"), it is grossly wrong. To the extent that this difference exists between my experience and theirs, the sense of denial that "Japanese (nonwhite) Americans" experience may be greater than what I have encountered. Nevertheless, it is clear that I am going to be an "other American" no matter how much I adapt to the "American" culture unless there is a change in the society that sees me as a "foreigner" because of my appearance.

Upon this somber realization, I then attempted to make sense out of my own "minority" experience as an "other American." My sensemaking process largely depended on learning the "Japanese (Asian) American" culture and its history. Because of my appearance I am perceived in the United States as either a "Japanese (Asian)" or a "Japanese (Asian) American." It was therefore sensible for me to examine the group of people with whom I was lumped together. It also meant claiming my own identity in the United States. As Kimoto (1997) asserted, cultural knowledge empowers one's identity by providing a basis to question, modify, and create a label for one's own identity.

As I began my studies of "Japanese American" history and culture, I realized that my experiences with prejudice in the United States are similar to what other people of Japanese origin have experienced throughout their history there. The more I learned about the prejudices and discrimination committed against "Japanese Americans," the more determined I became to do something about racism as an intercultural communication scholar. I conducted a research study about the "Japanese American" internment experience during World War II (Imahori, 1996) and began preparing myself to teach a course on intracultural communication.

In 1995 I encountered a film called *The Color of Fear* (Mun Wah, 1994). I went to see the film partly to decide whether I could use it as a teaching tool, and also to find confirmations for my own experiences with racism. In the film, eight men of different racial backgrounds discussed their views about racism. One "European American" man kept denying that racism is a problem in the United States. He exhibited a complete lack of awareness about how "people of color" are treated and made to feel because of racism. I could easily identify with the seven other men, who were trying to convince this "white man" of the seriousness of racism. I had had experiences similar to theirs. While viewing the film, however, I realized that I was also the equivalent of the "white man" in Japan, as I was the "mainstream." Curiously, I found that

I had two contradictory cultures living inside of me: a "majority" (as a "Japanese" in Japan) and a "minority" (as a "Japanese" in the United States).

In my earlier phase of cultural adaptation I struggled with the paradox of being at the same time "American" and "Japanese." Now I was also struggling with simultaneously being a "majority" and a "minority." What helped me understand the consequences of being a majority or a minority was the concept of "white privilege."

McIntosh (1995) offers a list of privileges whites in the United States enjoy. The list includes assumptions or conditions that apply (or do not apply) in daily life. Examples include: "I can turn on the television or open to the front page of the paper and see people of my race widely and positively represented" (p. 79); "If my day, week, or year is going badly, I need not ask of each negative episode or situation whether it has racial overtones" (p. 81). If I considered these two examples as an "other American," as a "minority" in the United States, I would answer "false" to both of them. If I responded to them as a "Japanese male," a "majority" in Japan, I would answer "true" to both of them.

McIntosh lists 46 such privileges. As an "other American" in the United States I answered "false" to 42 of them. The four conditions I could answer "true" were largely due to my "model minority" status[1] in the United States. As a "Japanese" in Japan I responded "true" to 43 of the 46 privileges. The three "false" responses were due to global-level racism and the relative status of the "Japanese" in the world's racial hierarchy.

When I looked at my answers to McIntosh's list, I was saddened by how far I was from the privileges of the "white American" in the United States. Conversely, I became unsettled as I realized how much privilege I am granted in Japan as a "majority Japanese male" and how much and how long I had taken such privileges for granted. I have also generalized McIntosh's list to include gender preferences, sexual identity, and physical disabilities. Every time I examined the privileges I did or did not have, it crystallized in me an understanding of the prejudices that exist in the society around me. I also understood more clearly the suffocating power of prejudice. My own prejudices kept me from interacting competently with others. The prejudices around me suffocated me by keeping me outside and oppressed. When I acquired this awareness about what it meant to be a "majority" and a "minority," I was able to see my world from multiple perspectives: "Japanese," "U.S. American," "majority," and "minority."

Becoming an "Other Japanese"

As much as I have become an "other American," I have also become an "other Japanese" who can now examine the prejudices and privileges of the "mainstream Japanese" as an "outsider" with a "minority" consciousness. I am still a member of the "mainstream Japanese" in appearance. I would still be a member of the "mainstream" if I hadn't come to terms with my own prejudices and hadn't committed myself to changing the prejudices that lift the "mainstream" unjustly while oppressing racial, gender, and other "minority" groups. My values concerning diversity (e.g., gay marriage rights) further make me a "minority" in Japan.

I am also an "other Japanese" because I have transformed culturally. My "Japanese" family, friends, and colleagues in Japan expect me to be different from them as a result of my cultural transformations. Some of the cultural transformations resulted from consciously choosing an acquired value (e.g., an individual's right to choose) over my original "Japanese" cultural value (a duty to maintain group harmony), whereas other transformations were mostly unconscious (e.g., my initial instinct to avoid public confrontations with others). Not only have I changed some of my cultural beliefs and values, but I have also acquired an ability to examine "Japanese" culture from an "outsider's" view by taking the "American" perspective.

My identity as an "other Japanese" mirrors my identity as an "other American." Although I am not accepted fully as a "mainstream American," I can no longer be accepted fully as a "mainstream Japanese." As much as I am "foreign" and looked on suspiciously in U.S. society, I am perceived as "strange" and treated with polite caution by the "Japanese." Although I hold an outsider's view of "American" culture, I am able to see "Japanese" culture from the outside as well. The difference, however, is that I am an "other American" because of my race and I am an "other Japanese" because of cultural transformations and my growth as an intercultural being.

As the "other" I am in a unique position to provide different perspectives as a "minority" in both the "Japanese" and the "American" "mainstream" cultures. In explaining the "minority" perspective I can also take on the "majority" perspective. In essence, by becoming both an "other Japanese" and an "other American," by having both "majority" and "minority" perspectives, I have become "intercultural."

On Being "Intercultural"

More than 20 years ago I came to the United States to become "American." Today I seek to be "intercultural." I say "intercultural" rather than "multicultural" because the latter term suggests to me that I am merely the sum of my multiple identities. However, although I can take on only one perspective at any given moment, I can move from that perspective into another instantaneously. I am "intercultural" in that I can shift easily between my different cultural perspectives. In looking back, Kim (1997) best summarized my personal adaptation experiences:

> Communicating across cultural identity boundaries is often full of challenges as it provokes questions about our taken-for-granted cultural premises, habits. . . . Yet it is precisely such challenges that offer us openings for new cultural learning, self-awareness, and personal growth. (p. 443)

I agree with Kim that I have grown personally, and in ways that are consistent with her model of adaptation (Kim, 1988). However, my adaptation was even more complex than what her theory suggests. It was directed to both my home and my host cultures. It also occurred between the cultures of "majority" and "minority."

The literature on intercultural adaptation suggests that I may yet attain an ability to transcend my perspectives, achieving what is referred to as the "third culture" (Gudykunst, Wiseman, & Hammer, 1977). For example, Yoshikawa (1978), a scholar who has a cultural background similar to mine, wrote: "I really am not concerned whether others take me as a Japanese or as an American" (p. 220). I cannot yet quite echo his sentiment. I care that others perceive me as "American," "Japanese," "Asian," "foreigner," "dominant," or "nondominant," because how others see me affects my perspective taking. I may or may not choose to agree with the identity they ascribe to me. I may loudly announce a different identity and "correct" their assumptions. Depending on my interactional situation, I have to decide constantly "who" I am going to be.

This identity shifting is highly stressful, but my ability to move across these multiple identities also allows me to become a change agent. I hope to be "close" enough to communicate appropriately and effectively with the "Japanese" or the "Americans" but be able to pull back far enough to be "other Japanese" or "other American" when an alternative perspective is needed. If I succeed in providing different perspectives in this manner, I can at least convince some individuals to examine their values and prejudices from contrasting points of view.

I now realize that my internal cultural stress, born out of my complex set of identities, is my resource as an intercultural person, scholar, and change agent. When I deal with my own prejudices and fears of cultural differences, I am able to be comfortable with my own identities. I am not sure if I have yet developed the "third culture" perspective, but what carries across my various cultural identities are both my attitudes toward cultural differences as a source of enjoyment and personal growth and my commitment to keep learning and providing different cultural perspectives. I hope that you will be able to share the same joy of learning about cultural differences by studying intercultural communication.

Postscript

Six months after I began writing the first draft of this essay, I find myself living and teaching in Japan. It was a drastic and "unbelievable" (as many of my friends said) decision to leave the United States and go to Japan after 19 years of absence (not "back to" because this is really a new adaptation and not a simple "reentry" process for me). I am adding this note to clarify that my move to Japan was not motivated by my dissonance of being an "other American" in the United States. Actually, I am now experiencing a great deal of dissonance with being an "other Japanese." For example, people often give me a sympathetic look when I play with my daughter at 10 o'clock on a weekday morning at a neighborhood park. Here in Japan, fathers are expected to work hard on weekdays. It's unusual to see a man in a park on a weekday. So perhaps the onlookers are thinking: "Look, he has no job. Poor man, poor girl." My days are now filled with these kinds of surprises and culture shocks.

I made the decision to move to Japan willingly, to experience being an "other Japanese" and to enrich my intercultural experience. I need to experience the feeling of otherness on this side of the Pacific Ocean so that I can make better sense of being a "Japanese," an "American," a "majority," a "minority," and above all an "other." So the tale of my intercultural journey continues.

NOTES

1. "Model minority" is a term often used for "Asian Americans." Because some "Asian Americans" have earned economic success and upward mobility in the United States, they are perceived as models for other "minority" cultures to "follow." The racist assumption in this term suggests that "Asian Americans" will forever be a "minority," and thus it maintains and accentuates the distance between "Asian Americans" and "mainstream America." At the same time, by elevating "Asian Americans" from other "minority" cultures, it also encourages a sense of distance and discord among the "minority" cultures.

REFERENCES

Gudykunst, W. B., Wiseman, R., & Hammer, M. (1977). Determinants of a sojourner's attitudinal satisfaction. In B. Ruben (Ed.), *Communication yearbook 1* (pp. 415–425). New Brunswick, NJ: Transaction.

Imahori, T. T. (1996, November). *Revisiting the responses 50 years later: Identity management of "yes-yes" and "no-no" boys.* Paper presented at the annual meeting of the Speech Communication Association, San Diego, CA.

Kim, Y. Y. (1988). Intercultural adaptation. In M. K. Asante and W. B. Gudykunst (Eds.), *Handbook of international and intercultural communication* (pp. 275–294). Newbury Park, CA: Sage.

Kim, Y. Y. (1997). Intercultural personhood: An integration of Eastern and Western perspectives. In L. A. Samovar and R. E. Porter (Eds.), *Intercultural communication: A reader* (8th ed.) (pp. 434–447). Belmont, CA: Wadsworth.

Kimoto, D. M. (1997). Being Hapa: A choice for cultural empowerment. In A. González, M. Houston, and V. Chen (Eds.), *Our voices: Essays in culture, ethnicity and communication* (2nd ed.) (pp. 157–162). Los Angeles, CA: Roxbury.

Madrid, A. (1988. May/June). Missing people and others: Joining together to expand the circle. *Change, 20* 55–59.

McIntosh, P. (1995). White privilege and male privilege: A personal account of coming to see correspondences through work in women's studies. In M. L. Andersen and P. H. Collins (Eds.), *Race, class, and gender* (pp. 76–87). Belmont, CA: Wadsworth.

Mun Wah, L. (Director), & Stir Fry Productions (Producer). (1994). *The color of fear* [Film]. (Available from Stir Fry Productions, 1222 Preservation Park Way, Oakland, CA 94612).

Nakayama, T. (1997). Dis/orienting identities: Asian Americans, history, and intercultural communication. In A. González, M. Houston, and V. Chen (Eds.), *Our voices: Essays in culture, ethnicity and communication* (2nd ed.) (pp. 14–20). Los Angeles, CA: Roxbury.

Takaki, R. T. (1993). *A different mirror: A history of multicultural America.* Boston: Little, Brown.

Yoshikawa, M. (1978). Some Japanese and American characteristics. In M. Prosser (Ed.), *The cultural dialogue: An introduction to intercultural communication* (pp. 220–239). Boston: Houghton Mifflin.

Belonging to multiple cultures can sometimes lead to an odd sense of juxtaposition. Keturah A. Dunne describes how it feels to be bilingual and bicultural, simultaneously European American and Latina. Her poem expresses the poignancy and precariousness of living in two cultural worlds.

10 La Güera

Keturah A. Dunne

> ¿Quién soy?
> Me dicen La Americana
> La güera
> Is the color of my skin
> Lo más importante?

What is most important in determining the culture to which one belongs? Is it the genetic influence of one's skin color? One's learned patterns of behavior? The categories into which people are placed by a seemingly omniscient society? The issue of culture is a delicate one, especially for those of us on the border between two cultures. To come to terms with my life as a cultural anomaly, I composed a poem to express and define—at least to myself—who I am and how my perceptions were formed.

In simple terms, I, Keturah Alegra Dunne, appear to be of European American descent. In other words, I'm *güera,* or light skinned. My ancestors came to the United States from Ireland, Scotland, Germany, Australia, England, and Norway. Add to this heritage a great-great grandmother from the Blackfoot tribe. Such are the genetic facets creating my outward appearance. Yet culture is not genetics. To complete my cultural "profile," I must accurately state that I am a European American Latina.

How is it that I am a Latina when I have no such ancestors? Why is it that both Spanish and English can be considered my native tongues? Allow my poem to explain:

> Desde la infancia
> Spanish was the language
> de mis amigas
> mi comida
> mis hermanos

> y bailes folklóricos
> "La Raspa," "Jesusita En Chihuahua,"
>   "La Bamba"
> With energy I danced
> of places I never knew.

My parents were missionaries in El Salvador when I was conceived. Sociopolitical events prevented them from obtaining an extended visa, and I was born shortly after they returned to the United States. Because all of my family's religious activities have been centered in the Latino community, I was raised in a Latino environment from infancy.

When people discover that I speak Spanish, I tend to get various reactions. If European Americans find out that I speak Spanish, they often react with astonishment: "Oh, how do *you* know Spanish so well?" or "I was sure you were an American." In contrast, Latinos generally ask, "Where are you from?" or "You certainly don't speak Spanish like an American. How is it that you know Spanish?" I've even been told, "Why, you speak the language better than we do." To most inquisitive people of both cultures it seems incredible, almost implausible, that I've always spoken Spanish and that I can't remember ever "learning" the language.

Of course language, by itself, is not culture. This I discovered painfully in fifth grade, when I was uprooted from my bilingual classes and transferred into an advanced GATE (gifted and talented education) class populated solely by upper-class European American students.

> And then
> my reality was distorted
> 5th grade
>   al pozo de los leones fuí
> to a class of cliquish "smart" rich kids
> Entré
>   They stared
>   and
>   looked me up
>   and
>   down,
> You're not one of us they silently whispered
> ¿Cómo soy diferente?
> I was white wasn't I
> just like them
> No entendí
> Me trataban como si fuera invisible
> ¿Quién soy?

My rude awakening to the fact that I was no longer a "typical" European American girl shocked me. I was perplexed; I could not understand why my classmates so despised me. I cried a lot that school year. Now that I look back,

I can see that the first nine years of my life had created such an indelible imprint on me that I was having serious trouble communicating with individuals outside my culture. Of course, I didn't realize this at that tender age. All I knew was that I was somehow different from my new classmates and that it hurt a great deal to be ostracized.

Although I felt isolated at school, I was confident that I still had my Latina friends and nothing could change or alter our friendship—or so I thought.

> Pero Hey!
> tengo mis amigas hispanas
>   right?
> Y de repente
>   vino el junior high
>   and you were too cool for me

Junior high school created more chaos. Unbeknownst to me, there is a secret transformation that occurs in almost all Latina girls as they enter junior high. In sixth grade we were free to jump, skip, or play tag, but with junior high the game plan changed. We were now expected to begin practicing to become full-fledged women. Thus I was no longer accepted as a part of my Latina group because I had no interest in makeup, boyfriends, or other culturally acceptable activities for my age group.

So where am I presently? The good news is that I wasn't permanently expelled from the Latino community. Although many of my childhood friends are now married, we've somehow come to terms with one another. I still enjoy doing many hours a month of volunteer work in the Latino community. As for my relationship and communication with my university peers, most of them don't realize that I speak Spanish or was brought up in a Latino community. Since I am used to being different, I find that I am now rarely bothered by negative or insensitive comments regarding my biculturalism:

> My skin betrays my culture
>   No soy Americana
>   ni Mexicana
> I stand precariously between
> 2 peoples
> A cultural anomaly

Here is the complete poem, as I originally composed it.

"La Güera"

> ¿Quién soy?
> Me dicen La Americana
>   La güera
> Is the color of my skin
>   Lo más importante?

> Desde la infancia

Spanish was the language
    de mis amigas
    mi comida
    mis hermanos
    y bailes folklóricos
    "La Raspa," "Jesusita En Chihuahua,"
        "La Bamba"
With energy I danced
of places I never knew.

And then
my reality was distorted
5th grade
        al pozo de los leones fuí
to a class of cliquish "smart" rich kids
Entré
    They stared
            and
    looked me up
            and
    down,
You're not one of us they silently whispered
¿Cómo soy diferente?
I was white wasn't I
just like them
No entendí
Me trataban como si fuera invisible
Quién soy?
La poderosa niña
    transformada
    crying wet salty tears
    lágrimas . . .
Pero Hey!
tengo mis amigas hispanas
    right?
Y de repente
    vino el junior high
    and you were too cool for me

Ana M.
compartimos
    tap dancing lessons
    sleepovers
    quesadillas
    "Sabado Gigante"
Now you want nothing to do with me
No soy

     tú type
     I was not mature
"¿Por qué no te gustan los chicos?"
      she repeatedly asked,
"¡Yo nunca me casaré!"
      I defiantly stated;
"Mijita, tú cambiarás,"
      Ana's mom chided when I was 12,
"y un dia iré a tu boda."
Pero fuí terca
  and instead of me
Tú, Ana, a los diecinueve
  ya eres en verdad mujer
  y tienes esposo
  que te cuida
  'til death do you part

Y yo me he quedado atras
    Or have I?
Y tú, Elizabeth M.
  con tu copete
  varnizado con hairspray
  y tu chola stance
You told me
    in my face
  I wasn't one of you
"¿Porque no te pintas?"
    you asked
Are you a baby
  a mama's girl
  a schoolie
Why can't you be normal?
¿Pero qué era ser normal?
Were you normal Elizabeth?

I didn't understand
  would make-up
  a boyfriend
  copetes
  tight dresses
make me one of you?
Why couldn't I wear
  my long skirts
  and bobby socks
  and skip

My mother said:
  "Sticks and stones

will break your bones
                but
words will never
        hurt you"
But these words
        did

10 años han pasado
Y un viaje a México he realizado
Could it be so?
Was I truly discovering my roots?
Now I listen to
    Radio Latina
            with confidence
    Speak Hebrew
    Cook Equadorian Llapingachos
            and smile

My skin betrays my culture
            No soy Americana
            ni Mexicana
I stand precariously between
2 peoples
A cultural anomaly.

Peter O. Nwosu provides an account of an African immigrant's experiences in the United States. The narrative describes and explains some of the problems he encountered and the intercultural growth that occurred on his American journey. The narrative style of the essay reflects the nonlinear approach to story telling that is common among Africans. African narratives include interconnecting ideas; the story typically begins somewhere, breaks off into another but related subject, and eventually returns to the main body of the narrative. This essay provides both an example of the African narrative style and an analysis of the ingrained cultural patterns that one brings to intercultural interactions.

Cultural Problems and Intercultural Growth: My American Journey

Peter O. Nwosu

The entire family gathered to wish me farewell. Little did they realize that I would probably be spending quite some years in the United States. In keeping with family tradition my mother, the matriarch of our large and extended family, had organized a reception in my honor and had invited many people to see me off.

I had been offered a graduate fellowship by Nigeria's Federal Agricultural Coordinating Unit, a World Bank program to manage all of the bank's integrated rural development projects in the country. The fellowship enabled me to pursue a master's degree in liberal studies, with a specialization in communication and instructional media technology, at Towson State University. Towson State, in Baltimore, is a predominantly European American institution. Later I went to the mainly African American Howard University in Washington, D.C., to pursue doctoral work in human communication studies, with an emphasis in communication processes across cultures.

My arrival at Dulles International Airport near Washington, D.C., on September 19, 1985, was accompanied by mixed feelings and perceptions. The flight had lasted nearly 13 hours. I had a great curiosity about a land I had been told flowed with "milk and honey." The things I saw upon my arrival seemed to confirm my expectations: a magnificent airport infrastructure; huge paved roads that I observed as I trucked along the freeway with an in-law who had come to the airport to greet me; numerous high-rise buildings; and lighted streets. It was as if the roads had been swept. Truly, it appeared to be a land flowing with milk and honey. Yet in the midst of this grandeur, I had flash-backs of stories I had been told of race relations in the United States. I re-called the negative images of blacks that were portrayed on Nigerian televi-sion, images of the buffoonery behavior of J.J. in the old-time sitcom *Good Times,* images of blacks in subservient or supporting roles. Those images heightened my initial fears about living in the United States, and I wondered about the opportunities that would be available to a person with my back-ground. I also wondered about the nature of relationships that would emerge between my African American relatives and me.

I had left Nigeria with the impression that African Americans were con-fined to a life of silliness and crime in America, and that the experience of slavery had wrought considerable havoc on the psyches of blacks. My experi-ences in Nigeria with some African Americans living and working there (my boss was African American, as was one of my good high school friends) did lit-tle to alter the very negative perceptions reflected in media images that had become the prism through which I saw life in America. My initial interactions with African Americans upon my arrival in the United States were therefore filled with curiosity, because I wanted to get to know them, and caution—one could even say fear—because of the negative media portrayals. Such fear was manifested in my polite refusal of an offer from a young African American male staffer to assist me with my luggage at Dulles; yet I felt safe when a sim-ilar offer came, moments later, from a white male attendant! For most new-comers into a foreign land, their knowledge of a place is typically informed by media images. Clearly the distorted depictions of blacks helped to condition my perceptions of and relationships with that group upon my arrival in the United States. Fortunately, those perceptions had changed by the time I went to Howard University for my doctorate.

At Towson State University I continued my American journey. A predomi-nantly white institution located on a pristine campus, Towson had more than 16,000 students; when I was there I was the only black face, or one of the very few black faces, in several of my classes and on the campus. I had never been exposed to such a sea of white faces in my life! It was there that I encountered some initial cultural problems. They came in many shapes and sizes. The first was in the use of the English language.

In my initial interactions with U.S. Americans, I had difficulties related to use of verbal and nonverbal codes, including the meanings assigned to various actions or behaviors. One such difficulty arose during my first encounter with snow. I had never seen snow until I came to the United States. There is no word in Igbo (my language) for it.

My knowledge of snow came from watching television and from classroom discussions at St. Mary's Elementary School (later renamed Niger Close Pri-mary School) in Enugu, Nigeria. The teacher would liken snow to ice forma-tions in one's refrigerator. For someone who has not experienced snow, that description does not capture the phenomenon. My sister had warned me of the need to be careful during winter,[1] since large tracks of snow tend to turn into ice. On one particular morning in Baltimore I woke to the sight of snow and was clearly enthused by it. My college friend, Sam, who is African American, had joined me at my apartment as I prepared for class that morning. A few minutes later, we both left the apartment and walked down the stairs, which had been partially covered by the snow. Not remembering my sister's warning, I tripped and rolled down to the bottom of the stairs. I was in pain, and of course I expected my friend to say that he was sorry about the incident while assisting me up from the ground. Instead, he kept asking "Are you all right, Peter? Are you all right?" The more he asked the question, the angrier I became. When I finally managed to get up, I wasted no time in telling him how inconsiderate he was. Sam could not understand why I would expect him to say "sorry" when he was not responsible for my fall.

Years later, at Howard University, when I was able to reprocess that interaction, it became clear that our remarks regarding appropriate behaviors and linguistic norms were a function of our cultural backgrounds. I began to feel a sense of both awareness and understanding of these differences—a sense of intercultural growth. Among Africans, when a person is hurt, regardless of the circumstances, it is appropriate for the others who are present to indicate their sympathy by saying "I am sorry." The phrase is not an indication of responsibility; rather, it is one's way of showing concern. Duty also requires one to assist physically in extricating the injured person from the source of the pain. Among U.S. Americans, however, the predominant cultural norm is that a person should display concern through questions like those Sam asked. How a question is posed—its tone, pitch, and rate—indicates the degree of concern. In fact, if one is badly injured, the cultural rule in the United States is that the person would call for medical help, since any attempt to assist physically might exacerbate the pain or injury. There are a few exceptions to this rule, as in the case of administering cardiac pulmonary resuscitation (CPR) when needed.

In spite of my proficiency in British English, American English, for the most part, was incomprehensible to me because of differences in pronunciation and the use of words. There were numerous instances of miscommunication when I felt embarrassed because my accented speech was misunderstood or the way I pronounced or used words was wrong. For example, what the British pronounce *schedule (shedyool)* is pronounced *skedyool* by most American students. Once I used the word *stroke* to explain intrapersonal/interpersonal communication in one of my classes. The students were clearly confused by the term because the U.S. American way of saying intrapersonal/ *(stroke)* interpersonal communication would have substituted the word *stroke* with the word *slash*. It was another lesson for me in communication, whose goal is shared meaning. In addition, my accent was different from the U.S. norm, and in the company of many U.S. Americans, it was a constant reminder that I was an outgroup member who did not belong. It was a struggle to understand both my instructors and my classmates. In numerous instances I laughed at jokes when I did not understand their meanings or their cultural contexts, simply to cover my "deficiency."

Another equally perplexing issue centered on the use of first names to refer to people in authority or who were higher in status or age. I could not understand the general informality of my new environment, and I wondered why people would be so "disrespectful." Why, I asked rhetorically, would fellow classmates address the instructor by his or her first name? My relationship with authority figures and with people older than me was guided by an expectation that they should be treated with deference, which is displayed, in part, through one's greeting styles (handshakes, bowing, or kissing the hand or forehead). To observe students address the instructor, an authority figure, without such deference was perplexing. In contrast to these experiences of white students' relationships with their instructors at Towson State, I saw a profound difference in the way African American students related to their instructors—referring to them by their formal titles—at Howard University. At California State University, Sacramento, where I now teach, it took me a while to refer to my colleagues by their first names, since doing so (given my cultural background) was a sign of disrespect. In fact, during the initial period of my teaching, the chair of my department insisted (although jokingly) that he would stop speaking to me if I continued to address him using the honorific title Doctor! In spite of my growth and adjustment in this area, I am still somewhat uncomfortable when students refer to me or to other instructors by first name.

The initial period of my American journey included other instances of communication failures. At the college cafeteria and at public restaurants, I always ordered the same meals. On public transportation, I paid my fare with large bills to mask my ignorance of the currency. I felt too embarrassed to ask questions, since my accent would give me away and expose me to vulnerabilities. On a few occasions I had to withdraw from the sources of pain because, as for so many immigrants who come to the United States, the transition involved not just a tremendous adventure but, at times, near overwhelming stress, feelings of alienation, and low self-esteem. At no time did it occur to me that the frustrations I experienced on a daily basis were a symptom of the stress associated with adjustment to a new environment, or the phenomenon commonly known as "culture shock."

When I first left Nigeria I believed, like most African-born immigrants, that my life and experiences in my country had prepared me fully for life in another country. After all, when I graduated from college my parents had encouraged me to accept employment in the western part of Nigeria, in an area inhabited by Yorubas, who are one of the major ethnic groups in the country. My parents, who are Igbos,[2] had lived in western Nigeria, and they speak the Yoruba language fluently. The Igbos represent one of the three major ethnic groups in the country. My parents also lived for more than a quarter of a century in northern Nigeria, where I was born. The North is inhabited largely by Hausas and Fulanis, and my parents also speak the Hausa language fluently. However, the rise of ethnic antagonisms against the Igbos in the region a few years after Nigeria's independence in 1960 compelled my parents to return to eastern Nigeria, their place of origin. In 1967 eastern Nigeria seceded from the rest of the country to form the Republic of Biafra. Following the collapse of talks to resolve the crisis between the East and the Nigerian government, a bloody civil war ensued. The war, which lasted nearly 30 months, claimed more than one million lives. The period of the Biafra-Nigeria conflict (1967–1970) was a very dark chapter in the country's history, and many accounts of that ugly experience have been written. Just as the history of slavery shaped black-white relations in the United States, the history of the Biafra-Nigeria war shaped interethnic relations in Nigeria. Communication in such areas as politics, education, the military, the economy, and infrastructure development has been tainted by these historical circumstances, yet it was difficult for me to recognize the profound impact of my country's history on my perceptions of race relations in the United States. I will return to this point later.

Although I was born in the northern region of Nigeria, I cannot claim that as my place of origin. According to Igbo custom, one's father's place of birth (not one's mother's) is the person's place of origin. In other words, my father's place of birth, in the eastern region of Nigeria, is my place of origin. In the same manner, my father's place of origin is his father's place of birth. Consider, for example, the following: according to my culture, if my father was born in California and I was born in Arkansas, California would constitute my place of origin. However, if my grandfather was born in California, my father was born in New York, and I was born in Arkansas, both my father and I would hail from California, which is my grandfather's birthplace. This is how Africans generally maintain their family lines and group identities from one generation to the next. In the United States a person's own place of birth is his or her place of origin. Thus, if someone is born in California, that state would constitute the person's place of origin, regardless of where his or her father was born. Initially I had difficulty and a sense of disconnection in my conversations with U.S. Americans because I could not comprehend their sense of casualness about something as important as origins and group identities.

In any case, my period of residence in the North, East, and West of Nigeria exposed me to three vastly different cultures in the country. My work with the World Bank project, in the western part of the country, provided further exposure to other cultural and ethnic groups, as I had the opportunity to travel to 18 of Nigeria's 19 states.[3]

At the World Bank project, I worked with many expatriate workers from several countries, including Ghana, the United States, the United Kingdom, Canada, India, Pakistan, Bangladesh, and China. My daily interactions with these workers, in addition to my exposure to the various cultural and ethnic groups in Nigeria, convinced me that I was fully prepared to deal with the challenges of life in another society. But this was not the case.

My world view collided with fundamental teachings about what is viewed as logical and illogical in Western society. For example, old age in African society is valued positively and held with a high degree of respect, whereas most

U.S. Americans place a high value on youth rather than old age. The value placed on communal or group responsibility for rearing a child ("it takes a village to raise a child") contrasts with the Western notion of individualism ("only parents can raise their child"). The Igbo value placed on the extended family system contrasts greatly with the value placed on the nuclear family in the United States. The most fundamental principle in Igbo society is "I am because we are; since we are, therefore I am." One does not exist in isolation from the group. The unbridled individualism in the United States is therefore hard to comprehend, especially for a new immigrant from a communally based culture.

An equally perplexing experience for me was the reaction of most U.S. Americans to my family background. I come from a fairly large extended family with some history of polygyny. Polygyny is the union between a man and two or more wives. (Polygamy, a more general term, refers to marriage among several spouses, including a man who marries more than one wife or a woman who marries more than one husband.) Polygyny is an accepted and respected marriage form in traditional Igbo society. My father, Chief Clement Muoghalu Nwosu, had two wives. My paternal grandfather, Chief Ezekwesili Nwosu, was married to four. My great grandfather, Chief Odoji, who also married four wives, was the chief priest and custodian of traditional religion in my town, Umudioka town, a small rural community in Anambra State of the Federal Republic of Nigeria.

My maternal grandfather, Chief Nwokoye Akaigwe, was from the royal line of the Akaigwe clan and was the traditional ruler of Enugwu-Ukwu, which is a medium-sized community in Anambra State. Chief Akaigwe was known for several firsts (the first warrant chief[4] in Enugwu-Ukwu, the first to own and ride a bicycle, the first to own a car in eastern Nigeria, and the first to build a "zinc" house—metal roofing as opposed to a thatched roof—in Enugu-Ukwu). He was married to 24 women! I found myself explaining to my curious, and sometimes amazed, U.S. friends that the traditional economic structure in Igbo society dictated this familial arrangement whereby a man would have more than one spouse and produce several children, who would then assist him with farm work, which is regarded as the fiber and glue of economic life in traditional Igbo society. Each wife and her own children live in a separate home built by the husband. Each wife is responsible for the upkeep of her immediate family, with support from her husband.

One of the traditions of my extended family is the family reunion, held every two years. Families who are unable to attend for any reason are required to send pictures so that other members of the extended family, who are present at the reunion, may know them. The goal of the family reunion is to encourage unity, promote awareness of one another, and prevent the potential for incest or marital union between and among family relatives, considered an abomination in Igboland.

In traditional Igbo society it is acceptable for a man to marry many women to support the economic well-being of the family. In an agrarian lifestyle, where peoples' livelihoods depend on subsistence farming, it makes sense that the institution of polygyny would be a fundamental pillar of traditional Igbo economy and society. Indeed, marriage to more than one wife was often regarded as a measure of a man's wealth and status. Today, however, a man marries more than one wife mostly only if his first wife fails to conceive a male child, which is a requirement for perpetuating the family and ancestral lineage.

Although the extended family system exists in the United States, it is typically much less important than in Africa. During the initial period of my journey, it was clear that in the United States the nuclear family was the norm, although other kinds of families (e.g., single-parent families) did exist. I was surprised to learn that most U.S. couples were not concerned whether their unborn child was male or female. This is certainly not the case in Africa.

A related and perplexing issue centered on my perception of differences in matrimonial life between my culture and that in the United States. Among the Igbos, marriage doesn't just bring husband and wife together into matrimonial life; it also unites two families into a stronger relationship. Couples do not establish independent families; instead, they enter into already existing ones. The U.S. ideal of exclusivity, of mutual love just between spouses, was an aberration to me. In the Igbo culture, family love is multidimensional. One enters into love not only with one's spouse but also with all members of both families. Marriage for the Igbo people is a community affair, a joyful reality, a covenant between two *umunnas* (extended families), not merely an arrangement between a man and woman.

In the United States a core value of social life is a sense of personal freedom and a commitment to oneself. As an African, it was difficult for me to contrast this personal freedom and commitment to self with the commitment to interdependence and community affiliation that are at the core of social life in Africa. The nonindividuality of the African, which is such a vital part of the African cultural ethos, often is responsible for the numerous misperceptions and misinterpretations of U.S. cultural values.

Let me now return to the profound impact of historical forces on my initial interactions in the United States. These forces include slavery, conflict, war, colonialism, famine, and prosperity. To deny or ignore that history is to deny the experience of the group to which that particular history occurred. To deny the Holocaust, for example, is to deny the experience of the Jewish people and a major historical force that shaped how Jews have come to view the world around them. To deny the internment experience for the Japanese is to deny their suffering in the United States during World War II. To deny the discrimination experiences of the Irish in the 1840s in Boston is to deny a major historical force that shaped their lives in this country. In the same manner, to deny or ignore the experience of slavery for blacks is to deny or ignore a major historical force that shaped and continues to shape the collective wisdom of African Americans in the United States. There is considerable evidence to show that people bring their histories to their communication events. When

African Americans react negatively to Ross Perot's choice of the words "you people" in an address to them in Texas during the 1992 presidential campaign, their reaction stems from the experience of slavery, in which a "master-servant" relationship existed between blacks and whites. The term "you people" is a reminder that they (blacks) are different, and are often regarded by whites as lower in status.

Some of my initial cultural problems in the United States emerged from a lack of a deep sense of understanding of some of the forces of history that have shaped U.S. domestic relations, and their implications for competent communication in a variety of contexts. I recall my encounter with an African American classmate at Howard University. I had used the term "old boy" in referring to him during a conversation. While in Nigeria this is regarded as a positive term in referring to friends, my African American friend took offense at what appeared to suggest a master-servant relationship. During and after the slavery period in the U.S., Africans were referred to as "boy" by the white master. However, through discussions we were able to recognize that no offense was intended, and we both grew from the experience. One of the major indicators of intercultural growth when one confronts a cultural problem must be a willingness on the part of those involved to engage in genuine dialogue, which helps to sort out the cultural differences that created the miscommunication. Through such dialogue, intercultural understanding is enhanced.

As a newly arrived African-born immigrant from a society in which race was not necessarily an issue, initially I had difficulty understanding why both intellectual and lay discussions about domestic relations were so much anchored by race. For most Africans, ethnicity and national origins, rather than colors, were the critical factors. My experience living in the United States has made me look for deeper meanings. The perceptual differences between black Americans and native Africans stem, perhaps, from the fact that in Africa, black people under the control of Europeans were subjected to the institution of colonialism, an institution that while very limiting allowed certain basic freedoms and protections under the law. In the United States, blacks under the control of Europeans were subjected to the institution of slavery, an institution that denied them every right under the law. To understand why black Americans may view reality from the perspective of race, one must put the experience of slavery in its proper historical context.

Overall, growth for me throughout my American journey has produced a greater degree of adaptability, such that I am now able to experience cultural differences with better understanding while at the same time functioning well in my host culture. Although my expectations are still grounded in Igbo cultural values, nevertheless they have become shaped through frequent travels and interactions with host culture nationals in both small communities and large cities across the United States. I have visited more than 30 states since my arrival in the United States, from large urban cities such as Washington, New Orleans, New York, Chicago, Los Angeles, San Francisco, Miami, and Atlanta, to mid-sized towns such as Sacramento, Portland, Nashville, East

Lansing, and Albuquerque, to small communities such as Oakdale, Myrtle Beach, and Plains (hometown of former President Jimmy Carter). I have participated and immersed myself in the various historical, institutional (government and religious), and community events that cut across racial, ethnic, and cultural boundaries—events such as church services of other faiths, Latino Cinco de Mayo celebrations, African American Juneteenth, Native American Pow Wows, German Oktoberfests, Chinese New Year's festivities, East Indian weddings, and Thanksgiving dinners.

In fact, it is safe to say that I have become so functionally adapted in the United States that when I return home to Nigeria I experience the stress of reverse culture shock as I readjust to my own culture. The stress results because the new ideas that I have acquired living in the United States often are in conflict with my native customs and traditions. For example, during my father's funeral in 1995 a number of the native beliefs and values regarding funeral rites seemed very strange to me, but I quickly adapted, after a few days, with help from family members still living within the culture.

When I first entered the United States, I was a stranger in this land. I was unsure how to behave properly, and I was anxious and insecure about what I would experience. Through prolonged and varied experiences, I have gradually acquired the communication skills necessary to cope with the challenges and to realize the promises of my new environment. This, for me, has been and continues to be a wonderful American journey.

NOTES

1. There are four seasons in the United States—winter, spring, summer, and fall—but there are only two seasons in Nigeria: the dry season, which lasts from November through February, and the rainy season, which runs from March through October.

2. The Igbo people of Nigeria rank as one of the largest ethnic groups in Africa. Their population ranges from 15 to 25 million, according to various estimates. They occupy a land area that encompasses 7 of Nigeria's 36 states and stretches from the southeastern corner to the midwestern part of the country. The Igbos are a tenacious, adaptable people who also maintain a considerable presence beyond this geographical region.

3. Nigeria's four regions—North, West, East, and Midwest—were initially divided in 1967 into 12 states as a way to end interethnic tensions and bring the government closer to the people. Successive military governments in Nigeria have created more states since then, bringing the total to 36, including the Federal Capital Territory in Abuja, which is considered a state.

4. The institution of warrant chief was introduced in eastern Nigeria by the first British governor-general of Nigeria, Lord Frederick Lugard, as a system of indirect rule (governance through proxy) of subject territories.

A move from the racially segregated but predictable world of Mississippi to northern California thrust Chevelle Newsome into a different cultural realm. It also set in motion a series of events that would allow her to understand the causes and consequences of prejudice, discrimination, and marginality. Chevelle recognizes that, in all likelihood, she will always operate from a position of marginality; but she has learned to draw strength and purpose from that place. Her story is that of a successful African American woman who has encountered, and continues to experience and combat, many forms of racism.

12 Finding One's Self in the Margins

Chevelle Newsome

When I was in high school in California, I discovered that I had the same birthplace—a small town on the Gulf Coast of Mississippi named Moss Point—as Michele, who was my high school academic counselor. Like most towns in the south, Moss Point was segregated in the early 1960s when Michele and my mother graduated from high school. Michele and my mother had been high school homecoming royalty the same year in Moss Point, but in different high schools. While they had only lived five miles from one another, because of racial segregation they attended different schools. Their lives would intersect again, some 20 years later and some 3,000 miles away from our common birthplace, through their relationships with me.

During my senior year in high school I was crowned homecoming queen, an event that, at least on the surface, symbolized for Michele, my mother, and me a bridge between the racially segregated world in which we were all born and the ostensibly desegregated world we lived in some 20 years later. My coronation seemed to blur the lines that had separated them when they were young women. Michele's words to my mother when I was crowned homecoming queen indicate their sense of progress and change: "This is the way it should have been back then. That's our girl up there." Her words suggested progress and change for African Americans away from segregation, discrimination, and racism. Though I understand the hope and optimism in Michele's statement, what she did not realize was that I still experience, on a daily basis, marginalization born from racism and discrimination as I move between the segregated world of my birthplace and the seemingly integrated world of modern-day California, where I now live.

Writing this essay has triggered for me an awareness of the struggles I have experienced as I made the journey between two worlds, both pivotal to my identity and both demanding that I explain myself, because success and comfort in one world inevitably render me marginal in the other. In this essay I share my experiences and offer others who are similarly torn between different cultural worlds an understanding of the quest for cultural identity grown and nurtured on the margins of dual cultural worlds.

My story is about finding myself as I made the transition between a rural town in Mississippi, where segregation was the norm, and a city in northern California, where physical integration is tolerated. In the search for my own cultural identity I struggled to understand the complexities of race, ethnicity, discrimination, and communication between people from different cultural groups. As I sought to understand my own experience, I read the works of many African American scholars and discovered the words of Franklin Frazier, which helped me to understand the similarities between my situation and those of other African Americans. Frazier (1957) wrote:

> What may appear as distortions of American patterns of behavior and thought are due to the fact that the Negro lives on the margins of American society. The very existence of a separate Negro community with its own institutions within the heart of the American society is indicative of its quasi-pathological character, especially since the persistence of this separate community has been due to racial discrimination and oppression. (p. 234)

I have had to reconcile the discrepancies between living in segregated and integrated communities, and the words of Frazier have helped me to do this.

Neighborhoods in Moss Point remain segregated to this day. During the 1960s civil rights movement, Michele, my mother, and I resided in a small town where the lines between the black minority and dominant whites were clearly marked. As a child I watched members of my family's older generation, my second cousins and grandparents, quietly cross the boundaries between the racially segregated worlds to work in factories and to clean the homes and offices of European Americans. Some of those who crossed the boundaries during that time supported the idea that the boundaries were beneficial. As a child I heard comments such as "You can't trust them white folks; they ain't got nothin' for us. It's better we stay on over here and they stay over there." The arguments of the separatists, in both the black and the white communities, have been that the separation of the races helps to maintain each group's traditions and cultures. Such ideas resonated with some members of each culture, including some of the older members of my family. However, it was the oppression and devaluation of blacks as human beings that sharply marked the divergence of the ideas of the black and white separatists. As members of our community moved between the two worlds the physical segregation was tolerable, and in some instances welcomed, but it was the economic oppression and abusive language—products of racism—that were and still are intolerable.

Many of the children who were born in Moss Point have, like me, moved on to other places. Moss Point is a town where the residents still live in the shadows of the segregated South. About a decade ago, when my grandmother died and the funeral home personnel were being very difficult, my father, who was born and raised in California, suggested that we have my grandmother's body moved to the "white" funeral home that had opened on the highway. His suggestion would seem reasonable to most people, but to the other members of my family and to me, it was inconceivable. In our town, "black folks" would never allow a "white mortician" to handle the bodies of their loved ones. It was an unwritten rule that even the cemeteries were supposed to be segregated. We lived "outside" the boundaries of the dominant European American culture in that town, and we would never consider crossing that boundary. In death as in life, we operated under a set of rules that placed us outside the mainstream social structure.

I have a vivid image of a European American man who gave me one of my first lessons in racism and the marginalization of my people. My parents and grandparents were moderately educated. Both of my parents had graduated from high school, and in our town that was an accomplishment. Although my parents were employed, there was not an excess of money for medical and dental treatment. Thus, when a group of dentists came to our area to do community service and to provide free dental check-ups, my parents took me to see them. Despite my fears of this strange place, my parents were not allowed in the dental examination room. The dental assistant was friendly and attempted to make me feel comfortable in this unfamiliar environment. Her efforts worked until the dentist entered the room, and then the atmosphere changed. He entered the room, slammed the door, and stated, "I'm tired of these poor nigger children. They're like li'l rats." Needless to say, the words and tone assured disaster. During the examination he was rough and cut the inside of my mouth with his cleaning instrument. I retaliated by biting his finger. He responded by pinching my nose to force me to take a breath and open my mouth, thus releasing his finger from the clutches of my teeth. He rattled off several obscenities and racial slurs and refused to finish the cleaning. The comfort and carefree attitude that I had developed in my segregated community had not prepared me for the reality of an interaction with an individual who openly expressed racist views against a group to which I belonged. From this encounter, I learned quickly and forcefully that racism creates boundaries and margins between my cultural group and that of the dominant European American culture.

Recognizing the lack of economic opportunities in Mississippi, in the early 1970s my parents moved to California, which represented economic opportunity. California also presented an opportunity for me to live in an integrated neighborhood and to attend an integrated school. In that environment I met people from different cultures and explored my own cultural identity in new ways. I vividly remember the song "California Girl," and as I sang along with the record my pride in being viewed as a Californian was palpable. For me the song represented a shift in my cultural identification. I was a girl with new-found allegiances to her adopted home state.

Despite my enthusiasm to meet new people and learn more about them and their cultures, I also longed to return to the comforts of my original home and people in Mississippi. When I visited Mississippi during the holidays and summer vacations, I experienced divided loyalties. I felt conflicted because California had taught me to fulfill many of the behavioral expectations of my European American friends, but in order to fit in with members of my culture from Mississippi I had to relearn many of my old behaviors and language choices.

The marginalization I experienced in moving between my worlds in Mississippi and California is linked to the language used by members of the dominant European American culture. The language we learn and use helps us to develop our social reality. For example, in the United States we learn to associate white with good things and black with bad things. The image that "black" is dirty is pervasive. One day I entered a store and the sales clerk refused to allow me to try on a dress after my European American friend had just done so. She stated, "Your skin might soil the dress." The implication was that my "black" skin might rub off on the fabric. This example illustrates how conceptions of color marginalize African Americans. The clerk's conception of color turned a day of shopping with friends into an event marked by blatant racism.

While the experience with the sales clerk illustrates the detrimental effects of color labels, my own use of language shows me the cultural margins in which I operate. While in California, I had become formally socialized into using standard American English, and I had dropped my southern accent. Members from my southern culture began to tell me that I spoke like a "white girl." They viewed me as an outsider to the culture we once shared, and I began to adjust to the idea that there was one "best" form of English to use. Thus, language that had once bonded me to my culture was becoming divisive. The conflicting messages I was receiving caused me to question my identity as a person and as an African American.

In my search for cultural identification as an African American, I had fallen victim to one of the pitfalls that Frazier had written about years ago. Frazier argued that African Americans are socialized to forget their heritage and to embrace the ideology of the dominant group. In California I had been socialized to believe that I could attain success only by discarding the language and behaviors of my African American cultural group in Mississippi. In the process of being socialized, I was being separated from the poor and disenfranchised in my culture—my family members who crossed the racial barriers in my hometown.

Through my experiences and education in California, I had learned to adapt my behaviors, values, and attitudes to accommodate to the views of the dominant culture. Though my parents tried to maintain my connection with Mississippi by sending me there during summers and other holidays to visit with relatives and friends, I was immersed in a new environment for the majority of the year. In this new environment I had to learn to tolerate—and in some respects to accept—a world that excluded the people I knew back home.

When I began studying rhetoric, learning about political communication, and reading the works of Frazier, Asante, hooks, and other African American scholars, I began to understand fully that although I had been living the middle-class life provided by my parents, I was still operating on the margins of the European American culture and world. It was not only the lower-income African Americans who were marginalized by the language and behaviors of the dominant class, but also people like me who were socialized to accept the language of the dominant class and in so doing to give up part of our racial and cultural identities. I thought about my European American friends and realized that many of them did not see me as an African American. In their eyes, I was not like the African American elevator operator who took us to our offices in the state capitol each morning, or the African American janitor who cleaned our offices and worked double shifts to earn the money to meet his mortgage payment each month. Those hard-working African American individuals, with whom I so closely identified because they reminded me of the people in my family and my neighborhood in Mississippi, were not viewed as being from the same community as me. They were somehow different because the color of their skin was darker, they were not college educated, and their speech did not always conform to standard European American English. I understood then that not only were they marginalized, so was I.

This idea troubled me, because I had worked so hard to represent my culture and attain an education and status in the dominant culture. By not being recognized as a member of a culture that I so passionately thought defined me as an individual, I was once again forced to realize that the margins created by racism do exist. At that moment, I was back in that dentist's chair and again felt the dynamics of racism. I was reminded of Angela Davis's observation that social marginalization often creates political activism. African Americans fought for the right to be politically active within the formal political structure, and they were given the right to vote by legislation, but the dominant group subverted their rights by using verbal and physical violence. In my case, members of the dominant group attempted to strip me of my cultural identity by denying that I was an African American. Some of my European American friends, who considered me to be "one of them," thought their attitude was proof that they were not racist. From my perspective, however, it was a sign of cultural insensitivity at best, and racism at worst. As an African American, I was clearly *not* one of them. To ignore or deny my reality forced me to the margins of the European American culture, from which I had to operate every day.

In an effort to assert my cultural identity as an African American, I was called to political activism. I had an intense need to explain the value of my cultural identity to myself, to my African American friends, and to my friends from the European American culture. I began to read and examine the practices of dominant groups in dealing with members of minority groups. I also began a reflective process in which I examined my actions in dealing with my friends from my culture in Mississippi.

Many of my friends and relatives have left our small town in Mississippi, and my visits there are far less frequent than when I was a child. However, in that town I discovered my community of origin and a recognition of the differences between two cultures. While I may represent progress in overcoming discrimination, which Michelle expressed when I was crowned homecoming queen so many years ago, I am also an individual who, because of racism, constantly speaks from the margins. As a person of African descent, I cannot afford to lose touch with my heritage. Because of a renewed interest and quest for knowledge about the plights and successes of members of other cultural groups, I frequently share information and debate social issues with friends and colleagues from other cultures. It is a healthy dialogue that allows me to reaffirm my own ethnic identity.

In a discussion with a European American woman about the status of affirmative action, long before the issue became publicly controversial, I was urged to withdraw my support of affirmative action programs because "there would soon be too many others like you and then you would not be special." Her comments devalued my racial identity by supporting tokenism, and it marked me as marginal to her world. It was once again clear to me that racism draws boundaries and creates margins, so that I must validate my cultural identity and speak in support of those who, as I do, operate and live along the margins.

The study of language use among African Americans illustrates the need for self-validation. Scholars have reported on the African use of pidgin language by slaves on the plantations. When white scholars studied pidgin, they reported that it was obvious that African Americans used pidgin because they were inferior and incapable of learning the English language. Labeling African Americans as inferior allowed and justified their mistreatment. In my life I have watched and experienced how language is used to degrade and demean people. I have only to think back to that dentist in Mississippi to learn this lesson again. The language he used allowed him to categorize me as insignificant. I was no longer a small child who needed dental care, but a nigger, a rat, a pest, and, in his view, insignificant. When people are marginalized through racism, as I was, then it is acceptable to deny them the right to live in the neighborhood of their choice or to feel comfortable in a particular store.

Language is often used to create and shape a hierarchical structure that maintains power and control. However, I have learned that, just as the dominant group can use language to maintain control, the dominated group can use language to gain control. For example, in the late 1960s and early 1970s, there was an offshoot of the Civil Rights movement called the Black Power movement. Leaders of the movement, in conjunction with popular music artists and many ministers, used language to empower African American people. Songs such as "I'm Black and I'm Proud," and chants such as "Black Power," were heard across the United States and in my home. I vividly remember the Afros and dashikis worn by members of my family, including me. The clothes, music, and chants served as elements of empowerment. As I reflect back, I now understand it as a self-affirmation by the members of a marginalized culture.

By immersing myself in the history and rhetoric of the leaders of my culture, I recognized the important role that higher education has and can play in helping people to develop their cultural identities. I was exposed to ideas and interests that I had not fully considered. I recognized how I was being and had been oppressed by language. For I believe that understanding the power of language was a key component in the development of my cultural identity and my understanding of my role as a person on the margins.

bell hooks calls for minorities to use the margins as a catalyst for rebellion. According to her, the margins—and not the center of the dominant culture—are where the dialogue for equality should originate. For minority groups, their social marginalization is also based on their status in relation to the dominant group, which in the United States is typically comprised of European American males. For African Americans, in particular, marginalization creates an ongoing battle that began when the first slave arrived. It continues to this day. As Angela Davis, Franklin Frazier, and bell hooks proclaim, African Americans have made many advances, but the fight against oppression and racism must continue. As my life demonstrates, the margins can be used to rebel and to become an activist for this cause.

My search for cultural identity is both challenging and fulfilling. In that search, I am becoming a strong African American woman who speaks from the margins as a representative for herself and for others who are similarly marginalized.

REFERENCES

Asante, M. K., & Asante, K. W. (Eds). (1985). *African culture: The rhythms of unity*. Westport, CT: Greenwood Press.

Davis, A. Y. (1981). *Women, race & class*. New York: Random House.

Davis, A. Y. (1990). *Women, culture, and politics*. New York: Vintage Books.

Frazier, E. F. (1957). *Black bourgeoisie: The rise of a new middle class in the United States*. New York: Free Press.

hooks, b. (1990). *Yearning: Race, gender, and cultural politics*. Boston: South End Press.

The consequences—both positive and negative—of living in multiple cultures is the central theme of this essay by Ringo Ma. Belonging, comfort, predictability, and "fitting in" are all emotional states that can be rare for those who live extensively within cultures other than their own. While Ringo acknowledges the hazards of multicultural living, he also makes a passionate argument for the benefits that result from an ability to function within multiple cultures.

13 "Both-And" and "Neither-Nor": My Intercultural Experiences

Ringo Ma

A question that I have been asked repeatedly and do not know how to answer is "Where is your home?" When asked, my answer is that "home" is the place where I currently live and work. To those who ask, however, "home" refers to the place where I was born and raised. The question also implies that one's place of birth and residence remain the same for most of one's life. Because I have lived in many places and among several cultures, my response is not the one that most people expect. My multicultural experiences have blurred my sense of "home," as well as my cultural identity, in many ways.

Born and raised in Taiwan, I spent my childhood in three different cities and completed my undergraduate studies there. I came to the United States for graduate studies; taught in Canada and the United States; lectured in the People's Republic of China (PRC); and visited numerous countries in Africa, Asia, and Europe. I did miss my "home" in Taipei, Taiwan, at the beginning of my intercultural experiences, but my attachment and belonging have gradually faded as my stay outside Taiwan has been prolonged. The process of becoming familiar with new cultures has also moved me away from my "home" culture.

People describe the consequences of their intercultural experiences differently. Some describe them as "broadening their horizons" and "enlightening." Others associate their intercultural experiences with being "marginalized," "disfranchised," and "muted." Still others view their experiences with greater complexity, with their intercultural experience initially exciting but later frustrating as the novelty and curiosity wear off. All three views explain my experiences over the past two decades, and all are necessary to understand my evolving sense of belonging to multiple cultures.

I believe I will never be fully accepted as a community member in Canada or the United States because of my appearance, accent, and cultural naiveté. During the first year of my graduate studies in the United States, a European American told me how he feels about Asians: "Although blacks look different from us, I know how to deal with them. But I don't know how to handle Asians. Asians are so different and can be more threatening to me."

I was not offended by the remark, because I thought it was more genuine than an insincere and patronizing statement. Instead, I tried to understand the meaning of his words from his perspective. I understood him to be saying that because African Americans had lived in the United States for centuries, many European Americans were more familiar, and thus more comfortable, with African Americans' behavioral patterns; the two groups also share many cultural values and behaviors. I also heard him say that because I was Chinese, I was too different and too unpredictable for him to feel comfortable around me. Certainly, Chinese value systems and the resultant communication behaviors are at odds with the prescriptions of the European American culture. For example, I was trained as a child to be considerate and to refrain from expressing my preferences directly. I was encouraged *not* to stand out in a group and *not* to tell others what I really wanted. In the United States, however, children are encouraged to express their own desires. When I was in graduate school, this cultural difference frustrated me because, whereas my fellow graduate students would directly tell me what they wanted from me, I never could tell them what I wanted from them. This put me in an ever-giving and never-taking position.

When I lived in Canada, I felt I had to insist on being treated with respect in many situations. For example, in a department newsletter article to introduce new faculty members, I was the only one referred to by first name, while all the others were presented as "Doctor." Occasionally people in the community showed the same lack of respect, addressing my colleagues as "Doctor" and me as just "Ringo." I experienced similar unequal treatment in nonprofessional contexts. In a store one day, my request for a rain check was ignored, despite a note posted in the store to encourage customers to take a rain check for on-sale merchandise that was out of stock. I had to raise my voice and show displeasure on my face in order to get the clerk's attention. Of course, what was annoying to me in each of these instances was not the absence of the title "Doctor" or being ignored. It was, instead, the unequal and inconsistent treatment that I received in comparison to others; usually the "offender" didn't even notice that something was "wrong."

It has been very difficult to handle situations such as these. First, I am not accustomed to and do not feel comfortable requesting "respect" or equal treatment from others. Second, if I complain about unequal treatment, I risk being accused of "making too much of it." However, if I avoid dealing with the offense, the situation may repeat itself in the future. So what am I supposed to do? Hint? Sometimes that works and sometimes it does not. Ignore what happened? I can do that occasionally, but not always.

Barriers to communication between people from different cultures can be related to race or cultural differences or both. I have found that prejudice, hostility, and unequal treatment are often race related, whereas misinterpretations of verbal and nonverbal behaviors and inappropriate responses are related to differences in culture. Prejudice and cultural misunderstandings are not mutually exclusive but interact with each other. Prejudice, for instance, can develop from frustrations due to an inability to understand what someone is trying to communicate—a combination of both race-related and culture-related problems. Many of the problems I experienced could be related both to my physical appearance and to my communication behaviors. The situations I face tend to be different from what American-born Chinese (Chinese Americans) face. European Americans and Chinese Americans are less likely to misinterpret each other's behaviors because they share a common educational system and speak the same language. Similarly, Chinese Americans are familiar with such icons of popular culture in the United States as professional sports, television, radio, and other media. Taiwanese-born Chinese, like me, suffer not only from our Chinese appearances but also from our naiveté about appropriate cultural behaviors. There is less tolerance and acceptance of my inability to perform cultural rituals perfectly, yet there are so many cultural rules that I fear it is impossible for me to learn them all! A simple ritual like kissing the hostess's cheek at the end of a dinner party, for example, is done so intuitively by members of the culture but can never be performed competently and comfortably by me.

Did my sense of belonging return when I paid a return visit to Taiwan, the place where I was born and raised? Yes, but only to a limited degree. After spending so many years in North America, I am no longer completely Chinese or Taiwanese, and this change sometimes makes me a stranger in many social situations in Taiwan. Whenever I phone old friends and express my desire to see them, they almost always begin to arrange a dinner for me. I enjoyed their dinner invitations at the beginning, but gradually they have become a burden. In my daily life in the United States I eat very little for lunch and do not eat out often, because I try to avoid eating MSG and high-sodium foods. In Taiwan, however, if one turns down a dinner offer for no "legitimate" reason, he or she is perceived as unfriendly or socially inept. A time conflict because of another social obligation is a "legitimate" reason, but simply not wanting to eat out is not an acceptable excuse. The dilemma I face is that I want to see my friends but do not want to eat with them. Some times I was dragged to a restaurant even though I had told my friends, "No, I do not want to eat." They didn't believe me. Instead they thought I was trying to be polite. After living in North America for many years, I did mean "No" when I said "No." I had to repeat my "No" message to them many times and use facial expressions to validate my "No" message before they finally accepted that I really did not want to eat.

I had the same communication problem with my mother—she did not accept my "No" messages when food was to be served. She would ask me, "Do you want to eat anything now?" Whether I said "Yes" or "No" didn't make any difference to her. She would just go ahead and prepare some food for me, even though I told her I was not hungry and didn't want to eat anything at that moment. She thought I was just trying to be considerate, because I would have given her "trouble" had I said "Yes."

When I visited friends' houses, I tended to stay for a relatively short period of time. My friends would expect me to stay for dinner and would feel guilty if they could not persuade me to stay. Having adjusted to the United States, where social engagements are planned and time and purpose are negotiated ahead of time, I was not comfortable acting spontaneously and "staying for dinner."

I found I could no longer tolerate the complexity of many Taiwanese social rituals, though I am still familiar with them. I have discussed this cultural reentry problem with other Taiwanese-born people who decided to work in Taiwan after studying and working in the United States for many years. They all identified similar disruptions and discontinuities in displaying appropriate social behaviors. One man mentioned that he had spent six months learning to drive in Taiwan, though he had driven in the San Francisco area for almost 20 years. He said that driving in Taiwan was quite different in terms of the distance one is expected to maintain between cars, the right of way, and how to cope with parking problems. Because my return visits to Taiwan were for relatively brief stays, my ability to regain a level of comfort there has been severely constrained.

In the summer of 1995 I was invited to lecture at eight universities and colleges in Hubei and Sichuan Provinces in Central China. This was my second trip to the People's Republic of China (PRC), or "mainland China." Because my first visit in 1991 was brief and I did not have a chance to visit any academic institutions, I was quite excited. This visit also constituted a valuable and exciting experience in my life for other reasons. First, my parents were born and raised in mainland China and moved to Taiwan before the Communist government was established in the late 1940s. Ever since I was a little child, I have heard numerous stories about this "big" China. I also have many relatives there. Until the 1980s, however, Taiwanese were unable to visit mainland China because of the military confrontation between the Communist government in Beijing and the Nationalist (Kuomintang) government in Taipei. Yet Taiwan and mainland China share a common cultural heritage, in spite of their different political ideologies and systems. Mandarin is the official dialect in both Taiwan and mainland China. Furthermore, people on both sides are familiar with each other's history and customs. In other words, we are familiar with each other, yet we are distant because of the political situation.

In addition to different political ideologies and systems, the characteristics of mainland Chinese social life are different from the Taiwanese social life in many important ways. After living in North America for years I was unprepared for the treatment I received in the PRC. For example, due to the lack of privacy in the PRC, I felt a little uncomfortable at the beginning of my visit. When I stayed in a university hostel for international teachers, I was not given a key to my room. The service people, however, could enter my room at any time. One day a service person entered my room without even knocking on the door, and then she said without apology, "Oh, I thought you were already gone." My phone calls were often monitored, and the operator sometimes interrupted my conversation. On a few campuses, the door to my room was expected to be open for most of the evening because those coordinating my lectures were continually shuttling between the rooms. On almost every campus, my year of birth was included in my visiting schedule. Furthermore, in most rural areas, using a public squat toilet is a group-oriented activity; people of the same sex squat next to each other and are separated only by waist-high walls.

I quickly learned, however, that there was a more benign explanation for these differences than I had originally thought. The lack of concern for privacy, for instance, is not necessarily associated with unfriendliness. In the PRC, hotel rooms are monitored and all tenants are required to register with official identification. A man and a woman are not allowed to sleep in the same room unless they are married. In most university hostels, the main entrance is closed at 11:00 P.M. The purpose of this policy is to prevent prostitution and crime. In other words, it is a way to protect tourists. Monitoring phone calls was not necessarily for the purpose of spying. In at least one of my hotels in the Hubei Province, my coordinators made an effort to ensure that my phone connections were trouble free. They asked the operator to pay special attention to my phone connections. Thus, they monitored my phone to ensure that there would be no breaks in the service. By the same token, shuttling between my room and theirs was a gesture by my hosts to indicate that "my services are at your disposal." I also learned that a special guest's year of birth in the PRC is treated with reverence, which is why it is usually announced at the beginning of a reception. Obviously, hiding one's age is a learned behavior that is not found in every culture! There are several other things that made me uncomfortable in the PRC. While I was expected to share a lot of information, including facts about life in the United States, details of U.S. society, and how I felt about issues of international relations, my Chinese hosts did not tell me much about themselves and their lives. I also found that although I was treated as a fellow Chinese on the surface level, I was actually viewed as an outsider—"Mr. Ma"—instead of as "Comrade Ma," the insider. The "unequal" treatment, I realized afterward, was largely due to the unique political and social situation in the PRC, rather than a reflection of their attitude toward me personally.

From the frustration and alienation I experienced in Canada, the People's Republic of China, the United States, and even Taiwan, it is not difficult to understand my "homeless" feeling. Although I am associated with the four countries and cultures in various ways, there is no place that gives me a strong sense of belonging. Nowhere am I an insider. In the United States I am an "Asian faculty member" on campus, a "resident alien" to the U.S. Immigration and Naturalization Service, and an "Oriental" to the community. In Taiwan, I am an "overseas Chinese" (that is, someone who does not reside in Taiwan) or an Americanized Chinese. Others expect my behavior to differ from theirs, and it does.

So, you might ask, have my intercultural experiences produced only liabilities with no rewards? The answer is an emphatic "No." My multicultural identity and bilingual skills are a valuable asset in all facets of my life. After experiencing diverse lifestyles in different cultures, I believe that I have a broader and deeper understanding of life and its circumstances than those who have not been exposed to "other" cultures.

In North America, for example, my Chinese cultural background, with its emphasis on subtle, nonverbal cues, sometimes allows me to see and understand what many others do not. I can also provide alternative evaluations of right and wrong, and good and bad, and can provide stories and examples that illustrate multiple interpretations of a single event. I think that when I teach, my intercultural experiences enrich my lectures, and students regard them favorably. For example, when I describe for my students that different cultures have different attitudes about the importance of verbal communication, I tell them the following story from an ancient Chinese book:

> A student asked his teacher whether it is good to talk a lot. The teacher replied by saying, "The toad in the field makes noise throughout the day and nobody cares to hear. The rooster crows only once a day but people are enlightened by it."

I then provide a contrasting story that was told to me by a colleague and is derived from the European American cultural framework:

> The codfish lays thousands of eggs and the hen lays only one egg each time. The hen is much more appreciated because she cackles whenever she lays an egg.

So the "moral" of the Chinese story is that "More talk just makes talk less valuable," while the European American story emphasizes that "It pays to advertise." Students tell me that they do not often hear such stories and that they appreciate them. From my perspective as a professor interested in having my students learn, I know that if they remember the two stories, they have learned important cultural differences in communication from me.

Having learned to adapt my teaching style to U.S. students who expect greater openness and less formality, I found my experiences in China to be more positive than they might otherwise have been. Certainly as a professor and scholar, I find continual benefits from my ability to draw on a deep knowledge of two different cultural traditions. My research has also been positively informed by my bicultural knowledge.

I would summarize the advantages and disadvantages of being an intercultural person in two phrases: "both-and" and "neither-nor." "Both-and" is the joy of functioning effectively in dual cultures. "Neither-nor," on the other hand, is the agony of being rejected by both one's old original and one's new culture. There are also two Chinese idioms that can represent these contrary feelings: *zhu1 ba1 jie4 zhao4 jing4 zi3, li3 wai4 bu4 shi4 ren2* ("When the pig spirit [in the popular novel *Pilgrims to the West*] looks in the mirror, he found no humanity both in and outside the mirror") and *zuo3 you4 feng2 yuan2* ("Be able to achieve success one way or another" or "Gain advantage from both sides").[1] The abilities to see "no humanity both in and outside the mirror" and "gain advantage from both sides" are actually developed from two facets of the same process. When blue changes to purple, it is not as blue as before, but it is redder. The resulting color can relate to both blue and red, but it is neither pure blue nor pure red.

The process of moving toward a "purple" area through intercultural experiences is a mixed blessing for many people. To become a profoundly happy intercultural person requires the ability to maximize the "both-and" experience and to minimize the "neither-nor" feeling. It is my hope and professional goal through teaching intercultural communication that a multicultural world can be created in which "both-and" is the dominant experience and people from all cultures appreciate the cultures of others.

NOTES

1. The *pinyin* system of Romanization is used to transliterate the Chinese terms. The number immediately following each transliterated word represents the tone of the word when pronounced in Mandarin Chinese.

While acknowledging that he speaks from the privileged position of the white U.S. American male, William Starosta describes his identity as one that draws on multiple cultural perspectives. Bill lives and interacts among multiple cultures: teaching at a predominately Black university, relating in an intercultural marriage, socializing with Asian Indians, and working as a scholar seeking (and sought out) to interpret and understand Chinese cultural patterns as they influence communication. Yet he recognizes that he is often, ultimately, the "outsider" in many of these intercultural interactions.

14 dual_consciousness@USAmerican.white.male

William J. Starosta

The domain "USAmerican.white.male" (UWM) receives hits almost daily from scholars investigating gender, culture, ethnicity and nationality. Various visitors to this site carry away observations about power, patriarchy, resistance, hegemony and ethnocentrism. (For many visitors, UWM is not a pretty site to see!) Remarkably, however, few UWMs enter their own domain to examine themselves as enculturated communicators.

Consequently, this analysis represents a visit to the UWM domain by one member of that domain. It relates the experience of one USAmerican. white.male who has spent most of his adult life amidst those of contrast cultures. Questions that occur to me concern the construction of identity, the consciousness of identity by those within and without that identity, and the search for a middle perspective from which to assess issues of identity.

I

"Your brother teaches at Howard? You don't look black!"—Midwest coworker

I have been on many sides of the looking glass during more than 50 years spent as a white USAmerican male. My formative years indoctrinated me into the naturalness of being anglophone, of speaking the "standard" form of U.S. English, of coming from the "first" world, and of internalizing the privilege of being a white male. In ways that I do not yet understand—since a culture is often the most invisible to one who lives in it—I am a profoundly USAmerican specimen, culturally baptized into the "original sin" of racism, sexism, and nationalism.

My middle years were spent learning of South and East Asia. Mine was the only doctoral minor in Asian studies at my graduate institution, as I prepared myself to understand India, Sri Lanka, and China in some depth. As a graduation requirement, I was tested on two Asian languages. From my time spent executing research in India and Sri Lanka, and as a byproduct of 30 years of a bicultural marriage to a north Indian, a side of me has become identifiably Indian. I have lectured and written on Indian philosophy, meditated, become completely vegetarian, recoiled from Indian regional and communal bias, and adopted the nonviolent philosophy of Mahatma Gandhi *(satyagraha)* that came to inspire many who sought redress from oppression globally. My social circle is mostly north Indian.

For the most recent two-fifths of my life I have taught at an historically black (college or) university (HBCU). Within and without the classroom I have negotiated or shared attitudes, worldviews, values, and assumptions with African American students and faculty. When I leave the classroom for home gatherings, I am met with incredulity that I left a famous white school to teach in a black university. "Um, how are the students there?"

Of still more recent vintage, I have rekindled an interest in Chinese culture(s). By some mechanism unknown to me, I became identified as a person who has an interest in things Chinese. Soon I was responding to, presenting on, or chairing conference panels dealing with conflict resolution, relationship formation, or linguistic practices among those of the Chinese diaspora.

This peculiar mixture of cultural elements led me to initiate a professional journal that deals with gender, culture, and ethnicity. The journal is probably too black for Asians, too Asian for African Americans, too Hispanic for Anglophone readers, and pleases Europeans little if at all. In this sense, the journal parallels my identity: it can be described in a few words, but those few words really describe too little.

As I reflect on my identity, I see that I am an anomaly. I appear, when or if I wish, or even if I do not wish, to be a white USAmerican male. But I chafe at racial and communal slights and have come to take them personally. I socialize with Asian Indians, but I feel their resentment that I have married into their community, though I am told that "I am more Indian than most Indians." To reduce the social gulf between Indians and me, I speak, sing, write, or listen to jokes in two Indian dialects. I recognize this is not enough—I am still the outsider who is treated only on the surface as an insider by the local Indian community. Similarly, I teach at an African American university, but I do not feel I should try to become an administrator there. ("Some people are born into a religion; others convert. Some are born black; some, I am beginning to think, convert.") I sit down to dinner with Chinese Americans and am told that a person cannot stay balanced or healthy by eating no meat. The body needs certain qualities only meat can provide.

Always, I am the outsider who is treated, from friendship or social duty, as a pseudo-insider. Yet, at unprotected moments, I see that I can socially penetrate into other communities only to a certain degree. I have worked hard at gender inclusiveness, and can be accepted as a friend, maybe even as a fellow traveler, but I see that a gulf stands between many feminist-leaning female white professionals and me. I see that I can do many things to project an interest in, and an identity with, other groups, but admission to these groups is priced beyond my means. No matter how I try to project an identity over and above my native UWM one, the other sees me only as a member of my "domain," USAmerican.white.male.

II

The questions that occur to me following cultural introspection rest on identity. I have argued elsewhere (Chen & Starosta, 1996) that a major difference between intercultural communication competence and competence within a single culture is that interactants must make judgments about which cultural identities are in play and which are not. The best introduction to the question of the clash of cultural identities comes from W.E.B. Du Bois, who coined the term "double consciousness" in *The Souls of Black Folk* to describe the competing demands placed on African Americans who walk a fine, wavering, and perilous line between black and white. In a sense, what follows is a footnote to the thinking of the first detailed intercultural communication identity theorist, W.E.B. DuBois:

> One ever feels his two-ness—an American, a Negro; two souls, two thoughts, two unreconciled strivings; two warring ideals in one dark body. . . . The history of the American Negro is the history of this strife, this longing to attain self-conscious manhood, to merge this double self into a better and truer self. In this merging he wishes neither of the old selves to be lost. He would not Africanize America, for America has too much to teach the world and Africa. He would not bleach his Negro soul in a flood of white Americanism, for he knows that the Negro blood has a message for the world. He simply wishes to make it possible for a man to be both a Negro and an American.

Similarly, Frederick Douglass asserted a lack of common identity with white Americans in his address on the slave having little reason to celebrate the Fourth of July, while Sojourner Truth asserted a common identity with white women in her speech "Ain't I a Woman?" Intercultural identity issues ever punctuate the black experience in America.

It is relatively straightforward to pose the dilemma of culture for the African American. Should one try to aim for parity and success in the white world? If so, he or she succeeds only to the degree that mainstream society permits. One's destiny is placed in the hands of a sometimes unwilling other. But if this attempt to orient to the white world is perceived by the black community as assimilation, the person risks being taken as a "Tom" (based on *Uncle*

Tom's Cabin). He or she can be viewed by some members of the black community as abandoning blacks, of trying to forget his or her blackness, and he or she will be called to return back to a black orbit. (Some in the community remark "Didn't I say so?" when they see the best efforts of white-oriented African Americans fail.) In short, neither the white nor the black community forgets black skin tone. Social forces pull and push from one side and the other, and they offer few convenient answers to the problem of dual consciousness. The double bind of dual identity stays with the person from birth to death.

The point to be explored is whether such a sense of dual consciousness is also the legacy of the USAmerican.white.male. Is he, too, destined to be stigmatized according to both gender and skin tone? If he asserts his Americanness and his whiteness, he claims unfair privilege; but if he disavows these personal characteristics, he is distrusted by other whites and foreign expatriots, and he is tested by those of color. White maleness is not something to be given away, since it and its meanings rest simultaneously in the mind of the beholder as well as in the man himself.

III

Experience is individual, but its interpretation shows evidence of cultural patterning. In sifting through my own adult experience I hope to locate some sites where my training as an Indian, as an African American, as a Chinese, and as a white male have come to the fore. Indeed, these identities probably will be seen to supplement one another or to clash at times.

Sifting through personal data poses the question of objectivity. How can a person put the self into perspective? My answer comes from the lessons of other experience-close studies: what is lost in distortion should be gained in verisimilitude, richness, and detail. What I make of my own experience cannot be "bias," since it is the only available measure of my own meaning. (It can, of course, suffer from deliberately selective reporting or from my inability to translate the subtleties of my experience into terms that others can comprehend.) I hold out the hope that others of the UWM domain and elsewhere will "see themselves" in some way in my personal data. I start my inventory with an attempt to uncover where, if at all, I have grown into an African American perspective.

I find myself believing, as do many—perhaps most—African Americans, that prejudice is "alive and well" and that racial equality in USAmerica is anything but accomplished. From my teaching perspective alone I have been told of three recent instances from Louisiana, California, and Montreal that support my perception: in two cases, African American students were told by a high school guidance counselor not to go on to college, to attend a two-year vocational program, and/or not even to attempt to enter the University of California system. ("Ha-ha! You aren't remotely qualified!") These students moved on to a 3.9 undergraduate average, in one instance, and to graduating with honors from the University of California system in the other. The third student had the chance to see a reference that was written for her only to find the words, "She isn't very capable, even for a black student." She is now a successfully published doctoral student. These are only a few of a multitude of pertinent cases gleaned from daily conversations with African Americans students.

A case reported by a sensitivity trainer makes a similar point. She and another trainer accepted an assignment to put on a workshop in a small city outside Philadelphia. After completing the morning session, one workshop participant came up to her and related, "Ma'am, that sure was pretty, what you said. But if I was you, I would be out of town before dark!" She found the threat credible, since the KKK had an active local chapter.

One more case is offered in support of my perception. A black Ph.D. took up a university teaching job in Kentucky. Her young son was at the head of his class before she moved there. Once settled there, though, she and the only other parent of a black child in that parochial school class received notices at home from one instructor that explained that the two children were unteachable and would not succeed in school. Turning the letters over, the parents found the letters were written on the back of KKK stationery. The school authorities issued an apology, but the teacher remained on the faculty to repress future students of color.

These instances and others are not firsthand, in that I did not live the original experiences. But they happened for persons who are for me very real and very important. Why else would I have felt personal anger when a panel of regional communication journal editors "looked right through" an African American woman in the front of the room, only to call repeatedly on white males of greater fame elsewhere in the room? And why did I feel a personal insult when a second such panel at a national convention related, "[We] would like to place more minorities on our editorial board, but we can't find enough who are qualified." As I looked at four white questioners who were charged with asking the journal editors "tough questions," I asked if this same logic prevented the panel from locating qualified minority questioners?

Beyond attitudes and worldview, though, I find myself learning new habits and mannerisms. I perform frequent greetings (even of strangers), downplay parliamentary rules in meetings to seek consensus, state my personal opinion on topics that are under consideration, spend time getting to know my students personally, talk about a student's personal circumstances before talking business, become more attentive to nonverbal qualifiers in verbal messages, enjoy verbal interruptions in the classroom, "call on" students with facial gestures, rely heavily on friendship networks and brokers, raise the emotional level of my discourse, and accept the education of young African Americans almost more as a "mission" than as a salaried "job." These and other behaviors I would not have assimilated, were it not for my extended sojourn at an HBCU.

IV

I will open the windows of my house to breezes from all the directions, but I will not be blown from my feet by any of them. —Mahatma Gandhi

Every person who enjoys extensive contact and interaction with others of differing heritages and nationalities heightens his or her self-consciousness about identity. Although I could extend my analysis to recount in some detail how I have consciously and unconsciously refashioned myself as an Asian communicator, I would rather consider the juggling of various identities that are acquired through interethnic and intercultural interaction.

It is instructive to view the person who has engaged in extensive intercultural communication as someone who cooks from a recipe book. Early in life, we cook and eat what we were taught to cook and eat from childhood. We reproduce that cooking behavior, as best we are able, and we think of "eating" as that which is drawn from a familiar universe of cuisine. For a picnic, a party, a banquet, we come programmed with a set variety of responses. We can, of course, improvise with a touch of spice, or perhaps with a garnish. But food critics would recognize the result as the product of a certain culture—that is, as a product of our food identity.

Then we invite a person over to eat, but discover she is vegetarian. We rush to our cultural cookbook, only to find little beyond macaroni and cheese and grilled cheese sandwiches to serve the guest. Our cultural recipe book is revealed as lacking in its capacity to respond to a certain task. Indeed, the more suitable cookbook may be written in Hindi, Italian, or Arabic. If we go through with the task of preparing a meal from a new cookbook (though some would still serve steak, cancel the dinner, or "eat out") we raise our consciousness of new possibilities. Now we can cook from several books in several languages, and we have further ideas on how to improvise in the future. Indeed, we reach a point where we prepare food from various cuisines because it is more interesting, because we are curious, or because we want to showcase our new cooking skills. The real test of our skills is when we are told by a native that they recognize our dish, that it is just as it used to be prepared at the guest's own home.

Earlier writers looked at a new identity as something that tramples an older one. If enough identities were learned, the person might become "multi-phrenic" and have no cultural base of operations to which to return. Perhaps these writers critiqued identity from a standpoint of ethnocentrism: each was comfortable with his or her own identity and was convinced of its "correctness." They feared a bad result cooking with an unfamiliar book. They felt that visitors, whether vegetarian or Jewish or Muslim, should "eat steak," or pork, or not visit. For every person who embraces new alternatives in identity, there is another who offers resistance. Further, issues of sampled new identities create moments of misunderstanding and confusion: "Salmon is vegetarian" or "You eat onions and garlic, so do not say you are vegetarian." Our new identity may have a certain permanence, or it may be temporary. It may be reinforced or rejected by persons who are significant for us. It may be practiced in places where it is not rewarded.

Resistance

In a multicultural society, eventually someone of a differing ethnicity or nationality or religion or sexual orientation enters our orbit. Such persons differ in socialization, and they practice different communication behaviors. They may have different notions of the roles of supervisors. They may "look over our shoulders" when we do our work, whereas we are accustomed to working on our own unless we encounter a problem. They may single out individuals for praise or blame, or credit an entire unit with achievements more traceable to individuals. They may be slow to ask for help or may seek help perpetually. They may associate mostly with others like themselves. They may want holidays that we do not recognize, or wear a turban or facial covering at work. They may not be able to "take kidding." They may complain about things we take for granted. They may seem to "want special treatment."

Some percentage of those who formerly defined the "mainstream" may never want to "open a new cookbook." They may assert that it is the duty of those "who cook from a different cookbook" to "eat like us." They will see no reason—enhanced flexibility, provision of scarce skills, access to other markets, the chance to compare different techniques, the gaining of fresh voices, the chance for synergy—that would justify making adjustments for the new entrants. ("Is this sensitivity effort at work going to be optional or required? If it's optional, I won't get anywhere near it!") What others may view as delicacies will be for them "raw fish."

Confusion

For some amount of time cues are misinterpreted. A meeting "at 2:00" means literally 2:00. A majority vote may leave disgruntled losers as a consensus might not, but business moves on. Finding fault in the work of subordinates may, in the minds of some Greek, Chinese, or West Asian supervisors, make the unit look bad; but in the local context, it speaks to the evaluator's keen eye as a supervisor. Entering the conversation while another person is still talking may be considered rude, not enthusiastic. Being made to write frequent reports may be viewed as the company "keeping a suspicious eye" on the new worker. The arrival of a worker of color is viewed as "affirmative action," even when the new worker has comparable credentials. Other workers give the new worker extra space and deny him or her a needed sense of corporate belonging.

Especially for the new entrant into the context, the rules are unfamiliar. He or she may talk with a supervisor with whom smooth interpersonal relations have been established, only to be accused of "going behind someone's back" or "skipping levels." The question "Can you do this?" may sound patronizing. In a thousand ways, the new setting is unfamiliar just where it should be clear. Too many cues can be taken in multiple ways; indeed, this may be the sarcastic intent of an associate.

Permanence

Some sojourns are temporary, and the trainee or student expects to return "home." The incentive decreases for such persons to learn new recipes or ways of coping. For so long as misunderstandings and confusion do not prevent the acquisition of desired knowledge, life will be tolerable. Similarly, some workers are "loaned" to a branch elsewhere. Even though they may have a limited understanding of the new context, both parties may decide to "suffer through" a temporary assignment.

Life in a multicultural society is more permanent. Various projections see white and nonwhite workers in USAmerica reaching parity in about 50 years. In a seemingly permanent relationship, both parties are called on to make adjustments. My model of third culture building (Starosta & Olorunnisola, 1995; Chen & Starosta, 1997) moves from stages where impressions are fleeting through other stages where changes in communication become permanent. In the parlance of this essay, foreign cooking comes to taste better than the home cuisine. The new recipes are taught to the next generation as standard fare.

Reinforcement

Some companies in search of a new multicultural identity establish incentives and penalties for those who advance company policy. Similarly, some exclusionary choices are sanctionable in court. Fundamentally, however, the force behind an accepting attitude toward multiculturalism is largely individual. Mahatma Gandhi believed that each person must make him- or herself answerable for deeds that are committed against others. Scripture should never be used as an excuse to countenance the oppression of others; "I decline to be bound by any interpretation [of the Scriptures] if it is repugnant to [my individual] reason or moral sense. . . . I would rather be torn to pieces than to disown the suppressed classes" (Gandhi, 1929). Nor would Gandhi say the problem is "with them," and not his concern. Gandhi's goal in life was to free himself from rebirth, but "I prayed that if I have to be reborn . . . I should do so . . . as an [untouchable]" (1921).

The answer to those who repressed others was to act with "transparent morality," and to reflect the deeds of the other back to the perpetrator. The person who holds a spark of morality will not long be able to stand his or her reflection in the mirror if that reflection betrays a moral flaw. Gandhi's movement of "truth force" goes from a committed individual to commitment on the part of those surrounding that individual. Finally, a whole society is moved in the direction of greater virtue. The most potent reinforcement for a positive reception for culturally diverse individuals takes part in individual minds. The impulse for inclusion starts as an individual impulse. It continues even when courts and workplace evaluators are not looking. This outlook of individual accountability and its methodology, "transparent morality," alone can achieve and expand inclusive communication conduct.

Reward

In recognizing that the workplace, particularly in high-tech fields, must draw on the skills of workers from a variety of cultures, some computer firms put incentives in place to reward those in the firm who seek out, consider, hire, and promote nontraditional workers. Turning to the cultural natives of a region to avoid naming an auto (a Chevy Nova) with a word that means "no go" in the local language, or knowing not to tell people to "put a tiger in your tank" in areas where tigers are scorned produces economic outcomes that are visible to a savvy company. Latinos and African Americans make up a sizable section of the USAmerican market, and it would be wise to seek input from persons of these cultures and others to decide how best to tap this market. That is, some rewards for inclusiveness are tangible and self-evident.

Arguably, it is the nontangible reasons for including others that offer an individual his or her first real choice. "Synergy," "telling a better story," "knowledge," "new horizons," "alternatives," "adventure," "culture learning," "fair play," and the like are not, in themselves, totally convincing reasons to include others with parity in everyday interactions. They sound vague and remote. Medical studies have demonstrated that it is the innovations with less tangible and visible benefits (boiling water, spacing children, getting a vaccination, quitting smoking) that are the hardest to introduce. The richest rewards for multicultural inclusion may be like those for preventive medicine: the innovative practice (cultural inclusion) must take place now to realize the harmony, synergy, liberation, and new possibilities of the future.

V

Experiencing dual_consciousness@USAmerican.white.male, as is the case for the black and Asian and Native American domains, is neither a blessing nor a curse in itself. At most, it presents a host of expanded possibilities.

Dual consciousness is a fluid moment where identities flow and collide. Some of the consequences are delightfully fortuitous; others are bitter. Few are predictable with great fidelity. The same set of raw materials can be used to build towers or dungeons. Worse still, the materials may be returned unopened, their potential untapped and unrealized.

Dual consciousness is a vantage point from which new outcomes become thinkable and old possibilities appear outmoded and antiquated. It is a point of unsettled perspective, of shifting allegiance, of new linguistic possibilities, of racial antithesis, of sexism, of hegemony, of hope. Those who visit the USAmerican.white.male site, as well as every other contested site, will take away, in great measure, that which they bring to the site. The site can magnify intolerance and it can liberate. The difference between the two rests in the identity or identities of the individual beholder.

PART THREE

Othering

Racism and Prejudice

AmongUS

Cultural Biases and Intercultural Communication[1]

Myron W. Lustig and Jolene Koester

Interaction only within one's own culture produces a number of obvious benefits. Because the culture provides predictability, the threat of the unknown is reduced. When something or someone that is unknown or unpredictable enters a culture, the culture's beliefs, values, and norms tell people how to interpret and respond appropriately, thus reducing the perceived threat of the intrusion. These cultural patterns also allow for automatic responses to stimuli; in essence, cultural patterns save people time and energy.

Intercultural communication, by definition, means that people are interacting with at least one culturally different person. Consequently, the sense of security, comfort, and predictability that characterizes communication with culturally similar people is lost. The greater the degree of interculturalness, the greater the loss of predictability and certainty. Assurances about the accuracy of interpretations of verbal and nonverbal messages are lost.

Terms that are often used when communicating with culturally different people include *unknown, unpredictable, ambiguous, weird, mysterious, unexplained, exotic, unusual, unfamiliar, curious, novel, odd, outlandish,* and *strange.* As you read this list, consider how the choice of a particular word might also reflect a particular value. What characteristics, values, and knowledge allow individuals to respond more competently to the threat of dealing with cultural differences? What situations heighten the perception of threat among members of different cultural groups? To answer questions such as these, we need to explore how people make sense of information about others as they categorize or classify others in their social world.

Social Categorizing

Three features in the way all humans process information about others are important to your understanding of intercultural communication. First, as cognitive psychologists have repeatedly demonstrated, people impose a pattern on their world by organizing the stimuli that bombard their senses into conceptual categories. Every waking moment, people are presented with literally hundreds of different perceptual stimuli. Therefore, it becomes necessary to simplify the information by selecting, organizing, and reducing it to less complex forms. That is, to comprehend stimuli, people organize them into categories, groupings, and patterns. As a child, you might have completed drawings by connecting numbered dots. Emerging from the lines was the figure of an animal or a familiar toy. Even though the form was not completely drawn, it was relatively easy to identify. This kind of recognition occurs simply because human beings have a tendency to organize perceptual cues to impose meaning, usually by using familiar experiences.

Second, most people tend to think that others perceive, evaluate, and reason about the world in the same ways they do. In other words, humans assume that other people with whom they interact are like themselves. Indeed, it is quite common for people to draw on their personal experiences to understand and evaluate the motivations of others. This common human tendency is sometimes called "ethnocentrism."

Third, humans simplify the processing and organizing of information from the environment by identifying certain characteristics as belonging to certain categories of persons and events. For example, a child's experiences with several dogs that growled and snapped are likely to result in a future reaction to other dogs as if they will also growl and snap. The characteristics of particular events, persons, or objects, once experienced, are often assumed to be typical of similar events, persons, or objects. Though these assumptions are sometimes accurate, often they are not. Not all dogs necessarily growl and snap at young children. Nevertheless, information processing results in a simplification of the world, so that prior experiences are used as the basis for determining both the categories and the attributes of the events. This process is called "stereotyping."

Please note that we are simply describing these human tendencies, not evaluating them as good or bad. Their obvious advantage is that they allow people to respond efficiently to a variety of perceptual stimuli. Nevertheless, such organization and simplification can create genuine obstacles to intercultural competence because they may lead to prejudice, discrimination, and racism.

Ethnocentrism

All cultures teach their members the "preferred" ways to respond to the world, often labeled "natural" or "appropriate." Thus, people generally perceive their own experiences, which are shaped by their own cultural forces, as natural, human, and universal. This belief that the customs and practices of one's own culture are superior to those of other cultures is called *ethnocentrism*.

Cultures also train their members to use the categories of their own cultural experiences when judging the experiences of people from other cultures. Our culture tells us that the way we were taught to behave is "right" or "correct," and that those who do things differently are wrong. William G. Sumner, who first introduced the concept of ethnocentrism, defined it as "the view of things in which one's own group is the center of everything, and all others are scaled and rated with reference to it."[2] Sumner illustrates how ethnocentrism works in the following example:

When Caribs were asked whence they came, they replied, "We alone are people." "Kiowa" means real or principal people. A Laplander is a "man" or "human being." The highest praise a Greenlander has for a European visiting the island is that the European by studying virtue and good manners from the Greenlanders soon will be as good as a Greenlander. Nature peoples call themselves "men" as a rule. All others are something else, but not men. The Jews divide all mankind into themselves and Gentiles—they being the "chosen people." The Greeks and Romans called outsiders "barbarians." Arabs considered themselves as the noblest nation and all others as barbarians. Russian books and newspapers talk about its civilizing mission, and so do the books and journals of France, Germany, and the United States. Each nation now regards itself as the leader of civilization, the best, the freest, and the wisest. All others are inferior.[3]

Ethnocentrism is a learned belief in cultural superiority. Because cultures teach people what the world is "really like" and what is "good," people consequently believe that the values of their culture are natural and correct. Thus, people from other cultures who do things differently are wrong. When combined with the natural human tendency to prefer what is typically experienced, ethnocentrism produces emotional reactions to cultural differences that reduce people's willingness to understand disparate cultural messages.

Ethnocentrism tends to highlight and exaggerate cultural differences. As an interesting instance of ethnocentrism, consider beliefs about body odor. Most U.S. Americans spend large sums of money each year to rid themselves of natural body odor. They then replace their natural odors with artificial ones, by using deodorants, bath powders, shaving lotions, perfumes, hair sprays, shampoos, mousse, gels, toothpaste, mouthwash, and breath mints. Many U.S. Americans probably believe that they do not have an odor—even after they have routinely applied most, if not all, of the artificial ones in the preceding list. Yet the same individuals will react negatively to culturally different others who do not remove natural body odors and who refuse to apply artificial ones.

Another example of ethnocentrism concerns the way in which cultures teach people to discharge mucus from the nose. Most U.S. Americans purchase boxes of tissues and strategically place them at various locations in their homes, offices, and cars so they will be available for use as needed. In countries where paper products had historically been scarce and very expensive, people blow their noses onto the ground or the street. Pay attention to your reaction as you read this last statement. Most U.S. Americans, when learning about this behavior, react with a certain amount of disgust. But think about the U.S. practice of blowing one's nose into a tissue or handkerchief, which is then placed on the desk or into a pocket or purse. Now ask yourself which is really more disgusting—carrying around tissues with dried mucus in them or blowing the mucus onto the street? Described in this way, both practices have a certain element of repugnance, but because one's culture teaches that there is one preferred way, that custom is familiar and comfortable and the practices of other cultures are seen as wrong or distasteful.

Ethnocentrism can occur along all of the dimensions of cultural patterns. People from individualistic cultures, for instance, find the idea that a person's self-concept is tied to a group to be unfathomable. To most U.S. Americans, the idea of an arranged marriage seems strange at best and a confining and reprehensible limitation on personal freedom at worst.

One area of behavior that quickly reveals ethnocentrism is personal hygiene. For example, U.S. Americans like to see themselves as the cleanest people on earth. In the United States, bathrooms contain sinks, showers or bathtubs, and toilets, thus allowing the efficient use of water pipes. Given this arrangement, people bathe themselves in close proximity to the toilet, where they urinate and defecate. Described in this way, the cultural practices of the United States may seem unclean, peculiar, and even absurd. Why would people in a so-called modern society complete two such contradictory functions next to each other? People from many other cultures, who consider the U.S. arrangement to be unclean and unhealthy, share that sentiment. Our point here is that what is familiar and comfortable inevitably seems the best, right, and natural way of doing things. Judgments about what is "right" or "natural" create emotional responses to cultural differences that may interfere with our ability to understand the symbols used by other cultures. For example, European Americans think it is "human nature" to orient oneself to the future and to want to improve one's material status in life. Individuals whose cultures have been influenced by alternative forces, resulting in contrary views, are often judged negatively and treated with derision.

To be a competent intercultural communicator, you must realize that you typically use the categories of your own culture to judge and interpret the behaviors of those who are culturally different from you. You must also be aware of your own emotional reactions to the sights, sounds, smells, and variations in message systems that you encounter when communicating with people from other cultures. The competent intercultural communicator does not necessarily suppress negative feelings, but acknowledges their existence and seeks to minimize their effect on his or her communication. If you are reacting strongly to some aspect of another culture, seek out an explanation in the ethnocentric preferences that your culture has taught you.

Stereotyping

Journalist Walter Lippmann introduced the term *stereotyping* in 1922 to refer to a selection process that is used to organize and simplify perceptions of others.[4] Stereotypes are a form of generalization about some group of people. When people stereotype others, they make assertions about the characteristics of all people who belong to a given category. The consequence of stereotyping is that the vast degree of differences that exist among the members of any one group may not be taken into account in the interpretation of messages.

To illustrate how stereotyping works, read the following list: college professors, surfers, Marxists, Democrats, bankers, New Yorkers, Californians. As you read each of these categories was it relatively easy for you to associate particular characteristics and traits with each group? Now imagine that a person from one of these groups walked into the room and began a conversation with you. In all likelihood you would associate the group's characteristics with that specific individual.

Your responses to this simple example illustrate what typically occurs when people are stereotyped.[5] First, someone identifies an outgroup category—"they"—whose characteristics differ from those in one's own social ingroup. Next, the perceived dissimilarities between the groups are enlarged and accentuated, thereby creating differences that are clearer and more distinct. Sharper and more pronounced boundaries between the groups make it more difficult for individuals to move from one group to another.[6] Concurrently, an evaluative component is introduced, whereby the characteristics of the outgroup are negatively judged; that is, the outgroup is regarded as wrong, inferior, or stigmatized as a result of given characteristics. Finally, the group's characteristics are attributed to all people who belong to the group, so that a specific person is not treated as a unique individual but as a typical member of a category.

Categories that are used to form stereotypes about groups of people can vary widely, and might include the following:

- Regions of the world (Asians, Arabs, South Americans, Africans)
- Countries (Kenya, Japan, China, France, Great Britain)
- Regions within countries (northern Indians, southern Indians, U.S. midwesterners, U.S. southerners)
- Cities (New Yorkers, Parisians, Londoners)
- Cultures (English, French, Latino, Russian, Serbian, Yoruba, Mestizo, Thai, Navajo)
- Race (African, Caucasian)
- Religion (Muslim, Hindu, Buddhist, Jewish, Christian)
- Age (young, old, middle-aged, children, adults)
- Occupations (teacher, farmer, doctor, housekeeper, mechanic, architect, musician)
- Relational roles (mother, friend, father, sister, brother)
- Physical characteristics (short, tall, fat, skinny)
- Social class (wealthy, poor, middle class)

This list is by no means exhaustive. What it should illustrate is the enormous range of possibilities for classification and simplification. Consider your own stereotypes of people in these groups. Many may have been created by direct experience with only one or two people from a particular group. Others are probably based on secondhand information and opinions, output from the mass media, and general habits of thinking; they may even have been formed without any direct experience with individuals from the group. Yet many people are prepared to assume that the stereotype is an accurate representation of all members of a specific group.[7]

Stereotypes can be inaccurate in a three ways.[8] First, as we have suggested, stereotypes often are assumed to apply to all or most of the members of a particular group or category, resulting in a tendency to ignore differences among the individual members of the group. This type of stereotyping error is called the *out-group homogeneity effect* and results in a tendency to regard all members of a particular group as much more similar to one another than they actually are.[9] Arab Americans, for instance, complain that other U.S. Americans often hold undifferentiated stereotypes about members of their culture. Albert Mokhiber laments:

> If there's problem in Libya we're all Libyans. If the problem is in Lebanon we're all Lebanese. If it happens to be Iran, which is not an Arab country, we're all Iranians. Conversely, Iranians were picked on during the Gulf War as being Arabs. Including one fellow who called in who was a Polynesian Jew. But he looked like what an Arab should look like, and he felt the wrath of anti-Arab discrimination. Nobody's really free from this. The old civil rights adage says that as long as the rights of one are in danger, we're all in danger. I think we need to break out of our ethnic ghetto mentality, all of us, from various backgrounds, and realize that we're in this stew together.[10]

A second form of stereotype inaccuracy occurs when the group average, as suggested by the stereotype, is simply wrong or inappropriately exaggerated. This type of inaccuracy occurs, for instance, when Germans are stereotypically regarded as being very efficient, or perhaps very rigid, when they may actually be less efficient or less rigid than the exaggerated perception of them would warrant.

A third form of stereotype inaccuracy occurs when the degree of error and exaggeration differs for positive and negative attributes. For instance, imagine that you have stereotyped members of a culture as being very efficient (a positive attribute) but also very rigid and inflexible in their business relationships (a negative attribute). If you tend to overestimate the prevalence and importance of the culture's positive characteristics, such as its degree of efficiency, while simultaneously ignoring or underestimating its rigidity and other negative characteristics, you would have a "positive valence inaccuracy." Conversely, a "negative valence inaccuracy" occurs if you exaggerated the negative attributes while ignoring or devaluing its positive ones. This latter condition, often called *prejudice,* will be discussed in greater detail below.

The problems associated with using stereotyping as a means of understanding individuals is best illustrated by identifying the groups to which you belong. Think about the characteristics that might be stereotypically assigned to those groups. Determine whether the characteristics apply to you or to others in your group. Some of them may be accurate descriptions; many, however, will be totally inaccurate, and you would resent being thought of in that way. Stereotypes distort or hide the individual. Ultimately, people may become blind to the actual characteristics of the group because not all stereotypes are accurate. Most are based on relatively minimal experiences with particular individuals.

Stereotype inaccuracy can lead to errors in interpretations and expectations about the behaviors of others. Interpretation errors occur because stereotypes are used not only to categorize specific individuals and events but also to judge them. That is, one potentially harmful consequence of stereotypes is that they provide inaccurate labels for a group of people that are then used to interpret subsequent ambiguous events and experiences involving members of those groups. Ziva Kunda and Bonnie Sherman-Williams note:

> Consider, for example, the unambiguous act of failing a test. Ethnic stereotypes may lead perceivers to attribute such failure to laziness if the actor is Asian but to low ability if the actor is Black. Thus stereotypes will affect judgments of the targets' ability even if subjects base these judgments only on the act, because the stereotypes will determine the meaning of the act.[11]

Because stereotypes are sometimes applied indiscriminately to members of a particular culture or social group, they can also lead to errors in one's expectations about the future behaviors of others. Stereotypes provide the basis for estimating, often inaccurately, what members of the stereotyped group are likely to do. Most disturbingly, stereotypes will likely persist even when members of the stereotyped group repeatedly behave in ways that disconfirm them. Once a stereotype has taken hold, members of the stereotyped group who behave in nonstereotypical ways will be expected to compensate in future actions to "make up for" their atypical behavior. Even when some individuals from a stereotyped group repeatedly deviate from expectations, they may be regarded as exceptions or as atypical members of their group. Indeed, stereotypes may remain intact, or may even be strengthened, in the face of disconfirming experiences; those who hold the stereotypes often expect that the other members of the stereotyped social group will be even *more* likely to behave as the stereotype predicts to "balance out" or compensate for the "unusual" instances they experienced. That is, stereotypes encourage people to expect future behaviors that compensate for perceived inconsistencies, and thus allow people to anticipate future events in a way that makes it unnecessary to revise their deeply held beliefs and values.[12]

The process underlying stereotyping is absolutely essential for human beings to function. Some categorization is necessary and normal. Indeed, there is survival value in the ability to make accurate generalizations about others, and stereotypes function as mental "energy-saving devices" to help make those generalizations efficiently.[13] However, stereotypes may also promote prejudice and discrimination directed toward members of cultures other than one's own. Intercultural competence requires an ability to move beyond stereotypes and to respond to the individual. Previous experiences should be used only as guidelines or suggested interpretations rather than as hard-and-fast categories.

Prejudice

Prejudice refers to negative attitudes toward other people that are based on faulty and inflexible stereotypes. Prejudiced attitudes include irrational feelings of dislike and even hatred for certain groups, biased perceptions and beliefs about the group members that are not based on direct experiences and firsthand knowledge, and a readiness to behave in negative and unjust ways toward members of the group. Gordon Allport, who first focused scholarly attention on prejudice, argued that prejudiced people ignore evidence that is inconsistent with their biased viewpoint, or they distort the evidence to fit their prejudices.[14]

The strong link between prejudice and stereotypes should be obvious. Prejudiced thinking is dependent on stereotypes and is a fairly normal phenomenon.[15] To be prejudiced toward a group of people sometimes makes it easier to respond to them. We are not condoning prejudice or the hostile and violent actions that may occur as a result. We are suggesting that prejudice is a universal psychological process; all people have a propensity for prejudice toward others who are unlike themselves. For individuals to move beyond prejudicial attitudes and for societies to avoid basing social structures on their prejudices about groups of people, it is critical to recognize the prevalence of prejudicial thinking.

What functions does prejudice serve? We have already suggested that the thought process underlying prejudice includes the need to organize and simplify the world. Richard Brislin describes four additional benefits, or what he calls functions, of prejudice.[16] First, he suggests that prejudice satisfies a *utilitarian* or adjustment function. Displaying certain kinds of prejudice means that people receive rewards and avoid punishments. For example, if you express prejudicial statements about certain people, other people may like you more. It is also easier to simply dislike and be prejudiced toward members of other groups because they can then be dismissed without going through the effort necessary to adjust to them. Another function that prejudice serves is an *ego-defensive* one; it protects self-esteem. For example, people who are unsuccessful in business may be prejudiced toward groups whose members are successful. Still another advantage of prejudicial attitudes is the *value-expressive* function. If people believe that their group has certain qualities that are unique, valuable, good, or in some way special, their prejudicial attitudes toward others is a way of expressing those values. Finally, Brislin describes the *knowledge function* as prejudicial attitudes that people hold because of their need to have the world neatly organized and boxed into categories. This function takes the normal human proclivity to organize the world to an extreme. The rigid application of categories and the prejudicial attitudes assigned to certain behaviors and beliefs provide security and increase predictability. Obviously, these functions cannot be neatly applied to all instances of prejudice. Nor are people usually aware of the specific reasons for their prejudices. For each person, prejudicial attitudes may serve several functions.

Discrimination

Whereas *prejudice* refers to people's attitudes or mental representations, the term *discrimination* refers to the behavioral manifestations of that prejudice. Thus discrimination can be thought of as prejudice "in action."

Discrimination can occur in many forms. From the extremes of segregation and apartheid to biases in the availability of housing, employment, education, economic resources, personal safety, and legal protections, discrimination represents unequal treatment of certain individuals solely because of their membership in a particular group. Teun van Dijk conducted a series of studies of people's everyday conversations as they discuss different racial and cultural groups. Van Dijk concluded that when individuals make prejudicial comments, tell jokes that belittle and dehumanize others, and share negative stereotypes about others, they are establishing and legitimizing the existence of their prejudices and laying the "communication groundwork" that will make it acceptable for people to perform discriminatory acts.[17]

Racism

One obstacle to intercultural competence to which we want to give special attention is racism. Because racism often plays such a major role in the communication that occurs between people of different races or ethnic groups, it is particularly important to understand how and why it occurs.

The word *racism* itself can evoke very powerful emotional reactions, especially for those who have felt the oppression and exploitation that stems from racist attitudes and behaviors. For members of the African American, Asian American, Native American, and Latino cultures, racism has created a social history shaped by prejudice and discrimination.[18] For individual members of these groups, racism has resulted in the pain of oppression. To those who are members of cultural groups that have had the power to oppress and exploit others, the term *racism* often evokes equally powerful thoughts and emotional reactions that deny responsibility for and participation in racist acts and thinking. In this section we will introduce some ideas about racism that illuminate the reactions of both those who have received racist communication and those who are seen as exhibiting it.

Robert Blauner has described racism as a tendency to categorize people who are culturally different in terms of their physical traits such as skin color, hair color and texture, facial structure, and eye shape.[19] Dalmas Taylor offers a related approach that focuses on the behavioral components of racism. Taylor defines racism as the cumulative effects of individuals, institutions, and cultures that result in the oppression of ethnic minorities.[20] Taylor's approach is useful in that it recognizes that racism can occur at three distinct levels: individual, institutional, and cultural.

At the individual level, racism is conceptually similar to prejudice. Individual racism involves beliefs, attitudes, and behaviors of a given person toward people of a different racial group.[21] Specific European Americans, for example, who believe that African Americans are somehow inferior exemplify individual racism. Positive contact and interaction between members of the two groups can sometimes change these attitudes. Yet as the preceding discussion of prejudice suggests, people with prejudicial beliefs about others often distort new information to fit their original prejudices.

At the institutional level, racism is the exclusion of certain people from equal participation in a society's institutions solely because of their race.[22] Institutional racism is built into such social structures as the government, schools, and industry practices. It leads to certain patterns of behaviors and responses to specific racial or cultural groups that allow those groups to be systematically exploited and oppressed. For example, institutional racism has precluded both Jews and African Americans from attending certain public schools and universities, and at times it has restricted their participation in particular professions.[23]

At the cultural level, racism denies the existence of the culture of a particular group;[24] for example, the denial that African Americans represent a unique and distinct culture that is separate from both European American culture and all African cultures. Cultural racism also involves the rejection by one group of the beliefs and values of another, such as the "negative evaluations by whites of black cultural values."[25]

Though racism is often used synonymously with *prejudice* and *discrimination,* the social attributes that distinguish it from these other terms are oppression and power. *Oppression* refers to "the systematic, institutionalized mistreatment of one group of people by another."[26] Thus racism is the tendency by groups in control of institutional and cultural power to use it to keep members of groups who do not have access to the same kinds of power at a disadvantage. Racism oppresses entire groups of people, making it very difficult, and sometimes virtually impossible, for their members to have access to political, economic, and social power.[27]

Forms of racism vary in intensity and degree of expression, with some far more dangerous and detrimental to society than others. The most extreme form of racism is *old-fashioned racism,* in which members of one group openly display obviously bigoted views about members of another group. Judgments of superiority and inferiority are commonplace in this kind of racism, and there is a dehumanizing quality to it. African Americans and other cultural groups in the United States have often experienced this form of racism from other U.S. Americans.

In *symbolic racism,* the form currently prevalent in the United States, members of one group believe that people from some other group threaten their traditional values, such as individualism and self-reliance. Fears that the outgroup will achieve economic or social success, with a simultaneous loss of economic or social status by the ingroup, typify this form of racism. In many parts of the United States, for instance, this type of racism has been directed toward Asians and Asian Americans who have achieved economic success.

Tokenism as a form of racism occurs when individuals do not perceive themselves as prejudiced because they make small concessions to, while holding basically negative attitudes toward, members of the other group. Tokenism is the practice of reverse discrimination, in which people go out of their way to favor a few members of another group to maintain their own self-concepts as individuals who believe in equality for all. While such behaviors may increase a person's esteem, they may also decrease the possibilities for more meaningful contributions to intercultural unity and progress.

Aversive racism, like tokenism, occurs when individuals who value fairness and equality among all racial and cultural groups nevertheless have negative beliefs and feelings about members of a particular race, often as a result of childhood socialization experiences. Individuals with such conflicting feelings may restrain their overt racist behaviors, but they may also avoid close contact with members of the other group and may express their underlying negative attitudes subtly, in ways that appear rational and that can be justified on the basis of some factor other than race or culture. Thus the negativity of aversive racists "is more likely to be manifested in discomfort, uneasiness, fear, or avoidance of minorities rather than overt hostility."[28] An individual at work, for instance, may be polite but distant to a coworker from another culture but may avoid that person at a party they both happen to attend.

Genuine likes and dislikes may also operate as a form of racism. The cultural practices of some groups of people can form the basis for a prejudicial attitude simply because the group displays behaviors that another group does not like. For example, individuals from cultures that are predominantly vegetarian may develop negative attitudes toward those who belong to cultures that eat meat.

Finally, the least alarming form of racism, and certainly one that everyone has experienced, is based on the *degree of unfamiliarity* with members of other groups. Simply responding to unfamiliar people may create negative attitudes because of a lack of experience with the characteristics of their group. The others may look, smell, talk, or act differently, all of which can be a source of discomfort and can form the basis for racist or prejudicial attitudes.

Overcoming Cultural Biases

Ethnocentrism, stereotyping, prejudice, discrimination, and racism are so familiar and comfortable that overcoming them requires a commitment both to learning about other cultures and to understanding one's own. A willingness to explore various cultural experiences without prejudgment is necessary. An ability to behave appropriately and effectively with culturally different others, without invoking prejudiced and stereotyped assumptions, is required. Although no one can completely overcome the cultural biases that naturally exist, the requisite knowledge, motivation, and skill can certainly help to minimize the negative effects of prejudice and discrimination.

As inhabitants of the twenty-first century, you will no longer have a choice about whether to live in a world of many cultures. The forces that bring people from other cultures into your life are dynamic, potent, and ever present.

The tensions inherent in creating successful intercultural relationships, communities, and nations are obvious. Examples abound that underscore how difficult it is for groups of culturally different individuals to live, work, and play together harmoniously. The consequences of failing to create a harmonious intercultural society are also obvious—human suffering, hatred passed on from one generation to another, disruptions in people's lives, and unnecessary conflicts that sap people's creative talents and energies and that siphon off scarce resources from other important societal needs.

To improve your intercultural communication by building positive motivations, or emotional reactions, to intercultural interactions, take an honest inventory of the various ways in which you categorize other people. Can you identify your obvious ethnocentric attitudes about appearances, foods, and social practices? Make a list of the stereotypes, both positive and negative, that you hold about the various cultural groups with which you regularly interact. Now identify those stereotypes that others might hold about your culture. By engaging in this kind of self-reflective process, you are becoming more aware of the ways in which your social categorizations detract from an ability to understand communication from culturally different others.

There are no simple prescriptions or pat answers that can guarantee competent intercultural communication in all settings. Nor has anyone discovered how to eliminate the destructive consequences of prejudice, discrimination, and racism. Nevertheless, the joys and benefits of embracing an intercultural world are many. As the world is transformed into a place where cultural boundaries cease to be impenetrable barriers, differences among people become reasons to celebrate and share rather than to fear and harm. The opportunities to understand, experience, and benefit from unfamiliar ways are unprecedented.

The intercultural challenge for all of us now living in a world in which interactions with people from different cultures are common features of daily life is to be willing to grapple with the consequences of prejudice, discrimination, and racism at the individual, social, and institutional levels. Because "prejudice" and "racism" are such emotionally charged concepts, it is sometimes difficult to comment on their occurrence in our interactions with others. Individuals who believe that they have perceived discriminatory remarks and actions often feel that they cannot risk the resentment of their coworkers, fellow students, teachers, or service providers that would likely occur should they demand interactions that do not display prejudice against them. Conversely, those who do not regard themselves as having prejudiced or racist attitudes and who believe they never behave in discriminatory ways are horrified to learn that others might interpret their attitudes as prejudiced and their actions as discriminatory. While discussions about prejudice, discrimination, and racism can lead to a better understanding of the interpersonal dynamics that arise as individuals seek to establish mutually respectful relationships, they can just as easily lead to greater divisions and hostilities between people.

The need for an intercultural mentality to match our multicultural world, the cultural biases that must be overcome in the quest of such a goal, the excitement of the challenges, and the rewards of the successes are summarized in the words of Troy Duster:

> There is no longer a single racial or ethnic group with an overwhelming numerical and political majority. Pluralism is the reality, with no one group a dominant force. This is completely new; we are grappling with a phenomenon that is both puzzling and alarming, fraught with tensions and hostilities, and yet simultaneously brimming with potential and crackling with new energy. Consequently, we swing between hope and concern, optimism and pessimism about the prospects for social life among people from differing racial and cultural groups.[29]

We urge you to view your intercultural experiences as steps in a lifelong commitment to make the world a place where people from all cultures can live and thrive.

NOTES

1. Excerpted and adapted from Myron W. Lustig and Jolene Koester, *Intercultural Competence: Interpersonal Communication Across Cultures,* 3rd ed. (New York: Longman, 1999).

2. William G. Sumner, *Folkways* (Boston: Ginn, 1940), 27.

3. Sumner.

4. Walter Lippman, *Public Opinion* (New York: Harcourt Brace, 1922), 25.

5. See Carl Friedrich Graumann and Margret Wintermantel, "Discriminatory Speech Acts: A Functional Approach," in *Stereotyping and Prejudice: Changing Conceptions,* ed. Daniel Bar-Tal, Carl F. Graumann, Arie W. Kruglanski, and Wolfgang Stroebe (New York: Springer-Verlag, 1989), 183–204.

6. Henri Tajfel, *Differentiation Between Social Groups: Studies in the Social Psychology of Intergroup Relations* (New York: Academic Press, 1978).

7. Marilynn B. Brewer, "When Stereotypes Lead to Stereotyping: The Use of Stereotypes in Person Perception," in *Stereotypes and Stereotyping,* ed. C. Neil Macrae, Charles Stangor, and Miles Hewstone (New York: Guilford, 1996), 254–275; Diane M. Mackie, David L. Hamilton, Joshua Susskind, and Francine Rosselli, "Social Psychological Foundations of Stereotype Formation," in *Stereotypes and Stereotyping,* ed. C. Neil Macrae, Charles Stangor, and Miles Hewstone (New York: Guilford, 1996), 41–78; Charles Stangor and Mark Schaller, "Stereotypes as Individual and Collective Representations," in *Stereotypes and Stereotyping,* ed. C. Neil Macrae, Charles Stangor, and Miles Hewstone (New York: Guilford, 1996), 3–37.

8. See Charles M. Judd and Bernadette Park, "Definition and Assessment of Accuracy in Social Stereotypes," *Psychological Review* 100 (1993): 109–128; Carey S. Ryan, Bernadette Park, and Charles M. Judd, "Assessing Stereotype Accuracy: Implications for Understanding the Stereotyping Process," in *Stereotypes and Stereotyping,* ed. C. Neil Macrae, Charles Stangor, and Miles Hewstone (New York: Guilford, 1996), 121–157.

9. Marilynn B. Brewer, "Social Identity, Distinctiveness, and In-Group Homogeneity," *Social Cognition* 11 (1993): 150–164; E. E. Jones, G. C. Wood, and G. A. Quattrone, "Perceived Variability of Personal Characteristics in In-Groups and Out-Groups: The Role of Knowledge and Evaluation," *Personality and Social Psychology Bulletin* 7 (1981): 523–528; Charles M. Judd and Bernadette Park, "Out-Group Homogeneity: Judgments of Variability at the Individual and Group Levels," *Journal of Personality and Social Psychology* 54 (1988): 778–788; P. W.

Linville and E. E. Jones, "Polarized Appraisals of Out-Group Members," *Journal of Personality and Social Psychology* 38 (1980): 689–703; Brian Mullen and L. Hu, "Perceptions of Ingroup and Outgroup Variability: A Meta-Analytic Integration," *Basic and Applied Social Psychology* 10 (1989): 233–252; Thomas M. Ostrom, Sandra L. Carpenter, Constantine Sedikides, and Fan Li, "Differential Processing of In-Group and Out-Group Information," *Journal of Personality and Social Psychology* 64 (1993): 21–34.

10. David Barsamian, "Albert Mokhiber: Cultural Images, Politics, and Arab Americans," *Z Magazine* (May 1993): 46–50. Reprinted in *Ethnic Groups,* vol. 4, ed. Eleanor Goldstein (Boca Raton, FL: Social Issues Resources Ser., 1994), art. no. 73.

11. Ziva Kunda and Bonnie Sherman-Williams, "Stereotypes and the Construal of Individuating Information," *Personality and Social Psychology Bulletin* 19 (1993): 97.

12. John J. Seta and Catherine E. Seta, "Stereotypes and the Generation of Compensatory and Noncompensatory Expectancies of Group Members," *Personality and Social Psychology Bulletin* 19 (1993): 722–731.

13. C. Neil Macrae, Alan B. Milne, and Galen V. Bodenhausen, "Stereotypes as Energy-Saving Devices: A Peek Inside the Cognitive Toolbox," *Journal of Personality and Social Psychology* 66 (1994): 37–47.

14. Gordon W. Allport, *The Nature of Prejudice* (New York: Macmillan, 1954).

15. John F. Dovidio, John C. Brigham, Blair T. Johnson, and Samuel L. Gaertner, "Stereotyping, Prejudice, and Discrimination: A Closer Look," in *Stereotypes and Stereotyping*, ed. C. Neil Macrae, Charles Stangor, and Miles Hewstone (New York: Guilford, 1996), 276–319.

16. Richard W. Brislin, *Cross-Cultural Encounters: Face-to-Face Interaction* (New York: Pergamon, 1981), 42–49.

17. Teun A. van Dijk, *Communicating Racism: Ethnic Prejudice in Thought and Talk* (Newbury Park, CA: Sage, 1987).

18. For a discussion of the effects of racism on various groups of people, see *Racism in America: Opposing Viewpoints,* ed. William Dudley and Charles Cozic (San Diego: Greenhaven, 1991).

19. Robert Blauner, *Racial Oppression in America* (New York: Harper & Row, 1972), 112.

20. Dalmas A. Taylor, "Race Prejudice, Discrimination, and Racism," in *Social Psychology,* ed. A. Kahn, E. Donnerstein, and M. Donnerstein (Dubuque, IA: Wm. C. Brown, 1984); cited in Phyllis A. Katz and Dalmas A. Taylor, "Introduction," in *Eliminating Racism: Profiles in Controversy,* ed. Phyllis A. Katz and Dalmas A. Taylor (New York: Plenum, 1988), 6.

21. Katz and Taylor, 7.

22. Blauner, note 19.

23. James M. Jones, "Racism in Black and White: A Bicultural Model of Reaction and Evolution," in *Eliminating Racism: Profiles in Controversy,* ed. Phyllis A. Katz and Dalmas A. Taylor (New York: Plenum, 1988), 130–131.

24. Jones, 118–126.

25. Katz and Taylor, note 20, 7.

26. Jenny Yamoto, "Something About the Subject Makes It Hard to Name," in *Race, Class, and Gender in the United States: An Integrated Study,* 2nd ed., ed. Paula S. Rothenberg (New York: St. Martin's, 1992), 58.

27. For discussions of racism and prejudice, see Benjamin P. Bowser, Gale S. Auletta, and Terry Jones, *Confronting Diversity Issues on Campus* (Newbury Park, CA: Sage, 1994); John C. Brigham, "College Students' Racial Attitudes," *Journal of Applied Social Psychology* 23 (1993): 1933–1967; Richard W. Brislin, "Prejudice and Intergroup Communication," in *Intergroup Communication,* ed. William B. Gudykunst (London: Edward Arnold, 1986), 74–85; Brislin (1981), 42–49; Charles E. Case, Andrew M. Greeley, and Stephan Fuchs, "Social Determinants of Racial Prejudice," *Sociological Perspectives* 32 (1989): 469–483; Samuel L. Gaertner and John F. Dovidio, "The Aversive Form of Racism," in *Prejudice, Discrimination and Racism: Theory and Research,* ed. John F. Dovidio and Samuel L. Gaertner (New York: Academic,

1986), 61–89; David Milner, "Racial Prejudice," in *Intergroup Behavior,* ed. John C. Turner and Howard Giles (Chicago: U. Chicago, 1981), 102–143; Albert Ramirez, "Racism Toward Hispanics: The Culturally Monolithic Society," in *Eliminating Racism: Profiles in Controversy,* ed. Phyllis A. Katz and Dalmas A. Taylor (New York: Plenum, 1988), 137–157; David O. Sears, "Symbolic Racism," in *Eliminating Racism: Profiles in Controversy,* ed. Phyllis A. Katz and Dalmas A. Taylor (New York: Plenum, 1988), 53–84; Key Sun, "Two Types of Prejudice and Their Causes," *American Psychologist* 48 (1993): 1152–1153; Ian Vine, "Inclusive Fitness and the Self-System: The Roles of Human Nature and Sociocultural Processes in Intergroup Discrimination," in *The Sociobiology of Ethnocentrism: Evolutionary Dimensions of Xenophobia, Discrimination, Racism, and Nationalism,* ed. Vernon Reynolds, Vincent Falger, and Ian Vine (London: Croom Helm, 1987), 60–80.

28. Brigham, 1934.

29. Troy Duster, "Understanding Self-Segregation on the Campus," *The Chronicle of Higher Education,* September 25, 1991: B2.

Richard Morris, John Sanchez, and Mary Stuckey confront directly arguments made in response to the controversies surrounding the use of Indian names as mascots for sports teams. Taking as their text Internet responses that were initially written in opposition to Native Americans' objections to the appropriation of Indian names in athletics, Richard, John, and Mary argue passionately for a recognition of the ongoing, systematic, and insidious racism that underlies the commercial use of Indian names in modern-day America. Because their article captures the dilemmas and difficulties of living in a multicultural society, their arguments may make some people uncomfortable.

16 Why Can't They Just Get Over It?

Richard Morris, John Sanchez, and Mary E. Stuckey[1]

> When I go around America and I see the bulk of the white people, they do not feel oppressed; they feel powerless. When I go amongst my people, we do not feel powerless; we feel oppressed. (John Trudell, Santee Dakota (Sioux), as quoted in Churchill & Vander Wall, 1988, 388)

In 1763, British colonists, many of whom owed their lives to the kindness and generosity of nearby members of the Lenni Lanape nation,[2] repaid that kindness and generosity by knowingly sending their benefactors smallpox-infected blankets; their "gift" had "the desired effect" of killing nearly all of their neighbors and rendering the nearby lands conveniently "vacant" (O'Brien, 1989, 47). In 1811, members of the U.S. Army celebrated their victory over Tecumseh, the great Shawano[3] leader, in the last battle of what Bil Gilbert has called the "first American civil war" by skinning Tecumseh and awarding various pieces of his skin to the troops as trophies of the battle. In 1864, the men led by Kit Carson cut off the breasts of Diné[4] women and played catch with them while ridiculing the people they had thus wantonly butchered as "savage" and "uncivilized." In 1891, shortly after the much valorized and romanticized seventh Cavalry slaughtered more than 300 unarmed Minneconjou[5] men, women, children, and infants at Wounded Knee in South Dakota as retribution for their earlier defeat at the hands of Sitting Bull, the United States government awarded 21 medals of honor to soldiers who had "distinguished" themselves in the massacre.

Roughly one hundred years after the massacre at Wounded Knee, as thousands of fans gathered in Cleveland to commemorate the fiftieth anniversary of Jackie Robinson's entrance into major league baseball and the "breaking of the color barrier," the grinning visage of Cleveland's mascot, Chief Wahoo, pervaded the proceedings. As the image of a smiling Indian[6] boy unrelentingly served as the iconographic representative for a carpet company's sale at a local store in Memphis, Tennessee, mainstream society endlessly reinvented the "Indian Wars" in film and on television through presentations of media heroes who continued to fight hordes of screaming European Americans who were pretending to be savage Indians. Against this fantastic backdrop, children in towns and cities across Native America once again returned home in tears that reflected yet another torment-filled day brought about simply because—unlike Chief Wahoo, the Mohawk Carpet boy, and Hollywood's savages—they *are* Indian.

What unites such events and phenomena is not simply that they poignantly characterize the longstanding relationship between Indians and the larger society. Because the history and lived experiences of Native Americans (and others,[7] needless to say) are so incoherent and unintelligible in public memory, they are typically unavailable for individual reflection and/or consideration, which allows members of the dominant society—earnestly, and with little hope of arriving at a satisfactory answer—to pose questions like the one that titles this essay. With only a distorted context, which was created primarily to bolster nationalism and obscure harsh and often reprehensible realities, and with little or no understanding or appreciation of the lived experiences of contemporary Native Americans, members of the mainstream are left to conclude that Native Americans can't get over "it" because they are hampered by one or more serious intellectual, cultural, or character flaws.

These are difficult issues, embodying as they do many of the racial and cultural tensions that have come to define our time. Rather than treat the question that titles this essay lightly so as to avoid such tensions, however, we think serious consideration of the problems, meanings, and misunderstandings behind the question will prove considerably more illuminating. Drawing on our own experiences, the experiences of friends and family, and various scholarly works, we want to consider some remarks that citizens offered in response to a *USA Weekend* Internet poll.[8] Before turning to our analysis of the issues, however, we think it important to offer up several preliminary observations about this poll.

First, we selected this particular poll precisely because, as we explain in greater detail below, it focuses on what many regard as a "trivial" issue—namely, whether sports teams should use mascots and/or team names that Native Americans find offensive.[9] Second, we have retained the original spelling and syntax, not to put the writers of these opinions in a poor light but because we want to preserve the authors' intentions and because we recognize that members of the cybercommunities that occupy the Internet typically regard such matters as unimportant. Third, the real and oftentimes heated opinions recorded by this poll need to be considered thoroughly if we are to understand the equally real and heated issues from which they emerge. Finally, 33 percent of the 2005 people who weighed in with their opinions "think a sports team should change its name, mascot, or both because Native Americans find them objectionable," while 66 percent "think a sports team should not change its name, mascot, or both simply because Native Americans find them objectionable." With these points in mind, we now want to give serious consideration to a series of typical responses.

It's an Honor

As the following passage illustrates, many of those who responded to the Internet poll insisted that Indians should feel honored by being chosen to represent sports teams:

> Being chosen as a symbol that represents a team should be considered a compliment. Who would choose a symbol that was derogatory to the team image. The comic Logos are nothing more than caricatures that are eye pleasing. Tell protesters to find a cause worth fighting for they are what people are laughing at not Chief Yahoo. (Butch vandiver Anniston, Alabama)

Of the various things one might say about this response, two are immediately important. First, this individual clearly believes that he knows far better than Indians do what is and is not complimentary. The widespread belief that Indians are intellectually inferior serves as the basis for a great many such remarks, of course; but here that belief serves, first and foremost, to announce that Indians have neither the intellectual capacity nor the right to make such judgments for themselves. Paternalistically, such a response serves to "correct" those with "poor" analytical abilities, who cannot see that what they "think" is racist isn't racist at all.

Beyond the obvious paternalism, however, is a form of disrespect that is difficult to fathom. Allow us to step out of our authorial character for a moment and direct a question to you, the reader: If your mother (or father or anyone else for whom you have great respect) asked you not to refer to her in a particular way, would you seriously "correct" her by informing her that you planned to continue to refer to her in the same way and that if she were "smarter," she would be able to recognize that the reference is "really" a compliment, regardless of how she felt about the matter? We think not.

Why is the same thing not true in the present case? Because as long as individuals continue to insist that Indians are incapable of making sound judgments, they can also continue to insist that more complicated issues (e.g., land management, local government issues, resource management, and so on) are well beyond the judgmental capacities of Indians. Such a belief serves as both justification and as motive for insisting that Indians should remain "wards" of the state; so long as the state regards Indians as "wards," the state can continue to make decisions that benefit non-Indians. In order to retain the state's power to make decisions for Indians, then, it is imperative that people continue to believe and attempt to persuade others to believe that Indians are not the intellectual equals of non-Indians. Continually representing Indians as childish and less than human—as cartoonish, as buffoons, as savages, as primitive—significantly aids in maintaining the absurd but widespread belief that Indians are too incompetent even to run their own lives.

This Is Trivial

Another type of response that people often articulated in the Internet poll is that naming teams after Indians is a nonissue, as the following passage illustrates:

> What has the world come to? We have thousands of people arguing about whether a name, a grouping of letters, is offensive or not. People question everyday what the "PC" term for blacks or Asians is. I am ashamed to hear this. The name Redskins or Indians isn't used to be offensive, it is used to suggest a feeling of strength. Men like Geronimo and Crazy Horse were true men and the sports team simply wish to capture that feeling. This whole argument is ridiculous to the point of insult. With millions of people starving in the U.S. and abroad, wars raging, killing innocent people, and corrupt men ruthlessly running governments and ruining lives, can't you find something more important to fight for? Shame on you. (Scott Alexander Hartsville, SC)

Like the previous passage, this passage presumes that Indians are incapable of knowing what does and does not honor them and, thus, preserves the right of non-Indians to disrespect Indians for material purposes. Here, however, two additional issues serve to justify the author's conclusion. The first issue emerges in the fifth sentence, where the author subtly obscures and berates the existence of contemporary Indians by drawing attention to famous Indians of the past. Presumably, "Men like Geronimo and Crazy Horse," who lived long ago, would have been "honored" by the fact that sports teams bear "Indian" names and mascots; whereas the poor contemporary counterparts of these great relics of the past presumably have proved that they are not "true men" (or "true women") since they find such things offensive. We have no evidence whatsoever to indicate that Geronimo or Crazy Horse (or anyone else, for that matter) would have thought any such thing, of course; but that is of little concern to the author. What apparently is of great concern, on the other hand, is the moral distinction between those who are and those who are not "true men." The markers are obvious: "true [Indian] men" belong to the past and, like the author, would have had the moral integrity to know what is honorable and what is not. If any contemporary Indians wish to distinguish themselves as honorable, therefore, they must adopt attitudes like those that distinguish the author. Put simply, anyone who has moral integrity is distinguishable because, like the author, he is a white male.

The second issue is more conspicuous: When juxtaposed with issues such as starvation, wars, murder, corruption, and the like, the fact that sports teams bear "Indian names" and represent themselves through cartoonish mascots must be regarded as trivial and a waste of time. Along with feeding into the belief that Indians aren't smart enough to see what "true men" would be able to see without any difficulty (e.g., that being turned into a mascot is an honor), the implication here is that "true men" would spend their time in more worthwhile ways. And there is a ring of truth to this, which is what makes the argument enticing. Presumably, then, the author (and others who resort to this argument) would be willing to grant that his next pay raise, his children's education and health, his home, the death of a friend, and a thousand other "personal" issues are not worthy of his time (or ours) since they pale in comparison to global issues.

In the grand scheme of things, of course, turning Indians into mascots is *not* an earth-shattering issue. Solving world hunger would be of far greater benefit than changing the names of sports teams. But choosing between one or the other is not the point. We need not address *either* one or the other issue. Presenting a false dichotomy thus turns out to be a ruse since this is a reasonable choice only insofar as it reveals an ideological predisposition toward other human beings: Human beings should *neither* be treated with disrespect *nor* be expected to starve.

Rather, the question before us concerns a matter of balance. Consider the matter this way: Suppose there are 100,000 negative images and 100,000 positive images of a certain group, where each image weighs one pound. Sensibility dictates that adding another image of one sort or the other would not significantly upset the balance. But when there are 100,000 negative images and 100 positive images of the same group, the addition of even one more negative image of that group represents the weight of all 100,001 negative images. Even in "the grand scheme of things," this kind of imbalance is impermissible in any society that considers itself just.

I'm Not a Racist

A third typical response from those who participated in the Internet poll represents a defensive posture that reveals how deeply they felt the need to announce that they were not racist:

> I think this is ridiculous. I can't see this as being disrespectful. I've struggled most of my life with the issue of race in our world and pride myself on not referring to anyone in any type of stereotype. There are many teams that have been named after all sorts of peoples, even one that's been named after a blue collar worker (Packers). I've talked to many Native Americans, and I'm sorry

for using that title because some find that disrespectful. It's a never ending battle. Stop singling yourselves out and learn to join the global community, and not try to find fault in everything, try to look for good instead. I don't find the Cowboys, Patriots, Piropits, Padreas, Vikings, Yankees, Fighting Irish, Orange Men, 49ers, Pakers, Giants, disrespectful, there are names for people of strength, courage, as is Indians, Redskins, and Warriors, (the latter being the most obvious) I don't see anything disrespectful about being related to that. (Bruce Phoenix)

Like the previous two responses, this response emerges from and seeks to perpetuate the beliefs that Indians are not sufficiently intelligent or moral to make sound judgments and that such a "trivial" matter would not emerge if those who complain about such things would simply think in larger terms (i.e., globally). But the impetus for this response appears to derive from a fear that some might think that turning Indians into mascots is a racist activity and, therefore, that its supporters are racist by association. This is a curious fear, particularly if the activity *isn't* racist. Yet, because there is no way to escape the fact that this is a racist activity, a great many people, like this author, find themselves in the awkward position of having to insist that they are not racist and that an obviously racist activity is also not racist.

Although one might conclude that such responses serve simply to cover over individual racism and/or feelings of guilt, there is a deeper matter afoot here. Assume that individuals who employ such responses earnestly believe that racism is wrong and that their position is *not* racist. Assume further that they are genuinely surprised to learn that such activities are unavoidably racist. How is it that someone could not see the obvious parallel between naming a sports team, say, the Naperville Niggers, the Susanville Sluts, the Jacksonsonville Jews, the Redding Racists, the Sacramento Spics, the Memphis Mysoginists, the Hoboken Honkies, or the Chico Chinks and other equally racist and offensive names such as the Washington Redskins, the Atlanta Braves, the Cleveland Indians, the Kansas City Chiefs, or the (insert the name of your local high school) Warriors? How is it, in other words, that individuals can so readily see the obvious racism and sexism embedded in some names and yet not see the obvious racism embedded in names and mascots associated with Indians?

The answer, unfortunately, is that racism directed at Indians is still very much socially acceptable and systematically encouraged. Think of the cigar shops and restaurants that feature wooden Indians; of the textbooks that not only exclude Indian achievements but also continue to portray Indians as stupid and lazy and drunken while simultaneously portraying Cortez, Columbus, Andrew Jackson, Custer, and a host of others who made their livelihoods from murdering Indians as "bold," "courageous," "fearless," and fundamentally good human beings (see, for example, Knopp, 1997); of the films and television shows that slide between portraying Indians as depraved, noble, and/or mystical; of the businesses that use Indians or caricatures of Indians to sell their products; of the fact that the United States government continues to run and ruin the lives of Indians and Indian resources, as if the government were still at "war" with Indians. The fact that such negative images of Native Americans are so pervasive is *not* a sign of their acceptability but a sign that racism toward Native Americans is pervasively accepted.

We Won!

Another response that merits attention insists that Indians have no right to complain about such matters (or presumably any matters) because they are "conquered" peoples:

> I tend to think that all this noise about mascots offending certain groups of people is taking up valuable time and effort that could be directed at solving important issues. And besides the indians lost the war and therefore it is our right to make fun of them. (At least we gave them welfare and a place to live) (Bill Smith, El Paso Texas)

Like previous respondents, this respondent insists that such matters are trivial. Beyond that appeal, however, the author approaches the matter with a firm, perhaps even calcified sense of "history" that is no doubt reinforced by both popular and "official" mythologies, which consistently have portrayed and continue to portray the "winning of the West" as a "war" in which the "superior" forces of a "superior" people inevitably conquered the "inferior" forces of an "inferior" people. Rarely in such accounts does one find acknowledgment that this supposed contest was conducted primarily through the agencies not of warfare but of deceit, dishonesty, diseases introduced by European invaders, calculated murder by military forces (often of unarmed men, women, children, and infants), and ruinous butchery by citizens. Even more rarely do we find non-Indians willing to acknowledge that Native Americans are not and never were in any sense inferior to the people who willingly and, in a deplorably high number of documentable cases, happily committed such atrocities.

On the contrary, the author here even points to the supposed "generosity" of the "conquerors" toward the "conquered." Like many other people, the author's misunderstanding of the relationship between Native nations and the United States government allows him to believe that the government is doing what it does out of a sense of generosity rather than out of a series of obligations incurred as a result of explicit international agreements. This is how stolen and ceded lands become a gift and how financial remuneration becomes welfare. Such a reversal of actualities not only allows individual citizens (including politicians) to boast of the government's great generosity toward Indians, it allows them to indict Indians for being ungrateful and lazy. Only when people come to understand the *international* relationship between Native nations and the United States do they begin to understand that the government has taken a great deal more than it has given or will ever give.

I Didn't Do It

Another kind of response that people who participated in the Internet poll often articulated is that they are not responsible for past injustices. As one respondent put it,

> I think the red man is going too far to have these things done. It was their and our ancestors that done the trading for properties and principal so we could have the right for this freedom. So, Mr. Red Man get off of the other people and the government for what our ancestors did before our time. Thank you. (LeRoy Harder, Kenton, Ohio)

There is in such responses a curious distancing from history, as if the things that make life what it is for any given group are so distant that they could not possibly have any impact on the lives of contemporary members of that group. This brings to mind an equally curious situation in which one of the authors found himself. During a lecture, a member of the audience stood to address a question to the speaker: "If my grandfather was a horse thief, and even if my father was a horse thief," the man wanted to know, "does that make me a horse thief?"

The response came easily and with a smile: "I don't know. Do you still have the horses?"

Clearly, many members of the mainstream are utterly unaware that they *do* still have the horses—that stolen land, stolen resources, threatened sovereignties, destructive policies, unilaterally broken treaties, and the like do not cease to be stolen, threatened, destructive, or broken merely with the passage of time. Moreover, these same people seem equally unaware that the sorts of unethical activities they so comfortably place in a "distant" past not only are *not* part of a "distant" past, but also are incessant. Not a day goes by when Native American lands, resources, treaties, sovereignty, and rights are not threatened; not an hour goes by when Native American lives are not put at risk by policies and actions that have been in place and ongoing from the beginning of that "distant" past; not a minute goes by when individual Indians do not face individual and systemic acts of racism and oppression. If those who offer up such responses genuinely believe that the "distant" past has or should have no bearing on the conduct of contemporary affairs, then surely they would be equally willing to grant that, say, the Bill of Rights does not apply to them because it was written "before our time."

I'm an Indian

Another kind of response that emerged frequently came from people claiming Indian heritage:

> KEEP IT!! I am part American Indian, and I do not find offense with the name of the team. I am not a baseball fan, but think the name deal is going too far,

surely there are more important things to worry about than the name of a sports team. I get tired of the big deal made about the "White Man" doing so many bad things to the Natives here. They also brought us many things that make our lives so much better today than they were then. From the people who invaded our country we gained metal, the wheel, a written language and much more. I am Cherokee and Chactaw with some "White" thrown in for flavor. I like to feel some of my ancestors were on the boat and some of them met it. The one thing we all have in common is we are "Americans." Go "Cowboys"! (Anna, Livermore, Ca.)

There is a curious logic at work in such responses. In one sense, the response invites us to believe that "being" Indian is merely a matter of having a particular ancestry—certainly not a matter of living according to specific codes, of participating in particular ways of life, of maintaining certain beliefs, or even of physically and spiritually belonging to the nation from which her heritage derives. This is rather like someone claiming to be an automobile mechanic because his or her parents are or were automobile mechanics. The parallel is incomplete, of course; without intending any disrespect to automobile mechanics, *being* Indian involves considerably more than knowledge—even extensive knowledge—about a particular subject. Individuals who rely on such "blood logic"—even when their claim to a particular heritage is true—are being either disingenuous, at best, or simply deceitful, at worst.

In another sense, such a response invites readers to believe that the author is in a position to speak for *all* Native Americans. Alternatively, one also might insist that some Indian somewhere doesn't find a particular activity offensive. The existence of such an "Indian" voice presumably serves to negate the fact that other people *do* find the same activities hurtful. The complete implausibility—in fact, pretentiousness—of either sense of this claim is obvious, given the fact that there are more than 500 distinct Native American cultures. No one, regardless of lineage, speaks for all Native Americans, and alert readers will instantly be on guard against anyone who claims to speak for all the members of *any* group.

Not Enough "Real" Indians Object

A related response comes from those who insist that a sufficient number of Native Americans must object to such practices or the claim is empty. As one respondent put it:

Your question is emotionally loaded and designed to get a yes response. On what possible basis can you say that Native Americans find this offensive? Certainly not because one woman in Santa Fe alleges that to be the case. Come on—give it up. Your readers see through your cheap ploy. . . . How many demonstrators in Cleveland today—not very many I'll wager. In fact, I'll bet that I can count them on the fingers of my hand. . . . (Maury Blu Kalihi)

Among other things, what appears to be behind such a response is the belief that something must be offensive to a sufficient number of people and that the people who register their objections must be authenticated—presumably so that "inauthentic" people won't be counted. The numbers argument, of course, allows people to argue that change can occur only after a full accounting. Knowing full well that Indians will not be gathering at someone's home to take a vote on the matter in the foreseeable future, people who use this argument apparently believe that they have "legitimately" forestalled resolution of the issue. On the one hand, we frequently hear individuals defending this posture on the basis of fairness: In all fairness, the argument goes, we must wait until we *know* that such activities are in fact hurting sufficient numbers of people. What remains unclear is how stopping an obviously hurtful activity immediately would in any way be unjust. Then, again, no one seems willing to say just how many constitutes a "sufficient" number.

On the other hand, we just as frequently hear people defending this stance on the basis of effort: Changing the way we refer to and think about Indians, the argument goes, would require too much effort. Here, the exact amount of "effort" remains unclear, as does the matter of what might be the consequences of expending "so much" effort. Whatever the defense, the numbers strategy consistently results in maintaining the status quo, prohibiting any sort of advancement in cultural and racial relations, perpetuating ignorance among yet another generation, and silencing the voices of those who are victimized by society's systematic racism.

And if the numbers argument fails, the fallback position is that the numbers are not representative of "real" Indians. So even if someone could demonstrate that a large percentage of Native Americans does in fact object to racist activities that debase and demean Indians, one can always argue that the "vote" was "rigged" or improperly conducted. Stated back to back, these twin arguments effectively make it impossible for any minority group to be heard. Again, simple matters of respect would dictate that something that denigrates an entire group of people—regardless of whether the members of that group are allowed to voice their discontent—has no place in a society that continues to think itself "superior."

This Is a Matter of Free Speech

A final type of response that respondents infrequently articulated in the poll but that we have heard often enough to merit comment is that team names and mascots are protected by the Bill of Rights:

> I am sure that some people may find this a little rude, or the other word I can't remember, but this IS America. I feel that the logo, etc. is protected under our great Bill of Rights. If the N.A. used a "white man" would they ("white men") get upset? I doubt it! (Chris Jingozian, Norman, OK)

Freedom of speech is a powerful and much beloved concept in the United States—rightly so. Throughout the years citizens have turned time and again to the First Amendment, often as their only defense against assaults on other rights and privileges. At the same time, we recognize that there necessarily are limits even on this exceedingly important right. Unless they wish to incur often very stiff penalties, for example, individuals cannot yell "FIRE!" in crowded places, cannot speak or write lies or rumors about others, cannot utter certain expressions toward others without reprisal, cannot advocate the violent overthrow of the government or the assassination of government officials, and so forth. What counterbalances our right to freedom of expression is the rights that others have to live their lives unmolested; your right to stick out your arm, in other words, ends where the other person's face begins. Since the kinds of team names and mascots we have been considering here obviously serve to molest very identifiable individuals and communities, the First Amendment unequivocally does not apply.

But there is a further curiosity about this line of reasoning that also applies to each of the other responses we have considered. If team names and mascots are so obviously trivial, so blatantly unimportant, why would people trot out such a cherished principle as the First Amendment—indeed, why would they be so fervent in articulating their positions? Surely people who honestly believe that an issue is utterly insignificant do not register their opinions with such force, such intensity, and in such great numbers. Part of the answer, of course, is that these *are* significant issues; those who so fiercely advance arguments that either wittingly or unwittingly preserve the dominant society's "right" to demean, debase, and disrespect Native Americans do so precisely because these are significant issues. And they are significant issues precisely because, by preserving this so-called "right," members of the dominant society also thereby preserve their "right" to keep the horses.

Conclusions

> I often feel like I'm invisible to the larger society. The things I represent are relegated to a position so far in the past that they might as well not be there. It's like a curio, a museum piece, a throwback to some childlike form of life— you're alive and you're Indian, aren't you cute? (Janine Pease Pretty on Top, 1990 NIEA educator of the year, President of Little Big Horn College, as quoted in Crozier-Hogle, et al., 1997)

We do not suppose that the responses we have considered here are exhaustive. Nor do we imagine that our analyzes of those responses are in any sense complete. On the contrary, we recognize that there is a great deal more to say. Even within the confines of such a brief discussion, however, several conclusions stand out.

First, it is important to understand that much of society's racism and racist activities is conducted beneath the surface and that individuals often are completely unaware of their racism or that their activities are racist and perpetuate systematic racism. We offer this not as an excuse, but as a clue. In one sense, it is a clue that allows us to understand some of the racial tensions that have come to mark our time. Those who are the objects of such racism sometimes seem "hypersensitive" because they deal with racism and racist activities continuously, while those who are unaware of their own contributions to such tensions are often confounded and frustrated because they are not trained to see or hear or feel the Other's pain.

In another sense, our clue points to a harsh reality: Racism in the United States is systematically perpetuated despite the best intentions and exertions of a great many people of all colors and cultures. How is it that successive generations have continued to hold essentially the same distorted views of Native Americans, despite the looming mountain of evidence to the contrary? How is it that, as a whole, the United States has made remarkably little progress in the way the mainstream citizenry regard and treat Native Americans?

A partial answer to these questions is that, on the whole, members of the dominant culture in the United States have learned how to substitute guilt for action. The relationship of guilt to action is much like the relationship of sympathy to empathy: The former is a counterfeit, a fraud of the latter. Sympathy is a greeting-card response to crisis, whereas empathy is an involvement in crisis; sympathy is the expression or feeling of a "heartfelt" concern, while empathy *is* concern. Similarly, guilt is a superficial response to turmoil, whereas action requires a great deal more. And the reason that guilt so readily substitutes for action is that the stakes are high. Consider but one among a myriad of possible examples: Were the United States government to live up to the more than 400 *international* treaties it has with Indian nations, there would be an enormous redistribution of wealth, population, and power.

Another part of the answer is that members of the dominant culture generally have adopted a view of time that disallows continuity. Collapsing time privileges a particular view of "history," as well as particular views of what are and are not important issues. This, in turn, privileges the status quo since one must accept the status quo's terms of debate to enter into the argument. But the terms of the debate *are* the argument; having accepted these terms, the debate is already over before it even begins. By definition, no other position is possible. Indian preferences regarding team names and mascots (or anything else) are inadmissible because they are not expressions of the majority or because "they lost the war" or because members of the dominant society do not wish to be inconvenienced. Thus, no one "really" bears responsibility for the continued abrogation of Indian sovereignty, for the continued violations of treaty rights, and for the continued political, spiritual, and cultural oppression that Indian people face every day. No one "really" needs to worry about these things if members of the mainstream can continue to convince themselves that, contrary to all the available evidence, these issues were "finally" resolved at Wounded Knee 100 years ago.

Such constructions create and sustain generalizations about Native American communal and individual identities, and these generalizations contribute mightily to the confusion surrounding those identities. The tendency to render "Indian" as a generic category thus works to conflate the enormous cultural diversity that is Native America into one amorphous category, which in turn further violates and contains individual Native American identities and experiences. Like the European American insistence on referring to Indian nations as "tribes" as a keystone of Native identity, collapsing all Native nations into a singular and readily identifiable "Indian" image allows for both containment and control of that identity and the persons subsumed by that identity. Such a collapsing of Native identities also allows for the imposition of European American–generated categories on Native experiences in ways that transform and delegitimate those experiences.

Do these things have real consequences for real people? Do these issues go deeper than the tears of a "few" children? Beyond question. Consider some statistics: "Recent research points to Native American student performance that is below the national average: 52 percent finish high school; 17 percent attend college; 4 percent graduate from college and 2 percent attend graduate school" (Myers, 1996–1997). When barely half of a growing and thriving population manages to survive high school, clearly something is wrong. According to all the available data, what is wrong is that schools are not prepared for, nor do they deal well with, their Indian students (Sanchez, Stuckey, & Morris, 1997).

Indian children—specifically the 85 percent who are educated by non-Indian teachers in public schools—continually are forced to decide between their resident tribal identity and assimilation into the dominant culture. In most cases these are children who are enrolled members of federally recognized Native nations, who have been attending traditional tribal councils and ceremonies since birth, who have names that reflect their cultural heritage, who speak and pray in the language of their nation, and who are intimately knowledgeable about the customs and traditions of their nation. Their parents and grandparents and aunts and uncles typically hold traditionally significant positions within their nation.

Forced to choose between their national identity and an alien identity that ultimately will help to alienate them from their own family members and friends, Indian children experience severe ethnostress from the beginning to the end of their schooling. Gradually, sometimes almost imperceptibly, they either give in to the incessant pressures from school teachers and administrators and classmates to assimilate, thereby replacing their national identity with a "white" identity they can never fully claim, or they turn away from educational processes that have no room for difference. Yet even those who turn away too often are forever changed. Their eating habits change; their attention turns away from learning science and math and reading and toward escapist activities that no longer challenge their minds or threaten their identities. Escapist activities in too many cases become ways of life—not because of any inherent character flaw or cultural deficiency, but because they must live their lives in the midst of constant racist assaults on their cultural identities, people, character, laws, traditions, customs, appearance, religion, government, and existence. Escapism becomes a form of self-medication: "Lack of resolution of the repressed issues are continuously manifested in symptoms that require some type of medication. If the person does not medicate him/herself, then the only defense left in the light of pain is dissociation. The person no longer has an awareness of who or where s/he is, thus rendering them nonexistent" (Duran and Duran, 1995, p. 40).

After more than 500 years, Indians continue to experience pressures and stresses imposed by the dominant culture that make it exceedingly difficult to maintain their religions, traditions, customs, languages, and national identities. What happens when there are no more Indians to assimilate? How do we stop this continual, shameful assault on Indian cultures? What would you do? What *will* you do?

NOTES

1. All authors contributed equally to this essay, and no inferences should be drawn regarding the order of authorship.
2. Otherwise known as the Delaware Nation.
3. Otherwise known as the Shawnee Nation.
4. Otherwise known as the Navajo Nation.
5. Otherwise known as the Sioux Nation.
6. We use the terms "Indian/s" and "Native American/s" interchangeably.
7. Although we restrict ourselves to our experiences as and with Native Americans, we feel confident that many (if not all) of our observations and conclusions apply equally to other marginalized or oppressed groups and individuals.
8. The purpose of the poll was to determine people's opinions about whether certain sports teams should change their logos in response to complaints from Native Americans who find such logos offensive (Quick Poll, 1997).
9. Ward Churchill (1994) provides a superb treatment of these and related issues.

REFERENCES

Bolls, P., Tan, A., & Austin, E. (1997). An exploratory comparison of Native American and Caucasian students' attitudes toward teacher communicative behavior and toward school. *Communication Education, 46*, 198–202.

Churchill, W. (1994). *Indians are us? Culture and genocide in Native North America*. Monroe, Maine: Common Courage Press.

Churchill, W., & Vander Wall, J. (1988). *Agents of repression: The FBI's secret wars against the Black Panther Party and the American Indian Movement*. Boston: South End Press.

Crozier-Hogle, L. Wilson, D., & Leibold, J. (Eds.) (1997). *Surviving in two worlds: Contemporary Native American voices*. Austin, TX: University of Texas Press.

Duran, E. & Duran, B. (1995). *Native American postcolonial psychology*. Albany, NY: SUNY Press.

Gilbert, B. (1989). *God gave us this country: Tekamthi and the first American civil war*. New York: Antheneum.

Knopp, S. (1997). Critical thinking and Columbus: Secondary social studies. *Transformations 8*, 40–65.

Meyers, B. (1996–1997). Keys to retention. *Winds of change college guide, 63:* 65. Boulder, CO: AISES Publishing.

Morris, R. (1997). Educating savages. *Quarterly Journal of Speech, 83,* 152–171.

O'Brien, S. (1989). *American Indian tribal governments*. Norman, OK: University of Oklahoma Press.

Quick Poll. (1997). On Indian mascot issue. http://www.usaweekend.com/cgi-bin/qp1.p1.

Sanchez, J. (1997). *Diversifying America's classroom: A view from Indian country*. Paper presented at the National Communication Association's summer conference on diversity. Washington, DC.

Sanchez, J., Stuckey, M., & Morris, R., (1997). *E pluribus unum: American education and Native American values*. Paper presented at the conference on North American Indian Values: For a New Millennium. Hattiesburg, MS.

What does it mean to be black in the United States? How black is black enough? Mark McPhail and Karen Dace describe the pressures to conform to the prevailing interpretations of political and social events that reflect on a cultural group. Though they write from their experiences as African American scholars, Mark and Karen explore issues that pertain to all cultures. Who can speak for the members of a particular culture? Who can be critical of members of a culture? What social expectations govern what can and cannot be said?

17 Black as We Wanna Be: From Identity Politics to Intercultural Competence

Mark Lawrence McPhail and Karen Lynette Dace

In his book *Bad as I Wanna Be,* Dennis Rodman asserts his right to define his own identity by challenging many of our most basic assumptions about race, gender, and difference. Admired by many, and criticized by just as many others, Rodman discusses his life before and after becoming a celebrity and provides interesting insights into what we will call in this essay "identity politics": that is, the tendency of marginalized or oppressed groups to establish notions of "authentic" identity that are used to determine who is and is not included in the group. For African Americans, identity politics is expressed in the idea that some of us are "not black enough" to be considered a part of "the community," and therefore the insights and observations that we have to offer are neither representative nor relevant. This exclusion creates an identity dilemma that Rodman addresses in these words: "Before I got the fame and the money, I wasn't accepted by black people, and I wasn't accepted by most white people. I wasn't the right color for any situation I found myself in. I'm sure a lot of kids and young people go through that. They think like I did: I want to be the right color."[1]

One of the most important lessons that the study of intercultural communication teaches is that the belief that there is a "right" color is at best wrong and at worst dangerous. Consequently, we wish to explore the issues raised by Rodman and consider how they have affected us both personally and professionally. As intercultural communication scholars (and fans of the Chicago Bulls), we would like to expand on Rodman's insights by examining how students and scholars, when engaging in identity politics, run the risk of rejecting ideas that can increase their understanding of intercultural and interracial communication.

The issues we address are certainly not limited to specific cultures, communities, or shared identities. Rather, our extended story should be viewed more generically, as an exemplar that provides insights into the predominant assumptions about the nature of race, culture, gender, and the prevailing orthodoxy that can be used to silence ideas requiring critical self-reflection within a community. We speak from our own experiences as African American communication scholars who have advanced positions that critically analyze ideas about gender and race in contemporary African American culture. We also speak as scholars whose work has been dismissed and resisted because it explores issues that some do not want us to address.

Our story begins with an essay on interracial communication that we wrote together and was rejected by an intercultural communication anthology because it incorporated "white" scholarship. We then explain how the rejection of that essay evolved into a larger conflict with an editor of the anthology; this experience, we believe, illustrates the danger of identity politics. Finally, we offer some conclusions and suggestions for students and scholars of intercultural communication that we believe will help facilitate a richer and more inclusive agenda for understanding and appreciating identity, difference, and diversity.

The Politics of Inclusivity: Blackness, Whiteness, and Intercultural Exclusivity

The conflict we recount here began several years ago, when we were invited to submit an article to an intercultural communication anthology that solicited essays dealing specifically with biracial relationships. Before submitting the essay we spoke with one of the editors about an idea we had that looked at how communication can function positively in interracial communication. Mark McPhail's portion of the essay focused on how performance could be used to bridge racial divisions, and Karen Dace's portion of the essay examined her friendship with a European American man she had known for several years. Initially we were told that the essay would work well in the anthology; after submitting it, we received an email from the editor who had invited us to submit it that said that it had been received, and that offered a tentative evaluation of our work: "I love it," was the response from this editor, and so we looked forward to the publication of our work.

Several months later, however, we received a letter indicating that the editors could not include our essay in their anthology. We were informed that, after careful consideration and discussion, they had decided the essay would not be appropriate because it incorporated and validated those types of scholarship they felt were at odds with the basic assumptions of their project. Specifically, they criticized Mark's portion of the essay because it affirmed and incorporated the insights of white men and focused on the notion of "empathy," which the editors believed was an inadequate concept for the development of "authentic" intercultural understanding. "Doesn't Mark's personal narrative reinforce the claim that white men espouse 'universal' ideas that 'speak' to everyone, but that persons 'limited' by 'nonwhite' ethnicity can only absorb, not contribute, such universals?" asked one editor. A second added, "Not only is the conceptualization of empathy problematic for us, but also the 'essay ends where it begins, as it hints at how to perform empathy interculturally.' " Although the essay evidently could be read this way, Mark suggested in conversations with both editors that what they had done was basically the same thing they accused white men of doing: rejecting positions because they did not fit into a predetermined agenda. One editor candidly acknowledged that this might well be the case, but the other responded by saying, "I never thought of myself as someone with an agenda."

One thing intercultural communication teaches us, we believe, is that we all have agendas. Fortunately, the essay fit into the agenda of another group of intercultural scholars,[2] who agreed to publish the same essay after minor revisions, none of which involved the critiques we had received from the editors of the first anthology. These latter scholars, whose anthology aimed at integrating the diverse voices of intercultural scholarship (including those of white men), believed that the essay made an important contribution to our understanding of intercultural communication and interaction. Still, we felt that the issues raised by the rejection of the essay by the first group of editors needed to be examined more fully, so we attempted to address them in a second essay, which was presented on a panel at a communication conference. One of the editors of the first anthology was a respondent to that panel. The panel addressed the concerns of African American men as communication scholars, and the invitation to appear on the panel included a quotation from an African American feminist scholar, bell hooks, who suggested that the voices of black women as well as black men need to be heard if we are to "redefine in nonsexist ways the terms of our liberation."

We saw this invitation as an excellent opportunity to incorporate both of our voices in an essay that addressed our concerns about racial exclusivity in intercultural communication. Although we did not mention our earlier essay, we explored how assumptions about the nature of race and gender in African American communication scholarship can be used to silence research that calls for critical self-reflection. We have included both narratives, as they were presented on that panel, below. Our story continues with Karen Dace's narrative, which focuses on issues of gender in contemporary African American culture, and Mark McPhail's, which deals with resistance to the theoretical perspectives he has developed in response to an important concept in African American communication scholarship known as Afrocentricity.

Karen Lynette Dace: Disciplining Black Feminism

In their essay "Disciplining the Feminine," Carole Blair, Julie Brown, and Leslie Baxter examine how scholarly norms in the field of communication can, when accepted uncritically, affirm the notion that "institutional or professional power are deemed superfluous to the substance and character of our scholarly efforts."[3] My own experience, like theirs, suggests otherwise, and I believe that issues of power and control are as much at work in academic institutions and practices as they are in the society as a whole. While their analysis focuses on issues of gender, my concerns relate to those situations in which gender and race intersect, and issues of domination become somewhat more complex. One example of this intersection was revealed in the confirmation hearings for Supreme Court Justice Clarence Thomas, where issues of race, class, and gender were so deeply entwined with each other that issues of power and control became somewhat obscured: for some, the hearings were about male domination; for others, they were about racial discrimination; and for others, the hearings were a site of intraracial conflict. It is this last consideration, I believe, that provides important insights into the problems and possibilities of complicity in intercultural communication inquiry.

My entrance into feminist scholarship as it intersects race began not with the Clarence Thomas Supreme Court confirmation hearings, however, but with the Mike Tyson rape case. Both Clarence Thomas and Anita Hill were vital, vocal, and active members of a conservative power structure that excluded most folks like me—African American and female. Although the hearings were an alarming and sad event in American and African American history, the discourse surrounding Mike Tyson and Desiree Washington (the then 18-year-old woman who charged the boxer with rape) was even more disturbing. Conversations with friends and family revealed sympathy for Tyson and contempt for Washington. An examination of cultural artifacts, including African American publications, music, and television programs, pointed to a deep sense of commitment to Tyson at the expense of Washington. The result of that research was a conference paper titled "Let's Set the Bitch on Fire: The African American Community's Response to Desiree Washington." The title of the paper came from a scene from Spike Lee's film *She's Gotta Have It,* in which several African American women are discussing the film's lead character, a woman named Nola. Nola is depicted as a "threat" to these women, and as they discuss how she should be dealt with, one of the women states "Let's set the bitch on fire." The sentiment seemed similar to the responses that I heard from some of those who criticized Washington, who felt that she somehow constituted a threat to African American unity by accusing Mike Tyson of rape. It was this notion of African American unity that troubled me, since it seemed to suggest that women should be silenced, even dominated, for "the good of the race."

I found that the silencing of women within the race was not simply a matter of patriarchal domination; it also revealed how notions of "black authenticity" obscured issues of gender domination within some segments of various African American communities. In an attempt to understand and challenge this rigid notion of "blackness," I looked to "revolutionary feminist thinking," which according to bell hooks is "more concerned with how sexism and sexist oppression are perpetuated and maintained by all of us, not just men."[4] The paper that emerged provided an analysis of African American discourse concerning the Tyson case. Great and powerful institutions and people, including the National Baptist Convention, Louis Farrakhan, and an assortment of popular cultural institutions, joined together to communicate "community" support for Mike Tyson. As for Washington, the possibility that her accusations were true were discussed within the community. The prevailing messages about her behavior were (1) she should have known what to expect from this "strong, active black man" (the racism inherent in that reasoning was ignored by the speakers) or (2) Washington should remain silent in order to show African American solidarity and support Tyson. Many within the culture seemed "convinced that the struggle to 'save' the black race is really first and foremost about saving the lives of black males."[5]

Writing the paper on Mike Tyson was both therapeutic and enlightening. Ever concerned with uplifting the race, I found that many African Americans, both male and female, made the leap in reasoning that Tyson, too, must be saved and lifted out of the hands of his jailers. He needed the community to rescue him from an unjust judicial system and a certain conviction that would rob him of what could be his most viable boxing years. Tyson was an African American hero, and the discourse suggested that there are far too few African American males who wear that label. I felt that the essay provided some important insights into the complex character of African American responses to situations in which race and gender become intertwined, and that the essay at least provided some useful directions for scholarly inquiry. As the essay evolved from a convention paper to an article submitted for publication, however, I began to see the complexity of the very issue I had attempted to study in the responses of reviewers from two journals, the first of which focused on intercultural communication and the second on issues of gender.

The essay was first presented during a national communication convention in 1994, and it has been submitted to two scholarly journals, one of which rejected the essay outright and the second of which invited revision and resubmission. Perhaps the comments I received after its initial presentation shed some light on my failure to find a publishing outlet. Immediately after the convention presentation and throughout the remainder of the conference, African American women approached me to offer their congratulations on the paper. Many were impressed with my "courage," saying: "I'm so glad you said what you said," or "A lot of us feel that way," or, my personal favorite, "I can't believe you actually wrote what so many of us have been feeling." Reflecting on these remarks, it becomes apparent that these women recognized that the essay made a connection between theory and practice, between revolutionary feminist thought and how it applies to our everyday lives. As scholars we seek to explore, analyze, critique, explain, and sometimes predict. When our explorations, analyses, critiques, explanations, and predictions go against or call into question the status quo or deeply held convictions, they become problematic.

After making revisions and readying the paper for publication (with the assistance of my colleagues), the essay was sent to an intercultural communication journal that emphasizes African American issues, culture, and sensibilities. The first review that arrived (normally all reviews arrive together) charged me with racism, a bias against African American men, and a lack of understanding of the culture. My sense is that the author of that review believed I had to be one of those European American feminists who has no right to explore issues African American. The implication was that no self-respecting or "authentic" black woman would write such an analysis. The reviewer recommended against publishing the analysis because it was "highly generalized," without a "detailed method," and because it "contradicted its own conclusions." The failure of the reviewer to accept feminist analysis, introduced on page one, as an appropriate method was something I had expected. But the tenor of the critique was not: the essay was likened to "a gossip column," and at one point the reviewer asked, "Is this a letter to the editor?" The reviewer rejected the essay as "more a broadside than a piece of scholarly research." The second review arrived several weeks after the first. It contained no remarks or commentary on the manuscript, simply circles on a form identifying the work as "weak" and unworthy of publication.

When sent to a feminist journal, the essay was not rejected; instead, the editor enthusiastically encouraged me to revise the essay, to include more background information about feminist scholarship, and to resubmit it for possible publication. I am in the process of working with these reviews in hopes of finally seeing this piece published. It is apparent that its "acceptance" by the feminist journal is the result of reviewers acknowledging and embracing black feminist scholarship. The analysis of the Mike Tyson rape case was approached from a black feminist standpoint that deconstructs the experiences of oppression and the asymmetrical relationship of power from the perspectives of the women who live such experiences. While the intercultural communication journal claimed to provide a voice for scholars not always available in other places, it became clear that my voice needed to toe a new color line where race, as it intersects gender, is concerned. When that intersection suggests some flaws within African American culture, the author must be reprimanded and silenced. As I attempted to illustrate how complicity undermines intracultural understanding, I encountered an interesting double jeopardy. Indeed, I received the same message that Desiree Washington had received: "To be black is to unite at all cost; you are expendable for the greater cause."

This double jeopardy places African American women and all women of color in the impossible position of having to choose between race or gender. My refusal to make the choice in a manner that satisfied the reviewer of my work offers important insights about how the intersection between race and gender can disrupt our rigid notions of identity. The message I received from my "brothers" was that to be authentically "black" meant to be silent, while my "sisters" heard the authenticity of my voice in their own experiences with gender domination. Like me, they seemed to be more willing to explore how race, culture, and gender might be seen as entwined with each other, and not simply in conflict with one another. Rejected as a "race traitor" by some within the race, I was well received on the other side of the color line and encouraged to contribute my voice to a conversation that continues to challenge our understanding of difference and domination. This is a challenge that I believe intercultural communication students and scholars will increasingly face as we struggle to address the problems and possibilities of gender, race, and ethnicity in communication theory and practice.

Mark Lawrence McPhail: Afrocentricity and Complicity

I first encountered Afrocentric thought while in graduate school, and I found that it offered a powerful commentary on the dominating or "hegemonic" character of traditional Western thought. As I delved deeper into the theories and philosophies associated with Afrocentricity, I began to notice how much of the scholarship associated with it tended to establish and sustain divisions between Afrocentric and Western or "Eurocentric" ways of knowing and being. At the same time, Afrocentric scholarship claimed to be inclusive and integrative, qualities allegedly missing in Eurocentric theories and perspectives. There seemed to be a basic contradiction at work here, and I began to look for connections between Afrocentricity and Eurocentricity. The result was an essay presented at the National Communication Association Convention titled "Afrocentricity and Complicity: An Ethnophilosophical Analysis."

The basic position that I took in the essay was that distinguishing between Afrocentric and Eurocentric thought as essentially different was neither useful nor justifiable. The distinction is not useful because it tends to perpetuate the very tendencies for which Afrocentric theorists criticize Eurocentricity: it creates rigid and sometimes false divisions, and it tends to privilege one position at the expense of the other. The distinction could not be justified because much of the research that influenced the Afrocentric perspective in communication was conducted by Europeans, thereby making distinctions based on racial or ethnic heritage somewhat suspect. I suggested that intercultural communication researchers might instead focus on the points of similarity between the two perspectives, and integrate these points of commonality, so that each position might strengthen or support the other. The individual scheduled to respond to my paper and those of the other members of the panel was an internationally recognized scholar on Afrocentricity, and I expected that whether or not my position was affirmed, it would certainly receive an engaged and insightful critique.

Unfortunately, my expectations were not met, as the scheduled respondent did not appear, and the individual who did respond to my essay basically dismissed it with the statement "everyone knows that Afrocentricity is not hegemonic." He went on, however, to make a much more telling comment that was both troubling and enlightening: troubling because it revealed a peculiarly "Eurocentric" type of racial reasoning, and enlightening because it further supported my thesis. In responding to a critique of Afrocentricity by the African philosopher Anthony Appiah, he remarked that Appiah was "a very troubled man:" "I think," the respondent continued, "that one of his parents is white." Here was an Afrocentric scholar rejecting the scholarship of a respected African philosopher on the basis of a subjective and irrational argument: on the basis of racial classification. This is the same basis upon which Afrocentric scholarship was once rejected: it reflects the same type of racial reasoning that would deny any individual or group a legitimate intellectual voice because of gender or ethnic identity. It was invoked to silence Appiah and, in the process, to silence me.

I continued to work on the essay, however, and submitted it to a scholarly publication in intercultural communication. Almost a year later I received a letter from the editor rejecting the essay, accompanied by a single half-page review recommending major revisions and resubmission. "The irony here is the fact that Afrocentricity seems under attack for its failure to realize an unspecified goal," explained the reviewer, "when, in fact, Afrocentricity, admittedly, more closely reaches the implied goal that (sic) does Eurocentric hegemony." The reviewer went on to suggest that I might be "unfairly ascribing to Afrocentrists" a "deliberateness of motive" by suggesting their complicity in sustaining the "Eurocentric hegemony" they call into question. The reviewer, like the respondent at the convention, accepted the claims of Afrocentric thinkers as axiomatic, that is, as "givens." My critique of those claims, though having some "merit," showed "unclarity of purpose" and failed "to usher in the subtle prescription within the essay, arrived at in its end." Everyone knows that Afrocentricity is not hegemonic. Everyone, evidently, but me.

My lack of knowledge led me to submit the essay again, unrevised, to a "mainstream" journal of communication. My efforts resulted in an "enthusiastic" recommendation that I revise the essay as described by the responses of the editor and two reviewers, one of whom remarked that it was "an important essay that has the potential to transform not only how we think of Afrocentricity and multiculturalism, but also how we conceive of cultural relations." It was an essay, the reviewer wrote, "that should be read by many." Perhaps it will, since the essay has since been published.[6] Regardless of whether the essay is read by many, however, the concerns that motivated me to write it continue to be a focus of my intellectual energies, and in my opinion pose an important challenge to students and scholars of intercultural communication. If the expressed values of Afrocentricity are inclusivity and openness, then those values must be translated into tangible practices. The same is true for the discipline of communication in general, and for intercultural communication inquiry in particular, which can only benefit from increasing the number of our voices that we invite to participate in conversations and dialogues that challenge static notions of difference, identity, and diversity.

Disciplining Blackness: Oppositionality and the "Embrace of Whiteness"

One of the values intercultural communication scholarship promotes is the importance of inclusivity and the valuing of diverse voices. Our story continues through an examination of how the narratives that we presented illustrate how difficult it can be to translate principles into practice, even for communication scholars whose research has emerged as a response to the exclusivity of traditional social science approaches to the study of identity and culture and who emphasize the importance of self-reflexivity in an understanding of difference. Because we believed that the respondent to our panel was one such scholar, we hoped that our essay would be seen as an opportunity to have a public conversation about the tension between inclusivity and exclusivity in intercultural communication research. Although we did not mention the essay that the respondent had rejected earlier, it did come back to haunt us in a very personal and public way. In the response to the essay presented on the panel, Mark was singled out and admonished to "come back to [your] black masculinity," and not to "embrace whiteness." Both of these statements seemed to be coded personal attacks directed at Mark because his wife is European American. This belief was confirmed by another participant on the panel, who said that the respondent had told him that the comments were meant to be "double edged."

When Mark confronted the respondent with the accusation that her critique was a veiled attack on him that was based on her inability to deal with his relationship with his wife, however, he was told that this was a conflict of "intellectual perspectives" that had nothing to do with his personal life. Shortly afterward, an email message was sent out to a public list to which both Mark and Karen are members that explained the respondent's position. In response to Mark's accusation that the comments were directed at his personal life, the respondent wrote:

> Is that true? Is that the "bottom line" of my criticism that, unlike [the other members of the panel], Mark appeared in his paper not as a "live black man" but only as a "disembodied intellectual"—raceless and genderless? Is that all that lies behind my caution to Mark and Karen not to get so lost in the "white embrace" of work that was not well-received, or not universally well received by Black scholars, that they forget that such "white embraces" can be motivated by anti-black intellectual politics?

While the respondent noted that "in a sense [Mark was] correct," the response to the paper was ultimately defined as a conflict of intellectual visions.

That conflict was related back to our earlier essay, and an apparently new issue was raised: why had Mark not, when given the opportunity, written about his relationship with his wife? As the respondent recalls,

> I simply asked if you'd write about a positive, close personal relationship with someone of another race or culture, hoping that you would CHOOSE to write about your marriage. Imagine my surprise when you chose to write about the positive influence on your intellectual development of Robert Penn Warren (a long-dead white male poet!).

Somehow the conversations about the essay that occurred before it was submitted, in which Mark clearly explained what was intended (an earlier version of the essay had been presented publicly at a communication conference, and the respondent was aware of it), and the first email that we had received in which the respondent wrote "I love it," had been erased from memory. Mark was guilty of "the erasure of race" because he had chosen to write about something other than his marriage, and his silence was viewed as an indication of his wife's undue influence, his unwillingness to embrace his own "blackness," and Karen's unwillingness to do the same! The respondent continued:

> After reading that essay, I said to myself, "Mark simply prefers to keep his private life private." Yet I think I read into the fact that you were silent about your marriage in a space where there was the opportunity to speak about it positively, the influence of one of those black man-white woman relationships that I "can't deal with." This was exacerbated by your (and Karen's preference, in both the proposed chapter and the NCA paper,) for intercultural perspectives that emphasize "empathy" and "understanding" over those that deconstruct "oppression," "power asymmetry" and "difference." Surely, this was the influence of a guilt avoidant white woman!

The attack on Mark's wife continues, despite the respondent's acknowledgement that "I don't know your wife—or ANYTHING about her except her race," and concludes that the critique of our paper "was not centrally about the 'black man-white woman thang' (not ee-ven close.)" The respondent acknowledges having read into Mark's silence

> the presence of an imagined white woman with attitudes that I "can't deal with." Shame on me for doing that! I apologize to you for doing that (although for nothing else I said or did!). AND shame on you for leaving that space—among so many others that would locate you as black and male as well as intellectual—as a gaping void.

Because of the public character of these criticisms, we do not feel that it is improper to repeat them here. In responding to them we attempted to move the discussion beyond antagonism and debate and toward dialogue. Although both Karen and Mark were indicted by these public accusations, it was clear that they were largely directed at Mark, so he alone responded publicly, acknowledging his own role in sustaining the argumentative character of the interaction and apologizing for attributing to the respondent motives that may or may not have been the basis for the critique of our work. Mark suggested that the work that Karen and he have done together illustrates their commitment to including diverse voices, while at the same time being "critical of the notions of authenticity that have circumscribed what we define as 'real' blackness, or maleness."[7] Further, Mark explained that he would "continue to embrace whatever forms and perspectives that help us better understand that character of human antagonism and how we might be able to transform it for the better of all people. If that means embracing whiteness, as well as blackness, then I am guilty as charged."

In response to the accusations of guilt and "shame," however, we felt that something more needed to be said. Mark concluded the response with the following statement that, though phrased in the first person, reflects the position of both of us:

But I hope that we can get beyond guilt, and shame. While we may not always agree, I believe that we can continue to be friends and colleagues, and to support and nurture each other in ways that advance our common goals and aspirations. I believe now, and always will, that it will be people who are willing to question our most basic assumptions about domination, identity, and difference who will set the example for creating the moral and spiritual knowledge that will guide us in the future as we cross the color line into the next millenium. I have always admired your willingness to be one of those people. Thank you.

This conflict was eventually resolved in a civil and professional manner, but the issues it raised, and those that we have attempted to address in this and other essays, will continue to confront students and scholars of intercultural communication.

Black, White, or Brown as We Wanna Be: From Identity Politics to Intercultural Competence

Our story ends with some important lessons that our experience can offer students and scholars of intercultural communication. We believe that the most significant lesson is that we need to address the problems of "identity politics" if we are truly committed to the possibility of achieving intercultural competence. Identity politics assume that some voices are more authentic than others, and they speak to issues such as oppression, power asymmetry, and difference in ways that are more useful and acceptable than others. Intercultural competence helps us to understand that to deal effectively with the historical and social realities of cultural divisions and antagonisms, and with the problems of oppression and inequality, we must be willing to listen to those voices that are different from our own and that do not necessarily fit our personal and cultural beliefs and biases.[8] The irony of the conflict issues described above is that we have always addressed them in our work, which has been accepted by scholars and students of diverse backgrounds, although perhaps not in ways that all of our colleagues believe are legitimate.

Nonetheless, we believe that our voices, and the insights they offer, are just as important as those perspectives that define intercultural and interracial communication in oppositional terms. Indeed, we believe that the challenge we face as intercultural communication scholars and students is that of moving beyond oppositional stances and facilitating inclusivity in intercultural communication in practice as well as theory, and thereby establishing an enlarged understanding of difference and identity. One way of doing this is envisioned in what Dolores Tanno describes as "dialogue," an approach to communication that goes beyond debate and accusations, as it works toward inclusivity and reconciliation. "If we are truly going to address the issues of intolerance and stereotyping and discrimination," she writes, "we have to develop a history together (really we have to acknowledge we already have a history together!), commit ourselves through time, be inclusive of all voices, and invest both our minds and our souls to the dialogue for solutions."⁹ The need to include all voices, we believe, is one of the most important challenges that intercultural communication theory and practice will encounter as we enter the next century.

The notion that our race, or gender, or intellectual perspective defines us in some essential way inhibits our ability to communicate not only across cultures, but within cultures as well. The experiences we recount in this essay have reinforced this belief, but we recognize that our understanding of the complexity of cultural difference and diversity will always be limited by our own peculiar personal and professional agendas. Still, we remain confident that the challenge that our discipline faces today is one that has defined it from the beginning: the challenge of communicating competently across and within our differences, and celebrating the diversity of all of our voices, regardless of race, culture, or beliefs. We have tried in this essay to tell our own story of this struggle and the impact it has had on our lives. We believe that these experiences, despite being uncomfortable and at times discouraging, have also helped us to understand better both the problems and the possibilities of intercultural inquiry.

As students and practitioners of intercultural communication, we all must come to grips with the implications of how we choose to understand our identities and our differences. We must also confront in ourselves the willingness to accept the differences of others despite the fact that they may not always conform to our own preconceived agendas. This, in intercultural interaction, is the difference between communication and competence. If we simply view "blackness," or "maleness," or "intellectualness" as fixed, static, and unchanging markers of who we are, we may miss one of the most important lessons that the study of intercultural communication can teach us: regardless of what others wish to impose on us, we already are the right color. Intercultural communication can help us understand that we have the right to be as black, or white, or brown, as we wanna be, as long as we are willing to extend that same courtesy to others. It is at this point, we believe, that we are able to erase the divisions between empathy and oppositionality, understanding and deconstruction, and move beyond intercultural communication toward intercultural competence.

NOTES

1. Dennis Rodman with Tim Keown, *Bad as I Wanna Be* (New York: Dell Publishing, 1996), p. 178.

2. Our essay, entitled "Crossing the Color Line: From Empathy to Implicature in Intercultural Communication," appears in *Readings in Cultural Contexts,* ed. Judith Martin, Thomas Nakayama, and Lisa Flores (Mountain View, California: Mayfield Publishing, 1998).

3. Carole Blair, Julie Brown, and Leslie Baxter. "Disciplining the Feminine," *Quarterly Journal of Speech 80* (1994), 383.

4. bell hooks, *Killing Rage: Ending Racism* (New York: Holt, 1995), p. 62.

5. hooks, 1995, p. 88.

6. The essay appears as "From Complicity to Coherence: Rereading the Rhetoric of Afrocentricity," *Western Journal of Communication 62* (1998), 1–18.

7. Our analysis of these issues can be found in our essay "Complicity and coherence in Intra/Intercultural Discourse: Alberto Dialogue," in (eds.) *International and Intercultural Communication Annual* ed. Alberto Gonzalez and Dolores Tanno (Beverly Hills: Sage, 1997), 27–47.

8. See Myron W. Lustig and Jolene Koester, *Intercultural Competence: Interpersonal Communication Across Cultures.* (New York: Longman, 1999).

9. Dolores Tanno outlined her position in "A Characterization of Dialogue," presented at the Western States Communication Association Convention, Portland, OR, 1995, p. 5.

Using remembered and sometimes painful events from her own life, Gale Young examines the unacknowledged, uncontested, and unmentioned privilege of being white in the United States today. Her stories challenge those with White privilege to recognize and become uncomfortable with such unfair and un-earned power over others. Gale also summons us to think about the difficult and complicated consequences of race in the United States. Through an analysis of our family stories, we can understand our taken-for-granted beliefs and actions, thus making connections between our personal experiences and the larger polit-ical and social world.

18 Leonard's Yard: Pulling at the Roots and Responsibilities of My Whiteness

Gale Young

I sat on the stone ledge surrounding my parents' garden, which contained the 50 roses my father had planted nearly 50 years earlier. They were the roses he liked to prune and pamper while I tagged along with a willing ear, first as a child listening to his tales of garden gnomes and later to his gentle sugges-tions for coping with my adolescent gyrations. This was the rose garden that bloomed on my wedding day, out of season, and that brought my mother so much pleasure in the years after my father's death. This was the rose garden that looked out over the San Francisco Bay, Mt. Tamalpais, and what had years ago been "Leonard's yard." In those moments by the garden, myriad memories flashed before me, rearranging themselves like pieces in a kaleido-scope, offering multiple views of my middle-aged life.

The memory pieces I want to share with you expose an emerging aware-ness of my whiteness. They are intentionally personal and presented as iso-lated instances. After 19 years of teaching intercultural communication to stu-dents and faculty from many ethnicities, I've come to believe that the way we learn about the differences that race/color and culture make is through gath-ering what may at first appear to be unrelated stories that we can then exam-ine through the lenses of race and culture.[1]

The difference between a personal story and an ethnic story is not so much the pieces that are chosen but the expanse of the context. A personal story em-phasizes the particulars of individuals and families. An ethnic story places the memory pieces in a racial and ethnic context that highlights the impact the social-political and cultural power structures have on individuals and their families.

Most white, Anglo, western European Americans in the United States don't feel their color or culture each moment, because they are not in contrast to it. So it is not uncommon for European Americans to say, "I don't have a culture," "When I look in the mirror I see a human being or just a man or a woman," and "I don't have any white privilege; I work just as hard as the next guy." These statements are true in the sense that they mirror the emphasis that European Americans put on their experience. But what is left out of these statements is also true: that they reflect the unconscious and unearned privilege that comes with being racially similar to other members of the dominant group (Bowser & Hunt, 1997; Wildman, 1996). Conversely, people of color in the United States are forced, at an early age, to experience the contrast between the dominant racial domain and their own. Herein lies the foundation of the racial divide and, paradoxically, the ability to envision a bridge across it.

In the act of recalling, collecting, and inquiring into what may initially appear as fragments of memory about what was said, seen, and unspoken, we can understand how our race and ethnicity weave into our identity. As you read my memory pieces, look for the personal feelings of being different and in contrast to others. Notice the recurring theme of wanting to belong, and variations such as feeling left out, favored or rejected, or feeling tolerated but not fully accepted juxtaposed with my lack of awareness about being part of the ingroup. Notice the growing self-consciousness and confusion about being white and the sense of feeling responsible for and embarrassed by other whites.

Each person's experiences, when focused through the lens of power, culture, race, and social institutions, provide the landscape for perceiving the ingroup/out-group dynamics that drive sociopolitical policies and practices. In our families, we respond in various ways to the rules of politeness, protocol, secrets, and silence that are perpetuated across generations. By so doing we engage in the personal version of the social power to dominate, deny, respond, resist, rebel, and assimilate. When we learn to see and situate our place within these patterns, we can then acknowledge our feelings (such as how frustrated, sad, angry, hurt, and/or overwhelmed we feel) about our own circumstances. Paradoxically, being able to view and respond to our situation as personal provides the possibility of comprehending that the collective version of these dynamics has an exponential effect on the members of racial groups who are different from the dominant culture. Furthermore, that exponential effect varies in relation to the ways in which the dominant culture categorizes each ethnic group.

The memory pieces that follow represent many others that touch the tenderness and vulnerability behind the dilemmas, dissensions, and tensions surrounding diversity—my own and those of others. They remind me that experiencing our ethnicity occurs moment by moment, and those of us who are members of the dominant group can choose when to conceal and when to reveal our racial roots.

Powdered Milk and Silver Pitchers: Learning about Socioeconomic Class

Living on the periphery of a blended family, I am seven when I ask my mother, "Why do we kids drink powdered milk?" What I really want to ask is why she gets whole milk and we don't. She declares it nutritionally superior and prompts me to serve it in a silver pitcher. I am left wondering if whole milk is bad for her or just bad for kids, or only good in silver pitchers, or if something is left unsaid. My mother—English, French, and Scot—can trace her U.S. ancestors back to the 1600s. She was raised and educated in the upper-class traditions of the East Coast establishment. Her father was tax commissioner for then Governor Franklin Roosevelt; as a young woman she and her father often dined at the White House once Roosevelt became president. Now, however, she lived in Northern California and was married to an under-employed artist who brought four children from two previous marriages with him into the household. She was unwilling to tell me that, though our lower-middle economic class meant that we couldn't afford "whole" milk for the children, we could serve our "poor" milk in the silver pitcher of her higher social class. Further, as an adult, she could treat herself to the enriched milk.

This experience marks the beginning of my wondering about what I would come to understand as the nature and consequences of who has power and privilege and who does not. Whole milk, store-bought (not hand-me-down) clothes, and gentle attention were scarce resources in my childhood. Much later I would learn about other scarce resources such as money, education, position, and housing. The split between my mother's upper-class social values and our lower middle class economic condition meant that I wasn't accepted by the "rich kids" and my mother wouldn't let me play with the "poor kids." Spending much of my free time feeling left out, I would often hang out with the available adults: playground directors, community-based leaders, and Leonard.

Leonard: My First Mentor of Color

While I might have seen other African Americans in the integrated Richmond-Berkeley area where I lived, Leonard, as it turns out, becomes my first mentor of color, but that's not why I began talking with him. He would come to mow the neighbors' lawn each Wednesday afternoon, and I would look forward to his kindly ways. My baby brother was clearly "the family favorite" and my older stepbrothers were getting into so much trouble that my parents were just relieved to have me "out of their hair," as they would say. So they began paying Leonard to watch me, a weekly arrangement that continued for several years.

Leonard did not raise the topic of race when I complained that the kids at school teased me because of my dark eyes, hair, and freckles. Nor was race mentioned when I pined to be blond and blue-eyed like Daun Stone, because she was popular and everyone said she was pretty. Nor, in fact, did he mention race when I told him that my favorite older brother was sent away to live with another mother, and no one wanted to hear what I had to say about it. But somewhere along the way, Leonard did tell me that his relatives were working in the Civil Rights movement down south. I probably asked the dear man so many questions that he finally decided to try to explain a bit of U.S. racial history to this little white girl, all the while hoping that he wouldn't get into trouble with her parents. I can't now recall most of my questions or many of his responses. But I do remember that he used my self-consciousness about not looking like the other kids, and the experience of having my brother sent away without my wishes being heard, to introduce me to what life was like for lots of people "whose faces were brown all over, not just in freckles." In that moment, I remember viewing him simultaneously as more and less like me than I had before, when his being older and more attentive than my parents, peers, and siblings was all that had mattered. I knew his skin color was darker but I hadn't attached any particular meaning to it.

One hot summer day, I invited Leonard into my house for lemonade. My mother fluttered with too much friendliness, and my grandmother told tales of "how much she loved her colored cook and chauffeur." Leonard smiled but got really stiff. I didn't know why and didn't ask any questions; thereafter, I just brought the lemonade outside. It was the first instance of a feeling that now often reappears: being embarrassed by how my own kind acts when they are with or talking about people of color. To this day, in certain situations I tighten and wait for a white friend or stranger to say or do something that is racially insensitive. Like Wendell Berry (1989),

> I am trying to establish the outlines of an understanding of myself in regard to what was fated to be the continuing crisis of my life, the crisis of racial awareness—the sense of being doomed by my history to be, if not always a racist, then a man [or woman] always limited by the inheritance of racism, condemned to be always conscious of the necessity *not* to be a racist, to be always dealing deliberately with the reflexes of racism that are embedded in my mind as deeply at least as the language I speak. (pp. 48–49)

A few years later, Leonard listened as I learned a family secret: I had a biological father of Eastern European gypsy and Jewish descent who had returned "to get to know me." Leonard told me a story of similar happenings in his family. Then he added, "It happens a lot to blacks." I don't remember what happened after that, except that I wanted to ask him a slew of questions but didn't: Did blacks have gypsy-Jew fathers who showed up halfway through their childhood, or was there something else Leonard meant? Of course it was the latter, but I don't remember ever seeing Leonard again. It has taken me years to acknowledge that I never got to say goodbye to my first adult friend, nor told or asked for his last name, though I knew and usually referred to all the white adults in my life by their last names.

Looking back, I see the ways in which my parents kept Leonard at the margins of my life, which mirrored the social-political borders for blacks. Although Leonard and my family shared the same economic class, we were separated by the color line—a line that separated his caring for me from his becoming a family friend. It was a separation not of overt racism but of what Merton (1957) terms "nonprejudiced discriminators" or "fair-weather liberals."[2]

Family Secrets: Silence, Power, and Politeness

By the time I was 13, I had been molested by my birth father and an adult neighbor, and sexually harassed almost nightly by an older stepbrother. I believed that to tell about these events would create a mess that could bring punishment. I also feared that it was my fault and that if others found out I'd be sent away from the family. So I never directly told my parents or anyone, choosing instead to imply again and again that "I just wasn't comfortable with. . . ." I can now see how my parents were raised to be blind and deaf to the clues I persistently gave them.

It has taken me years to uncover and heal from the wounds inflicted by my parents' inability to acknowledge the sexual abuse, let alone protect me from it. But I now appreciate the connection between family secrets of sexual and physical abuse and the national secret of racial abuse. Secrets have a way of stealing and profaning personal power and memory. Only when I descended into my own awareness, pain, and rage could I imagine what it must be like to feel the daily onslaught of racial harassment and abuse—to feel unsafe in your own home country. I understand now that the subtle rules for silence and politeness that help to maintain family secrets are the same rules as those that perpetuate the national secret: "Don't talk about messy situations that might make you look bad and get you into trouble," and "Don't make the parents—whites—feel uncomfortable." The insidiousness of this dynamic is that those with the power to enforce the rules create the context for the rules to be internalized by the victims. Further, the inability of white America to acknowledge fully the racial abuse of the past and the present is disabling for all Americans. Stephanie Wildman (1996) and Benjamin Bowser and Raymond Hunt (1997) develop further this thesis.

Big "D" and "Big G": Learning Personal and Institutional Rules

Raised in integrated Berkeley, in the San Francisco Bay area, I knew I was white long before I was in high school. But one experience initiated my lifelong inquiry into the written and unwritten racial rules, the formal and informal bases of power, and the institutional and personal consequences of one's behaviors. I can't remember exactly when or where I met Danny, an African American classmate, only that we felt like we had been best friends forever. We nicknamed each other "Big D" and "Big G," though neither of us cleared

5'5". We were in high school classes together, he as a star football player and student body president, and I as the vice president. We talked often about such topics as our classes, homework, his girlfriend, my boyfriend, and ideas for class activities. The yearbook included pictures of us handcuffed together, participating in a "slave auction" to raise money for senior activities. At the time I remember feeling weird and strange, but I didn't question or examine the situation, choosing instead just to go along with the show.

"Big D" had a white girlfriend and, being nosy, I asked him why he never held hands with her. He said that he did, but only in private. I queried, "Why not around school like the other couples?" He said, "Because she is white." I asked him if there was a written rule about that; he said "No," but he just knew that he and his girlfriend would get into trouble if they held hands in public. In a spontaneous act I took "Big D's" hand and kissed him on the cheek in front of the oldest, whitest, and most prudish English teacher around. She hauled us off to the dean's office, where "Big D" sat and said, "What did you have to go and do that for?" and the dean warned us of consequences for "our inappropriate behavior."

With a rebel's confidence that I hadn't known before, I told the dean that I wanted my mother—a popular English and journalism teacher at the school—to witness whatever came next. I didn't know how my mother would react. She could easily turn me over to the wolves; after all, I had created quite a scene. But I guess I wanted to give her a chance, this time, to defend us, or at least Danny. She walked in with her blue-blood Anglo disdain for messes written all over her face and listened politely while the dean and I explained what had happened. I didn't know which way her sword-swift tongue would fall. With a strength and dignity I had only feared in her before, she told the dean that "in no way was interracial hand-holding and kissing legally, morally, or socially wrong." Her dramatic exit suggested legal and journalistic action if the dean intended to do anything other than let us go. Perhaps at that moment she recalled that she had been disowned temporarily by her family when she married my birth father, a Jew. Whatever the reason this time, she chose to use her informal organizational power to expose an unwritten racist rule.

Danny and I sighed and didn't speak of the incident until much later, when he said that all he remembers is hearing his mother's voice inside his head repeating, "You know better than to be holding hands with a white girl."

The Color Line: Feeling White

In college I was part of an interracial group of friends who were studying race in sociology classes. I remember feeling as if "I was part of something that mattered" and "I could help." As the Civil Rights movement intensified and the differences between Malcolm X and Martin Luther King, Jr., became sharper, the interpersonal tensions in our group mounted. I began to "feel white." Darcy and I spent a lot of time together, inviting each other to go places or to just hang out. And then she became less available. The friends she chose over me were all black, and I noticed. When the pressure between us finally surfaced, all I remember is the agony, shame, and harshness I felt when she said, "Take your condescending ways and go help your own kind." We never talked again.

Looking back, this was the first of what I would come to know as an opportunity for a difficult interracial dialogue. While I wish I could have maintained a friendship with Darcy, her challenge to me to understand the what, where, and why of her message has stayed under my skin to this day, and I thank her for it.

Who's the Teacher Here? Intersecting Differences

It is my first teaching experience, a course in public speaking that is included in a special program at UCLA for recently returned Vietnam veterans, mostly African American or Latino men, all older than me. On the first day a student calls out, "You don't look old enough to be my baby sister, let alone my teach." There I was, a 23-year-old European American female hippie doctoral candidate, away from my nursing baby for the first time, trying to conceal the leaking breast milk and my stand against the War, in a room full of men who had just returned from it. Their experiences and views of the world were radically different from my own. I realized that if I was to contribute in any way to their learning, I had to learn about them from their perspective. But how?

I can still smell the sharpness of feeling so white, so female, and so underprepared to teach. To this day, I can't recall how I got through that first class period. But I went on to learn that, as W. E. B. Dubois (1973) contends, for education to be relevant it must grow out of the experiences of the students being educated. I went into class the next day and said, "I know a lot about what the authors of your textbook have to say about communication. And I know how it relates to my life. But in order for you to learn from this course we need to figure out how it is relevant to your world." That I taught in the program for three years remains the brightest star in my learning career, because I learned far more than I taught. I am also struck by how I stuck to the "concepts" discussed in the texts and steered the discussions toward the personal and gender dynamics but away from the racial domain. I was perpetuating the racial rule of silence.

A White Woman Mentor

When I was in graduate school at UCLA I was fortunate to serve as a research assistant for Andrea Rich, a young European American professor, the author of the first communication text on interracial communication, the author of the "Interracial and Intercultural Communication Model" (Rich, 1973), and the first female professor in the department. She chose to work interracially with scholars of color and was not afraid to study, discuss, and teach about race relations in the United States. Her lectures and models cracked open my cognitive understanding of the difference that whiteness and color make in the United States. Working with Dr. Rich marked the birth of my passion for inquiring into the issues surrounding race relations. When Dr. Rich left the department there was no longer anyone with expertise in that area, so I pursued another topic for my doctoral dissertation. However, her knowledge, courage, and honesty in confronting these difficult issues served as a model for me of the work that white people could do to understand and improve race relations.

Cultivating Allies

With my doctorate in hand, I moved back to the San Francisco Bay area. A single parent, I left behind a group of friends and colleagues, the majority of whom are white. I needed a rest and wanted to spend time with my daughter and my dying stepfather. But soon after arriving I was offered and accepted a temporary position at Cal State University, Hayward, with the specific charge to develop the area of intercultural communication.

I did not have the confidence of my role model, Andrea Rich, and I wasn't sure where to find it. Although I had read and thought about the theories, perceptions, and stereotypes regarding whites and people of color and the dynamics of interracial communication, I had not dealt consciously with my own emotional connection to the issues, nor did I have a clue how to facilitate others' feelings. I was terrified of anger—my own and others'—and I knew that the issue of race relations was a lightning rod to an emotional ocean. Furthermore, teaching this course to a diverse group of students brought up all my fears and vulnerabilities about making messes and being told I didn't belong.

Something told me there might be some truth in my fear; maybe I really didn't know enough and I couldn't get it from books. I sought out the student service staff who worked with racially and culturally diverse students and the faculty who taught race- and culture-related courses. I asked them what they would like to see taught in a course focused on interracial and intercultural communication. These conversations, as grace would have it, allowed me to meet other colleagues who shared my interests, to hear their concerns and perceptions about the racial climate on the campus, to learn their perspectives on advising and teaching, and to plant seeds for cultivating allies.

Somewhere along the line, Terry Jones—an African American professor, sociologist, and political activist who was the associate dean at the time of our meeting—ended up on the commuter train with me. To pass the time we chatted, discovering that we lived near each other, our kids went to the same schools, our fathers had worked at the same shipyard, and we taught similar classes.

Soon thereafter, the dean asked Dr. Jones and me to attend a conference on "mainstreaming the multicultural curriculum," after which we cowrote a grant proposal, which was funded. Along with the chair of Ethnic Studies, I subsequently codirected the funded program, along with the chair of the ethnic studies program, which was designed to help faculty integrate multicultural perspectives into their general education courses. These experiences marked the beginning of what would become my professional path: working in multicultural teams for multicultural issues. It was during this time that Dr. Jones mentored me in the politics of race in the university. By 1984 we had established the Center for the Study of Intercultural Relations (CSIR) as a means of institutionalizing the gains made by our first grant. CSIR's accomplishments are quite impressive, and the roots of my whiteness continue to be pruned and its responsibility nurtured by the richly intellectual and multicultural faculty at the center.

Mom and Derrick Bell

Shortly after my mother's death, I am leading a one-day seminar for a multiracial and multicultural group of business folks on ways to engage in difficult dialogues about race, culture, and gender. It is the first time I am teaching this particular course without a cofacilitator of color. I feel confident in my knowledge of the material but tender and bit uneasy about being "just white." This feeling, while never fully welcomed on first appearance, has been around so often that I no longer shrink from or defend myself against it. I know it is here to stay for the day, and I hope I can befriend it and use it as my W. E. B. Dubois reminder that we are all in the world in different ways and that that in-ness affects everything.

While the participants work in small groups, I look over the books I hastily pulled from my shelf for examples and potential resources that the students can pursue. Amid the stack is the paperback edition of Derrick Bell's (1992) *Faces at the Bottom of the Well: The Permanence of Racism*. I reach for it, one of my favorites, thinking to myself, "I own the hardback. Where did the paperback come from?" I open it up and see a note written to my mother from David, an African American and one of her former students. As I read the note, my hands began to tremble:

> Thought you would need both of his books to get the complete picture. *And we are not saved* [Bell, 1987] is a little more dense to read—need to keep a finger in the back with the references. They are both written in the same allegorical style. *Faces* moves quicker and is easier reading. Hope my relaying of the "story" about Dominican shows how much you taught me about being respectful—yet maintaining the desired "edge" to the conversation. Enjoy it! Politics! Yum, Yum! See you soon, David.

With tears welling in my eyes, I struggle to maintain my public composure. I am filled with empathy for my mother who, both despite and because of her upbringing and experiences, was willing, at least in moments, to stay open-minded up until the end of her 80-year life. I saw her spend many afternoons talking with and listening to David. And when Irene, a recent Chinese immigrant she tutored, encountered difficulty understanding the assigned Cornel West's (1992) *Race Matters,* my mother asked me many questions about race relations in the United States. I was surprised at how quickly she caught on and without being defensive. We even discussed ways to explain to Irene enough of the history of race relations for her to be able to critique the text.

Like most whites in the United States, my mother could choose when and where to be aware of her racial place, yet I know that she had been more willing to see and learn about race, power, and privilege than *her* mother. In turn, I hope that my daughters will be more conscious, knowledgeable, and responsible than I am. I realize that each of our stories and insights is always incomplete.

Returning to the Rose Garden

The rose garden, and with it the family home in which my brothers and I were raised, was "on the market"—empty of all the objects that carried the Gale Graves Young stories. I felt blessed, though a bit overwhelmed, to inherit so many items, not because of their material worth, which was minimal, but because they evoked the stories I didn't want to forget. But what would arouse the stories of Leonard's yard? I sat on the ledge wondering whether to continue pulling at the entangled and deeply embedded roots so I could transplant, in my own garden, the "first rose bush" and my parents' favorite, "Mr. Lincoln."

In the end, I left the rose bush there, knowing that I couldn't really rip out the history and roots of my upbringing. The reminders of my heritage, and with them my whiteness, my blindness, my perceptiveness, my mentors, my unearned and earned privileges, and my institutional power, are everywhere. It is up to me, each day, to remain conscious and committed, so that I can contribute to the dismantling of unearned white privileges.

NOTES

1. The distinction I am making here is between *race* as the complexion that is a socially constructed marker to group and divide people and *culture* or *ethnicity* as the values, attitudes, beliefs, and behavior styles that are shared by groups of people and are transmitted from generation to generation. Clearly the intersection of color and culture includes the values, attitudes, beliefs, and behavior styles that are transmitted intergenerationally and that evolve when groups of people share similar experiences of living in a society that values or devalues their skin color.

2. Gudykunst and Kim (1997) characterize this type of prejudice and communication as being dominated by expediency. "When people around them discriminate or talk in a prejudicial manner, fair-weather liberals will take the expedient course of action and keep quiet. The major reason for the inconsistency between attitudes and behavior is the social norms of the situation" (p. 128).

REFERENCES

Bell, D. (1992). *Faces at the bottom of the well: The permanence of racism.* New York: Basic Books.

Bell, D. (1987). *And we are not saved: The elusive quest for racial justice.* New York: Basic Books.

Berry, W. (1989). *The hidden wound.* San Francisco: North Point Press.

Bowser, B. P., & Hunt, R. (1997). *Impacts of racism on white Americans* (2nd ed.). Newbury Park, CA: Sage.

DuBois, W.E.B. (1973). *The education of black people: Ten critiques,* 1906–1960. H. Aptheker, ed. New York: Monthly Review Press.

Gudykunst, W. B. and Kim, Y.Y. (1997). *Communicating with strangers: An approach to intercultural communication* (3rd ed.). New York: McGraw-Hill.

Merton, R. K. (1957). *Social theory and social structure.* New York: Free Press.

Rich, A. L. (1973). *Interracial communication.* New York: Harper & Row.

West, C. (1992). *Race matters.* Boston: Beacon Press.

Wildman, S. M. (1996). *Privilege revealed: How invisible preference undermines America.* New York: New York University Press.

The lessons to be learned from Veronica Duncan's stories are straightforward. First she describes her personal experiences with the pernicious consequences of the ever-present stereotyping and racism that are regularly experienced by African Americans, regardless of their profession, educational achievements, gender, or social class. Veronica then situates her story within an intercultural friendship to show how difficult it sometimes is even for friends to recognize the imposition of their own cultural practices on others. Finally, Veronica asks us all to recognize that, though virtually all U.S. Americans have unresolved issues about race in America, being blind to the racial dynamics does not produce competent intercultural interactions.

19 A Whole Lot of Milk with a Drop of Chocolate: An African American Woman's Story

Veronica J. Duncan

This essay shares two stories about my experiences as an African American woman. I do not presume to speak for ALL African American women, but I know that there are many whose experiences are similar to mine.

Before we begin, let me tell you a little bit about myself. I am a first-generation African American female college graduate and a professor of communication. I am a mother, wife, daughter, sister, teacher, mentor, protege, friend, colleague, and healer. You may wonder why all of this information is necessary. In other words, why am I telling you "all of my business"? This information is important because you are reading MY STORY. Throughout this essay you will hear MY VOICE, which I hope will help you to undertake a critical examination of your own beliefs, attitudes, values, and roles in the oppression of an "Other."

I chose the title "A Whole Lot of Milk with a Drop of Chocolate" because drinking milk with chocolate is a different experience from drinking milk alone. The chocolate gives the milk a little more flava'. Now, let's begin by examining individual racism.

Individual racism occurs when people of color, as a group, are regarded as inferior because of their physical characteristics. These physical traits, the individual racist believes, cause all who have them to be antisocial, morally decadent, and intellectually mediocre, which justifies and legitimates inferior social treatment directed against those individuals.

I will describe an incident that, for me, identifies how deeply ingrained individual racism is. As a new faculty member at a predominantly white university, I was leery of the kind of environment I would find. However, being the optimistic person that I am, I like to give people an opportunity to show me where they are coming from in terms of dealing with African Americans. Yes, I still believe that there is hope for humanity. The first week I was at this institution as a FACULTY member, the secretaries had money stolen from their purses. The structure of the department was such that we had a general department secretary, whom I will call Susan, and an assistant to the chair, whom I will call Betty. I am changing the names of these individuals not to protect the innocent but because, in talking to other African American and female faculty members, I know that the names may change but the behaviors are often similar. Anyway, I had noticed that Susan was acting rather strangely toward me, but I attributed it to her personality. She did not seem to be the happiest person in the world, for whatever reason. Then *it* happened.

I was trying to help Betty by getting some computer assistance from a technician. I had been told that the computer support people did not respond quickly to the secretary's calls, so I called to help her speed up the process. During the course of our attempts to take care of the computer issues, we needed some disks to complete the task. I asked Susan if she knew where the disks were kept. She told me that she didn't, so I went to look for them so that we could finish. When I went into the other secretary's office, which was also the department office, Susan followed me and stood in the doorway, watching me. By this time I was rather perturbed but chose not to dignify her behavior with a reaction. I went on "about my business," as we would say in the African American community. Once the task was completed, I had to go to the office to get something; the door was shut, but I heard whispering. By this time I was really feeling like something was wrong, but I couldn't believe that they might think that I STOLE THEIR MONEY! So I listened at the door. Talk about being the "spook by the door"; well, that was me. I wanted to know what was going on, and no one would tell me. I overheard Susan telling someone that "she just walked in the office like she owned the place. And I didn't know if your purse was out or not." I was LIVID. Who did they think they were? I was a PROFESSOR. I even had nearly finished my Ph.D. Me? A thief? I banged on the door. It opened and when people realized it was me, they scattered. Everyone got extremely quiet. Everyone, that is, except me. I let them have it. I told Betty, who was Susan's direct supervisor, that I was very offended at the way Susan had been treating me. I proceeded to let her know that I didn't appreciate Susan talking about me behind my back. If she had anything to say about me, then she needed to say it TO me. You may be wondering why I didn't just say these things to Susan, since she was in the next room and I was speaking loud enough for her to hear me. If I had said anything to Susan at that moment, I would have lost it. I knew I needed to cool down. I will tell you that all of the "street" in me would have come out. I actually wanted to hit her. That may seem stereotypically "black," but I am being honest here. I'm not a fighter, but I can be if I need to be.

Betty was terrified. Susan was gone, and the others had scattered. I told Betty that Susan and I needed to have a meeting, turned on my heels, and went back to my office. I'm sure that people could almost see the steam coming from my ears as I walked down the hall. If someone had placed a piece of ice on me, it would have melted so quickly and completely that by the time I reached my office there would have been no trace that it had ever existed. That is how HOT I was as I walked to my office.

Once I shut my office door, all of the hardness on the outside melted. I sat there and I cried. I cried for me because even though I was a PROFESSOR, they still thought I was a thief. I cried for my people because it seems that no matter how much we advance, we're still just NIGGERS to some white people. And I cried for them, because they obviously had missed out on the opportunity to learn some wonderful things about African American people and had only gotten the negative. One thing was certain: I cried out of anger, frustration, and hurt. But they wouldn't see me cry.

After I calmed down, I went to the office to schedule a meeting with Susan, but she was "gone for the day to a doctor's appointment." I don't know if she really had a doctor's appointment, but that meant I had more time to reflect and calm down. That additional time was not an accident; the Creator knew I needed it. I wrote a memo to Susan and copied it to Betty and to the chair, who was out of town at the time.

The next day, when it was time for our meeting, I called Susan to confirm it and find out if she was coming. She informed me that I needed to come to HER office. Who did she think she was? She obviously had her roles mixed up. I could have sworn that I was the faculty member and she was working for me. However, her perceptions of the situation seemed to be very different from mine. I told her that I would prefer it if she came to my office, to which she replied that she couldn't because she had to answer the phones. I asked her if Betty could do that, and she said that she wanted Betty in the meeting. Finally I told them that we could just meet in the chair's office. I went down armed—with my tape recorder. You see, I had learned the necessity of protecting myself in such settings. I asked if they would mind our taping the meeting, and they agreed that I could do so.

I began by telling Susan my perception that she had a problem with getting things that I requested, such as scissors, tape, pens, and pencils. She told me that I asked for things no other faculty member requested, such as a desk caddy for my office supplies. She also informed me that I acted arrogantly because I walked around with my head up. In other words, I didn't shuffle enough. I told her that I found our interactions strange, because I always had an excellent relationship with support staff wherever I had been. I treated them with respect and I expected the same thing in return. She was quiet but there was definitely an "attitude." I proceeded to talk about the missing money and the insinuations that I took it. I told them that it seemed to me that what was operating was the stereotype of blacks as thieves. Their response was "Yeah." I hadn't thought I could be shocked any more than I had already been, but that took the cake. They said "Yeah," and I was taping the meeting. They didn't even recognize the magnitude of the offense they had just committed. I could sue the university for discrimination, but they were oblivious to this fact. Then Betty started crying. All I could think was "What's wrong with her?" I wasn't even talking to her. "Maybe this is my fault. Maybe I accidentally said something that might have made her (Susan) think that you or Stacey (my African American graduate student) had done it," Betty sobbed. I was through, finished, worn out. Not Betty! Not after I had talked with her about the way Susan had acted toward me, and she responded so supportively. She stated that she didn't know why she (Susan) was acting that way, and that it was just the way she was sometimes. To close the meeting, I simply asked for respect and said that I would respond in kind.

I walked back to my office. Why was I here? Why me? I called a friend in the community and she answered those questions. "God has you here for a reason. Those people need you. They need to have the opportunity to be around us and you give that to them," she replied. "But why me?" I asked again. She told me that there was something about me. There was something about my spirit that drew people of all races to me. That spirit was a spirit of love. I wasn't feeling very loving at that point, but I knew that she was right. It had followed me everywhere I had gone. I connected with people . . . ALL kinds of people. And I knew my journey at that institution had just begun.

Those secretaries unknowingly identified their belief that African American people are thieves. And it doesn't matter how many degrees the African Americans might have. They are still thieves. That belief in the lack of moral character of African Americans is an example of individual racism. There were several things going on in my encounter with Susan and Betty. First, I was the first African American faculty member in that department. These women were obviously unaccustomed to dealing with African Americans in positions of authority. Second, I was young. I was only 28 at the time. Both Susan and Betty were at least ten years older than I was. How dare I tell them what to do, even if it was their job? And believe me, I have experienced this kind of age discrimination in other areas. Young people are not supposed to be in better positions than their elders, especially not African American women. Nor should young people know more about any subject than their elders. Third, I was attractive and feminine. Believe me, I am not making this statement out of arrogance. I have just noticed this negative reaction to attractive women. There is this unspoken belief that women in positions of authority should be plain and unattractive. God forbid they dress in flattering, feminine ways. This situation was new for these secretaries, and it was very complicated. Fourth, I was a woman. These women were unaccustomed to another woman in a position of authority over them, so our relationship may have disturbed them.

I think that it was not any one of these things, but a combination of them all, that best explains and describes my encounter with Susan and Betty. They were accustomed to plain milk, and my presence changed its flavor. You see, chocolate changes not only the way milk looks but the way it tastes. My presence changed the way the department looked and functioned, which was not necessarily comfortable for these women. And disruption of people's comfort levels has significant effects on interactions.

Discomfort occurs not only because of individual racism but also because of cultural racism. *Cultural racism* is a conscious or unconscious conviction, often held by the group that has economic and political dominance, that its culture is superior to those of other racial and ethnic groups. Thus, for example, there is a widely held belief among many European Americans that their cultural patterns and practices—their music, art, economic system, religious tenets, and other cultural artifacts—provide the standards against which all other cultures should be judged.

Though my experiences with cultural racism abound, I will provide just one example to show how it can play out. Remember that cultural racism is not necessarily conscious. I would wager that most people who engage in cultural racism are not aware of the implied superiority of their cultural patterns or practices.

When I was in graduate school, a European American female graduate student came over to my house one weekend afternoon. My husband (now ex-husband) and his brothers and cousins had assembled in the living room to watch a basketball game. My colleague arrived, and I met her at the door. We proceeded through the living room to the kitchen. The men, who were waiting for the game to begin, were listening to rap music. My colleague asked me how I could listen to that stuff. I asked her what she meant. She told me that rap was not music, it was just noise, and she asked me to change it. I told her that Rod Stewart was not music to me but when I was with her she still listened to it. I'm sure that she did not even think that what she was saying was "cultural racism," but it was. Her implication was that African American music was somehow inferior to European American music. I don't necessarily like all rap music, but she was saying that it was not music at all.

Now that I have told you what occurred, let me tell you what I was thinking and feeling. First, every day of my life, whether I like it or not, I am forced to listen to the musical choices of mainstream America. How could it be that this person, who said she was my friend, could not and would not tolerate a different type of music for a few hours? I felt hurt, betrayed, and belittled. I felt hurt that she would not make that sacrifice for our friendship and yet expected me to make sacrifices routinely. I felt betrayed because I did not think a real friend would do something like that. And I felt belittled because it was as though my music was somehow less than hers. I began to question whether she was really my friend and what our friendship meant to her. As if her claim that rap music was not music was not enough damage to be done on one day, she compounded it as she was leaving my house.

As soon as she got out the door and into her car, she made a comment about how the guys were all looking at her. Obviously she felt uncomfortable with African American men looking at her. So I told her that she had walked in front of the television and they were watching the game. I asked her what she expected them to do, since they were looking in that direction already. She gave an uncomfortable laugh and said, "Oh, yeah." But I could see the fear in her eyes. She was afraid of the men sitting in my living room. She was frightened that those men, who were part of my family, might jump up, grab her, and try to rape her. Why? Could it have been because the room was full of African American men who were all at least six feet tall? They weren't exceptionally big men, but they were black men. I could visualize all of the movies that have portrayed black men as rapists of white women. I could see and hear all of the stereotypes that are used to frighten white women into their place, which is not in the arms of any black man. This fear has been implanted in the psyches of so many European American women. But not my FRIEND! Again I was hurt, angry, and frustrated. You see, that is why I had limited the number of white people I allowed into this inner part of my world. I couldn't handle the rejection of my culture, my life, and my people. It hurt too deeply. Here I had opened my heart and my home to someone I believed to be my friend, and I was hurt . . . AGAIN! But I discovered something when I looked back on that incident. I discovered that the pain caused by those remarks and reactions doesn't go away just because the person didn't intend for it to hurt or didn't know that it would hurt. I also discovered that the opportunity to work through the thoughts and feelings behind those reactions can lead to understanding and healing. Interaction—REAL interaction—is crucial if we are going to change our perceptions of each other and our worlds.

My friend couldn't handle being the cultural minority. Her response was to assert, through her comments about the music, an unconscious belief in the cultural superiority of her own group. She was out of her element, and her discomfort led her to react without thinking about what she was saying. The situation at my home was different from me being at her home or us being in the office. It was okay when I was the cultural minority. It was okay for me to make accommodations. It was okay for me to deal with it. But, she was not supposed to have to make those types of adjustments. The milk had gotten significantly more chocolate than usual. It looked, tasted, and felt different. Yet it was still milk. It was just milk with a different flavor.

These two stories have a common theme that flows through them, much the way chocolate flows through milk. If I had not been on the faculty, the secretaries might not have had to deal with those beliefs they were holding about African Americans as thieves. If I had not been in graduate school and had not invited my friend to my house, she might never have been in an African American home and confronted her beliefs about rap music and African American men. I can't say that she would never have dealt with those issues, but she might not have had to do it. Often, European Americans have the luxury of avoiding African Americans. The luxury of avoiding the "Other" is one that most African Americans do not have. How often can European Americans go through a day without having to interact with an African American? How frequently do European Americans go a whole day without even seeing an African American? Have most European Americans ever been to an African American home? Do you think they're missing out on something if they haven't gotten to really know an African American? I can honestly say that even with the negative experiences described in the examples above, I would have missed out on some important lessons without them.

This essay has addressed some of the effects that an African American woman's presence has on European Americans. It is MY STORY and the story of many other sisters. We all have a story. I did not tell this story to isolate further European Americans and African Americans. To the contrary, my hope is that my story will help people to deal with themselves. So often much of our time is spent pointing fingers without recognizing, as my grandmother taught me, that when you point at someone else you have three fingers pointing back at you. So I will now reflect on how these incidents have affected me and my relationships with European Americans.

Everyone has racial issues. Often the difference between African Americans and European Americans is that African Americans are forced to deal with theirs, while many European Americans have the luxury of choosing not to. I am in the world as a change agent. I am hoping to change that European American luxury. I tell my students, for instance, that I am an African American woman (in case they hadn't noticed) and that I am fine with that part of who I am. Such a brief and simple statement often puts them at ease, because they know that race is not a dirty word or "politically incorrect" with me. It helps in the creation of a "safe" space for interaction. My goal is to provide an environment for healing, both for myself and for others.

It is time that we stop playing games that divide us from each other. It is time that we overcome our fears and take responsibility for our thoughts, words, and actions. It is time that we practice just thought, just speech, and just action. These are the ways that we will heal ourselves and assist in the healing of an "Other." It is only when we recognize our weaknesses and attempt to turn them into strengths that we grow as individuals. And it is only through individual growth that we can create the space for all voices and experiences to be heard without negating the pain or joy of others. Please hear my voice. Please give me my space for existence and experience. If you refuse, I will speak anyway. I will find other ways to create that space. You can only connect with me if you share my pain and joy, and I share yours. When we do, we have connected on the most basic level. Though our pains and joys differ, we all experience some, regardless of our race, gender, sexual orientation, abilities, religion, and other dividing lines. Remember, the most growth and the greatest joy often come from the worst pain. But it doesn't hurt forever.

The perils of silence and inaction in the face of racism, prejudice, and discrimination form the basis of Elane Geller's essay. Because of anti-Semitism and the genocide directed against Jews, Elane spent five years in concentration camps in Europe. While the descriptions of her experiences chill and horrify, her message is a call to vigilance and action whenever differences in culture, race, religion, or language become the basis for oppression. Geller reminds us that the Jewish Holocaust occurred and could occur again unless every individual assumes some responsibility to speak out about the moral character of our world.

20 The Holocaust and Its Lessons: A Survivor's Story

Elane Norych Geller

The Jewish sages say that, as human beings, we are obligated to leave this world better than we found it, and that we should dedicate our lives to this end. This directive may sound very lofty and intimidating, which would give us an excuse to ignore it. Actually, it is too simple to avoid. We are not expected to solve the world's problems with one grand deed. Quite the opposite, the sages instruct that we improve the world through the practice of decency in our daily behavior. Many people performing many small kind and decent acts on an everyday basis adds up to improvement on a global scale. Changing the world is within the reach of every one of us. Once we understand our capabilities, we cannot avoid our responsibilities.

I travel around the country sharing my story as a survivor of the *Shoah,* the Holocaust. I do not tell my story to win the personal sympathies of my listeners. Nor do I tell it in order to show that the Jews have suffered more than others. I tell it to teach the necessity of accepting personal responsibility for the world. While my "credentials" as a speaker come from my experiences as a Holocaust survivor, I speak not as a Jew, a woman, or a mother. I speak as a human being to other human beings of all creeds, colors, and religions. I am a witness to what can happen when humanity remains indifferent and silent in the face of intolerance. My goal is prevention.

For the most part I speak to students. Almost always I am approached by students after my talk who ask, "What can I do to prevent prejudice or intolerance?" Although we have this sense that the problem is too big for one person to do anything about, it is entirely curable—and it takes no special skills. Even young children have the skills. What it takes is the ability to judge between right and wrong, to care about the difference, and to speak up. I tell the students that it is in their power to combat intolerance of all kinds—they just need to say something, write a letter, make a phone call. It is actually that simple. It is only in an atmosphere of silent acceptance that these ills can flourish. To prevent something like the tragedy of the Holocaust from ever happening again, I hope to teach people, especially young people, that they do have the skills to eliminate racism, bigotry, anti-Semitism, and hatred of various kinds, and that it is simple to use their skills. Most of all, I believe it is our duty as human beings, as the beneficiaries of the gift of free will, to make the choices that will keep this planet ethically and morally safe for all of us.

I have to admit that I was not always an activist. Because I was a child survivor, I had the luxury of deferring the examination of my history. I was too busy becoming an American, going to school, running a household, and raising a family. About 20 years ago, when the revisionists surfaced, I knew I could no longer be silent. The revisionists are folks who say that the Holocaust never happened. What is especially scary about them is that they are "regular" people. They are not kooks. They are teachers, professors, mailmen, secretaries, and trash collectors. They are mainstream people who have decided for whatever reason that the Holocaust never happened and want to "set the record straight." When you think about it, it is a bit crazy to deny the Holocaust because much of what we know about the period comes from German archives. The Nazis were meticulous about keeping records. To a survivor, the kind of media exposure given the revisionists is very painful. In our media-worshipping society, the fact that such people appear on television or in the papers legitimizes their point of view. Picture, if you will, that tomorrow morning all the papers of the world say on the front page, "Eminent Harvard historian, after ten years of research, has concluded that there was no slavery in the United States" I would, of course, expect my fellow Americans who are black to be outraged. But if they were the only people who were outraged, I would be frightened beyond belief. This was the situation with the Holocaust revisionists. These people were going on talk shows and speaking at conferences, and their views were treated by the mainstream as though they were sufficiently grounded in reality to be worthy of consideration. I was outraged at the revisionists, but I was more terrified by the silent acceptance with which their views were treated by the general public. The silence is really the problem, because it allows the hatred to go unchecked.

Hitler's views were also met largely with silent acceptance. While information was available for the world press—the camps were not exactly hidden—the reports of the genocide appeared in the back pages of our newspapers. But it is important to acknowledge that there were some exceptions. Not absolutely everyone was silent. There were some good Poles, and there were some good Germans. There were also some good whites who helped black Americans during slavery. These people should be celebrated as heroes. But the existence of some people who behaved ethically and morally does not provide us with license to ignore the overall lesson of history. Mostly, people were silent and accepted the genocide of the Jews; otherwise it could not have happened.

It is essential to remember the political and economic contexts of the Holocaust. After World War I, Germany was suffering economically, and the people were desperate. It was a perfect climate for an extremist. Hitler came in through the ballot box with the answer to Germany's suffering. Then, all of a sudden, like magic a place called Auschwitz pops up. The people in the surrounding area could see the smoke of Auschwitz, smoke that smelled of human flesh burning, and suddenly they had jobs. They were making pillows out of human hair, and jewelry out of gold inlay, and fertilizer out of bones, and nobody said, "Where are these jobs coming from?" German businessmen went into government offices, bid on government contracts for extraordinary amounts of Zyclon B gas and striped cloth and barbed wire, and without question business was picking up for them. It played well because it played into already-existing anti-Semitism: get rid of the Jews and everything will be better. Because of the economic advantages, people wanted to accept Hitler's program despite the knowledge of the atrocities involved. They wanted economic stability so much that they accepted the idea of a master race of tall, blond, blue-eyed people that was given to them by a short, brunette man with brown eyes. This occurred in a country considered to be one of the most educated and most cultured in the world.

Of the six million Jews murdered, there were a million and a half children under the age of seventeen. An additional five and a half million non-Jews were also murdered in the camps: gypsies, gays, political dissidents, and Jehovah's witnesses, for example. Those souls are every bit as precious, every bit as missed as the Jewish souls. But again, we have to be aware of the politics. Only the Jews were targeted for genocide. I was four years old when the war began. From that time until I was almost nine, I was in one prison, one concentration camp or another.

I was born in a small town in Poland called Voygislav. The town had a healthy proportion of Jews; about 2,500 out of 4,000 people were Jewish. My family consisted of mother and father, two older brothers, an older sister, aunts, uncles, cousins, and grandparents. Of course, we all knew that this madman Hitler was loose, and that he was in fact conducting two wars: the war of conquest and the war against the Jews. We knew that the war was bad for everyone but that it would be worse for us. The Jews were persecuted in Poland long before Hitler. He did not invent anti-Semitism; he just perfected it. We were a dispersed people, without land or riches. Jews lived in Poland for hundreds of years; we paid taxes, we served in the army, we did everything required of good citizens, and yet we were never considered first-class Polish citizens. So we knew it would be worse for us, and of course it was.

What my father did in preparation, as did some other people in our community, was to hire a young seminarian to tutor me in the kinds of things that I would need to know to pass as a Christian child of age four in that setting; some bible stories, hymns, and prayers. I got a false birth certificate and a false baptismal certificate. An arrangement was made with a Christian family: should the Nazis come to our town, I would be taken to their home and left there until the war was over. At that time, whoever survived would come and claim me. These types of arrangements were not unusual. It is fair to say that many of these arrangements were carried out exactly as agreed on, and many were not.

The day arrived when the Nazis came into our town and began to gather all of the Jews on their knees in the town square. The earliest memory I have is my father dressing me in what seemed to me to be an enormous amount of clothing, so much that I could barely put my hands to my sides. We were to walk over quietly and unnoticed to the Christian home where he was going to leave me. On the way he noticed that here and there a door would open up with what looked to be the head of the household, a small child at his side. He would walk the child up to the SS and say, "I don't know who this is, this is not my child. It must be a Jewish child who wandered in here by mistake." The child was killed immediately. The family of the child was located and they were killed in front of everybody, as an example. My father decided at that point to keep me with him. He felt that, at least that way, he would know what my end was. As we survivors are getting older and there are fewer and fewer of us left, there is no doubt that some of us have gone to our graves not certain that the child we left behind wasn't either turned over to the Nazis at some point or hidden from the Jewish family when they came to reclaim the child after the war. Some families became very close to these children, baptized them and raised them, as their own. So my father decided to gamble and we joined my family in the town square.

By the time we got there—it took about 20 minutes—two of my uncles were already dead. My father's youngest brother had a loaf of bread under his arm and in that bread was some jewelry to be used as bribes for favors. The bread fell and broke open, and the SS saw the jewelry and killed him and my aunt's husband with him. Around the large group of Jews were smaller clusters of Jews who were pulled out of the community for various reasons. Maybe they were very strong men and they could dig ditches; maybe they were barbers or other artisans the Nazis needed. I could see that the Nazis were shooting at one of the small clusters near us. People were bleeding and screaming and dying and falling down. In that group were my grandparents and my mother. In the case of my grandparents, they were quite elderly and the Nazis did not consider it worthwhile to send them to a camp. My mother, I was told, was recovering from minor surgery. Again, the Nazis were not going to go through the effort to put her on a gurney and wait for her to heal. Hitler's motto was *Juden rein,* clean of Jews. Zero Jews. No soldier had to explain one less.

After the shooting and the chaos and the screams, we were moved out of town to a camp not far away. The camp was surrounded by electrified barbed wire. We were given armbands marked with yellow stars of David. This was the end of our freedom. Different family members were sent to different work camps or death camps. One had no idea where they were, or if they would ever be seen again. From that first camp, my 16-year-old sister was sent to Auschwitz, where she died in the ovens.

My father's sister—the one who was married to the uncle who was killed—and I were sent to another camp called Stekachine, not far away. My aunt was very courageous; she told the Nazis that she was my mother. This was courageous because the Nazis often sent mothers and children to the gas chambers together.

In the beginning, my father tried to keep us all together. From an incoming prisoner who knew the family, he found out where my aunt and I were. He bribed someone to have us sent to the camp where he was. He made an arrangement for my aunt and me to be sneaked out in the middle of the night. I was thrown over electrified barbed wire onto a large truck filled with coal. My aunt and I were buried under the coal and told not to sneeze or make any noises, because the vehicles were inspected with enormous searchlights. For a very brief time we were reunited with my father and brothers. We were all sent to an enormous work camp in Poland called Skarzysko. The camp had different sections, and it was so large that I never saw my father and brothers again until after the war was over. Indeed, they were not a fact of my life. I did not know whether they were in another camp or another country, or even if they were dead or alive. It was not an issue for me.

My aunt was put to work in a munitions factory, where they made guns and bullets. There were a few other children in the camp. We speculate that children were kept there as pets, since it was not a problem to kill us at any time. Possibly the higher officers missed their own children; they were far away from home and decided a few little children running around were okay. They probably enjoyed it. Still, my aunt would say to me, "When I'm not with you, stay in the barracks, don't be in anybody's way. Hide. Do not call attention to yourself." And I obeyed her or I would not be here today. Many times when children wandered out, we were forced to watch hangings. We were told to hold hands, and look up while they hanged rows and rows of people. For some reason this was very amusing to the young Nazi soldiers. One time when I wandered out, two bored SS soldiers looked at me and said, "Look at this hair, it's too pretty for a Jewish child." They shaved me bald. When my aunt came back and cried because she could hardly recognize me, they beat her with a rubber hose. Another time, for fun, the soldiers addressed a huge pack of German shepherds, talked to the dogs as if they were human and I was the dog. *"Menschen, bitss dem Hundt"* (People, bite that dog.) The dogs attacked me. I begged and pleaded for help and eventually, for reasons unknown to me, the dogs were called off. The physical scars are well healed, but the emotional scars are not. To this day I go nowhere until I make absolutely certain that the pet you love and cherish is behind a locked door. When I am confronted with a loose animal, I have a flashback, much like a soldier. I become that child of the Holocaust again, begging and screaming and pleading for mercy. As you can imagine, with it comes a loss of dignity. Sometimes I'm fine, but other times it takes me much longer before I am comfortable wandering out of my home.

From Skarzysko we were packed into railroad cars, the conditions of which I cannot even begin to describe. Suffice it to say that all one's bodily functions were performed right where one stood. What I remember most of all is my aunt's screams as she begged the other prisoners not to eat me alive. That train took us to a camp called Bergen-Belsen. Sometimes people ask if I knew Anne Frank, who died there. I did not know her. She was about nine years older than me and died very quickly after she got to Belsen. It was a very infested and diseased camp, probably one of the most infested. The trains stopped a great distance outside the barracks, and we marched to the barracks on ground that was solid ice. It was winter, and our feet froze so badly that when my feet began to thaw out, my aunt stuck her fist in my mouth so I would not scream and call attention to myself. Any excuse to silence a Jew was worth it, because the war was coming to an end.

When we arrived in Belsen there were women coming in from all parts of Europe: from Hungary, Romania, Czechoslovakia, Bulgaria, and France. Many of these women, if not all, had already lost their children, and the sight of a small child literally broke their hearts. By then I was a little past eight. I had been infected with typhoid, typhus, and tuberculosis; none of it was ever treated. I had lice and rats in my hair. I stole, I ate toothpaste, and I drank urine. I did whatever was necessary to fill my belly and stay alive. I would approach a broken-hearted mother and ask her to teach me a song in her native language. Then I would go off into a corner and practice it. When I thought I knew the song, I would go back to the woman and, with my palms open, I would sing to her so she would give me her food. She would cry and give me her food, although she needed it more than I did. The intake of a Holocaust prisoner was only 400 calories a day, consisting of a triangular piece of black bread and some dirty water in a squat aluminum container that passed as soup. I did not care one little bit that I was forcing them to give me their precious food. I was like a little animal trying to stay alive.

The British liberated my aunt and me from Bergen-Belsen. One of my brothers was liberated from Buchenwald. My other brothers and my father were liberated in Czechoslovakia in a place called Theresienstadt. We were then put into refugee camps. We needed medical attention and documentation. We needed to find a way to get off German soil. All the aid organizations of the world came there to help. My older brother put ads everywhere saying "I am Jacob Norych, I am looking for family in the U.S." My father had a brother who recognized the name and we came to the United States on the first boatload of refugees. I was almost nine.

This is not ancient history. It happened a mere 50 years ago. Also, for me this is not a horror story. My purpose is not to terrify, but to inform those who were privileged enough not to be living in Europe during that time what occurs when hatred and bigotry go unchecked by those who should know better. How can anyone remain silent when we know what can happen? They can and they will, but my goal is that more will speak up.

I believe that there are no mistakes in this world. The higher power created people of all colors and shapes and with all types of belief systems. I think there may always be racism and anti-Semitism and bigotry of various kinds. The degree to which they exist in our world is our daily challenge, all our lives. What this higher power gave us is free will. It is how we use our free will that is the challenge. One can become so angry that one is immobilized, or one can become empowered and an activist and do something to stop intolerance. As the Jewish sages say, it is very simple to speak up. When someone says "All blacks are this" or "All Asians are so and so," that is the start of the cancer of racism and bigotry. The horrible spread of the cancer is caused when people are silent in the face of these racist comments. A response is required. We need to say, "That is wrong. You do not know all Jews, blacks, Hispanics, or Asians." The spread of the cancer can be stopped in those small ways. As simplistic as that seems, it is a powerful start to leaving this world better than we found it.

When I came to this country everyone said America is like a large melting pot. I do not believe that that metaphor is accurate. I think the Reverend Cecil Murray of the First A.M.E. church in Los Angeles says it much better: America should be like a large tossed salad—all the ingredients retain their flavor. The peppers have different colors, the radishes, the tomatoes—everyone lives in harmony in one salad bowl with a common dressing. This is not to say that I expect an ideal world where everyone is in love. I do not expect everyone to like me. On one level it makes no difference. Even if the Nazis thought I was nice, they still would have killed me for being a Jew. More important than everyone liking each other and being friends is the goal of tolerance and decency toward every human being.

We can all see from the lessons of history what can happen when we abandon our efforts to maintain civility. We know the depths to which humans can sink. I know it personally, having been subjected to inhumanity in the camps, which in turn caused me to forage for food and steal and become less than human myself. We must accept that we are capable of such behavior, but we also must accept that we are capable of rising above it. We have no excuses, for we make the choices. We must choose to be vigilant in maintaining our civility every day. It is not enough that we have laws on the books that require that all people be treated equally. The fact that we have laws to protect our decency does not absolve us individually from the responsibility to make a continuous effort. After all, it is we who put those laws into practice. All must make their own individual commitments to be decent. It is a daily and lifelong pursuit. The power and the responsibility of our free will should be an honor, not a burden.

It is extraordinary to me that after all that I have witnessed and endured, I am nevertheless filled with hope for the planet. There was a time that as a Jewess from eastern Europe I would have feared living in a multicultural society. I am no longer in fear. In fact, I welcome it. I have heard from and met many, many people who take seriously their duty to improve the world by speaking out to their friends and in their schools and communities against hatred and intolerance in its many forms. I am therefore optimistic that if we continue to emphasize the dangers of silence and our responsibilities as human beings, we can greatly decrease the incidence of intolerance. I am pleased to have witnessed the many improvements that have been made in our society. But that is not a reason to rest. Protecting the quality of our humanity is a lifelong pursuit.

Can men and women work together effectively? Can an African American man and a European American woman sustain both a friendship and a business partnership? Why are others so fascinated and curious about competent intercultural communication that crosses both race and gender? What personal characteristics and communication practices support the development of competent task and social relationships for a man and a woman who come from different racial and cultural backgrounds? Business partners and friends, Ann Bohara and Patrick McLaurin offer their answers to these questions.

21 Friends and Partners

Ann M. Bohara and Patrick McLaurin

Eight years ago, against the advice of almost everyone with whom we talked, we decided to form a business partnership. The main theme of the advice we received was that such partnerships are notorious for ending friendships. Even worse, most of the business consultants we talked to about forming a partnership recounted horror stories of financial ruin and business failure. In spite of those dire warnings, however, we decided to challenge conventional wisdom by forming a partnership to do consulting and training in organizational change and management development.

After eight years, we can say the experts were right; remaining friends and partners has been much harder than we ever imagined. Everything they said about a business partnership was true; it pushes the limits of friendship and trust. At the same time, however, they were wrong; we are still here, as friends and partners. We found that by putting the friendship before the partnership, we have been able to withstand the many challenges we encountered as a small consulting business. What's more, we found that, in surviving the partnership, the friendship became stronger and more secure. We would like to talk about that friendship, not only because it has survived the partnership ordeal, but because the other unique aspect of the partnership, and perhaps another reason we were so counseled against working together, is that one of us is a white female and the other is a black male.

The intersection of race and gender in American society has always been a source of interest, if not a cause of uneasiness. From the country's earliest days, the fact that America was made up of men and women of different races has presented a dilemma: how would the "melting pot" ideal address racial and ethnic diversity when it came to gender? As a culture, our fascination with cross-race relationships has been explored in books, movies, and plays. Same-sex friendships across racial lines can be problematic enough, as Jim and Huck Finn might attest. But given people's responses to the relationship's romantic or sexual overtones, black males and white females are a particularly troublesome combination in U.S. social thinking. In our case, even as professional business partners we found that our racial and gender identities seemed to fascinate people.

The Business

We had known each other about three years and had done quite a bit of consulting together when we decided to form the business partnership. At the time, we were both teaching at an Ivy League university, and our offices were a few doors apart. In fact, Ann had been instrumental in Patrick's coming to the university, but the idea of working together in a business partnership was the farthest thing from either of our minds. We were teachers and researchers, struggling to meet teaching demands and publish articles.

As we found we had very similar research and teaching interests, we also began working outside the university, doing consulting and training for businesses. Most of this work we did as a team, and we found we liked working together outside the classroom. After a year or so of consulting as academic colleagues, we decided to formalize the association, despite those strong warnings from business consultants against forming a partnership.

Perhaps not surprisingly, much of our work both when we started and even today has to do with issues of race, gender, and other social dynamics as they relate to identity in organizations and communities. Some of this work focuses on organizational development to help organizations meet the demands of remaining competitive as workforce demographics change. Our consulting practice has been responsible for assessments that have led to substantial organizational changes and transformations. We have also worked with thousands of managers to give them the skills needed to manage today's changing workforce more effectively. Another aspect of our business has included work with international populations, focusing on issues of intercultural communication and management practices.

As a result of the business, we have traveled extensively throughout the United States and the world. We have worked with both Fortune 100 companies and small nonprofit organizations. No matter what the assignment or the location, however, we have always been fascinated by how people react to our partnership and our identities. At times surprise is visible on the face of a client who meets us for the first time. On other occasions it is clear the client finds our relationship intriguing by the way he or she keeps asking us about our partnership, rather than the business we have come to conduct. Sometimes the curiosity is more frank; we have been told by contacts inside organizations that "everyone is trying to figure out what it is with you two." When we ask what this means, the reply is usually that people assume we must be married or a couple in some form. On these occasions, we are reminded what an oddity our relationship is, as it seems to be hard to imagine a white woman and a black man working in a partnership for any other reason.

Often people with whom we work begin by assuming that one of us must be in the lead or controlling role and, therefore, that the other is the (less competent) assistant. But the usual labels cannot immediately be applied to this partnership, and people sometimes react with confusion. Is it the woman who is in the subordinate role, making the minority the leader, or vice versa, making the woman the "boss"? To whom should they be directing their conversation, and who is it safe to ignore? More confusing for those hoping to detect a power imbalance, we are, we believe, both very competent and well matched in our professional strengths. In business negotiations, as we became aware of how our relationship can put some people off balance, we learned to use this dynamic to our strategic advantage.

In less competitive business dealings, we have found that after the initial surprise, many of our clients and some of our coworkers begin to feel as if this cross-race, cross-gender relationship is a source of optimism for them as well. They often seem to want to be part of this relationship and to see it succeed. The partnership seems to become a kind of symbol of the potential for collaboration across racial and gender differences. It is as if we are "beating the odds" and are "lucky" in a curious kind of way. Of course, we can also use this dynamic to our advantage; often clients will bring extra energy and involvement to their work with us, which usually improves the outcome of the consultation all around. For us, these optimistic responses to the partnership can be amusing and sometimes disconcerting; we have learned that they have little to do with us and our work and more to do with the hopes and preconceptions of those around us.

The Friendship

When meeting us, most people immediately notice our obvious racial and gender differences. In our society, these social markers should indicate that we have very little in common. What most people don't realize, even after getting to know us, is just how similar we are despite our physical differences. As is often the case, what is not visible or noticeable is what really matters.

First, we are the same age, born the same year. One of us was raised on the East Coast and the other on the West Coast, but our upbringings were similar. Although we are of different races, both our families had about the same economic level, what could best be described as lower middle class. We both grew up in the suburbs in similar neighborhoods, only 3,000 miles apart. Although our families had their distinct, individual characters, we were raised in a time when most of America shared a common set of values and beliefs.

The shared American culture we grew up with was much less fragmented than in today's multichanneled cable world. We watched the same TV shows, saw the same movies, and listened to the same music on our transistor radios.

Even more significant than our upbringings is that today we both enjoy similar interests. We are voracious readers, and we discovered that we read many of the same books for enjoyment when we were young.

This is not to say that the friendship has been easy or without problems. In fact, we have had major fights concerning the business and how we relate to each other. Interestingly, most of our conflicts have not been as a result of the differences caused by our race and gender. Rather, our need to fulfill the responsibilities of our other social identities as "spouses" and "parents" has sometimes led to choices that have interfered with our work, and our work has sometimes interfered with our family responsibilities. Balancing these needs takes time and is a matter of trial and error, requiring the other partner (and our spouses) to be understanding and patient. Again, carrying us through these difficulties has been our trust in the value of our friendship, a friendship we both experience from a unique perspective.

Patrick's Perspective

Ann has been instrumental in my development as a professional and a person. When we started our partnership five years ago, it was difficult for me to talk to white people as a professional. I was insecure in thinking that they were noticing my race more than anything I had to say. Ironically, part of my professional work is in helping others overcome just this hurdle, so I know it is a fairly common problem for minority professionals. As a result of my insecurity, our early business practice usually consisted of Ann doing most of the talking whenever we met clients. I would chime in later, when I felt safer. Since then I have gained confidence and have become much more self-assured when talking, even to the most senior executives in corporate boardrooms. In the beginning, however, I was grateful to have Ann take the lead whenever we met new clients.

Much of our corporate work has been for very conservative organizations. I think that for me, our success in the very heart of white corporate America has a different significance than it does for Ann. Although I know she is proud of our accomplishments, she can't realize how meaningful it is for me to have had such success in these places where I probably would never have been hired. She might not understand what it feels like, as I work with the most conservative corporate types imaginable, to get to the point at which my race is not the issue.

Ann has also helped to fill the gaps in my understanding of mainstream culture. Like every school child in the fifties and sixties, I was educated by reading the classics, learning the history of the world from a Eurocentric perspective, and viewing mainstream European American culture as the norm. I was also very aware of my African American heritage and went through a period of discovery that left me with a sense of pride in and identity with my own ethnic culture. But that is not to say I rejected mainstream culture. On the contrary, as someone who studies cultures, I have always been fascinated with mainstream American culture, although I have not always understood it. One aspect of our friendship is that I use Ann as my cultural "guide" to make sense of Anglo-Saxon culture. In many ways, Ann has "explained" European and American literary culture and history to me.

I think that, to some extent, I serve the same role for her, helping her to understand African American culture. Unfortunately, I have trouble bringing her into my African American networks, primarily because I am not sure she would understand them or they her. I know this is an unfounded anxiety, and more my problem than hers, but I feel it nonetheless. In fact, she has always impressed me with her sensitivity and understanding of ethnic and minority issues and with her apparent comfort when she is the minority in a group of minorities. We do not talk about race or gender issues that much as part of the friendship, but when we do, I have always found Ann to be open, honest, and sincere.

Part of my unease comes from the realization that although our racial differences do not matter within our friendship, when we are around other African American professionals Ann's race and cultural background are more relevant and noticeable. African Americans are sometimes quick to label whites. I am afraid they will not understand her in the way I do, as a unique individual, and will not be able to get beyond her white skin and identity. This labeling is, in fact, a type of "reverse racism" not usually directed at an individual white person but aimed at some part of white culture in general.

Professionally, I know there are issues relating to race on which Ann defers to me when I am sure she would like to comment. Our work often concerns issues of race and culture. Like most majority people, there is much Ann does not know about minority or ethnic culture and experience. As a researcher, however, there is much she does know about multiculturalism and issues relating to social identity in a pluralistic society; still, on issues concerning race, she usually defers to my perspective.

Socially, I think Ann still does not quite feel comfortable admitting to me she dislikes some African Americans we meet, not because of race but simply because she does not like them as people. I think she is afraid I would take offense. I think she is also hesitant to comment on many of the social issues plaguing the black community, such as crime, drugs, and teen pregnancy. While we talk at great length about most social issues, these particular problems as they relate to the black community we often discuss at an abstract, distant level, not as if one of the people involved in the discussion was a part of that community.

There are times we both forget our major differences, race and gender, and are insensitive to each other. I can remember more than one occasion when Ann has been the only woman at the table when we have been out to dinner with colleagues or clients. On some of these occasions the talk becomes sexist, and I do nothing to support her, even though I know this kind of talk offends her. In fact, when she confronts me later and I apologize, I realize I had been thinking of her as "one of the boys" and not accounting for what it cost her as a woman to fit in socially with an all-male group. On another occasion, however, we traveled to Warsaw, Poland, together soon after the fall of communism as some of the first American educators to enter the country to teach Western business practices. In the week we were there, we never saw another person of color. But it was only toward the end of our stay that Ann became aware that people had been staring at me since our arrival, something I had noticed as soon as we got off the plane. After that, for the rest of our visit, while she could do nothing to change other people's behavior, she did her best to be supportive of me.

I think Ann struggles, as many majority members do, when trying to understand minority experience. Hard as she might try, there is a part of my identity that she can never truly know or experience. Although she understands, and can be empathetic, she cannot be in my skin or experience life as I do. What makes it worse is that I cannot explain it to her. I told her once that I had to raise my children as "black children," not just as children, as she was raising hers. She wanted to know what that meant and I couldn't explain it. I could not explain a 24-hour, seven-day-a-week process that takes a lifetime to learn and deals with both the most trivial and significant nuances of being a minority in this culture. Over the years, as her children and my children have grown, we have compared the different challenges we face as parents, and she has come to see what I meant; at the time, however, I could not put it into words.

I think for majority people who are sincere in their friendships with minorities, their friend's minority identity poses a dilemma. While wanting to become close friends, they are not sure how to share in that unique part of the identity of their friend. If the relationship is to be reciprocal, it is hard to find a comparable part of their identity to share. What I appreciate about Ann is that she is careful never to assume that she has access to that part of my identity simply because we are friends. I appreciate her understanding that my experience is a part of me that is uniquely mine. If she were to say she understood what it was like for me to be a minority because she understood minority experience in the larger sense or because we have been friends, I would be very disappointed. This is not to say that she doesn't understand my experience; in fact, she probably does to a large degree. But as part of our friendship, she never assumes or implies to me that she does.

Ann's Perspective

When Patrick and I first began working together, I had a relatively naive perspective about the impact of race, gender, and ethnicity on peoples' personal and professional lives. In fact, my ideas were unformed and untested; they were based on incidents of prejudice and favoritism viewed from a distance. For me, working as one half of a cross-gender, mixed-race team has been an unexpected and startling education in the nature and intensity of race and gender bias. Moreover, working alongside Patrick has taught me many ways of responding to that bias with grace and with the determination to learn and to succeed.

Initially what brought us together intellectually were shared research and teaching interests. Emotionally what mattered was that we both saw ourselves as outsiders in the almost wholly white, mostly male Ivy League school where we were teaching. We were nontraditional types in a very traditional, conservative environment. Almost from the start, we recognized a commonality of interests and found that we could help each other, whether facing challenges in the classroom or navigating through the shoals of departmental politics. We discovered that the two of us working together made a strong combination: those who would tend to discount me because of my gender still needed to deal with Patrick; those who would discount Patrick because of his race still had to deal with me; and those who would try to discount us both found it harder to do so with two of us to account for.

Historically and on a larger political scale, alliances between dispossessed minority groups often founder at this point: when despite this initial commonality of interests, joint progress toward recognition and growth reveals the many political and social issues on which these groups differ. They recognize many issues in which the stakes they hold are radically different or even in competition. Patrick and I have come up against our own small-scale versions of these challenges. I believe that what has kept us together as a team is Patrick's ability to see both his side of the issue and mine—and his willingness to persist in explaining these insights to me so that ultimately we are both able to see and respect each other's issues. When needed, we have put one person's interest ahead of the other's. We can do this only because we trust each other and believe in the long-term fairness and growth of our partnership.

Professionally, Patrick opened up a whole new discipline for me to understand and study. In addition, watching him teach has helped me improve my classroom persona and shape an open, interactive environment for my students. But it has been our consulting work together that has taught me the most about presenting myself as a woman and as a professional person in mainstream corporate and academic America. Patrick credits me with helping him understand white, mainstream high (literary) culture, but my parents were blue-collar, union, and lower middle class; neither had a college education, and both worked full-time. The ways and mores of the upper middle class, especially of corporate or business-centered America, were things I knew about only from books and movies.

So when we first walked into the offices of conservative corporate America to market our consulting services, it was foreign ground for both of us. Neither of us would have been there without the other.

Personally, I feel fortunate that our relationship has allowed me to understand something of what it is like to be the focus of racial bias. Traveling together on business, Patrick and I have often been stared at, asked to wait a long while to be seated for a restaurant table and then given the worst table in the house, and ignored by receptionists and secretaries. Even more telling are the smaller missteps: the airline check-in clerks who hesitate for a long moment before accepting that, yes, we are traveling together and would like adjacent seats; or the flight attendant on a client's private jet who greeted me cordially but stopped Patrick (in full corporate three-piece suit and tie) on his way into the cabin and began to ask him to put the luggage outside before realizing her mistake. While neither constant nor particularly problematic, such events reveal to me something of the frustration and fatigue that people of color often need to manage when they work in mainstream white environments. In our case, the bias encountered is not always white against black; it also comes from people of both races who resent us as a cross-race couple.

More fortunately, through our consulting I have met and worked closely with other African Americans, several of whom I now count as friends. My partnership with Patrick and these friendships have allowed me to feel, in a concrete way, how inextricably connected we all are. These people are not foreign to me, and they are neither exotic nor sinister. I have a stake in their future and they in mine. Through my relationship with Patrick I am learning to see people of color as *people,* not as "them" but as individuals, and I am learning to recognize at the same time that a significant piece of their unique, individual identity is embodied in their race. Holding these two perceptions simultaneously is a challenging mental and emotional balancing act for me as an observer; I can only imagine the challenge it is for the participants.

Earlier this year, Patrick's teen-age daughter Clairissa came to visit me for a day. I was supposed to advise her about some of her schoolwork. I did this, but we spent most of the afternoon going to lunch and browsing in the shops along the main street of the small town where I live. Like the curiosity that Patrick and I experience in our travels together, this combination of middle-aged white woman and young black girl caused a few stares, despite the racially mixed nature of the community. The fact that we were together was hard for some people to grasp. I found myself wanting to let shop clerks know that the girl was with me—was mine, at least for the day—and they didn't need to watch her so closely when we entered a store and separated to look at different things, as often happens with my own daughters. I felt a little angry and a little embarrassed. I wanted to protect her from the suspicious and even the casually curious stares. Yet I was helpless to do so. I am not sure that Clairissa even noticed. But for me the day represented two things: the growth of my own understanding since I first started working with Patrick, and the growth of his trust in me, to share his child with me for the day.

Conclusion

Writing this article about our partnership has given us a chance to reexamine what it is about this relationship that has made it "work" across the obstacles usually presented by race and gender. At heart, we respect and trust one another, a trust that has become stronger the more we have worked together. We hesitate, however, to draw any universal conclusions from our experiences. Clients and coworkers, observing how well we seem to work together, sometimes ask us for recommendations about building diverse teams, based on our own experiences. Yet we have always been reluctant to present our friendship as an example for anyone to follow. While it seems clear to us now that we have many commonalties in our backgrounds and views on many professional and personal issues, we are at a loss to explain what, initially, enabled us to see these similarities through the visible and real differences of race and gender. We are left with the realization that part of our success was the ability to focus on our commonalities and not let the potential divisiveness in racial and gender differences prevent us from seeing the other person.

PART FOUR

Crossing Cultures

Negotiating

Intercultural

Competence

22 Negotiating Intercultural Competence[1]

Myron W. Lustig and Jolene Koester

We begin with a word of caution. There is no guaranteed prescription that assures competence in intercultural interactions. The complexity of human communication in general, and of intercultural communication in particular, denies the possibility of a quick fix. Fortunately, there is not necessarily only one way to be competent in your intercultural interactions. Even within the context of a specific person and setting, there may be several paths to competent interaction. The goal is to understand the many ways that a person can behave in an interculturally competent manner.

Although there is some disagreement among scholars about how best to conceptualize and measure communication competence, there is increasing agreement about certain of its fundamental characteristics.[2] The following definition of communication competence provides the key components:

> Competent communication is interaction that is perceived as effective in fulfilling certain rewarding objectives in a way that is also appropriate to the context in which the interaction occurs.[3]

This definition provides guidance for understanding communicative and intercultural competence in several ways. A key word is *perceived* because it means that the people in the interaction are in the best position to assess competence. In other words, communicative competence is a social judgment about how well a person interacts with others. That competence involves a social perception suggests that it will always be specific to the context and interpersonal relationship within which it occurs. Therefore, whereas judgments of competence are influenced by an assessment of an individual's personal characteristics, they cannot wholly determine them, because competence involves an interaction between people.

Competent communication results in behaviors that are regarded as *appropriate* and *effective*. Appropriate communication means that people use the symbols they are expected to use in a given context, and their actions thus fit the expectations and demands of the situation. Effective communication means that people are able to achieve desired personal outcomes. Satisfaction in a relationship and the accomplishment of a specific task-related goal are examples of outcomes that people might want to achieve through their communication with others. Thus, communication competence is a social judgment that people make about others.

Competent intercultural communication doesn't happen by accident. It occurs as a result of the knowledge and perceptions that people have about one another, their motivations to engage in meaningful interactions, and their ability to communicate in ways that are regarded as appropriate and effective. To be interculturally competent, therefore, one must have sufficient knowledge of the cultures, contexts, relationships, goals, objectives, and messages that are used; suitable motivations to engage in intercultural experiences; and the skills to enact behaviors that are appropriate and effective.

An important concept for understanding how people negotiate what constitutes intercultural competence is that of *face,* or the public expression of the inner self. Face involves a claim for respect and dignity from others. Regardless of one's culture, all people have face and a desire to maintain and even gain more of it.[4] Face is negotiated in social interactions through the use of various interaction strategies that try to balance the competing goals of task efficiency and relationship harmony.[5]

Tae-Seop Lim suggests that there are three kinds of face needs: the needs for control, approval, and admiration.[6] *Control face* is concerned with individual requirements for freedom and personal authority. It is related to people's need for others to acknowledge their individual autonomy and self-sufficiency. The claim for control face is embodied in the desire to have freedom of action. *Approval face* is concerned with individual requirements for affiliation and social contact. It is related to people's need for others to acknowledge their friendliness and honesty. This type of face is similar to what the Chinese call *lien,* or the integrity of moral character, the loss of which makes it impossible for a person to function appropriately within a social group. Thus, approval face reflects the desire to be treated with respect and dignity. *Admiration face* is concerned with individual needs for displays of respect from others. It is related to people's need for others to acknowledge their talents and accomplishments. This type of face is similar to what the Chinese call *mien-tzu,* or the prestige acquired through success and social standing. Thus admiration face involves the need for others to acknowledge a person's success, capabilities, reputation, and accomplishments.

Intercultural competence is negotiated and maintained through *facework,* which refers to the actions people take to deal with their own and others' face needs. Everyday actions that impose on another such as requests, warnings, compliments, criticisms, apologies, and even praise may jeopardize the face of one or more participants in a communicative act. Ordinarily,

> people cooperate (and assume each other's cooperation) in maintaining face in interaction, such cooperation being based on the mutual vulnerability of face. That is, normally everyone's face depends on everyone else's being maintained, and since people can be expected to defend their faces if threatened, and in defending their own to threaten others' faces, it is in general in every participant's best interest to maintain each others' face.[7]

Thus, facework is concerned with the communication activities that help to create, maintain, and sustain the connections between people.

Competent facework, which lessens the potential for specific actions to be regarded as face threatening, encompasses a wide variety of communication behaviors. These behaviors may include apologies, excessive politeness, the narration of justifications or excuses, displays of deference and submission, the use of intermediaries or other avoidance strategies, claims of common ground or the intention to act cooperatively, or the use of implication or indirect speech. The specific facework strategies a person uses, however, are shaped and modified by his or her culture.

Stella Ting-Toomey[8] and Min-Sun Kim[9] both suggest that cultural differences in individualism-collectivism affect the facework behaviors people are likely to use. Indeed, Harry Triandis believes that the individualism-collectivism dimension is by far the most important attribute that distinguishes one culture from another.[10]

Members of individualist cultures believe that people are only supposed to take care of themselves, and perhaps their immediate families, because the autonomy of the individual is paramount. Key words used to invoke this cultural pattern include *independence, privacy, self,* and the all-important *I.* Decisions are based on what is good for the individual, not the group, because the person is the primary source of motivation. Similarly, a judgment about what is right or wrong can be made only from the point of view of each individual.

In collectivist cultures, decisions that juxtapose the benefits to the individual and the benefits to the group are always based on what is best for each group, and the groups to which a person belongs are the most important social units. In turn, each group is expected to look out for and take care of its individual members. Consequently, collectivist cultures believe in obligations to the group, dependence of the individual on organizations and institutions, a "we" consciousness, and an emphasis on belonging.

Huge cultural differences in facework behaviors can be explained by differences on the individualism-collectivism dimension. In individualist cultures, concerns about message clarity and preserving one's own face are more important than maintaining the face of others, because tasks are more important than relationships and individual autonomy must be preserved. Consequently, direct, dominating, and controlling face-negotiation strategies are common, and there is a low degree of sensitivity to the face-threatening capabilities of particular messages. Thus, people from individualist cultures are trained to speak out and are likely to use confrontational strategies to negotiate intercultural competence.

In collectivist cultures the mutual preservation of face is extremely important because it is vital that people be approved and admired by others. Therefore, indirect, obliging, and smoothing face-negotiation strategies are common, direct confrontations between people are avoided, concern for the feelings of others is heightened, and ordinary communication messages are seen as having great face-threatening potential. Thus, those with a collectivist cultural orientation are likely to use avoidance, third-party intermediaries, or other face-saving techniques.

The degree to which a given set of actions may pose a potential threat to one or more aspects of face depends on three characteristics of the relationship.[11] First, the potential for face threats is associated with the power or status differences among the participants. Interactions among people who differ widely in status and social power have a great potential to be interpreted as face threatening. For example, a verbal disagreement between a respected elder and her assistant will have a greater potential to be perceived as face threatening than will an identical disagreement among people who are equal in seniority and status. Second, relationships in which participants have a large social distance, and therefore less social familiarity, have a great potential for actions to be perceived as face threatening. Thus, very close family members may say things to one another that they would not tolerate from more distant acquaintances. Relationships where strangers have no formal connection to one another but are, for example, simply waiting in line at the train station, the taxi stand, or the bank may sometimes be seen as an exception to this general principle.[12] Third, face-threat potential is related to culture-specific evaluations that people make. That is, cultures may make unique assessments about the degree to which particular actions are inherently threatening to a person's face. Thus, certain actions within one culture may be regarded as face threatening, whereas those same actions in another culture may be regarded as perfectly acceptable. In certain cultures, for instance, calling an adult male "boy" may be regarded as an insult and therefore a threat to face; in other cultures, however, those same actions are perfectly acceptable.

A willingness to understand the face needs of people from other cultures and to behave in ways that preserve and enhance their sense of face is critical to intercultural competence. Always consider a person's need to maintain face in his or her interactions with others. Perceptions of autonomy, approval, and respect by others are important, as is meeting these face needs with facework that is appropriate to the other's cultural beliefs and values. Competence in negotiating intercultural relationships requires an understanding of the differences among people, a willingness to consider and try alternatives, and the skill to enact alternative relational dynamics.

Intercultural competence is, in many ways, an art rather than a science. Our hope is that you will use your artistic talents to make the United States a place in which people from many cultures can live and thrive.

NOTES

1. Excerpted and adapted from Myron W. Lustig and Jolene Koester, *Intercultural Competence: Interpersonal Communication Across Cultures,* 3rd ed. (New York: Longman, 1999).

2. For a discussion of the concept and measurement of communicative competence, see Arthur P. Bochner and Clifford W. Kelly, "Interpersonal Competence: Rationale, Philosophy, and Implementation of a Conceptual Framework," *Speech Teacher* 23 (1974): 279–301; Myron W. Lustig and Brian H. Spitzberg, "Methodological Issues in the Study of Intercultural Communication Competence," in *Intercultural Communication Competence,* ed. Richard L. Wiseman and Jolene Koester (Newbury Park, CA: Sage, 1993), 153–167; Charles Pavitt, "The Ideal Communicator as the Basis for Competence Judgments of Self and Friend," *Communication Reports* 3 (1990): 9–14; Brian H. Spitzberg, "Communication Competence as Knowledge, Skill, and Impression," *Communication Education* 32 (1983): 323–329; Brian H. Spitzberg, "Issues in the Study of Communicative Competence," *Progress in Communication Sciences* (1987): 1–46; Brian H. Spitzberg, "Communication Competence: Measures of Perceived Effectiveness," in *A Handbook for the Study of Human Communication,* ed. Charles H. Tardy (Norwood, NJ:

Ablex, 1988), 67–105; Brian H. Spitzberg, "Issues in the Development of a Theory of Interpersonal Competence in the Intercultural Context," *International Journal of Intercultural Relations* 13 (1989): 241–268; Brian H. Spitzberg, "An Examination of Trait Measures of Interpersonal Competence," *Communication Research* 3 (1991): 22–29; Brian H. Spitzberg, "The Dark Side of (In)Competence," in *The Dark Side of Interpersonal Communication,* ed. William R. Cupach and Brian H. Spitzberg (Hillsdale, NJ: Erlbaum, 1994), 25–49; Brian H. Spitzberg and Claire C. Brunner, "Toward a Theoretical Integration of Context and Competence Research," *Western Journal of Speech Communication* 55 (1991): 28–46; Brian H. Spitzberg and William R. Cupach, *Handbook of Interpersonal Competence Research* (New York: Springer-Verlag, 1989); Brian H. Spitzberg and William R. Cupach, *Interpersonal Communication Competence* (Beverly Hills, CA: Sage, 1984); Brian H. Spitzberg and Michael L. Hecht, "A Component Model of Relational Competence," *Human Communication Research* 10 (1984): 575–599; John Wiemann, "Explication and Test of a Model of Communicative Competence," *Human Communication Research* 3 (1977): 195–213; John M. Wiemann and Philip M. Backlund, "Current Theory and Research in Communicative Competence," *Review of Educational Research* 50 (1980): 185–299; John M. Wiemann and James J. Bradic, "Metatheoretical Issues in the Study of Communicative Competence," *Progress in Communication Sciences* 9 (1988): 261–284.

3. Brian H. Spitzberg, "Communication Competence: Measures of Perceived Effectiveness," in *A Handbook for the Study of Human Communication,* ed. Charles H. Tardy (Norwood, NJ: Ablex, 1988), 67–105.

4. Penelope Brown and Stephen Levinson, "Universals in Language Use: Politeness Phenomena," in *Questions and Politeness: Strategies in Social Interaction,* ed. Esther N. Goody (Cambridge: Cambridge University Press, 1978), 56–289; Penelope Brown and Stephen Levinson, *Politeness: Some Universals in Language Use* (Cambridge: Cambridge University Press, 1987). Though Brown and Levinson's ideas have been criticized on several points, the portion of their ideas expressed here are generally accepted. For a summary of the criticisms, see Karen Tracy and Sheryl Baratz, "The Case for Case Studies of Facework," in *The Challenge of Facework: Cross-Cultural and Interpersonal Issues,* ed. Stella Ting-Toomey (Albany: State University of New York Press, 1994), 287–305.

5. Greg Leichty and James L. Applegate, "Social-Cognitive and Situational Influences on the Use of Face-Saving Persuasive Strategies," *Human Communication Research* 17 (1991): 451–484.

6. We have modified Lim's terminology and concepts somewhat but draw on his overall conception. See Tae-Seop Lim, "Politeness Behavior in Social Influence Situations," in *Seeking Compliance: The Production of Interpersonal Influence Messages,* ed. James Price Dillard (Scottsdale, AZ: Gorsuch Scarisbrick, 1990), 75–86; Tae-Seop Lim, "Facework and Interpersonal Relationships," in *The Challenge of Facework: Cross-Cultural and Interpersonal Issues,* ed. Stella Ting-Toomey (Albany: State University of New York Press, 1994), 209–229; Tae-Seop Lim and John Waite Bowers, "Facework: Solidarity, Approbation, and Tact," *Human Communication Research* 17 (1991): 415–450.

7. Brown and Levinson, 66.

8. See Stella Ting-Toomey, "Toward a Theory of Conflict and Culture," in *Communication, Culture, and Organizational Processes,* ed. William B. Gudykunst, Lea P. Stewart, and Stella Ting-Toomey (Beverly Hills, CA: Sage, 1985), 71–86; Stella Ting-Toomey, "Intercultural Conflict Styles: A Face-Negotiation Theory," in *Theories in Intercultural Communication,* ed. Young Yun Kim and William B. Gudykunst (Newbury Park, CA: Sage, 1988), 213–235; Stella Ting-Toomey, "Intergroup Diplomatic Communication: A Face-Negotiation Perspective," in *Communicating for Peace,* ed. Felipe Korzenny and Stella Ting-Toomey (Newbury Park, CA: Sage, 1990), 75–95; Stella Ting-Toomey and Beth-Ann Cocroft, "Face and Facework: Theoretical and Research Issues," in *The Challenge of Facework: Cross-Cultural and Interpersonal Issues,* ed. Stella Ting-Toomey (Albany: State University of New York Press, 1994), 307–340.

9. Min-Sun Kim, "Culture-Based Interactive Constraints in Explaining Intercultural Strategic Competence," in *Intercultural Communication Competence,* ed. Richard L. Wiseman and Jolene Koester (Newbury Park, CA: Sage, 1993), 132–150; Min-Sun Kim, "Cross-Cultural Comparisons of the Perceived Importance of Conversational Constraints," *Human Communication*

Research 21 (1994): 128–151; Min-Sun Kim, "Toward a Theory of Conversational Constraints: Focusing on Individual-Level Dimensions of Culture," in *Intercultural Communication Theory,* ed. Richard L. Wiseman (Thousand Oaks, CA: Sage, 1995), 148–169; Min-Sun Kim, John E. Hunter, Akira Miyahara, Ann-Marie Horvath, Mary Bresnahan, and Hye-Jin Yoon, "Individual- Vs. Culture-Level Dimensions of Individualism and Collectivism: Effects on Preferred Conversational Styles," *Communication Monographs* 63 (1996): 29–49; Min-Sun Kim and William F. Sharkey, "Independent and Interdependent Construals of Self: Explaining Cultural Patterns of Interpersonal Communication in Multi-Cultural Organizational Settings," *Communication Quarterly* 43 (1995): 20–38; Min-Sun Kim, William F. Sharkey, and Theodore M. Singelis, "The Relationship of Individuals' Self-Construals and Perceived Importance of Interactive Constraints," *International Journal of Intercultural Relations* 18 (1994): 117–140; Min-Sun Kim and Steven R. Wilson, "A Cross-Cultural Comparison of Implicit Theories of Requesting," *Communication Monographs* 61 (1994): 210–235.

10. See Harry C. Triandis, *The Analysis of Subjective Culture* (New York: Wiley, 1972); C. Harry Hui and Harry C. Triandis, "Individualism-Collectivism: A Study of Cross-Cultural Researchers," *Journal of Cross-Cultural Psychology* 17 (1986): 225–248.

11. Brown and Levinson; see also Robert T. Craig, Karen Tracy, and Frances Spisak, "The Discourse of Requests: Assessment of a Politeness Approach," *Human Communication Research* 12 (1986): 437–468.

12. Ron Scollon and Suzie Wong Scollon, "Face Parameters in East-West Discourse," in *The Challenge of Facework: Cross-Cultural and Interpersonal Issues,* ed. Stella Ting-Toomey (Albany: State University of New York Press, 1994), 133–157.

A very common—indeed very ordinary—conversational sequence in which we all engage is the introduction. This conversational pattern is so "ordinary" and taken for granted that most of us tend to be unaware of how scripted and culturally grounded it actually is. Donal Carbaugh and Saila Poutiainen describe conversational introductions as cultural communication events. Their essay focuses on those events in which people are being introduced to each other by a third party. They present differences in Finnish and American cultural premises, sequences, and forms associated with introducing people. Note that they write about the cultural dimensions and features of communication practices, and not about the personalities of specific people. Though anyone from a particular cultural group may use, resist, deny, or exaggerate that culture's way of communicating, doing so relies partly on an understanding of those ways. Thus Donal and Saila call our attention to the subtle requirements that must be performed to interact in an interculturally competent manner.

23 By Way of Introduction: An American and Finnish Dialogue[1]

Donal Carbaugh and Saila Poutiainen

I (DC) had been anticipating my trip to the University of Suomi, in Finland, for a couple of weeks.[2] My family and I were living as foreigners in a city south of the University of Suomi, where I had begun my research and teaching at another university. I had been fortunate to receive a Fulbright professorship to Finland, with the Fulbright arrangement involving me in activities at universities there. So after settling in at our home, I was excited about traveling to Suomi, where I would meet the Finnish colleagues with whom I would be working over the next few months.

Upon arriving at the university, I marveled at the modern facilities and the advanced technologies available in classrooms and computer rooms. I also felt energized by the natural landscape—the main part of the university was located on a hill with views through pines onto a large lake. It was a beautiful winter day, with a deep blue sky above a snow-covered ground. I felt energized and was ready to go.

But I was not ready for what happened next. Upon meeting my Finnish host, Professor Silvo, we began walking through the building where my office would be located. As we moved down a hallway of office suites, I noticed that some people—upon seeing us—seemed to be avoiding us by moving into their offices. After this happened a couple of times, I asked my host if I'd be able to meet my future colleagues, especially Professor Virtanen. I knew we shared some interests in our studies and thought that perhaps I'd seen him out of the corner of my eye, going into an office. Professor Silvo replied that perhaps we could meet him at my next visit, in a couple of weeks.

Given my customary ways, these introductory events were, for me, puzzling and cumbersome. I wondered to myself, "Why can't Professor Virtanen at least say 'hi'? And why aren't the others here more forthcoming with their greetings?" I was accustomed to meeting people quickly, with perhaps a "hello" and a quick exchange of smiles, names, and pleasantries. But nothing of the sort was happening here on my first trip to Suomi. I was puzzled. Moreover, upon meeting someone, the exchanges seemed, at least to me at times, quite cumbersome. I had heard and read about "the silent Finn" and wasn't sure when I should step into a conversation. Moreover, when I did so, I wasn't sure what to say, how long I should speak, or what obligations I had to open or close the conversation.

What follows is a record of one such meeting that occurred upon this, my first trip to Suomi. The meeting involved me with a group of colleagues that I had only met that day, but who eventually, over the years, have become my good friends. The introductory event, on this occasion, involved a Finnish university administrator, two Finnish faculty members, and me. In particular, the event involved me in my role as an American Fulbright professor who was to meet this Finnish university administrator (Professor Jussi Virtanen, male). More specifically, in this exchange, I, the American professor (Donal Carbaugh, male), was being introduced to the administrator by a Finnish professor (Anna Silvo, female). We were accompanied by another Finnish professor (Jussi Levo, male). The event begins as the two Finnish professors escort me down a university corridor to meet the administrator, Jussi Virtanen. He is visible through a slightly opened door.

1. (Anna Silvo knocks on the door.)
2. Jussi Virtanen: Jaa. [Yes.]
3. Silvo: Hei, anteeks, voinko mä esitellä sulle meidän uuden Fulbright professorin? [Hi, excuse me, could I introduce to you our new Fulbright professor?]
4. Virtanen: Joo. [Okay.] (Virtanen rises from his desk, walks around in front of it so he is facing Silvo on his right, Carbaugh in front of him, and Levo on his left.)
5. Silvo: Jussi, I would like you to meet Dr. Carbaugh.
   And (Silvo looks at Carbaugh while gesturing to Virtanen) Professor Virtanen.
6. Virtanen: Hello. (Shaking hands with Carbaugh)
7. Carbaugh: Good to meet you.
8. (10- to 16-second pause)

9. Virtanen: So, uhm, when did you arrive?
10. Carbaugh: Well, we arrived in early January and we've been here for about a month now.
11. And it's been very good to be here. We've been able to see just a little bit of Finland but
12. what we've seen we like very much. We feel like we're at home. With the good help of
13. people like Anna and Jussi, they've made us feel even more at home.
14. (12- to 20-second pause)
15. Virtanen: Have you been meeting people here?
16. Carbaugh: Well, yes, uh, we met several people this morning and uh I've heard a little bit
17. about their research projects and that's been very interesting. It sounds like there are
18. many interesting things going on here. And uh I'm just so impressed with your physical
19. facilities. The buildings are so nice and your lab seems very well equipped.
20. (10- to 16.9-second pause)
21. Virtanen: So what are you going to do while you are here?
22. Carbaugh: Well uh mainly I have teaching obligations at another university. I have a
23. couple of lecture series. And then here at Suomi I'll be teaching and doing some
24. seminar work. And so most of my time will be spent teaching here and there.
25. (10- to 13.5-second pause)
26. Carbaugh: Well, it's been very good to meet you and I look forward to spending time at your university.
27. Virtanen shakes hands with Carbaugh, nods, smiles, and bows slightly. Silvo, Levo, and Carbaugh turn and leave.

As this event began, I felt rather comfortable, up through line 7 at least. However, at that point, as the event unfolded, I met what was for me a pause in the conversation that went well beyond any I had encountered before. As the seconds ticked by, and as is typical for me when sensing something may have gone awry, alarms began to sound in my mind. Perhaps I had done something wrong, or perhaps I was supposed to be doing something different, or saying something else. Why was this pause lasting so long? Finally, and thankfully from my view, Professor Virtanen filled the silence and asked me when I had arrived. I told him when we arrived and how things were going, and tried to indicate that Anna and Jussi had been fine hosts to me. I tried to offer some information that he could take up, ask me about, or build on. After doing this, however, there was no uptake on the matters I had mentioned, but instead an even longer pause—perhaps up to 20 seconds long! What was going on? Had I done something wrong? My collar began to moisten as I looked to

Jussi and Anna for nonverbal cues about what to do next. Both were delightfully calm, small smiles at the corners of their mouths. Were they smiling at me? All nonverbal indications from them seemed positive. Evidently, from their view, things were proceeding quite well, thank you. At the time, I found this hard to believe, especially when the next question from Professor Virtanen did not seem to relate to anything I had said earlier, but initiated another topic altogether, about the people I had been meeting.

And so the event went. As we cycled through the question-answer-silence sequence another time, it occurred to me that perhaps it was my responsibility to conclude our meeting. After all, I thought—perhaps unwittingly initiating an escape from the conversation—I may be taking too much of the administrator's valuable time. So eventually, after the fourth and shortest of the pauses I broke in with a closing, thanking Professor Virtanen for meeting me and indicating an interest in seeing him again.

Two weeks after this exchange, I was having lunch with Professor Silvo. We were discussing a student project about uses of silence when the exchange above came to mind. I asked her about it and she said, yes, the use of long pauses in conversation—at least longer "when compared to the ones you Americans tend to do"—is common in Finnish conversation. But also, she said, these pauses are especially long when conversing with Professor Virtanen, even by Finnish standards! After discussing this for a while, I asked her a question to which I thought I already knew the answer. "Should I have waited for Professor Virtanen to close the conversation?" She smiled kindly, said again how long his pauses tended to be. "You know," she said, "he's very Finnish." Then she answered my question: "Yes, it is up to him to close the conversation. He wanted to give the proper amount of time to meeting you." I had not known enough to give Professor Virtanen, and this event, the "proper amount of time."[3]

We have provided some initial reactions to this event as they were formed, early on, by the American (DC). Now let us add additional reflections about this same event from a Finnish view. How might the conduct of this event, and initial reactions to it, be formulated by a Finnish participant?

When I (SP) look at this exchange, I cannot help but hear some common and important features of Finnish communication. According to my experience, these features are present and active in many intercultural communication situations, like this one between Finns and others. For example, consider Professor Silvo's response to DC about pauses in Finland being longer "when compared to the ones you Americans tend to do." Professor Silvo's comment reflects her own considerable intercultural experiences and expertise, including living in the United States for several years. Clearly she knew firsthand how Finnish and American pauses differ in length. Perhaps more generally, comments as these may reflect the strong sense Finns have about their way of communicating and how it compares to the ways of others, such as Americans,

Germans, and Japanese. For various reasons, Finns are interested in knowing what others think about Finns and Finnish communication. The images Finnish people have about themselves, relative to others, are partly based on images of others they have contacted personally or, especially for the younger generation, perhaps seen in Finnish popular culture and television. Many popular American television programs are shown on Finnish television, thus providing a daily contrast between this mediated "American" world and the Finnish one. Based largely on these contacts and images, some Finns—especially those who have not traveled to the United States—may believe they "know" how Americans communicate, how they talk, and what they sound like. Thus, Finns may know that their pauses are at times much longer than those that are typical in "America." When considering this kind of intercultural encounter from the Finnish perspective, it is important to remember this: One's prior personal contacts, experiences, and exposure to mediated images may establish expectations about others' communication, for example of Finns as being relatively silent or of Americans as being talkative, with those expectations perhaps shaping parts of this kind of encounter.

A second important point to stress is the perceived language skills of the Finnish speakers. While often in situations of speaking a foreign language with cultural others, and in spite of an obvious fluency with a foreign language, Finnish speakers may lack confidence or assurance in using that foreign language.[4] In the scenario above, English is required of the Finnish speakers; this may be the second, third, or even fourth language of a Finnish speaker.[5] Recall, in this scene, that Virtanen has to speak English not only with a respected native English speaker (DC), but also in the presence of two of his coworkers, who are important to him.

To focus on the kind of interaction described above, one event that may have been taking place when DC first visited the Finnish universities might be called, from the Finnish perspective, "getting to know, or getting acquainted with the workplace or house" (in Finnish this is *tutustua taloon*). When "getting acquainted with the workplace," a main initial activity involves walking around and seeing the facilities, the important offices, and hearing from the host about the workplace, its history, the people, the relationships, and the preferred practical daily procedures. Perhaps Silvo and Levo, and other faculty, were engaging in activities that are deemed appropriate to that kind of Finnish activity—that is, to helping DC "get acquainted with the department, workplace, or house." In Finland such an activity doesn't necessarily involve verbal introductions with the people working in that department. The main activities in the Finnish activity of "getting acquainted with the house" would involve seeing the facilities and hearing about the workplace from a host or hostess. Naturally, of course, one might see people during such a visit, but here's an important point: in Finland, during this *tutustua taloon* activity among Finns, there would be no felt need to talk with visitors or to be verbally introduced to them. A nod, a slight smile, and/or a "hello" if passing them in the hallway would be quite enough. "Getting acquainted with the workplace"—that is, in this Finnish way—may require very little by way of verbal interaction with those besides the host that one sees. Minimizing verbal interaction can also be a way of not wasting DC's, and other participants' time in relatively "superficial" matters.

At this first visit, the host, Silvo, mentioned to DC that it may be best to meet some of her colleagues, including Professor Virtanen, after the first visit, at a later date. Indeed, Finnish readers of the introduction episode have called the event a "handshaking delegation" that can seem very distant and formal. Perhaps this is because of several reasons. Formal introductions are not part of the normal, daily professional communication in this Finnish scene, nor typically a part of initial visits. Formal introductions can require special preparation. As contrasted with a Finnish greeting such as an exchange of nods, a formal first meeting may—perhaps even should—involve exchanging information and ideas that are special and worthy of the occasion. To get to know someone, or to meet someone formally, takes more time and is usually done directly and concisely by discussing one's official affairs, business, and duties. Professor Virtanen may have wanted the time to prepare for his first meeting with Professor Carbaugh, a highly respected guest, and perhaps Professor Virtanen wanted to make sure that the first meeting would be rewarding and productive for both Professor Carbaugh and himself. That kind of Finnish interaction might involve the Finnish style of talking *asiaa,* or "matter-of-fact" speaking. This style, prevalent in scenes of education, consists not so much of small talk, pleasantries, and getting acquainted but of significant and substantial exchanges of important information on a variety of matters or topics. As such, talking *asiaa* involves direct, concise, and substantial discussion about one's official affairs, business, and duties.[6]

Notice then, from the Finnish perspective on these matters, several features: Finnish interactions of this kind can presume something about American speaking based on the ways Americans have acted in the past. As a result, in scenes like the one above, Americans may be relied on—by Finns—to talk a lot. Finns, on the other hand, may prefer to speak very little in such situations, especially when speaking a foreign language, including English. Accentuating these differences are Finnish folk events, such as "getting acquainted with the workplace." Only the assigned host is required to entertain the guest. Moreover, Finnish events like this one do not necessarily incur the obligation from others of verbal communication with the guest. As a result, workers may move into offices quite appropriately without speaking to a visitor. Further, when being introduced to a visitor in Finland, very little information needs to be exchanged verbally. If one is involved in a more formal meeting, this may take place one on one, in a small group, and at a specified date and time. Both third-party introductions and formal one-on-one meetings may be conducted through talking *asiaa,* which is rather straightforward, direct, and matter-of-fact, about official affairs and duties. Note that this is quite unlike American "small talk," which may involve lengthy exchanges of "pleasantries."

Being mindful of these few Finnish cultural features, then, a participant might monitor the above encounter somewhat differently than DC did initially. Perhaps Finnish communication, here, moves between actions one does when "getting acquainted with the workplace" and a more formal and meaningful meeting through the matter-of-fact, *asiaalinen* style. With it, participants may anticipate a direct style of speaking, exchange information matter-of-factly, and interpret ideas accordingly. Understanding the exchange in this way suggests the following additional insights about it.

After Silvo introduces DC and Virtanen to each other (lines 5–7), Virtanen asks DC about his time of arrival (line 9). DC's response to that question is on line 10, "we arrived in early January," but is followed by several more utterances about Finland, his feelings, and friends. Note how that same pattern is repeated as Virtanen asks his second question (line 15): "Have you been meeting people here?" DC's answer is on line 16, "we met several people this morning," but again is followed by additional descriptive commentary about research projects, physical facilities, and laboratories. From a Finnish perspective, especially one accustomed to a kind of talking *asiaa* that is concise and direct, DC has given a sufficient answer on line 9, and again on line 16. Such answers, like these, are what might be preferred as *asiaa,* something short, matter-of-fact, and directly responsive to the queries. No more speaking is required. As a result, the rest of DC's responses, while descriptive—and perhaps produced in a spirit of American "small talk" or exchanging pleasantries—are not so significant, at least to Finns. A Finnish listener might even wonder: why are these details forthcoming? In fact, a Finn might, indeed, ask silently: What is he talking about? Isn't DC saying something else than what Virtanen asked of him? For example, when DC says on line 12, "We feel like we're at home," or on line 13, "Anna and Jussi, they've made us feel even more at home," a Finnish listener might wonder if DC is indeed telling the truth and being honest. Having said so much in this way, DC may easily be heard, like those Americans seen on TV, as so very American, talkative, even exaggerating, and maybe even being stereotypically superficial ("Can he really feel at home, as he says?"). Is he speaking the truth or "just being nice"? From a Finnish point of view, especially one mindful of talking *asiaa,* he may easily be heard as saying more than was required in this situation and therefore be deemed guilty of stretching the truth a bit.[7]

Focusing for a moment on the Finnish pauses that are active in this exchange, we might ask why they are so long—at least when compared to those Americans might expect in their place. As mentioned above, one reason is this: Professor Virtanen is known for using long pauses, even longer than is typical by Finnish standards. More generally, pauses tend to be much longer in Finnish than in American communication. There are several reasons for this. First, it is customary for Finnish conversations to be punctuated by lengthy pauses, even if they are rarely as long as the ones in use here. Second, the long pauses might result from the Finnish speaker's speaking a foreign language, thus taking considerable time both to interpret the English being spoken and to formulate the proper responses in English. Third, introducing a foreigner (DC in this scene) is to create a scene that is perhaps a bit unusual to some Finnish participants. The foreigner may do something unusual, like the expressive "small talk" behavior, whereas a Finn might prefer or expect a more short, matter-of-fact talking *asiaa*. As a result, Finnish expectations must be adjusted, which takes time. Together, then, these features of the conversation lay some possible cultural ground for such long pauses in this situation.

What we have tried to do in our analysis is to notice features in one communication encounter that are deeply cultural. An American may notice people who are, in his words, not talking very much, not trying to avoid long pauses, and, when speaking, saying little. Perhaps unwittingly, the American produces an American folk version of communication, "small talk," and in so doing, does not quite meet the expectations the Finnish participants may have. A Finn may notice an American who, as expected, likes to talk a lot. Ready for verbal action, he says more than the occasion seems to warrant; he also says things other than expected, bringing informal affairs to a more formal occasion. Perhaps unwittingly, Finns may produce folk versions of communication including a Finnish form of "getting acquainted with a workplace" and "talking about matters of fact." To summarize with a metaphor, the encounter involves two scripts for the same play, two sets of lines for the same scene, and thus the stage is set for an intercultural drama.

We have come to understand the above encounter, and others that are similar, through American and Finnish cultural features that are active when a foreigner in Finland is being introduced by a third party. Introductory encounters, as this, can provide a kind of intercultural play. As such, we note the preparation and propriety that may be preferred for a Finnish version, as Professor Silvo said of Professor Virtanen: "He wanted to give the proper amount of time to meeting you." As a Finnish reader of this essay commented: "When meeting someone we want to make sure there is enough time to really talk about something." A proper, formal meeting, from the vantage point of this script, requires time and adequate preparation. When we discussed this kind of scene with other Finns, they made such comments as, "The whole scene certainly sounds very familiar! Slow pace, pauses, direct questions"; it sounds "delightfully familiar"; it "reminds me of formal parts of weddings and birthday parties"; and it is like "thousands of similar events when introducing foreign visitors to university officials. Very typical, delightfully typical." The intercultural dynamics seem to strike a chord. Yet understanding them is a tall order indeed.

Our understanding has come partly through ideas of propriety and preparation, in a Finnish version of the play. Propriety means that one should conduct a formal introduction in the proper way, with the appropriate degree of decorum and respect. If possible, one should give the event forethought, learning what one can about the visitor, and preparing questions that are fitting for the occasion. In fact, the questions used in this encounter—"When did you arrive," followed by "When will you leave," "Have you been meeting people," "What are you going to do while you are here"—are typically used in such exchanges between Finns and foreigners. Moreover, silence and patience in such exchanges are an acknowledged way of giving the occasion its proper due. Exchanges such as this should not be too short, and thus one expects silence as a sign that the occasion is being conducted properly, politely, and respectfully. As many Finns are quick to point out, good human relations, like Finnish coffee, take time to brew. Giving the event the proper amount of time makes it that much better, and one cannot hurry the process. So Finnish standards of propriety and preparation are active in silence, signifying that the visitor and the occasion are being treated respectfully and properly.

As a result of these cultural ideas, a Finnish interactional script can be produced during an introduction: pacing tends to be slower "than Americans tend to do"; verbalizations might be prepared ahead of time; and silence is quite comfortable and acceptable to prolong the situation and thus make it more meaningful and more respectful of social relations. Further, there are important nonverbal messages that may be difficult to notice in the conversation above but are nonetheless worthy of comment. Notice that Virtanen rises from his desk and walks in front of it to stand directly in front of DC. This is a gesture of respect from Virtanen for the occasion and the visitor. Further, Silvo and Levo are situated on either side of DC. This is a gesture of support by them. More nonverbal subtleties are also active here, including differing uses of the eyes and face. Noticing these nonverbal actions helps us understand how this event, and scene, was structured in a Finnish way to convey respect and support of DC, the other participants, and the occasion.

A popular American version of this play is different, for there are, of course, other features operating. Ideas perhaps active in American professional and business scripts may come to the fore, particularly with regard to introductory lines, quantity, and efficiency. Upon arriving, one may walk through a hallway and meet a large number of people, the feeling being that one has been greeted by, and introduced to, the whole group. Unlike the Finnish ideas of propriety and respect, an American idea may be "to get to know"—in this way—as many people as quickly as possible. Cultural notions of efficiency and quantity may be active. The American interactional script accompanying these ideas may be conducted at a quicker pace, with short pauses; spontaneous verbalizations play into the scene rather than prescripted comments; and the words, more than the nonverbal actions, tend to be the crucial site of communicative messages. Against this backdrop, within this American version of the play, silences of even a short duration, "compared to those Finns produce," can be sources of discomfort for some Americans. As one Finnish observer noted about the above exchange, DC "suffers from the pauses!"

We have offered a series of observations on some initial interactions and an intercultural encounter as they occurred in actual situations involving Americans and Finns. We have interpreted some of the features involved in this one encounter from Finnish and American perspectives. Based on several other similar events, we believe that these features suggest ways of structuring acts and sequences of this kind. We have thus noticed how these communication practices are shaped by cultural terms for those practices, such as "getting acquainted with the workplace" and talking *asiaa* in Finnish, or "small talk" in American English. Each draws attention to a cultural form of communication, through cultural terms, that perhaps identifies the kinds of communicative practices each produces. Further, we discussed various cultural premises about verbal and nonverbal action, about what is proper and preferred communication in such scenes in Finland and the United States. By focusing our attention on specific and actual intercultural interactions, by interpreting them through cultural terms, and by exploring some of the premises active in these interactions and terms, we have provided an admittedly partial and suggestive account of Finnish and American communication, by way of introduction. We hope also to have introduced, by discussing interactions and cultural terms, a way of understanding and enhancing intercultural communication.

NOTES

1. The authors acknowledge the helpful suggestions for improving the essay from several students of Finnish culture and communication, including Marjatta Nurmikari and Michael Berry among others. To them, we extend our heartfelt thanks but no blame.

2. The names of people and places that we use in this paper have been changed to honor the confidence of our colleagues.

3. We note here that uses and interpretations of silence vary not only by speaker but also by region within Finland. As a Finnish reader of this essay commented, "A Karelian Finn may have filled some of these pauses," unlike Virtanen, a Häme Finn.

4. This is especially difficult when native Finnish speakers are expected to do things in a second language, such as an American version of "small talk," that are not done quite that way in Finnish. On a related point, Finns themselves may be quite reticent in using their own language. This is a source of the oft-repeated joke, from Finns to others: "Why, Finnish people can be silent in several languages!"

5. It is not unusual for Finnish students to have studied and be fluent in English, Swedish, and German in addition to Finnish.

6. There is a special Finnish attitude associated with this style; it suggests that the discussion should be done "istua rauhassa," without any hurry. For these observations we are drawing partly on Richard Wilkins's dissertation work at the University of Massachusetts on "talking *asiaa*" in Finland.

7. In Finland and many European countries, "Americans" are often regarded as "superficial" because of such behaviors.

Zhong Wang and Rui Shen knew each other from their hometown of Beijing. They both came to the United States to study: Zhong on the East Coast, and Rui on the West. Their essay is derived from personal exchanges between them, and it shows the emotional, cultural, and linguistic difficulties that are often experienced in adjusting to a foreign culture. They describe the painful, joyous, busy, confusing, complex, and rewarding processes of acculturation to the United States.

24 Acculturation in a Foreign Land

Zhong Wang and Rui Shen

Rui: The First Attempt at Involvement

Dear Zhong,

It is really great that we have re-connected with each other in America.

I arrived in the United States two months ago. When I landed in Eugene, Oregon, it was one o'clock in the morning. The time difference from China to America's West Coast confused me about how long it took me to fly across the Pacific Ocean. Once I landed, a middle-aged couple warmly greeted me. Entrusted by the International Student Office of the University of Oregon, the couple would host me for my first two weeks in this new country. The hostess, Sheila, drove us "home" while we talked and laughed. After arriving at their house, she treated me with homemade pies and juice, and then we chatted some more for a while. When I went to the bedroom upstairs, I couldn't believe it was already daybreak.

Probably one or two hours after I fell into sleep, Sheila woke me up. She said: "Rui, a new Bible class will start today. You might be interested in going there with us." Thus, within six hours after I arrived in the United States, I seated myself in an American church. It was the first time I had gone to church throughout my life.

The woman preaching had a beautiful voice. She read a certain chapter of the Bible and explained it sentence by sentence. Then she read a letter from her friends who were American missionaries in Africa. We learned that her friends had built a church in a remote African village, and a lot of people there had accepted Christianity. The audience fervently applauded and was greatly moved. After the meeting, everybody filled in an application form to join Bible study class. I did too, because I thought, being "fresh off plane," the Bible class would help me get to know American society faster. A week later, I was informed that I had been accepted into the class. Some new friends, whom I only met once in church, called to congratulate me on my acceptance. I was touched by their warm and nice words. When I looked up at the bright-blue autumn sky above this new land, I felt blessed.

I went to the Bible class several times, but then I became too busy with my schoolwork to continue going. Whenever the class was over, some women I did not know very well would come over and hug me before they left: "Thank you for coming, I'm glad to see you again," they'd say.

Their kindness and piousness amazed me. Most of them were well-educated career women. After daytime work, they voluntarily came to the class. What motivated and called them to do so? A woman walked close to me and asked: "Ma'am, are you Christian?" I recognized that she was the other foreigner in our study group. She was from Iran. I wondered if we were the only two foreigners in the whole class.

"No," I shook my head quietly, "and how about you?"

"I was born into a Muslim family. Are you Buddhist?"

"No, I am not," I hesitated for a second, "I don't have specific religious beliefs. But I believe in Confucius and Lao-tze. They were great philosophers of my country. Their philosophies have been in existence for two thousand years. They told us to develop perfect morality and live with nature harmoniously."

I did not know how I could explain my religious perplexity and the rapid cultural changes that have happened in the recent decades of China. I couldn't tell her that when I hold the hymns with the red cover, I am suddenly reminded of my early childhood experiences in the "Great Proletarian Cultural Revolution" of the late 1960s in China. During that time, every Chinese, young or old, held Chairman Mao's red book and sang for him. I terrified myself with this analogy. In substance, Christianity did not share any similarities with the idolatry of Mao Zedong during the period of 1966–1976 in China. However, I found a similarity in power—the power of religion and quasi-religion. Good or bad, they both have profound social impacts. Eugene, a city with only 100,000 people, has over a hundred churches. All of these reminded me that in the new culture, there are too many layers to be fully understood immediately.

As you see, I have been busy since my very first day in the United States. I felt overwhelmed. In China I "learned" a lot about America from either academic channels or government propaganda. No matter what I learned, positive or negative, I never felt alien to the "America" that I constructed from those secondhand materials. But after I came here, I found I was totally a stranger.

I have suspended my church activities because I am getting really busy with my schoolwork. I noticed that American professors rarely lecture the whole class. Usually, they use fifty percent of class time to lecture and fifty percent to pose questions for discussion. At the beginning, I was very nervous and highly focused. Sometimes, I could only understand one third. I was especially lost when students conducted discussions. I was worried. I went to my professor after class. She consoled me: "Don't worry, Rui. One step at a time. You'll get better." But how long will it take me to "get better"? I don't know, but I can't wait to get there.

How are your studies? Are you OK? You've been here for a year. I guess you don't have language problems, do you?

—Love, Rui

Zhong: A Language Issue

Dear Rui,

You mentioned several times in recent letters about your difficulty with the language. In fact, I have also had painful experiences adapting to a new language environment. To the foreign students who study humanities or social sciences, the biggest challenge is language, linguistically, culturally, and academically. Once admitted, you are assumed to share the same language level with your American classmates.

It is said that most Asian students are quiet. I, unfortunately, fall into this category. I would not be very silent if I had strong confidence in my articulation. During the first two months, I felt bad whenever I failed to greet people well in a hallway, in a classroom, or in front of my office. For example, one day I encountered a woman from another department in the school elevator. She said: "Hi, how are you doing today?" Then I was stuck and I did not know how to go on. After an embarrassing three-second silence, she nicely offered a conversation topic. I wanted to respond to her in the same comfortable way, but before I could finish my process of translation, the elevator reached the first floor. She said "take care" and "bye" sweetly and I had to answer in a hurry without being fully detached from the translation process. I watched her walk away. I wondered how I became so slow? So dumb? So awkward? Yes, "awkward." This is the best word I can think of to describe myself during my first three months.

In China, language was an instinct. I never needed to organize my thoughts before speaking. In Chinese, I can talk properly, persuasively, and humorously. My humor was an intelligent one. It could make groups of people laugh. My talk showed my insights about life. My talk made me a pleasant, gracious, and delightful person.

Language, a thing that I've taken for granted for 26 years in China, became a luxury in America. Without the power of language, I felt I was disabled or abnormal. I identified myself with deaf-mute people. I dreamed about speaking English fluently. Words came out of my mouth, like a spring meandering along a mountain and merging into a long river.

Language is a resource that can externalize my inner self. I have a strong desire to articulate my ideas eloquently, logically, beautifully, and to be an accomplished scholar in English, my new language.

I have no doubt that I learned a great deal after I dove into a new culture. However, the more I learn, the more I notice how much more I need to learn.

I often ponder what it means to be "successful"? It means you figure out what you want to do, what you can do, and finally you do it. I guess to reach what we consider "success," we need to go through a painful process.

Tell me more about your life after you finish your final exam.

—Love, Zhong

Rui: School Life

Dear Zhong,

I finished my finals last week. The most important reward of my first term was acquiring a learning method, an active learning style. I was required to read almost 100 pages per day and write a book report every week. However, the purpose of reading is not merely for understanding but also for learning to think and critique. I am glad that now, whenever I read academic materials, I read them actively instead of passively.

The first term was very tiring. One professor required twelve textbooks for his class. The learning pace of the first ten weeks was like speeding. I worked very hard to keep up. Toward the end of the final exam, all my old illnesses that were healed years ago came back: stomach aches, serious headache, and insomnia. The rain is endless during winters in Eugene. Holding my books and notes, looking at the misty drizzles outside my window, I can't help asking myself: "Why am I here? Why did I bother to fly thousands of miles from China to Eugene? Yes, I am here to study. But why did I choose such hardship and misery?" I miss my husband, I miss my son, and I miss my home city.

Last Friday was my birthday. I finished my last exam of the term. I spent the whole day in the computer room typing. I was stressed and did not eat anything. I never touched a computer before I came to Eugene, so I had to learn everything from scratch and struggle every minute with frustration. I went out of the school building. It was rainy, windy, and chilly. Yellow leaves were scattered on the ground. I asked myself again: "Why am I here? Studying, reading, reading, and studying? Is this the life I am supposed to have? Having arrived in the United States for ninety days, I have not had a chance to go to any malls yet. I have no idea what American shopping malls look like. I do not have time to watch TV or videos. I do not have time to chat with old friends and make new ones. I do not even have enough time to sleep." This was my life for my first three months in America. This was the life I worked very hard to maintain and endure. This was the life I tried to treasure, because this was the life I chose.

I walked across the campus. In my mind, I whispered to my family in China. I talked to my husband, my son, and my parents. Life was hard and I was alone. I wanted to quit and go home.

I stopped before the Smith Family Book Store. The word "family" was dear to me. I walked in and climbed the old, narrow, steep stairs to the second floor. I walked between the bookshelves aimlessly. Suddenly, a familiar pocket picture jumped in front of my eyes: it was the picture of my favorite American woman poet, Anne Sexton. I squatted down and opened the book. A letter caught my attention. It was a letter written by Anne Saxton to her sixteen-year-old daughter Linda Sexton. And this letter was found after she committed suicide many years later.

> *Dear Linda,*
> *I am in the middle of a flight to St. Louis to give a reading. I was reading a New Yorker story that made me think of my mother and all alone in the seat I whispered to her, "I know, Mother, I know." (Found a pen!) And I thought of you—someday flying somewhere all alone and me dead perhaps and you wishing to speak to me.*
> *And I want to speak back. Linda, maybe it won't be flying, maybe it will be at your own kitchen table drinking tea some afternoon when you are 40—Anytime—I want to say to you.*
> *1st I love you.*
> *2. you never let me down.*
> *3. I know. I was there once. I, too, was 40 and with a dead mother whom I needed*
> *still.*
> *. . .*
> *I want to thank you for loving me!*
> *. . .*
> *This is my message to the 40-year-old Linda. No matter what happens you were always my bobolink, my special Linda Gray. Life is not easy. It is awfully lonely. I know that. Now you too know it—whenever you are, Linda, talking to me. But I've had a good life—I wrote unhappy—but I lived to the hilt. You too, Linda—Live to the HILT! To the top. I love you, 40-year-old Linda, and I love what you do, what you feel, what you are! Be your own woman. Belong to those u love. Talk to my poems, or talk to your heart—I'm in both if u need me—I lied, Linda. I did love my mother and she loved me. So there!*
> *—xoxoxo Mom*

While reading the letter, tears filled my eyes. At the moment when I felt terribly lonely, my favorite woman poet "came" and talked to me softly about loneliness, love, life, and hopes. Zhong, have you had a moment like this before?

—Love, Rui

Zhong: Homesickness

Dear Rui,

You are not alone. I have been there many times—I have been very homesick, too. It almost destroyed my faith in my capability of "hanging in there." That happened during my first two months here. . . .

One day, having finished a night class, I went back home. I still did not feel that I fully understood the content the professor lectured that day. I ate something tasteless. It was not appetizing food. I didn't have time to cook. After I washed my dishes, I lay on the bed, feeling very tired. I had very little furniture. The only things in my bedroom were a twin bed, a desk, a floor lamp, and two big suitcases that I brought from Beijing. The international air-lines only allowed two suitcases. I crammed them with several books, dictio-naries, as well as some clothes. Fortunately, I came to Florida, and I didn't have to bring winter clothes. I looked around the empty room and felt my mind was just as empty, unbearably empty. I felt myself shrinking, and at that moment, I needed someone's hand on my shoulder to keep me physically visible. I leaned forward, picked up my pillow, and held it tightly, as if the pillow was a life-saver and I was drowning in water. It was dark outside. I did not cry. The strong fear and homesickness held my throat. I picked up the phone and dialed. I heard Mother's voice, so clear and dear: "Weih—who is it?"

"Mom—" I answered with a trembling voice.

"Oh! IT'S ZHONG!" Mother raised her voice, stimulated and concerned: "How are you? Are you OK?"

"Yes, I am fine. Really, I am fine. How about you?"

"I AM FINE. Don't worry about me, Zhong. It is nice to receive your call. But you don't have to call me so often. I am really fine. I take care of myself very well. Forget about me and concentrate on yourself and your studies. How are your studies going this week? It must be very difficult for you in your first semester. It has been 35 days since you left. I count every day."

Tears fell from my eyes. I couldn't say a word. Being silent myself, I heard my Mom continue in a very soothing voice: "Don't be afraid. You will be all right. Nothing is too difficult if you put your heart into it. Try to make some friends. Try to talk to your professors if you have problems."

"Yeah, Mom, you are right. People here are very nice, actually. I probably spend too much time studying. I will try to socialize and relax a little bit." I tried very hard to keep my voice normal. I tried to calm down but the tears just trickled down my cheeks.

"Take care of yourself. Keep yourself in good shape. You wouldn't want to ruin your health for your degree, right? Don't worry too much about your stud-ies. Even if you do not perform ideally, you are still my daughter!"

"Thank you Mom." This time, the tears flooded.

I hung up the phone and buried my face into a towel. "Mom, Mom," I called in my mind. My dear, loving, supportive, aging, widowed mother. What a sin it is that I left her alone in China. How weak I felt without seeing her. In that moment, I thought about returning to China at once. I thought I would call the airlines that night and book a ticket. I must see her in two days. I couldn't wait. I felt my face burning. Was I crazy?

The next day, I recovered after an eight-hour sleep. I didn't go back to China. I went to school. I greeted people. And people responded with a high spirit. I was influenced. I greeted the next person in a very pleasant way. And I was responded to even more pleasantly. My mood changed. I went to my of-fice. How lovely my office is. My office mate, Christine, looked very beautiful that day. She brought me a book, *Handbook of Human Communication,* and said it might be helpful to me as a newcomer to the field. I chatted with her for a few minutes before she had to teach her class. I sat down. Recalling the pre-vious night, I realized that calling back home and crying did not help me ex-cept to let me unload some emotional burdens.

The homesickness became cyclical. But the next time I experienced it at home, I sat and calmed myself down, recalled something pleasant that occurred during the day, and thought about the tasks I had to do before the weekend. After a while, I got up, turned on the lamp, and spread out my books and notes. I reviewed and previewed readings until midnight. It seems the loneliness was peacefully overcome.

Dear Rui, believe me, you will be fine.

—Love, Zhong

Rui: Am I Too Critical?

Dear Zhong,

How have you been? Time went fast. It has been nearly a year since I came here. This term, I am a teaching assistant for two sessions of an undergraduate Chinese class. One day after teaching, Cathy ran into me. She is a graduate student majoring in Chinese Fine Arts History.

"Hi, Rui, imagine you drive your car into a gas station. While you have your gas filled, you run fast into McDonald's, bought a hamburger and a drink, came back in a hurry, pulled out, and drove directly to your work place. How is that?" Cathy asked.

"Doesn't sound bad," I replied pleasantly, without knowing her purpose.

"But if that happened in China, I mean if you ate fast food while driving cars in China, how does that sound?" she said.

"That sounds even better." I affirmed.

"Rui, I am not kidding!" Cathy looked serious: "I just read a report. It says China will step into the 'fast food culture.' Isn't that bad!"

"So, what do you expect of China's future?" I asked her.

"I don't know," She hesitated, "But definitely not 'fast food culture.' "

Cathy is getting her Master's degree this spring. She has been to China several times and fell in love with Dun Huang caves—the Chinese ancient art gallery in the desert, which is located at the west end of the ancient Silk Road. She just received an acceptance letter and a fellowship from a prestigious university and will start her Ph.D. in Chinese history next fall. The other day, several graduate students in our department, including me, got together in a Korean restaurant and celebrated with her.

I think Cathy is in love with Dun Huang caves—the great Chinese art of one thousand years ago. I hope her rejection of the Chinese "fast food culture" does not mean she expects China is still "primitive": Women wear traditional gowns, men marry many wives, people socialize in Peking Opera theater.

The other day, an undergraduate student selecting Buddhism Studies came to me and asked a very strange question.

"Ms. Shen, would you please tell me more about this? I heard there is a God or Goddess in Chinese religious legend. He or she is both male and female. It sounds fantastic!" the student said.

I was puzzled; what is he talking about? For a few seconds, I suddenly realized that he is talking about Avalokitesvara, a Bodhisattva in a famous

Temple in Zhejiang province, China. I replied: "Sorry, I know very little about Buddhism." I ended the conversation politely, but I felt sad that Chinese culture is often regarded as something novel or exotic. Am I too sensitive and too critical?

—Love, Rui

Zhong: Looking at Other and Self

Dear Rui,

Your story reminds me of Said's ideas about Orientalism, the knowledge of the "othered" culture constructed by European and American experiences, which is said to show relationships of power, domination, and hegemony. But I *don't* want to use this concept to name your stories. Rather, I would link this to ethnocentricity.

It is said that all human beings grow up and tend to rank themselves at the center of the universe and rank themselves over other ethnic groups accordingly. Both you and I were born in Beijing. I guess you still remember the sense of pride deeply rooted in the Beijingnese's minds. During my undergraduate years, I had a lot of students coming from remote provinces and cities. They were brilliant and diligent. However, a group of Beijingnese students in the class often made fun of their accents and expressions of their dialects. I never made fun of my provincial classmates, but I never tried to empathize with them. Now it's my turn to sound funny.

I study communication in America. One principle of communication is to respect the differences of diverse people and appreciate the rational and emotional commonalities among human beings. This philosophy makes me feel at home. For two years, I think I have benefitted a lot from this philosophy.

As time goes by, my homesickness, as well as language and cultural barriers, become less and less tormenting to me. I notice a lot of similarities between my American professors and my Chinese professors, as well as similarities between my American schoolmates and my Chinese schoolmates. These familiarities provide me with a sense of security, making my surroundings and future predictable.

Being a foreign student seems to be a mixture of both loss and gain, pain and joy. The homesickness and loneliness in a new place always intertwine with the joy of having new friends and a new cultural learning experience. The delight of surviving and thriving in a new educational institution also accompanies the fear of being a failure. The enrichment of learning another culture also brings the risk of transgressing my old cultural integrity and raises questions about who I am, what I can do, and who I will be.

I want to question why and how I became emotionally and intellectually vulnerable after I dove into a new culture. I want to inquire why my sense of self, which was based on where I came from, is challenged and re-constructed in a changing environment.

Let us continue our exchange on this topic. Take care.

—Love, Zhong

Learning about the beliefs, values, and norms of a culture is an essential step toward competent intercultural communication with people from that culture. Thomas Knutson's experiences in Thailand provide him with a rich understanding of the dynamics of Thai culture and the norms for interpersonal communication in that culture. He illustrates how the same words and nonverbal messages have different meanings for a Thai and a European American. His essay also illustrates the importance of affect and motivation in negotiating intercultural competence, because Tom's pleasure and comfort with Thai culture are clearly evident.

25 Tales from Thailand: Lessons from the Land of Smile

Thomas J. Knutson

Asking me to write about Thailand is like asking Julia Child to talk about cooking or Tiger Woods to describe golf. The Kingdom of Thailand, the "Land of Smile," has fascinated me for more than a decade and, I confess, I am enchanted with her beauty and many charms. I *love* Thailand; it's the most remarkable place I've ever lived. In short, don't expect an objective essay about Thai people, values, and norms. Instead, I'll try to explain the attraction of this beautiful culture in a way that I hope will inspire you to learn more about Thailand as well as intercultural communication. Thailand has so much to offer the world.

For the past several years, I've been a visiting professor in Bangkok at Chulalongkorn University, Bangkok University, and Assumption University. I've lived in Bangkok for a total of three years and have traveled throughout the country, a place that can teach everyone about civility, enjoyment, and life itself. If you haven't visited Thailand, you should; if you've been there before, you should return.

Thailand is located in Southeast Asia and is surrounded by Malaysia, Myanmar (Burma), Laos, and Cambodia. Roughly the size of Texas, Thailand is situated in the center of the world's most rapidly expanding economies. Although the Thai Baht has been recently devalued, most experts agree that Thailand will remain a major geopolitical force in the foreseeable future. You can actually feel the excitement of Thailand's new growth and determination. Bangkok's legendary traffic problems, the wild fluctuations in the Thai stock market, and the slow but sure development of a parliamentary system of government all contribute to an incredible laboratory for life in the modern age. Perhaps more than any other place on earth, Thailand epitomizes life in the new world order, completely involved in the intricacies of the global village.

Thailand must be the most sensual place on earth. The sights and sounds, the fragrances and feelings all combine to make every step in the Kingdom an exquisite encounter. Nowhere in the world will you find such awesome temples, towering golden spires glittering in the tropical sunlight inviting people to learn of Buddha. Traditional Thai music coexists with the sounds of Western tunes, traffic noise, and the persistent pleas of vendors in the countless markets. The scent of jasmine and the delicious aroma of Thai cooking make a stroll along any street in the Kingdom a unique pleasure. From the moment you arrive at Don Muang, Bangkok's modern international airport, the Thai "feeling" envelopes, encircles, and enchants every moment of your stay.

Of course, Thailand also provides challenges to the traveler. Bangkok has the worst traffic, the worst pollution, and the worst weather I've ever encountered. During the day, vehicles move through Bangkok traffic at a numbing speed of less than four miles per hour. Each day 550 new automobiles enter the traffic pattern. Carbon monoxide hangs in the air and the high temperatures coupled with the cloying humidity challenge even the most healthy sojourner. The Thai infrastructure teeters daily on the brink of collapse. Political corruption and an unequal distribution of wealth threaten government stability. You will find these problems met with a typical Thai insouciance, a confidence that relief will come soon. Even with these bothersome troubles, however, Thailand is the best place I've ever visited. Let me explain why.

More than any other attraction, the Thai people make their country the most civil and the sweetest place in the world. "The Land of Smile" is not just a tourist slogan; it's real. Thais are *nice* people. Other countries may excel in economic power, military strength, and technological ability, but Thailand surely leads the world psychologically. The gentleness and genuine charm of the Thai people serve as a model for the enjoyment of diversity and the acceptance of differences. Of course, we must recognize that not all Thai people behave consistently in a fashion compatible with Thai cultural values. Having made that disclaimer, however, I can say that the Thais I've been privileged to meet are the nicest people I have found in any of the more than 30 countries I've visited. My challenge is to explain that to you in a fashion consistent with intercultural and cross-cultural sensitivity.

You may have read about the various theories of social attraction, a popular variable in communication research. McCroskey and McCain (1974) provide an interesting method of describing the ways in which two people become attracted to one another. The technique adapts itself well to a preliminary examination of Thai people. McCroskey and McCain identify three dimensions of attraction: physical, task, and social. Physical attraction, which relates specifically to physical appearance, is considered the catalyst for conversation. Thai beauty is legendary. Countless visitors from around the world have been charmed by Thailand's "physically attractive people and their beguiling ambiguity" (Kulick & Wilson, 1992, p. 1). Thai people, with their ready smiles, dancing eyes, and impeccable personal hygiene, have little trouble attracting others for conversation. McCroskey and McCain explain that the physical attraction dimension is insufficient to maintain a relationship; the concern moves quickly to either social or task attraction. The international mark of friendliness, the smile, enables Thais to switch quickly to matters of social attraction. Spontaneous displays of happiness and sensitivity are hallmarks in Thai society, and visitors readily become fascinated with Thai hospitality. I have yet to meet a foreigner in Thailand who was not amazed at the quality of social relationships, the real "stuff" of interpersonal encounters. You will be astounded with the ease of talking with Thai people and their unique ability to display rhetorical sensitivity. The number one cultural value of Thailand is social harmony, a quality that can teach the world intercultural communication effectiveness. Thais are "other-oriented" in their conversations, an appealing characteristic for most foreigners. On the task dimension, Thais are noted for their long history of accomplishment. Work for the Thai, however, is insufficient motivation. To develop true task attraction, the Thai must have *sanuk* (fun) while engaged in chores and duties. Thailand taught me a big lesson about work. If I don't like to do something, I don't do it or I find someone else to do it. If I *must* do something I don't like doing, I make a rewarding and fun activity contingent upon completing an odious task. That simple lesson evaded me for years until I lived with Thai people.

You have read about several methods of comparing and contrasting various cultures. I will use some of these to illustrate for you my love for and fascination with Thailand. Of course, my experiences are not intended as an exhaustive description of Thai culture, about which I have written elsewhere (Knutson, 1994). My purpose here is to relate interesting anecdotes loosely organized around some of the intercultural taxonomies with which you are familiar.

Hall (1976), who received the Phi Beta Delta[1] award for international scholarship, described cultures as varying along a contextual continuum. In high-context cultures, interpretation of messages requires close attention to the physical environment in which a conversation occurs. Relatively little information is contained in the explicit message. Low-context cultures are just the opposite, with most of the information contained in the explicit message. Thailand falls in Hall's high-context category; most Western cultures are low context. This convenient dichotomy, although overly simplified, can best be illustrated by an example. My Thai friend Phan and I were enjoying a relaxing evening together at one of Bangkok's pubs. During the course of our conversation, Phan said, "My brother is coming to visit me." I replied, "You must be very happy since you've not seen him for a long time. When will he come?" Phan responded in one word: "Soon." As a Westerner, verbal messages are extremely important to me, and I found Phan's one-word comment quite perplexing, if not downright annoying. People from low-context cultures tend to see high-context communicators as evasive, indirect, and inscrutable. Thais, however, often stereotype Westerners as too direct, too talkative, and too loud.

One of the more delightful lessons Thai culture can teach involves Thais' cautious attitude toward words. In fact, there is no literal equivalent in the Thai language for the English word "no." In Thailand people say "not yes." Thais value moderate expression and avoid confrontational or negative messages, which is not surprising given their emphasis on social harmony. The meaning can be found in the environment, in the context, and through nonverbal cues. For example, when I first developed friendships with Thai people, they would often ask, "Dr. Thomas, why do you always say the obvious?" Well, it was obvious to them in their high-context culture, but it was not obvious to me. Another example of this all-pervasive high-context influence in Thailand can be seen in my "contractual" relationships with Thai universities, where I have taught as a visiting professor. I have never seen a written contract describing the parties' respective obligations and responsibilities. The contextual trust generated by social relationships is sufficient, a condition that causes my U.S. American colleagues to doubt my sanity. They often suggest that I should be worried about salary or working conditions not clearly and verbally specified (in their view of the world). My response leaves them glassy eyed and shaking their heads. I explain that the high-context Thai culture simply would not tolerate such an obvious interpersonal misunderstanding among friends.

Hofstede (1991), the Dutch management researcher, has had a profound influence on the analysis of cultural differences. His initial factor analyses revealed four dimensions on which cultures vary: individualism-collectivism, power distance, masculinity-femininity, and uncertainty avoidance. Bond (1987) later extended Hofstede's work to Asian populations and created a new dimension, unique to Asia, that he called Confucian Dynamism. These two researchers provide a loose agenda for the discussion about Thailand.

Gudykunst and Ting-Toomey (1988) note that Hofstede's individualism-collectivism dimension corresponds to Hall's ideas about low- and high-context cultures. The United States emerged as the most individualistic culture in the world, placing great importance on the "I"; Thailand is a highly collectivistic culture, emphasizing "we" in all aspects of communication. The most important Thai value, social harmony, contrasts sharply with the U.S. emphasis on success and achievement, which is often measured by the acquisition of material things. Buddhist teaching forms the basis for the Thais' genuine care and concern for others, an idea known as *nam jai* ("water of the heart"), which seldom allows Thais to see strangers as threatening or suspicious. The Thai term *kreng jai* refers to the desire to be "self-effacing, respectful, and extremely considerate as well as the wish to avoid embarrassing others or intruding or imposing upon them" (Fieg, 1989, p. 43). *Kreng jai* and *nam jai*, probably unique to Thailand, characterize every aspect of daily interpersonal relationships. Another anecdote will illustrate this attractive Thai attribute.

One night a group of us was happily enjoying beer and conversation. The Thais, coming from their collectivist background, displayed great rhetorical sensitivity and concern for others in the group. Suddenly, a huge and obviously intoxicated foreigner entered the area where we were sitting. This drunken oaf, unsteady of gait and talk, proceeded to proclaim loudly that he was the biggest and best man on earth. Although his behavior would have been seen as rude and impolite even in a low-context environment, the Thais viewed him as incredibly discourteous and disrespectful. My Thai friends watched the inebriated stranger with a combination of fright and shock, but they remained silent and discretely avoided any direct encounter. As the drunk shouted his personal attributes, his flailing arms frequently struck Phan's head, violating one of the biggest taboos in Thailand.[2] Throughout this humiliating episode, Phan remained stoic. Finally, when the sot left, I turned to Phan and said, "I'm sorry, Phan. We're not all that way." Phan turned to me with one of the special Thai smiles and said, "I know that. I know you. Anyway, he's probably a nice guy when he's sober." In Sacramento, where I'm from, this abusive behavior would not have been tolerated and the culprit would have been the victim of a firm and perhaps violent message. In Thailand, however, overt expressions of conflict are discouraged. Most Thais, including Phan, find something of value, even in the most difficult of situations. Overt displays of anger jeopardize social harmony in Thailand, and they indicate ignorance, immaturity, and vulgarity.

The Thai desire for smooth interpersonal relationships can be seen in the Thai expression *jai yen,* the talent of remaining calm and in control of one's emotions even during difficult situations. Komin (1991) observes the importance of *jai yen,* which is

> the core cognition behind the behavioral pattern of the everyday life social interactions of the Thai. And it is this value of smooth and pleasant interpersonal interaction that gives Thai people the image of being very "friendly" people, and Thailand, the "Land of Smile." (p. 148)

The soft-spoken politeness of the Thai can contribute to a greater understanding of interpersonal sensitivity throughout the world. The phrase you will hear often in Thailand, *mai pen rai* (contented, never mind, or "it doesn't matter"), and the condition of *arom dii* (always smiling), both show the great importance Thais place on social harmony.

Hofstede's (1991) dimension of power distance refers to the manner in which power is distributed in a culture. Thailand can be described as a culture that has a large power distance; power and wealth are distributed unequally. Differences in status are accepted in Thailand as useful signs of appropriate communication behaviors, and authority is given considerable deference and respect. Chantornvong (1992) describes the variation in Thai language use and proper linguistic form.

> Whereas English has "I" for the first person pronoun and "you" for the second person pronoun, a standard Thai speaker can choose up to 17 different forms of the first person pronoun and up to 19 forms of the second person pronoun, depending on the degree of politeness, intimacy, or role relationships and the relative status of the people involved. (p. 147)

My introduction to Thai power distance came on my first visit to Bangkok. I arrived 18 hours late, totally exhausted, and suffering from massive jetlag.

When I arrived at my hotel, I was stunned by the courtesy and efficiency displayed by hotel personnel in assigning me to a room. They knew I was tired, and a team of people installed me in a fresh and clean room, complete with fresh flowers and fruit. The room boy eagerly turned down the bed and attended to the various things that make a weary traveler comfortable. I watched him with fascination as he dealt with every detail in a most unobtrusive fashion, quickly and efficiently. When he finished, he turned to me, flashed that beautiful Thai smile, bowed, and gave a very respectful *wai*.[3] As a good and seasoned sojourner, I had learned a bit of the Thai language prior to leaving the States. What better time to try out my language skills, I naively thought. I faced the room boy, gave him a *wai* with my fingers touching my nose, and said, "*Khawp khun maak, khrap. Sawasdee, khrap*" (Thank you very much. Good bye). The room boy's reaction to my message startled me. He immediately crouched low to the floor, backed out of the room, all the while giggling hysterically. The door closed and I was left alone, pondering this bizarre scene. The next day I told a Thai friend who had spent a lot of time in the States what had happened. Soop looked at me with mock horror on his face and said, "Tom, in Thailand we never *wai* our social inferiors." That was the first of many lessons I would learn in Thailand, knowledge I would never have discovered at home. Later that week, through a third party,[4] I apologized to the room boy for my cultural insensitivity and gave him a gift. The next time I saw the room boy, he was wearing his new sweatshirt from California State University, Sacramento. He glanced at me quickly and delivered a beautiful smile and *wai*. I smiled back as Soop instructed, this time without a *wai* and with my exuberant Western feelings firmly in check.

Hofstede's masculinity-femininity dimension describes the degree to which a culture values achievement or social support. Cultures rated high on masculinity evaluate people based on their performance and acquisition of material things. Feminine cultures nurture people and emphasize the quality of life as central to their being. Given the Thai emphasis on social harmony, you should not be surprised to hear that Thailand falls on the feminine, or nurturing, end of Hofstede's masculinity-femininity continuum. Komin (1991) describes a successful Thai personality as "one of competence and substance, but most important of all, [it] has to have a soft and polite appearance, presentation, and approach" (p. 146). *Bunkhun* (the reciprocity of goodness) occupies a prominent place in Thai interpersonal relationships. Kindness elicits gratitude, and *bunkhun* is the very foundation of friendship. Klausner (1993) notes:

> To be *katanyu*, or constantly aware and conscious of the benefit or favor another person has bestowed, is a highly valued character trait in Thai society. To the contrary, one of the most reprehensible sins in the Thai social context is to be *akatanyu*, or ungrateful. (p. 275)

In Thailand, personal assertiveness, overt self-confidence, lack of feelings for others, and expressions of superiority elicit *mai sai,* a mixture of disgust and suspicion. Thai compassion and nurturing can best be seen in the Kingdom's schools and its system of education. Learning is seen as more valuable than material success, and people associated with knowledge and education are highly respected and esteemed. Teachers and professors occupy the top of the Thai social hierarchy.

Several years ago I befriended a Thai student attending classes at California State University, Sacramento. Tao was enrolled in my communication theory course, which is a requirement for majors, and she was committed and dedicated to learning, traits that would please any professor. Tao and I worked hard together and she appreciated the extra time I took to help her with all of her classes. I was amazed at her dedication and sacrifice to succeed as an international student. Tao mastered the English language quickly, successfully completed her bachelor's degree, and continued her education at the graduate level; she recently completed her MBA at the University of San Francisco. Our friendship grew over the years. Looking back, I now begin to grasp the meaning of *bunkhun*. Tao introduced me to her parents, Sawanit and Chavalit (they prefer to be called "Suzie" and "Charley"), who visited Sacramento many times, always bearing gifts and dispensing kindnesses and favors in a way I had never experienced. Suzie and Charley were never ostentatious, but their quiet and wonderful displays of appreciation and genuine affection made an indelible imprint on my life. When I went to Thailand as a visiting professor for the first time, Tao insisted that she inform her parents, who, she said, would "take care of all of my needs." Upon my arrival in Bangkok, Suzie and Charley overwhelmed me with Thai hospitality. They picked me up at the airport, which is a rigorous challenge given Bangkok's traffic, took me to their beautiful home, and insisted that I rest for a few days before they showed me their Thailand. Suzie and Charley treated me like family, taking me to all of the interesting sights in Bangkok and doing many marvelous and unexpected things to make my transition to Thailand enjoyable. One day Suzie and I were shopping in a jewelry store, as Suzie is fond of the exquisite Thai gems and intricate patterns of handmade Thai jewelry. While Suzie talked with the salesperson, a gold pendant displaying the Venerable Kasem, the influential monk, caught my eye. I asked Suzie if the pendant was indeed in honor of Kasem, and she seemed surprised that I knew of him. Later that night, Suzie gave me a small package, beautifully wrapped in red and gold, containing the pendant. My naive inquiry was interpreted by Suzie in her high-context environment as a marvelous way in which to display *bunkhun*. She was correct, and the sentiment surrounding that little piece of jewelry went far beyond its monetary value. When I moved from Suzie and Charley's house to my apartment at the university, they called weekly to inquire about my comfort and to invite me to numerous dinners and other uniquely Thai events. When I left Thailand to return home in 1993, Charley took me to the airport. We had a long farewell conversation that was filled with the bittersweet ambiguity about when we would meet again. As I got up to leave for passport control, Charley gave me an amulet dating to the Ayutthaya period (14th century, C.E.) and told me that it would keep me safe and cause me to return to Thailand. Charley was also correct. I wear that amulet today, and it has brought me back safely to Thailand many times since that auspicious introduction in 1993. More importantly, the friendship initiated by

Tao knows no boundaries. We are *phuan tai,* friends for whom it would be an honor to die. You see, now I must display *bunkhun* to Suzie and Charley, sure in the recognition that time and distance do not mitigate this sensitive point of Thai friendship. It's an honor few people outside Thailand can understand.

Hofstede identified the uncertainty avoidance dimension as relating to how cultures cope with ambiguity. People from high uncertainty avoidance cultures experience considerable anxiety and stress when faced with change and innovation. They establish rituals and rigid structural guidelines for dealing with uncertainty and reducing the threat created by ambiguity. In Hofstede's scheme, Thailand falls at the average; Thais neither excessively avoid nor strongly encourage uncertainty. For Thais, life consists of uncertainty, and their attitude toward the unexpected is one of passive acceptance: what will be, will be. Thais see themselves as subjugated by nature, and they accept life's events philosophically. Thais display a curious nonchalance when confronted by seemingly insurmountable problems, a response that frequently strikes outsiders as unfounded self-confidence. For example, when I was last in Bangkok, the Chao Prayha river was rising rapidly and the city was in grave danger of flooding. Thais continued to conduct their daily lives with little concern for the impending calamity and destruction. When the river at last spilled over its banks and inundated large sections of Bangkok, there was almost glee in wondering what would happen next. Thais deal with uncertainty by invoking the Buddhist notion of *karma,* a belief that destiny is ordained by previous existences and that no single individual can do much to change the course of natural phenomena.

Another example of the Thai ability seemingly to thrive on uncertainty involves my friendship with Dr. Pramote Nakornthab, president of the University Foundation of Thailand. Pramote is one of the most intelligent and creative people I know. He also most certainly has the highest tolerance for ambiguity of anyone I've ever met. We worked together in establishing a college in Nongkhai, located on the banks of the Mekong River across from Cambodia. The area was in desperate need of higher education, and Pramote was committed to providing opportunities to the people of Nongkhai, who had lived for a long time without complaint or hope. In the summer of 1995 we brought 20 U.S. American professors to Nongkhai to initiate the new school. When we arrived, there were no buildings, no classes, no computers, and no curriculum. There were, however, hundreds of people eager to study and learn. We spent several weeks socializing and making friends, reassuring everyone that school would begin soon. Government officials, professors, businesspeople, and a wide cross-section of the citizenry overwhelmed the U.S. Americans with their hospitality, but little seemed to be being accomplished in terms of establishing a college. One day, Pramote gathered all of the U.S. Americans together and empathetically announced that he was aware of our frustration that things were not progressing as quickly as they would in the States. He smiled and said, "You must be patient, my friends. The idea of the school was here long before the school. The people of Nongkhai haven't had a college for centuries; a few more months will be little bother." Drawing on the Thai importance of social harmony, Pramote explained that we had first to develop strong and trusting relationships with people before anyone could possibly take any action. The school, according to Pramote, would emerge based on the friendship and trust of everyone involved. There was a brief moment of argument before the U.S. Americans realized the importance of the cultural difference. In the States we don't waste time, we get things done, we establish and create, and we control the environment. In Thailand that kind of behavior is seen as impossible. Any achievement is founded on strong relationships, a condition that is far more important than anything Westerners would call progress. When I last saw Pramote, he was his typical smiling self, proclaiming friendship and trust to all who would listen, and advising everyone to avoid troubling themselves over future difficulties. He also mentioned, almost in passing, that buildings had been constructed in Nongkhai and a curriculum developed. The people have their college.

You have read of the difficulties in conducting intercultural communication research and the frustration often accompanying the interpretation of various findings. Bond (1987) felt that the Hofstede approach may have been guilty of a Western bias in describing cultures. His investigation using Asian scholars also resulted in four dimensions of cultural patterns, three of which were roughly equivalent to Hofstede's dimensions of individualism-collectivism, masculinity-femininity, and power distance. The uncertainty avoidance category described by Hofstede, however, did not emerge from the data. Instead, Bond and his colleagues added a dimension unrelated to Hofstede's earlier work, which they called Confucian dynamism. This added dimension emerged as a concept unique to Asian populations. A positive score on the Confucian dimension means that a culture prefers a long-term orientation toward life and includes such descriptors as persistence, status variation in interpersonal activities, and a sense of shame. Thailand's positive score on the Confucian dimension means that Thais prefer the Confucian value of a long-term orientation.

Perhaps more than other cultures, the Thai position on Confucian dynamism is easy to understand. Thais' score on Hofstede's uncertainty avoidance scale was average, perhaps referring to the relative unimportance to Thais of things ambiguous. Hofstede's uncertainty avoidance dimension relates to an individual's search for truth, something not considered so valuable in Thai culture. Rather, Thais search for virtue, a notion that can only emerge after an interpersonal history has been built. That's one of the reasons Thais prefer developing secure and trusting interpersonal ties before discussing matters of business or substance.

An example of the Thai importance of the long-term orientation to life can be seen in the manner in which my friend conducts business. Voravud and I have known each other for many years. He's a prosperous businessman in Bangkok and is involved in both the plastics and garment industries. On my last trip to Bangkok, I noticed that Voravud was doing much more business with the Japanese and less with the U.S. Americans. We talked about this change for a long time, and Voravud told me that the U.S. American products were equal in quality to the Japanese goods, and that in some cases he could strike better deals with the U.S. Americans. Since our friendship traces back years to when I met Voravud in the States, I felt comfortable asking him why he preferred the Japanese. His reply clearly illustrated the Confucian dynamism notion. Voravud explained that the Japanese businesspeople really *cared* for him and his company. The Japanese would come to Bangkok and enjoy many dinners with Voravud, play a lot of golf, and generally display the great interpersonal concern necessary for Thai business negotiations. Voravud explained, "Dr. Tom, I really like the Americans. After all, I studied there. But when the Americans come to my office, they want to deal only with profit and make deals quickly. They never send the same people and it's difficult for me to get to know anybody. I wish you were in the plastics business, Dr. Thomas. We could make a fortune together because of our friendship, and grow old knowing that we have little concern for the future." This simple yet profound idea was reinforced later that day when we walked together in the noontime heat of Bangkok. I was perspiring profusely, yet Voravud was fresh and seemingly unaffected by the high temperatures and humidity. As I recall, we were late for an appointment, and I was racing along in a hurry to get to our meeting. I turned to Voravud and said, "Why are you not sweating? I just can't get used to this heat." Voravud looked at me with a beautiful Thai smile and said, "You walk too fast. Slow down and we can enjoy our conversation." Voravud's care, genuine concern, and wisdom at that moment will stay with me forever. Why hurry to get some place when the journey itself can be enjoyable? I had avoided conversation that would build our friendship because I thought it was more important for me to arrive at our destination quickly. I turned to Voravud and said, "Let's stop for a coffee. It's okay to be a little bit late, right?" Voravud laughed and said, "Dr. Thomas, I think you were Thai in a previous life." You cannot imagine how much that observation meant to me.

This brief essay cannot identify all the wonderful lessons from the Land of Smile, but now you know some of the most noteworthy. Thailand can offer the world some amazing psychological techniques to improve the human condition and to increase intercultural communication effectiveness. The Thai ability to display gentleness and respect for all human beings can certainly improve our lives. The freedom from aggravation, the avoidance of criticism and conflict, the rejection of harsh words, the ability to find value in the moment, and the importance of friendship can make the world a more pleasant and a safer place. Culture is learned, and all of us can learn *kreng jai, bunkhun, jai yen,* and *nam jai*. These are simple but profound ways to manage the mysteries of cultural differences. You will likely meet more foreigners than you would have at any other time in the history of the world. Learning Thai values can help you to develop the harmonious relationships necessary for success in today's global environment. I wish you *sanuk, arom dii,* and *nam jai* on your journey, and I urge you to learn more about the remarkable lessons from the Land of Smile. *Sawasdee Khrap!*

NOTES

1. Phi Beta Delta is the honorary society for international scholars.
2. The head is the residence of the soul and virtually sacred in Thailand.

3. A *wai,* the traditional Thai show of respect, is made by placing the palms of the hands together with the fingers touching the nose. The placement of the hands shows the degree of respect. The higher the fingers, the more respect is displayed.

4. It would have been far too direct to approach the room boy in person.

REFERENCES

Bond, M. H. (1987). Chinese culture connection: Chinese values and the search for culture-free dimensions of culture. *Journal of Cross-Cultural Psychology, 18,* 143–167.

Chantornvong, S. (1992). To address the dust of the dust under the soles of the royal feet: A reflection on the political dimension of the Thai court language. *Asian Review, 6,* 145–163.

Fieg, J. P. (1989). *A common core: Thais and Americans* (E. Mortlock, rev.). Yarmouth, ME: Intercultural Press.

Gudykunst, W. C., & Ting-Toomey, S. (1988). *Culture and interpersonal communication.* Newbury Park, CA: Sage.

Hall, E. T. (1976). *Beyond culture.* Garden City, NY: Doubleday.

Hofstede, G. (1991). *Cultures and organizations: Software of the mind.* New York: McGraw-Hill.

Klausner, W. J. (1993). *Reflections on Thai culture* (4th ed.). Bangkok: The Siam Society.

Knautson, T. J. (1994). Comparison of Thai and U.S. American cultural values: "Mai pen rai" versus "just do it." *ABAC Journal, 14,* 1–38.

Komin, S. (1991). *Psychology of the Thai people: Values and behavioral patterns.* Bangkok: National Institute of Development Administration.

Kulick, E., & Wilson, D. (1992). *Thailand's turn: Profile of a new dragon.* New York: St. Martin's Press.

McCroskey, J. C., & McCain, T. A. (1974). The measurement of interpersonal attraction. *Speech Monographs, 41,* 261–266.

Charles Braithwaite gives us the opportunity to understand his experiences in crossing from his European American culture to that of the Navajo. This essay moves between descriptions of the communicative interactions he witnesses among the Navajo people and his interpretations of what might be happening. It provides a model for understanding a culture that is different from one's own. In your own intercultural experiences, do as Chuck does: begin by describing what you observe, in specific and nonjudgmental language. Then attempt to interpret and understand the rich dynamics of that other culture, always maintaining a sense of tentativeness and openness because your interpretations may not be accurate.

26 Roast Mutton, Fry Bread, and Tilt-a-Whirls: Cultural and Intercultural Contact at the Navajo Nation Fair

Charles A. Braithwaite

The Navajo Nation is the largest sovereign Indian nation in the United States. More than 200,000 Navajo live in an area the size of New England: seventeen million acres, which includes lands in Arizona, New Mexico, Colorado, and Utah. For 51 years the Navajo people have been attending the largest tribal gathering in the continental United States: the Navajo Nation Fair in Window Rock, Navajo Nation (Arizona). Around the first week of September, easily 150,000 people, more than 90 percent of whom are Navajo, gather for five days of powwows, rodeos, music, arts and crafts, food, midway rides, and other activities associated with "state" fairs. The Navajo Nation Fair Parade, which covers a two-mile stretch of road outside the fairgrounds, alone draws more than 80,000 people. For six years I have attended the Navajo Nation Fair, spending more than 150 hours participating in and observing the activities. Below I provide accounts of four important aspects of the Navajo Nation Fair to help you understand some dimensions of Navajo culture and intercultural communication. Each account has two sections: (1) a narrative description of events, and (2) a cultural perspective that includes contextual information and interpretative analyses that will help you understand the significance of what you are reading. You may choose to read the accounts in this essay in one of at least two ways. One way is to read the narrative section first, without being influenced by my analysis. The second is to read the cultural perspectives section first, thereby giving you a "lens" through which to view what you are reading.

1: Air Jordan and Walking Buffalo

As I head toward the Navajo Nation Fair from Gallup, New Mexico, about 25 miles from Window Rock, I tune in to KTNN ("The Voice of the Navajo Nation") on the radio. During the half-hour drive I hear songs by Garth Brooks, Van Morrison singing "Gloria," bluegrass music, traditional powwow music, and advertisements for local businesses in both English and Navajo. Just as I arrive in sight of the fair an old version of "Down in the Boondocks" comes on the air.

Entering the fair, the midway is straight ahead, with carnival rides to the right, and the Navajo Nation Warrior's Pow-Wow Arena on the left. Next to the arena, which is about one-third full of people listening to the drumming and singing, a booth is set up selling cassettes and CDs of a variety of Native Indian music: traditional powwow, peyote songs, song and dance, and contemporary Native American. Three young Navajo boys are lined up to make purchases. One is wearing a shirt with "Metallica" on the back, another wears a "Megadeath" sweatshirt, and the third has a Nike hat and an "Air Jordan" t-shirt. Each boy is buying two or three tapes of traditional powwow music from groups such as Walking Buffalo, Fly-In-Eagle, and Pipestone Creek. Later I see these same boys holding up microcassette recorders over the powwow drummers and singers to make their own recordings of the music.

As I look down the midway, I see a group of about 12 Navajo standing around an "old time" photo booth, the kind you see at almost all U.S. state fairs. Several families are patiently waiting for their turn to go into the trailer and change into costumes and have their pictures taken: the Navajo women and girls dressing up as "dance hall" girls, and the Navajo men and boys dressing up as "cowboys." Two of the Anglo workers from the booth are dressed as western gunfighters. They point their six-guns at little Navajo children while the parents smile and take pictures.

Cultural Perspective #1

The juxtaposition of different cultures is a common feature on the Navajo Nation. Although many Navajo still live far from the influence of Anglo culture, the vast majority of people readily embrace aspects of cultures that initially appear incongruent with Navajo life. There is a willingness, for example, to associate with "cowboys" (as evidenced by the 700-plus participants in the all-Indian rodeo that runs throughout the length of the fair), even though it was the Spanish, Mexican, New Mexican, and United States "cowboys" who have helped to steal land from the Navajo for the past 400 years. Navajo history is filled with examples in which the people borrowed and adapted aspects of those cultures with which they came into contact while simultaneously maintaining the important aspects of their traditional ways: corn was adopted from the Pueblo people; horses, sheep, and goats were adopted from the Spanish; and mining and forest development, which (at an estimated $50 million per year) provide the greatest source of tribal income in the United States, were learned from the U.S. Americans. Young Navajo apparently experience no cognitive dissonance when they listen to Snoop Doggy Dog on headphones while waiting for elderly Navajo women to finish up the fry bread competition so they can sample the tasty bread and honey.

2: Shorts and Sandals on Sacred Ground

The Navajo Nation Warrior's Pow Wow Arena includes a small stage, used mainly for public address equipment, and grandstands that hold more than one thousand spectators. Around the arena is a camping area where people from throughout North American and Canadian Indian Nations can stay when they come to participate in the intertribal dances. There are contests for adults, juniors, teens, and "tiny tots," which includes babies and toddlers who need assistance even with just walking. After the competitions judges tally scores but no awards are given out at the time, although partway through the fair a "powwow princess" is chosen and crowned. Groups of drummers and singers come from all over the United States and Canada and take turns playing for the dances and the "grand entries" that occur twice a day.

Of the few Anglos that attend the fair, most come to buy jewelry at the arts and crafts exhibit hall and to attend the rodeos. However, some do wander over to the Powwow arena. One reason the Anglos usually stand out is the way they are dressed. During one four-hour period, I saw ten Anglo women come to the powwow wearing shorts and halter tops. In all fairness, I should point out that the temperature was in the mid–80s at the time. Most of the Anglo men also wore shorts and carried cameras or camcorders, with which they walked into the arena to shoot pictures of the dancers. Sometimes the photographers would actually step out into the arena so they could take a picture. Few Anglos would sit more than about a half hour to an hour before moving on, even though the dances would go on from about 10:00 A.M. until sometimes 2:30 A.M. The day at the powwow arena would begin with a gourd dance, followed by the presentation of the colors (U.S., Navajo, and P.O.W. flags), followed by an invocation. One invocation was delivered by an elderly Navajo man in a wheelchair. Though using a microphone, he could barely be heard because he spoke so softly and occasionally let the microphone drop to the side. All the dancers and drummers in the arena stood for the speaker, and most of the people in the grandstand also stood, with the majority of men removing their hats. Even the Navajo teenagers showed respect, although with a slight air of indifference, too. However, most of the Anglos continued to film and talk and eat and often walked away when a speaker went on "too long."

Cultural Perspective #2

A powwow arena is a place for celebration by Native Indian people. It is an opportunity for Native Indian people from all parts of North America and

Canada to share their music and their communal beliefs in the nature of life. As one powwow host stated before an initiation ceremony for a young girl, "This circle (the powwow arena) is the Creator's circle. It's a sacred place." For many Native Indian people, attending a powwow has the same characteristics as attending church. However, most Anglos usually cannot see the analogy. A "religious" service has different qualities for Anglos, and the celebratory atmosphere of powwows, as well as the presence of contests and vendors and grandstands, makes it difficult for many Anglos to recognize the sacred nature of what is occurring in front of them. Further, when Anglos behave inappropriately at powwows by being scantily clad or by walking into the arena to take pictures, few Native people will overtly criticize their actions. This is especially true when visitors are perceived as "guests." Numerous times I was encouraged to move ahead of Navajos when waiting in line for activities, told as they moved aside, "You're our guest." There may often be disapproving glances toward the Anglos, especially from the elderly Indians, but no direct confrontations. Except for children and some teenagers, most Native peoples at the powwows wear long pants or long skirts and do not expose their bodies unnecessarily.

3: "Be Diné and Proud"

I remember attending state fairs with my parents, and the moment we entered the fairgrounds we split up: kids going in one direction and parents in another (after trying in vain to get the children to agree to a meeting place and time for later in the day). What catches my attention at the Navajo Nation Fair is the many groups of intact family units that walk around together: very elderly Navajo women wearing velvet dresses of turquoise or purple with many beautiful pieces of jewelry, holding the hands of very young children, followed by older children and parents or other adult relatives. The fair has numerous locations devoted to caring for the elderly and children: special tables reserved for elderly, special booths set up to give water and food to the elderly, and an extensive effort to make sure children are "tagged" (a name tag attached to each child's clothing) in case children stray too far from their families. What strikes me about the family interaction is how easy it appears to be for adults to cope with the few disruptions caused by children. I notice how remarkably quiet it is at the fair, given the thousands of people there. Few children or teenagers are running and yelling across the grounds, and few people are voicing the kind of complaints that are typical at events such as this (e.g., waiting in a long line, waiting for food, waiting for the bathroom). When a child does start to fuss, particularly a young child, it appears that an adult has simply to give the child "the look," often accompanied by a movement of the index finger in short sweeping motion, to silence the complaint quickly.

The prevalence of multigeneration groups is especially evident at the Navajo Nation Fair parade. Beginning as early as sunrise, Navajo people begin gathering along the fair route. Vendors of roasted corn, "kneel-down" bread, sno-cones, watermelon, and sodas stake out areas to feed the more than

80,000 people who will sit or stand in the sun until as late as 2:00 P.M. to watch the 250-plus entries: floats, bands, politicians, tribal agencies, and local businesses. Room is always made up front for the elderly to sit down, and the parade itself has many floats and groups that *feature* the respected elders of the tribe. Singled out for particular honor are groups of military veterans/warriors from World War II to Bosnia. The Navajo "code-talkers," U.S. Marines who spoke coded Navajo during the war in the Pacific and whose code was never broken by the Japanese, receive tremendous applause while leading a group of warriors. The crowd also shows great respect to veterans carrying a P.O.W. flag, which represents the men believed to have been left behind after the Vietnam War. The themes illustrated by the floats, most constructed on the back of trucks or small wagons, emphasize ideas such as "pride," "young people," "future," and "prosperity." As the various entries go by, it is common for the riders to toss hard candy into the crowd that is then chased down by the little children.

Cultural Perspective #3

The centrality of the family to Navajo life cannot be overstated. One's identity as a person is interwoven with one's place in a large family affiliation or clan. There are approximately 30 Navajo clans that emerged from the four original clans created by Changing Woman (one of the original holy people of the Navajo): Near the Water Clan (To'ahani), Tower House Clan (Kinyaa'aanii), Bitter Water Clan (Todich'iinii), and Mud Clan (Hastlishnii). The traditional Navajo way of relating is based on identifying oneself with the mother's clan, the father's clan, the maternal grandfather's clan, and the paternal grandfather's clan. When introducing themselves, even in writing, Navajo begin by stating their kinship—for example, "I am of the Honaghlaanii clan, born of Bitter Water, and my paternal grandparents are Naalani, my maternal grandparents are T'achiinii." A high value is placed on clan affiliation and on the teachings of one's elders. When asked to write an essay for a Navajo Nation Fair magazine, one Navajo author said he chose to get his information by talking to women who

> speak the Dineh (Navajo) language and speak limited English, and with none or limited Western/European education, those who possess livestock, a cornfield, participate in traditional Dineh ceremonies, who wear the traditional Dineh *tssii'* (hair bun), have a *hogan* (traditional Dineh home), and those who did not have all of the modern conveniences of indoor plumbing, electricity, cable TV, telephone, etc.[1]

Of the 40 lessons the above author learned from these women, at least 22 concerned the sense of family. The abandonment of Anglo elderly and the free rein given young Anglo children are sources of wonder and often disgust for many Navajo. The respect for the elderly holds true for the value placed on those who contribute to the tribe, such as warriors. Those who served and those who gave their lives in battle are highly regarded throughout the Navajo Nation. A large park near tribal headquarters is devoted to honoring all veterans. The Navajo believe a warrior takes into battle only two things that belong to him: his spirit and his shadow. For this reason, the veterans' memorial at the park will have large sheets of glass suspended horizontally over the ground, with the names of the fallen warriors inscribed in the glass. This is so you can look up through the glass toward the sky and the spirits; each man's name will appear as a shadow on the ground.

4: Juniper Berries

It is a 350-mile drive back to Phoenix, so I take off about halfway through the Navajo Nation Fair parade. I turn on the radio to listen to the announcers describe the floats and marching bands, which they do in both English and Navajo. Although I have a six-hour drive ahead of me, I want to make one more stop before leaving the Navajo Nation, so I head north toward Canyon de Chelly. At the base of the Chuska Mountains, along the Arizona–New Mexico border, are two canyons: Canyon de Chelly, which extends about 27 miles, and an 18-mile branch called Canyon de Muerto. The canyon walls range from 200 feet to more than 1,200 feet high. Rains and runoff water create washes throughout the canyon, which are sometimes completely dry while at other times surging with water that will submerge a truck. Throughout the canyons are farms that grow beans, corn, and squash and raise flocks of sheep or goats. Although designated a national park by the U.S. government, the canyons are home to many Navajo, who live on the rim during the winter and down in the canyons during the summers. I am always awed by the stunning beauty of the canyons: lush cottonwoods lining the wash; rocks in all shades of red, beige, black, and white; scattered patterns of crops and livestock; and a big blue sky ascending over the flat plateaus of the rim. The Grand Canyon is certainly better known, but I consider Canyon de Chelly to be the most spectacular site in the Southwest.

I drive to the extreme northeastern rim of Canyon de Muerto, to a place overlooking Massacre Cave. It was along this part of the canyon that Spanish troops cornered Navajo warriors, women, and children at a ledge high on the sheer canyon walls and killed more than 120 people. Almost 200 years later, bullet holes can still be seen where the Spanish soldiers fired into the cave. As I came down the path toward the canyon, I saw a woman and a very little girl sitting on sheepskins under a Pinon tree with a red Ganado blanket out in front of them. There were only three necklaces and one "dream catcher" displayed on the blanket, with a dirty piece of tape that said "$2." As I slowed down to look, I didn't expect to stop because I had seen and purchased jewelry from Navajo at the fair. However, as I was passing I saw a bandage on the child. Covering her right foot was gauze with the yellow stains of medicine or maybe infection. I then looked at the woman, who seemed to be somewhere between 20 and 40 years old, dressed in a faded blue velvet blouse and skirt with a small squash blossom necklace. As I looked, the woman and child stared at my face, which was an unusual sensation on the Navajo Reservation. What was more unusual was that I stared back in silence. After a minute she said, "Juniper berries." Looking down at the necklaces on the blanket I saw they were made of the dried brown seeds and a few bits of colored plastic or glass.

As I squatted down to take a closer look, the woman said, "They keep away evil spirits"; the entire time, the woman never took her eyes off my face. Then she pointed to the necklace in the middle. I got out three dollar bills and stepped over to pay her. When I looked at the little girl's foot, the woman told me that the child had stumbled into the fire that was heating up water for the child's bath, which is something they had to do because there was no running water in their hogan. But the mother said the child would be well soon, or so she was told by the nurse at the public health service in Chinle, 20 miles away.

Cultural Perspective #4

A sense of "place" is central to the life of most Navajo people. The people talk about how important it is to live among the "four Sacred Mountains": Blanca Peak to the east, San Francisco Peak to the west, Mt. Hesperus to the north, and Mt. Taylor to the south. Few places within the Navajo Nation carry as much significance as Canyon de Chelly. The canyon is central to many stories concerning the holy people, the deities in traditional Navajo beliefs, and the home of any Anasazi ruins, some more than 1000 years old. In addition, this place played a vital role in the Navajo struggles against Spanish and U.S. American invaders. Because of the sheer rock cliffs and winding tributaries, the canyon has been an important stronghold for Navajo who fought or needed to hide from those who came to take their land. It was into the canyon, in the 1860s, that Kit Carson and the U.S. Army drove many Navajo before forcing them to surrender and take the "Long Walk" to a reservation 500 miles away from the sacred mountains. To deprive their enemy of food and shelter, the U.S. Army destroyed all the crops and livestock they found in Canyon de Chelly, including 4,000 fruit trees, in less than a month. Today the land is being farmed again. Land is not held in private ownership among the Navajo of the canyon, but it is passed down through the mother's line based on family and clan relationships. Although there are rich places such as the Canyon de Chelly, poverty afflicts many on the Navajo Nation. Unemployment can be as high as 40 percent, and it is common to find homes without running water or electricity. The vast size of the Navajo Nation, as well as the continuing cutbacks of funds from the U.S. government and the Bureau of Indian Affairs, means that basic health services are hard to come by for many Navajo. However, there is much pride and hope for the future among the Navajo. The theme of the 1997 Navajo Nation Fair was *Yódi dó nitl'iz nihidahaazljágo bee nei'ni'ji'yiikahdoo* (Natural resources, spiritual wealth, and economic development create prosperity). The special relationship the Navajo Nation and the Navajo people have with Mother Earth and their Creator has sustained them through many years of hardship, and it appears to be a driving force in the continued success of the largest Indian nation in the United States.

NOTES

1. Navajo Nation Fair Office (1997). *Fiftieth Anniversary Program, Navajo Nation Fair.* Window Rock, AZ: Navajo Nation.

In Vicki Marie's essay, we witness the process by which an outsider attempts to understand and adjust to living within another culture. With enthusiasm and respect, Vicki moved to Micronesia, only to discover that her preferences about a variety of common social experiences (greeting others, resolving conflicts, desiring privacy, displaying courtesy and respect) have different meanings among her Micronesian colleagues and neighbors. Vicki's essay also introduces some of the ethical issues that inevitably occur when crossing cultures: how and when should one conform to behaviors that are inconsistent with one's own beliefs, values, and experiences?

27 Living in Paradise: An Inside Look at the Micronesian Culture

Vicki Marie

In 1988 I was an adjunct instructor at several nearby colleges and universities. One day, while commuting between campuses, it occurred to me that while I was waiting for a full-time position, I could be teaching abroad. I researched overseas teaching opportunities and sent out a dozen resumes. I received three job offers. The assistant professorship of language arts at the College of Micronesia was the most appealing. I accepted an 18-month contract, left California a few months later, and arrived on Pohnpei in January 1989.

Except for holiday travel, I had lived in California my entire life and knew little about Micronesia. I read eagerly about Micronesian history, geography, and culture, and talked with people who had lived in Micronesia and taught at the college. Yet I arrived in Pohnpei believing that my Micronesian students would be motivated by the same values and would aspire to the same goals that I considered worthwhile. I was surprised to discover that my worldview was uniquely European American and my attitude ethnocentric. Pohnpei became the classroom and textbook that taught me about cultural relativity and intercultural communication. I discovered I had much to learn about Micronesia and even more about myself.

Background

The U.S. and Micronesian governments have been intertwined since the end of World War II, yet many Americans are unaware of the vast northern ocean area of Micronesia. Micronesia, meaning "tiny islands," comprises a string of more than 2,100 islands and atolls lying in four major archipelagos: the Mariana, the Caroline, the Marshall, and the Kiribati islands. These islands are scattered across an area as large as the continental United States, yet they are so small that their combined land mass amounts to approximately 1,000 square miles, about the size of Rhode Island. The inhabited islands are home to more than 375,000 people, who make up five constitutional governments. While these political divisions also represent linguistic, ethnic, and cultural differences, the people native to the islands are all classified as Micronesians.

Despite 175 years of contact with foreigners, Micronesians have maintained their traditional politics, languages, and family organizations. Changes, though, are inevitable. As a result, I found island life to be an amalgam of traditional and Western influences. Micronesians wear Western-style clothing, drive imported cars, eat in Japanese restaurants, and socialize in American-style bars. Yet these same people are equally comfortable wearing traditional island *lava lavas,* reciting ancient folklore in native languages, and masterfully pounding *sakau,* the local kava drink.

Cultural Patterns

Although Micronesians can move easily between ancient traditions and modern ideas, they have distinct value systems unlike those in the West. I found that it wasn't always easy to consider—much less appreciate—our contrasting worldviews. And what huge differences in worldviews we had! The following list summarizes some of the significant differences in cultural assumptions that I encountered while living among Micronesians:

Micronesian	*European American*
Nature will provide for us in time.	We must change our world, control nature, and make it work for humankind.
What will be, will be. Human life is controlled by destiny.	We create our own future by what we do.
There's no use rushing away from what I'm doing now. There's always plenty of time.	I have to hurry and meet somebody now. See you later.
Worry about tomorrow when tomorrow comes.	Save for the future.
Work a little, rest a little. Whatever you do, try to keep other people happy.	If I work hard enough, someday I'll make it to the top.
What I have is yours. What you have is mine.	What's mine belongs to me.

The wise person is one who knows his place in the world, respects authority, and does what he is supposed to do.	Sensible people strike out on their own, learn to do things for themselves, and make their own decisions.
The feelings of others are more important than an honest answer.	Always tell the truth, no matter how much it hurts.
My life belongs to the family and God.	I am a god.

As you can tell from this list, the potential for intercultural misunderstandings is great. I found these cultural differences to be interesting, irritating, amusing, or stressful, depending on the situation.

As time passed, I moved through predictable and trying phases of adjustment and assimilation. The first few months I was euphoric just to be in Micronesia, and everything seemed perfect and beautiful. I walked around with a big smile on my face and wrote letters to my family that recounted every blissful event. My euphoria plummeted the morning I discovered two flat tires on my Jeep. As a prank, the boys in the village had let the air out of the tires. I took it very personally and cried. A few days later, someone stole my sandals off the porch. I wasn't sure what to expect next in my new surroundings. I coped with the uncertainty by writing letters to everyone I knew "back home," socializing primarily with American and European expatriates and occasionally retreating to the solitude of my bungalow. Eventually I settled into a routine in which uncertainty became entertaining more than threatening. I reached out to people with varied cultural backgrounds and broadened my social circle.

I enjoyed new cultural experiences. I drank *sakau* and ate eel at feasts, visited with neighbors, hiked in the rainforest, learned to scuba dive, and enjoyed the challenge of teaching English to Micronesian students. With each experience I gained valuable insights into the culture and into myself. As I learned about Micronesian ways, I came to better understand my own cultural conditioning.

My American assumptions were often laughable in the Micronesian context. I felt anxious about wasting time and reprimanded students who were late to class. I was impatient when meeting times were disregarded. I took pride in accomplishing a list of goals each day. Then one day a Micronesian dean questioned why another American professor always walked so fast. "What's his hurry all the time?" the dean wondered aloud. Knowing that I easily outpaced my American colleague, I realized the question was indirectly aimed at my own task-oriented style. I felt embarrassed about looking foolish to the dean, but it seemed right to use my time wisely.

My notions of being direct and straightforward also were challenged. One day my friend Maggie stood me up at the hospital. I had agreed to assist her by talking with a physician on her behalf. She had health problems that she didn't fully understand and agreed to meet me at the hospital for an 11 A.M.

appointment. I took a taxi and arrived at the hospital 10 minutes early. After reading a book for 20 minutes I roamed around the hospital, looking for Maggie. I was concerned and wondered if a problem was keeping her from being on time. After I'd been there 45 minutes, Maggie's brother found me, staring toward the main door, and told me that Maggie was sorry but she couldn't make it that day. I was disappointed and frustrated. Unlike the earlier interaction with the dean, the cultural implications were not obvious. Months later, after observing similar incidents between others, I realized that Maggie never intended to meet me that day. Apparently she felt that saying "no" would have insulted me.

Political Structure

Shortly after moving to Pohnpei, I discovered that an important key to understanding Micronesian culture lies in the pervasive traditional political structure, which is a hierarchical social system with strongly embedded political and relational values and social norms. Even when Micronesian communities are affected by the maneuvering of government politicians, the traditional system factors strongly into negotiations and outcomes of most political transactions. For example, the negotiations required for paving the road that encircled Pohnpei were lengthy and complicated. Government officials proposed a plan that had to be approved by each of the five districts' leaders. The negotiations for land rights took months of meetings, discussions, gifts, and other traditional courtesies. Eventually, after each traditional chief felt satisfied that his community had been sufficiently compensated, the road construction began.

Typically, each district on an island operates within a status hierarchy: hereditary nobility, landed gentry, and commoners. On Pohnpei, each island district is ruled by a *nanmwarki,* or "high chief." Below the *nanmwarki* is a group of high-titled nobles. A second set of nobles is headed by the *nahnken,* or "talking chief." Each male title has a female equivalent. The male leaders, however, are the decision makers and the most highly revered in traditional culture. They are bestowed with much respect; others must address them in a "high language," which is an honorific language with special vocabulary reserved for nobility and authority.

Commoners and outsiders like me are expected to stand when talking to nobility, to respond to rather than initiate communication, and to cast our eyes downward to convey humility and respect. One evening I was introduced to a *nahnken* who had entered the restaurant where I was dining with a colleague. As the *nahnken* approached us, my friend quickly coached me: "Stand up, shake his hand, and cast your eyes down." I reluctantly followed his direction, feeling very awkward. In that instance I was abiding by the local custom but violating behaviors that I considered to be courteous and comfortable. I prefer to use direct eye contact and a sincere smile and believe such gestures conveyed confidence, honesty, and mutual respect. At that moment, I struggled to avoid eye contact and felt resentment and a tightness in my stomach as I tried to abide by social norms that collided with my own standards of equality and status.

Gender Roles

Unlike in U.S. society, where equality is the desired value, the roles of men and women in traditional Micronesian cultures are quite well defined. Many gender roles were apparent. In the morning, women hung their laundry, prepared meals, and swept their living areas. Men returned from early-morning fishing outings to repair homes or head for their jobs in town. During the day, men built houses, repaired canoes, sailed, fished, and gathered breadfruit and coconuts. Women prepared meals, cared for the children, cleaned, and tended the taro patches. In the early evenings, men met at the "men's house" for socializing or all-male community decision making. After their homemaking chores, women played cards or walked through the village, visiting with friends along the way.

In business and government centers on the more developed islands such as Pohnpei and Palau, many women have moved into the workplace, operating businesses or working in government offices. As women's roles have changed, so have gender communication norms. Traditional hierarchies still dictate the intrinsic status of women, but the subtleties are not obvious to an outsider. I learned about social status by talking to Micronesian men and women.

Traditionally, social expectations in Micronesia dictate where and to whom women may speak, but norms have shifted as women have taken responsible positions in community affairs. In more traditional settings, however, predictable gender communication norms remain intact. Women, for instance, are not supposed to speak during village or community meetings. Above all, women should not challenge or confront men. As a European American woman, I found that notion foreign. I learned the hard way about hierarchical gender communication in Micronesia.

My bungalow was situated between a *sakau* bar and a beer bar in Porakiet village. Over the winter holiday season, both bars had ongoing parties. Because *sakau* is a soporific, the more the patrons drank, the quieter they became. The beer had the opposite effect on the patrons in the second bar. As the evening progressed, people and music became louder, and the noise continued until dawn. After two sleepless nights, I approached the bar owner with a direct but courteous plea to end the party at a reasonable hour. He reluctantly agreed to turn the music off by 10 P.M. and close the bar at midnight. I felt relieved, but that evening the music continued past midnight. I walked over to the bar, asked to speak to the owner, and pleaded with him to turn off the music. I made, I thought, a reasonable and polite request, but the music continued into the early morning.

On my way to campus that morning I was confronted by the owner's daughter, who accused me of casting shame on her father. Although the owner and I had had a private conversation, my directness was perceived as aggressive and disrespectful. I tried to explain my position to the daughter, but she wouldn't listen. As an outsider and a woman, I had overstepped my boundaries and never had a chance of persuading the owner to comply with my request. Interestingly, my landlord, a well-respected businessman, eventually intervened. From that night on, the owner conformed to a 10 P.M. curfew, and I finally got some sleep.

Even in family settings, women must temper their comments. A Pohnpeian colleague once explained that if she was bitterly angry with her brother's wife, she would not dare say anything to her brother about her feelings. To do so would be disrespectful to her brother and would cast shame on herself. She said she limits her conversations with her brother to "asking for his help or advice."

I learned that women who initiate conversations with men are considered forward or flirtatious. The college maintenance man went out of his way to help me set up my office and bungalow. I thought he was very nice—until he made a pass at me. I was informed that my outgoing personality and friendly small talk had been interpreted as romantic interest. I thought it was silly, so I just ignored the misunderstanding. To avoid an unnecessary conflict, however, I was courteously warned by my Micronesian friends about the man's jealous Chuukese wife and told to avoid him.

A similar situation occurred after I stopped one day to look at a hotel construction site near the lagoon. One of the owners, who was married to the college secretary, was on the premises. I was pleased to meet him and chatted about his new hotel. A few days later, his wife told me that he thought I was flirting with him. Thankfully, she didn't take him seriously. My Micronesian friends trusted me and guided me when necessary to avoid misperceptions. I was grateful for the support as I maneuvered my way through a new culture.

I learned, for instance, that despite the cultural constraint of gender, Micronesian women hold a position of power and community esteem in island life. When a dispute occurs, the first-born woman, who is the female head of her clan, is sent to settle the conflict and reconcile the two sides. Her judgments are almost always obeyed, because if they are not there is the risk that the conflict could reemerge to plague the community.

True to their collectivist nature, the Micronesian people consider social harmony an important cultural value that is critical to community welfare. Women are called on to ensure that such harmony prevails.

Family and Children

Like most European Americans, I tend to belong to several unrelated groups. Micronesians, however, belong to one relatively unchanging group: their family. Having grown up in a small family I found it intriguing that Micronesian families include all relatives in their clan. The extended family is composed of generations of matrilineal relationships. Several members of the extended family commonly share a single household. The larger clan is composed of descendants of a common female ancestor. As a Westerner, I was confused by the matrilineal nature of Micronesian families. Descendants always come through the woman and are considered members of the mother's clan. Children refer to their mothers, aunts, grandmothers, and other significant women as "mom." Their siblings and cousins are considered "brothers and sisters." When the girl next door told me that she had 19 brothers and sisters, I laughed because I thought she was joking. When I asked Millie, the daughter of my friend Maggie, how many brothers and sisters she has, she began counting on her fingers but finally threw up her and hands and exclaimed, " I don't know. A lot!"

Rank in the clan comes from birth order, not age. The children of the oldest daughter will have higher rank than the children of a younger daughter, regardless of their ages. For example, if the older daughter's son is 25 years old, and the youngest daughter's son is 35 years old, the older daughter's son would have the higher rank. He would be regarded as a big brother by the older but lower-ranking man. Rank for females follows the same pattern. Grandparents, by virtue of their position in the family, are highly honored and treated with great respect, love, and care by their children and grandchildren.

Respect is the most important value to Micronesians. It is expressed in the guiding rule to "be humble; don't put yourself up." This social rule, which extends to all relationships, discouraged our college freshmen from initiating conversation with sophomores. In some circumstances, though, such as in a classroom, students switched to an egalitarian style for practical reasons. But they did so with discomfort.

I asked my college students to explain status norms. One responded, "The rule about talking to higher-rank people is to be polite. We honor the higher-title person." Another said, "We use high language for leaders and important people like the elders. If you don't use appropriate language you are considered impolite and disrespectful. Following the rules in our culture is very important, which is why I don't like to communicate at feasts with traditional leaders."

In general, only a few expectations constrain children's behavior. Parents allow their children to do whatever they please as long as they display respect for others. One afternoon I sat visiting with my friend while her three young children played nearby. During our four-hour conversation, her children would stop to listen to us talk but did not once interrupt. Occasionally my friend or I would speak to her kids. They responded immediately to their mother but were more hesitant toward me.

Respect is the value embedded in the strict rules that prohibit children from initiating conversations with elders. An elder is loosely defined as anyone older than the child. When responding to an elder, children are expected to use "high language." They use honorific language to answer their parents, grandparents, or older siblings, especially the first-born son. Micronesian children will rarely vie for attention or interrupt adults. So, although children are included in all community events, they are typically "seen but not heard."

If a child does something displeasing, the parent will usually attempt to modify the behavior by making the child feel ashamed. For instance, if a girl uses her mother's money to buy something without permission, the parent may talk about the child within her hearing range to make the child feel ashamed for spending the family's money. Disputes among family members are strongly discouraged. Children are taught this value at a very early age and are made to feel great shame if a dispute occurs. Courtesy, respect, and politeness are constant themes found in each household and in the community. Intentional rudeness or malevolent behaviors are looked down on. A person exhibiting such behaviors is considered *amalgam tekia,* a Chuukese phrase meaning "haughty."

Micronesian parents do not praise their children for good deeds. Children might hear indirectly from a third party how pleased their parents are with their behavior, but Micronesians find it awkward to express and receive compliments directly. I would tell children how beautiful or talented they were and would be surprised to hear in reply "I'm not." My Micronesian friends were more likely to express their appreciation through caring, gifts, or favors. In fact, providing enough food is the primary way in which a parent shows affection for a child. Being hungry would imply to others that the child is not taken care of properly and is, therefore, unloved.

Family members who are hungry are expected to help themselves to food. But a hungry person may be too embarrassed to ask for food, for fear of implying that the family is neglectful. To avoid embarrassing family members, Micronesian people assume that any person coming into the house, including a visitor, is hungry and is thus greeted with an offer of food. Family members generally serve themselves from the communal bowl. Eating together goes beyond the mere intake of food to satisfy hunger. The spirit of sharing is a way of showing oneness and, more significantly, mutual trust and love.

Displays of affection among family members, as practiced by many groups in the United States, do not exist in Micronesian families. Children display affection for their parents through loyalty and by performing certain duties or responsibilities for the family, such as sweeping the floor without being asked. Although Micronesians seldom hug or kiss children, a mother will lovingly nuzzle her child's nose.

I attended a church wedding in Pohnpei and was surprised that the Western tradition of the husband kissing the bride was eliminated from the ceremony. I was told later that public displays of affection are considered inappropriate. Holding hands with others outside the family circle is more common, especially among those of the same gender. The only time one is likely to observe hugging and kissing in a family is when an adult is playing with a baby. In fact, children are not allowed to observe kissing. Millie told me that it made her *shake* (nervous) when she saw Americans kissing, because it was bad. I had seen her cover her eyes during a kissing scene in a film. She told me that her mother said she should never see kissing. In Pohnpei, I heard stories of teenage girls being punished for inadvertently witnessing Westerners kissing at the airport. The taboo is apparently a strategy for discouraging promiscuity.

Language

Many language differences exist in Micronesia, although each language derives from a common Malayo-Polynesian source. Several major languages, with dialect variations, are spoken in Micronesia. The islanders I encountered knew their native language and at least one other Micronesian language. On the islands that were heavily influenced by Japan, inhabitants know some conversational Japanese. Because of the diversity of native languages, English has emerged as the lingua franca used in government, education, and other intercultural contexts. For most Micronesians, English is a second language; for others, it is their fourth or fifth and, thus, the language with which they feel the least secure.

At the College of Micronesia students appeared confident when switching between Micronesian languages but seemed reticent when communicating in English to me. I spoke with students who had varying degrees of English proficiency. Some disclosed that they were afraid of appearing "stupid" to native English speakers.

I taught an evening class for two weeks before I realized that the majority of students didn't understand me. They pretended to understand by simply nodding and smiling. When I spoke to them individually after class, I realized that in fact they understood very little English. Micronesians who live and work in city centers and who have frequent contact with native English speakers are able to express themselves as clearly in English as they do in their native languages. When they speak fluent English, it is easy to forget that our cultural perceptions may actually block clear communication.

I sometimes wondered about the illusion of shared meaning that existed during my intercultural conversations. There were times I'd expect a particular outcome but it wouldn't occur. I learned, over time, not to take the language for granted. I tried to be empathetic toward students who spoke in a foreign language, especially when I heard them struggling to express themselves clearly. Actually, I admired their ability to speak multiple languages.

Communication Norms

Micronesians seem to be simultaneously extroverted and introverted. As a group Micronesians find it easy to talk with others, and they perceive themselves to be friendly, dramatic, and animated. They also appear interested in others, demonstrating goodwill when they communicate.

Because it is difficult to accept compliments, Micronesians generally do not openly give compliments. They admire people silently or indirectly. Generally, if a person wants to compliment another, he or she will pass the compliment through a relative rather than acknowledge the person directly.

When I praised our student clerk for a job well done she giggled, blushed, and turned away from me. I observed the same reaction when I openly praised students for well-written essays or other course work. One day in front of my office, I encouraged a young man to present his exceptionally good speech at our upcoming speech festival. He turned his body away from me as he flipped his hand chest-high in a gesture that meant to communicate "stop" or "go away," because it was difficult for him to accept the compliment. Each time I encountered these common nonverbal responses, they were coupled with self-effacing statements that were said with a smile, but it was quite clear that the student was extremely uncomfortable. One student explained: "People are uncomfortable with praise because they do not want to be perceived as thinking they are 'big' or better than anybody else." Modesty is an important characteristic of the Micronesian personality. Micronesians believe that it is generally virtuous to be quiet. Even in childbirth, a woman is expected to keep silent and show as little pain as possible.

Pohnpeians find very few situations in which they can show pride in their accomplishments or possessions without fear of criticism. This attitude was evident at the conclusion of our college speech festival, when all the student speakers disappeared immediately after the awards ceremony. The young man who won first place for his persuasive speech left to avoid criticism for pretentiousness or "acting big." Runners-up left because they felt ashamed. In a collectivist community where such public competition is rare, the fear of ridicule or gossip seems sufficiently strong to enforce an apparent pattern of exaggerated modesty, humility, and shame.

Micronesian communication style uses less verbal exchange and looks for implicit meaning in the situation. In contrast, my European American communication style is one in which talkativeness is valued and the message is conveyed explicitly. In everyday encounters I commonly misinterpreted silence as introversion, shyness, or disinterest. Over time, I better understood notions of context as I heard conversations similar to one between our department secretary and a European American professor. As the professor walked away from the exchange, the secretary grimaced. When I asked, "What's wrong?" she answered, "He talks too much." She explained that talkative people are less respected in Pohnpeian society. People who are reserved or quiet are admired. This greatly influences the way in which Pohnpeians conduct themselves in public. "Generally," she explained, "people rarely initiate conversations, particularly if they are meeting someone new. During childhood we are told not to speak to adults, and if we did speak we were to be careful of the language to be used." Talkativeness casts shame on oneself and one's family. Such perceived threats contribute greatly to Micronesians' willingness to communicate with others.

Nonverbal Communication

Differences in nonverbal communication, or body language, are often subtle and can be the source of intercultural misunderstanding. During my first few days at the College of Micronesia, the division secretary was on sick leave. When she returned I introduced myself and asked, "Are you feeling better?"

She answered "Yes" nonverbally by raising and lowering her eyebrows. I interpreted her response to mean "What did you say?" So I repeated the question a little more slowly, and again she raised her brows. I asked the question a third time, receiving the same nonverbal response. Out of frustration, I finally said, "I hope you are feeling better soon." About a week later, when I learned that raised eyebrows mean "yes," I realized that the secretary must have thought me dense for repeatedly asking the same question.

Micronesians use the same shake of the head as Americans as a way to say "no." A frown accompanied by a wave of the hand at chest level is an emphatic "no!" or "stop it!" Micronesians throw their heads slightly back and to the side to indicate "over there." Depending on the context of the question, the response could mean a few blocks away or the next island over. The apparent ambiguity of that particular response was sometimes confusing. Similarly, if I, as an outsider, were to summon a Micronesian by repeatedly curling my index finger upward, the gesture would imply that the receiver had the status of an animal. More than a few times, I had to control my impulse to use that common American gesture.

Much more difficult was remembering that the proper nonverbal gesture for summoning someone in Micronesia is to make a downward movement of the hand from the level of the head to the shoulder. The first time a Micronesian beckoned me in this manner, I thought he was telling me to "go away." I stood in utter confusion until he finally asked me to "come here."

Height

I often learned through my mistakes. I once reached out to ruffle a little boy's hair only to have my hand quickly pulled away by a colleague who saved me from cultural transgression. From my American perspective, I was expressing affection toward the child. I was surprised to learn that I was conveying the exact opposite meaning by violating a Micronesian perception of height, an important concept in Micronesian cultures. Generally speaking, the higher something or someone is, the more sacred it is. The head is the highest part of the human body; to touch another person's head is considered disrespectful, and such behavior is strictly prohibited.

Height also acts as a type of checks-and-balances system. When passing others who are sitting, Chuukese people say "Tirow" (excuse me) or "Tirow wom" (high language used to excuse oneself) to elders and others higher in rank. "Tirow wom" is usually accompanied by a bow from the waist, which demonstrates respect by lowering one's height in relation to the people who are sitting.

In the Chuukese culture, a woman is forbidden to be physically higher than a man at any time. I heard Westerners mistakenly categorize this behavior as sexist. From the Chuukese perspective, however, the behavior is practical: A woman should never stand when a man is sitting because she runs the risk of drawing attention to her thighs. A woman's thighs are considered sexually stimulating by Micronesian men. Therefore, her behavior would appear sexually suggestive.

If a woman's brother is sitting, she would either walk past him at a distance while bowing at the waist, walk past him on her knees, crawl, or simply sit down and wait for him to stand up. She would not, under any circumstances, directly ask him to stand up, because that would imply that he didn't respect her. She could, however, ask another person to point out her presence to him or wait until he noticed her. As an outsider, I was generally exempt from these strict cultural rules and was excused when I inadvertently violated social expectations. Still, I tried my best to be sensitive to cultural norms.

Before I left California, I read about the Micronesian perception of female thighs. I was prepared to teach while wearing long skirts and to play while wearing modest, knee length walking shorts. I found most outsiders to be equally sensitive toward this cultural norm. Peace Corps volunteers and other expatriate women adopted the Pohnpeian style of swimming in skirts. It was easier to swim or dive out on the reef, away from the island, because we could swim in bathing suits and cover up with *lava-lavas* (wrapped skirts) as soon as we got within sight of the island. One afternoon, while returning to the lagoon in our boat, some friends and I were engrossed in conversation and didn't remember to cover our legs. We snapped back to reality as we passed the docks and were jeered with whistles and wolf-calls. Interestingly, my friends and I felt very exposed and embarrassed and quickly learned to abide by cultural tradition.

Time

As members of a "doing" culture, European Americans are very concerned with time, compartmentalizing it carefully to avoid wasting it. Micronesia is a "being" culture. Micronesians are more likely to listen to their natural impulses—to eat when they are hungry and sleep when they are tired—than to the hands of a clock. Cooking, fishing, and other tasks are determined by mood, weather, or ocean tides. In the remote villages and outer islands, much time is spent relaxing and socializing. The men meet to discuss community affairs or play games. The women weave or socialize over a card game. I had difficulty relating to people in the village who appeared to spend a great part of the day just sitting around doing nothing. I would have been bored but, interestingly, the word "bored" does not exist in Micronesian languages.

In city centers, where people are expected to abide by work hours and class times, Micronesians find the transition to schedules unnatural and confining. It is not considered unusual or rude for Micronesians to come later than their appointed time. It would, however, be unusual to meet a Micronesian who was in a hurry or anxious over a deadline. Because European Americans typically view time as a commodity, the time issue causes many misunderstandings. It took most of the first semester for me to understand that student tardiness was not a sign of disrespect or apathy.

During the fall semester I was asked to present a communication workshop to local radio announcers. I had very little time to design the workshop, so I gave the support staff the course materials to duplicate and assemble. Two days before the workshop was scheduled I discovered the duplicating hadn't been completed. I expressed my concern about having the materials on time but was assured that they would be ready. I heard indirectly that if I was in such a great hurry I should do the job myself. Surprisingly, the materials were delivered one hour before I left for the radio station.

I arrived at the station ten minutes early and found only one person there. The general manager and three announcers trickled in over the next 20 minutes. As I was about to begin, the electricity shut down, leaving us without air conditioning or lights. The general manager suggested we move the workshop to the college campus. By the time we drove to the campus and settled into a classroom, 15 minutes were left of the scheduled time. I had time only for a brief introduction and an ice-breaker activity. I was disappointed that we lost virtually an entire session and that my preparation had been in vain, yet none of the participants seemed inconvenienced.

Space/Privacy

The Micronesian lifestyle is communal. Traditionally, many Micronesians live in shared areas where everything is used collectively. This idea is emphasized in the Chuukese proverb: "Meta aai epwe oomw, mea oomw epwe aai," or "What is mine is yours, and what is yours is mine." This notion remains an ideal cultural value but is mostly theoretical. In reality, Micronesians have personal property and regard it as such. Personal property may be loaned to others, but it is considered proper to ask the rightful owner for permission. Most of the time the owner will grant permission. In fact, about the only time the owner would withhold permission is when he or somebody else was using the object in question.

While the concept of private property does exist, Micronesians tend to be less attached to their belongings than are European Americans. Acquaintances who were Peace Corps volunteers on Pohnpei said this was a frustrating cultural difference that they found difficult to accept. They explained that if they wanted to keep personal possessions such as hair clips, books, or cassette players for themselves, they would have to put them away in a private place. Their Pohnpeian family's attitude toward such items was one of detachment, which is generally true for most Micronesians. For instance, if something is borrowed and subsequently lost or damaged, the owner will not express anger, because people are much more important than possessions. In contrast, European Americans tend to react to losing a possession with varying degrees of anger and, depending on the object, may perceive a loss almost as a loss of part of oneself. In the collectivist Micronesian societies, in contrast, the personality of each person is well known, but people express their individuality by their behaviors rather than their possessions.

The issue of privacy was a challenge for me in Pohnpei. As a typical European American, I highly value my privacy, but the concept of privacy is strange in Micronesian cultures because togetherness is the norm. Although most Micronesians have been exposed to American cultural patterns and accept them, they still do not fully comprehend the need for "quiet time" or privacy. Being alone is generally associated with strong emotions—for instance, avoiding an individual or group to keep from expressing strong anger toward others or hiding because of feelings of sadness or great shame. Micronesians may also think that someone desiring solitude is *mas* or "physically sick and wants to be alone."

The day I moved into my two-bedroom bungalow, the landlord sent his son over to make some repairs on the house. His three sisters followed him over, walked into my living room, tied up the curtains to let the breeze in, and sat down for a chat among themselves. They were as relaxed and natural as if they were in their own home. I, on the other hand, didn't quite know what to do. Should I offer them something to drink? Make small talk? Try to entertain them in some way? The young women were fully engaged in their conversation in Pohnpeian language, so I retreated uncomfortably to my back room to work until everyone was ready to leave. On other occasions, the children in the neighborhood would pile onto my back porch to watch the video playing on my TV. They seemed as interested in what I was doing as in the plot of the film. After some time, I noticed my boundaries relaxing, but I was never fully comfortable with the territorial differences. The most disturbing violations of my privacy were when the young men in the neighborhood looked into my windows at night. The nocturnal habits of a single *menwai* (outsider) woman were apparently entertaining.

Night-Crawling

The Chuukese term for night-crawling is *teefan*. This is the behavior in which a young man sneaks to a young woman's house at night to meet her. Strictly speaking, the man could go night-crawling only when the couple had made an arrangement. It is expected that the woman will help the man in their attempts to get together. In days gone by, the process was much easier. Houses were thatched, and all the man had to do was poke his carved wooden "love-stick" through the thatched wall and await an answer. The woman could either invite him in or ask him to wait outside by a simple push or pull of the stick. It was obviously necessary that the woman know the love-stick design of her intended lover.

Today the ritual is complicated by cinder-block or wooden walls that make the love-stick ineffective. Night-crawling continues but with an arrangement made between the lovers. Frequently I discovered evidence of such trysts near my bungalow. Large banana leaves had been used to pad the ground where young couples met. Crawling around without such prearrangement constitutes *inkikich* or peeping. The boys in my village occasionally whistled into my windows and on one occasion actually invited my visiting mother to join them in the night air. She just laughed. But night-crawling can be risky, and a man who night-crawls should expect to meet challenges. It is perfectly acceptable for the man to be beaten up by the woman's relatives if he is caught.

Conclusion

I moved back to California in 1990, when I accepted a teaching position at San Joaquin Delta College in Stockton. The first day on campus I met a visiting professor who had been a Peace Corps volunteer in Micronesia. He encouraged me to teach intercultural communication because, he said, "It's an important course, great fun, and a forum for Micronesian tales."

I am glad I took his advice, because each time I share a story with students I am transported to Pohnpei. I remember the riches I gained by living among Micronesians: I was able to move beyond my ethnocentrism and better understand and value variations of human behavior. I became aware of the culturally programmed beliefs, values, and norms that determine my behaviors. Most importantly, I developed lasting intercultural relationships.

Recently, my husband and I invited Millie, now eleven years old, to live with us. She arrived from Micronesia eighteen months ago and is attending the elementary school near our home. These months together have been joyous for us all but particularly meaningful to me. Millie is Maggie's daughter—Maggie, my dear friend and former student in Pohnpei. I consider Pohnpei my second home and Maggie and her children my Micronesian family.

Now that Millie is with us, I have a renewed sense of connection with my Micronesian home and family. Each day with her brings discoveries about our life experiences and cultural assumptions. As I help her learn about American culture, I develop a deeper dimension of love for Micronesia and a greater appreciation for cultural diversity and relativity.

Study tours to other cultures allow students to learn firsthand about the relativity of cultural beliefs, values, and norms. Such excursions inevitably provide insights into some of the moral and ethical dilemmas characteristic of those who cross cultures. Thomas Steinfatt's trip to Northern Thailand with a group of U.S. college students provided him with an opportunity to explore issues about cultural differences and the appropriate behaviors of visitors to another culture. Tom guides your understanding of these issues by providing a series of questions that are linked to his narrative. You might want to read this essay twice. The first time, skip the questions that are set apart from the narrative. Then read the story again, along with the questions, and think about your answers to them. Doing so produces an understanding of the original story that is different from the simple description of an excursion by touring U.S. college students.

28   The Shower

Thomas M. Steinfatt

Encountering another culture can occur in locations that vary from the everyday to the exotic. Different value systems and past experiences, as well as different languages and different cultural notions of right and wrong, can create situations in which the intercultural participants are annoyed at each other's reactions and at each other's apparent interpretations of the situation. One such situation occurred a few years ago.

I often teach summer courses in intercultural communication to culturally diverse groups of U.S. college students in Southeast Asia. Part of the course involves the study of hill tribes—indigenous peoples somewhat akin to Native Americans—who live within the countries of Asia yet apart from the dominant culture both geographically and in ways of thinking and behaving. Two of the larger hill tribes in Thailand are the Hmong and the Karen.

Most of the Hmong regard Laos as their original homeland. But the traditional beliefs of the Hmong include the concept that the Lao people and government want to steal their land. These beliefs were exploited by America's CIA during the Vietnam War period. The CIA convinced the Hmong to fight against the Pathet Lao communists, who now control Laos. Thus the Hmong believe that they would receive a most hostile reception in Laos were they to attempt to return—likely an accurate perception of reality. The Lao government exerts consistent pressure on the Thais to treat the Hmong as a hostile foreign group. Foreigners often subdivide the Hmong into the White Hmong and the Blue Hmong, according to the predominant color of the women's dress.

Burma is the Karen homeland. The Karen dress less colorfully than other hilltribes, and the Karen are the only group with no identifiable ties to Chinese culture. They are the most willing hilltribe group in adopting lowland agricultural methods. Thai Karen immigrants are usually Sgaw Karen and Pwo Karen, but scattered Padaung Karen live in the area of Mae Hong Son in northwestern Thailand. By tradition, Padaung Karen girls born on a full moon Wednesday have their necks stretched with rings. The rings force the head away from the body during growth. An elongated neck is a much-prized sign of beauty among the Padaung Karen.

> Is beauty an element of nonverbal communication? Which standards of beauty are universal across cultures and across history, and which are variable? Why might a culture adopt a standard that a long-necked woman is beautiful?

A mature Padaung woman may have 24 rings, with a maximum of 32. By the 1980s, demand promoted by tourists wanting to see the "long-necked people" led the Padaung to ring the necks of most of the village girls, regardless of the circumstances of their birth.

> Should tourism to foreign countries be regarded as an ethical issue? Would you apply the answer to that question equally in the opposite direction? That is, Miami depends on tourist income just as the principal source of foreign income for Thailand is tourism. If tourism to Thailand is an ethical issue, can the same be said about tourism to Miami? Why or why not?

The Karen and Hmong both live high in the hills, with the Karen usually choosing the higher elevations. Karen houses are always on stilts and lack a shrine. A common shrine to the local god of the land and water is located on a main path into the village. Both groups are skilled in agriculture, usually of the slash-and-burn variety during the nomadic periods of their histories. As the jungle has gradually disappeared, the nomadic ways and slash-and-burn tactics have given way to more permanent settlements and less transitory methods of agriculture. Poppies are the prized crop for both groups, who both use the opium and trade it for goods. Both Karen and Hmong smoke frequently, often every day, sometimes all day. The women wear a headdress made of a long thin cloth wrapped in layers around the head, from which a pipe may almost always be seen protruding.

> Drugs that are commonly used in one culture may be illegal in another. What do you think about the use of "illegal" drugs? Why did the British fight two "opium" wars with the Chinese? Were the British trying to stop Chinese drug use? Are you familiar with the history of attempts to suppress the drug trade in Asia? What were the results of several hundred years of attempted suppression? Do the lessons of Asian history apply to the West? Some people believe that drug use is immoral. If you encountered drug use in a hilltribe culture, how would you react to it? How should one react to it?

Early one morning, during one of our student trips, a group of four men and three women from U.S. universities left Chiang Mai in Northern Thailand with me. Two male Karen guides, Chi and Nong, rode with our group in the back of a pickup truck. Nong was bilingual in Karen and Hmong, and Chi spoke Karen, Thai, and limited English. The truck took us about 35 kilometers on twisting earthen roads, stopped at the edge of the jungle, let us out, and left. While I had cautioned everyone to bring enough water, several had listened to Chi's promise from the night before to provide enough water for everyone, a feat that would have been most difficult to accomplish. The water would be too heavy for one person, Chi tended to be on the forgetful side with respect to supplies, and Chi's water consumption estimates, though he was familiar with foreigners, were based on Karen norms. The Karen are used to arduous mountain treks. Westerners tend to be larger and softer, regardless of the physical shape they are in—or believe themselves to be in. It is particularly common for Western males on such trips to overestimate their physical abilities, and then to be too macho to admit it and ask for help. Females generally simply stop and say they have to rest.

Chi is represented as forgetful. Is this a characteristic of an individual or of a culture? While the text states clearly that it is Chi who is forgetful, some readers may make the inference that this is a characteristic of less developed peoples in general, or of the Karen. Though such an inference is unwarranted, some students have suggested that the characteristic of forgetfulness should not be ascribed to Chi since such an ascription may lead to the attribution by some readers that all less developed peoples are forgetful. What do you think? Should individual characteristics be described accurately, or should "political correctness" be invoked? If you argue for "political correctness," on what basis would you propose distinguishing between when accuracy versus political correctness is most important? Are the characteristics of "large, soft, and macho" politically incorrect? Does it matter? What if the ascribed characteristics were positive rather than negative, such as the Thai smile referred to later in the story? Should the positive or negative direction of the comments make a difference?

A 30-minute wait ended with unmistakable sounds and movement of the ground, and eventually of the trees, vines, and ferns, that only a herd of elephants can produce. Actually there were only five, and one was a nursing infant, but it sounded like a herd from ground level. Each adult elephant had been fitted with a rectangular basket mounted across the forward part of its back. The mountainside where the truck had let us off was steep enough at points that the students could get on the elephant from the uphill slope. Each elephant had a mahout, a boy or young man who lives in a symbiotic relationship with his mount. Our mahouts were Karen, who also tame and train elephants, practices not found in other hilltribes. Elephant and mahout need each other for protection and for survival in a human-dominated environment. In the city the mahout sells bananas to tourists and city dwellers, who then feed the elephant by hand. The mahout uses the proceeds to eke out a living and to buy more bananas and other food for the elephant. Most Thai elephants with a mahout find survival easier in the city than in the countryside. Elephants without a mahout are driven away from villages and are often hunted down and killed in response to the damage they do in trying to find food.

> What does it say about the moral superiority of humanity over other animal species that humans have created a society in which many species can no longer live in their traditional environments and without the support of humans?

At first we followed a narrow path weaving up the side of the mountain, elephants and baskets lurching from side to side along with their occupants. As the path became treacherous and slippery in spots, the elephants veered off it and through virgin jungle. This slowed our progress, since it was now more difficult for the mahouts to keep their charges from devouring the foliage they were uprooting and pushing aside as we moved slowly through the jungle. It was at this point I recalled that I had once again failed to apply "Steinfatt's First Law of the Jungle," learned on many previous journeys but temporarily forgotten: *Always ride on the front elephant.* Food appears to go through an elephant rather rapidly.

To control their mounts, the mahouts use a long bamboo stick as a whip around the animal's feet. If that and threatening yells don't work—and they usually don't—the mahouts use a pick, which is a piece of wood about half a meter in length that has a sharp, curved metal spike tied at a 90° angle to the wood. As I watched, blood seeped from half a dozen spots on our elephant's head where the mahout had applied the pick. The students appeared clearly upset, both at the flailing picks and at me for not "doing something." One student had tears in her eyes. We had a brief discussion of this point while lurching through the brush, and a more extended one later in the day.

After several hours, the mahouts stopped their beasts and urged us off. From here on up, the trail was too steep and rocky for elephants. I alighted from my elephant and placed my camcorder on the ground while gallantly attempting to help one of the women down from her basket. She assured me that she did not need any such help. Unfortunately, the camcorder's designer had not anticipated that its user might place it on the ground next to an elephant.

> Was I wrong, insulting, or "genderist" for offering to help a woman down? Was the woman wrong or insulting for refusing the offer?

Elephants are normally quite cautious and gentle about where they step, but when they step, they step. While my university was quite gracious after we returned and responded to my request for a new camcorder, I got some rather strange looks as people read the section of the report explaining how the damage had occurred: "An elephant stepped on it."

Do you see any problems with using a camcorder or a camera in intercultural settings? How does one decide between respecting the rights of people not to be photographed, and the rights and desires of an individual who wishes to record the experience? Does the fact that the persons on the trip are university related give them more rights, fewer rights, or equal rights to anyone else to take such photographs? Are you familiar with your university's institutional review board (sometimes called a human subjects committee) and its position on this point? Should students and professors have fewer rights to photograph, record, and videotape than other U.S. citizens and citizens of the world?

An hour's climb and walk led to a Hmong village where Nong was able to negotiate a refill of our water bottles for some of our food. Potable water, which might be "free" elsewhere, is a precious commodity when it is scarce. We parted with very little in exchange for the water, and a student suggested that we should pay for the water with Thai baht, another ethical decision to be discussed the following day.

How does one decide the worth of a trade in intercultural settings? Is it acceptable to simply let the individuals involved come to a mutually acceptable agreement? Would you be willing to apply that standard to Native Americans selling Manhattan to Europeans for trinkets?

It was afternoon by now. Beautiful as the jungle was, and as interesting as the birds, monkeys, and other assorted wildlife we encountered were, fatigue began to set in, along with the inevitable "Are we there yet?" comments. Our water was gone by now, and the small springs and streams of the jungle were tempting. But Chi steered us away from them as unwise, saying good fresh water was just ahead. Diseases associated with snail larvae are commonly associated with some jungle water supplies. Chi continued for more than two hours to say that fresh water was just ahead, which was perhaps a good persuasive tactic on his part. Eventually we topped a ridge and all of Northern Thailand seemed to spread out below us. Only a kilometer down the other side, a spring gushed forth with icy water that formed a small and rapidly flowing stream. All drank deeply but for Chi and Nong, who just looked on in puzzled amusement.

Several hundred meters further down, someone had apparently discarded a plastic milk jug right in the middle of the stream. A student went to pick it up and put it in our ever-expanding trash bag, but Chi stopped him with a gentle hand on his arm. Chi pointed to the plastic pipe taped on to the mouth of the bottle. The bottom of the jug had been cut away and was facing upstream. It was the source of the fresh running water supply for the Karen village, which soon appeared out of the growing evening mist, a half-kilometer below.

Since things may not be what they seem in another culture, how does one decide how long to wait and whom to ask and to believe when encountering events such as the apparent "trash" of the milk bottle?

Wearily—except for Chi and Nong, who were as fresh and talkative as they had been that morning—we entered the village and followed a diminutive pipe-smoking Karen woman, who greeted us with a killer smile worthy of a Thai, to an empty bamboo hut set off the ground on bamboo stilts. The double-sloped thatched roof formed most of the walls as well, and the hard, uncovered bamboo floor felt as soft and welcome to us as might your favorite overstuffed couch. Half the group was all for skipping dinner and going to sleep immediately, and they were making significant progress in that direction. The rest wanted to look around by firelight and see what were the sources of some of those delicious smells wafting through the air from other huts.

This debate was halted by the reappearance of the tiny woman, still puffing away, who gave us a five-minute speech of welcome, translated by Chi. The essence of the speech was the honor our visit had bestowed on the village, woven together with how cold it gets in the village at night. Indeed, a chill had already settled in, as I pointed out in whispered tones to the three sleeping beauties, gently nudging them from their prone positions to upright but exhausted stances as I did so. I was not sure of the Karen norms on sleeping through a speech of welcome, but I felt reasonably sure that upright had to be more acceptable than "prone and drone."

> Suppose a foreigner who walked into your home went straight to sleep in the guest room. What would you think? Would you be likely to attribute rudeness to the individual, or rudeness to the culture that the stranger represents? Or would you be more generous and assume the individual was just tired? How would your attributions change if the person was quiet and uncommunicative in the morning? Is the existence of a language barrier sufficient reason to avoid communication with people from another culture?

The speech reached its climax by pointing out the obvious: none of us had sleeping bags or blankets, since Chi had said they would be provided by the various villages where we would stay. The village would provide two blankets for each person, said the little woman, one for under and one for over. At this point I had the feeling that Chi was translating into more polite form the woman's words that, from her nonverbal behaviors, seemed likely to indicate "smelly foreigners who do not bathe before going to sleep." But Chi simply said that anyone who wanted blankets had to bathe, and now.

> How universal is the assumption that foreigners "smell funny"? Would knowing that other cultures sometimes regard Americans as unclean and smelly make Americans less likely to regard other cultures as "bad" because of their different smells?

Though quite a reasonable request, after the woman left it was met with limited enthusiasm within our group. It was already cold, several people pointed out, and taking a shower would only make us colder. And besides, where was the shower?

That proved to be the key question. Mustering my most authoritative manner, I strongly suggested the displeasure I would feel toward anyone who declined to accept the Karen's kind offer of a shower. Glumly, the troop followed Chi through the smoke of the cooking fires to the single water outlet in the village. It was the other end of the milk bottle pipe we had seen earlier, a series of right angles of PVC pipe ending in a spigot about a half-meter off the ground. "Of course it's going to be cold," I said, "but just get it done so we can all eat and get some sleep." The males met this comment, which seemed reasonable to me, with acquiescence, but it was met from the females, who stared at me with a unified and purposeful glare, with a silence colder than even the piped water was likely to be.

Not totally certain of the cause of this apparent displeasure, I looked around. The spigot was the central feature of the village, with the majority of the huts facing it, perhaps 10 to 20 meters away. As we stood there, a young woman from the village approached, smiled at us, and washed her body, while deftly and easily keeping the bits of cloth she had with her between herself, the foreigners, and the other villagers. The latter were going about their business as she was going about hers, with no one except the foreigners paying much attention to the events. She finished, dried herself, and walked off, with only limited compromise to her modesty.

I wanted to say, "See, that's how it's done," but thought better of it. The males in our group began to strip and shower, shivering from the cold water and holding up towels as the young woman had done with her cloth. The females in our group made a point of turning their backs and looking away. The presence of a group of foreigners in the middle of the village, all strangely dressed and acting in an unusual group manner, must have attracted attention, and it was after dinner by this time so the villagers were beginning to gather on their porches.

The men in our group were finished showering, but the added attentions of the villagers now upped the ante for the women students. All village eyes were fixed upon the spigot and the obvious discomfort of the foreigners. I thought of trying to explain that many cultures find no shame in the exposure of the human body in nonsexual circumstances. It seemed a reasonable comment from my perspective, knowing that students dutifully take in stride such cultural points in on-campus classroom settings. Professors always want to give lectures. But I held my tongue, guessing that such pedantic comments would not be particularly helpful while we were immersed in the actual situation.

How should nudity be viewed in this and other intercultural settings? Whose norms apply? The individuals involved are Western, yet the circumstances, culture, country, and village are not. Is nudity simply wrong? Is the fact of embarrassment of some individuals an important consideration? How important? Why would women be more embarrassed then men? Would this be true in other cultures? What of the Karen woman who bathed?

The resolution was for the male students to hold up towels in front of the female showerers while averting their eyes. This behavior in itself brought peals of laughter from the villagers, who likely would not have left this show to watch TV, had that option been available to them.

> Do you regard the laughter of the villagers as impolite or as normal? Would you regard Americans laughing at foreigners, in a situation that the foreigners perceived as embarrassing, as impolite? Are your answers the same for both cases? What do your answers say about your perception of "political correctness" norms?

The laughter only increased when it became apparent that it is difficult to coordinate the behavior of one's hands holding towels when one's eyes cannot see where the towels are and where the towels are moving versus where they are supposed to be. No slapstick comedy could have been better, I was later told by several villagers through Chi as they watched the towel holders respond to the squeals of the shower-takers that the towels were moving out of place. The response, quite naturally, was to look to see where the towels were. These efforts were met with even greater squeals by the showerers, along with a resounding slap or two, which did little to steady their hands and the towels they held. Eventually the showers were finished, the blankets distributed, and the cold night passed with our group huddled together for warmth on the hard bamboo floor, open to the wind both through the walls and up through the floor itself.

We awoke to the sounds of the pigs and chickens living beneath our hut as they rooted in the dirt searching for food, and the barking of the dogs whose job it was to keep the other animals from straying. Students were talking about the stream we would follow to the next village, and the promised pools and waterfalls. At a breakfast of fresh eggs and vegetables, which Chi cooked, the little Karen lady was able on request to come up with a few cans of warm Coke. Many villagers came by, bowed, nodded, and smiled, taking the opportunity to thank the comedy troop of foreigners for their wonderful performance the night before and assuring us that the village would welcome a repeat performance any time we chose to return.

About the Authors

Ann M. Bohara is associate director of the communication program, Wharton School of Business, University of Pennsylvania, and a partner in the consulting firm Resources for Change, which specializes in diversity management and conflict resolution.

Charles A. Braithwaite is a visiting professor of communication studies at the University of Montana-Missoula. He specializes in ethnographic studies of communication and has a special interest in Native American higher education.

Donal Carbaugh is a professor in the department of communication, University of Massachusetts, Amherst.

Patricia Covarrubias completed her doctorate at the University of Washington, where she specialized in cultural/intercultural communication with an emphasis on organizational contexts. She was born in Mexico City and moved with her family to the United States when she was eight years old.

Karen Lynette Dace is a professor of communication at the University of Utah.

Veronica J. Duncan is a professor of speech communication at the University of Georgia, Athens.

Keturah A. Dunne is a law student at California Western School of Law and a graduate of San Diego State University.

Samuel M. Edelman is a professor of communication arts and sciences at California State University, Chico.

Elane Norych Geller lives in Sherman Oaks, California, and is one of the youngest survivors of the Holocaust. She regularly tells her story throughout the U.S., including the Museum of Tolerance in Los Angeles.

Alfred J. Guillaume, Jr. is the vice chancellor for academic affairs at Indiana University, South Bend. He formerly served as vice president for academic affairs at Humboldt State University and at St. Louis University.

Tadasu Todd Imahori is a professor of communication studies in the department of foreign languages at Seinan Gakuin University, Fukuoka, Japan. He has also taught at San Francisco State University and Illinois State University in Normal.

Young Yun Kim was born and raised in Korea and now lives in Norman, Oklahoma, where she is a professor of communication at the University of Oklahoma. Her research has been primarily aimed at explaining the role of communication in the cross-cultural adjustment process of immigrants, sojourners, and native-born ethnic minorities.

Thomas J. Knutson is a professor of communication studies at California State University, Sacramento. A Fulbright scholar, he has taught and done research in Thailand and has also studied and lectured in Korea and Russia. He is a past president of Phi Beta Delta, the honorary society for international scholars.

Jolene Koester is provost and vice president for academic affairs, as well as professor of communication studies, at California State University, Sacramento. Despite her primarily administrative responsibilities, she is deeply committed to the importance of teaching and researching intercultural communication issues. She is coauthor of *Intercultural Competence: Interpersonal Communication Across Cultures.*

Mei Lin Swanson Kroll recently received her B.A. in speech communication from the University of Minnesota. She regularly consults and does workshops on transracial adoptions.

Wen Shu Lee grew up in Taiwan and taught herself English by listening to the Voice of America. She teaches at San Jose State University and her research interests include critical intercultural communication and postcolonial feminism.

Michael John Lewis is professor and chair of the department of special education, rehabilitation, and school psychology at California State University, Sacramento.

Myron W. Lustig is a professor of communication at San Diego State University. He writes actively in the areas of intercultural and interpersonal communication and is coauthor of *Intercultural Competence: Interpersonal Communication Across Cultures.* He likes talking with people, working with data, and eating Thai food.

Patrick McLaurin is director of human resources for diversity at the management consulting firm Booz-Allen & Hamilton, New York.

Mark Lawrence McPhail is a professor of communication at the University of Utah.

Ringo Ma is an associate professor of communication at State University of New York College at Fredonia. Born in Taiwan, he completed his B.A. there, and his M.A. and Ph.D. in the United States. His major research area is communication and culture in East Asia and North America.

Vicki Marie teaches communication at San Joaquin Delta College and has taught at the College of Micronesia. Among her passions in life are world travel and teaching intercultural communication.

Richard Morris, whose Indian name is Four Hawks, teaches at Arizona State University-West.

Chevelle Newsome is a professor of communication studies at California State University, Sacramento.

Peter O. Nwosu is a professor of communication studies at California State University, Sacramento. His research and consulting interests include multicultural training and development.

Saila Poutiainen is a graduate student in the department of communication, University of Massachusetts, Amherst. Her home country is Finland.

John Sanchez is an assistant professor of broadcast journalism at The Pennsylvania State University and a consultant in intercultural communication in Indian country. As a multiculturalist, he is deeply involved in providing non-Native America with a more balanced perspective of American Indian cultures.

Rui Shen is a Ph.D. candidate in English and comparative literature at the University of Oregon. Her home country is the People's Republic of China.

William J. Starosta works and teaches at Howard University in Washington, D.C. In 1973 he received the nation's first doctorate specifically designated intercultural communication.

Thomas M. Steinfatt is a professor in the school of communication, University of Miami.

Mary E. Stuckey teaches in the department of political science at the University of Mississippi.

Zhong Wang was born and raised in the People's Republic of China and is a Ph.D. candidate in communication at the University of South Florida. She now works in private industry and lives in San Diego.

Gale Young is a professor of speech communication at California State University, Hayward, where she codirects the Center for the Study of Intercultural Relations. She recently completed a fellowship from the American Council on Education in which her focus of study was improving intercultural relations in American higher education.